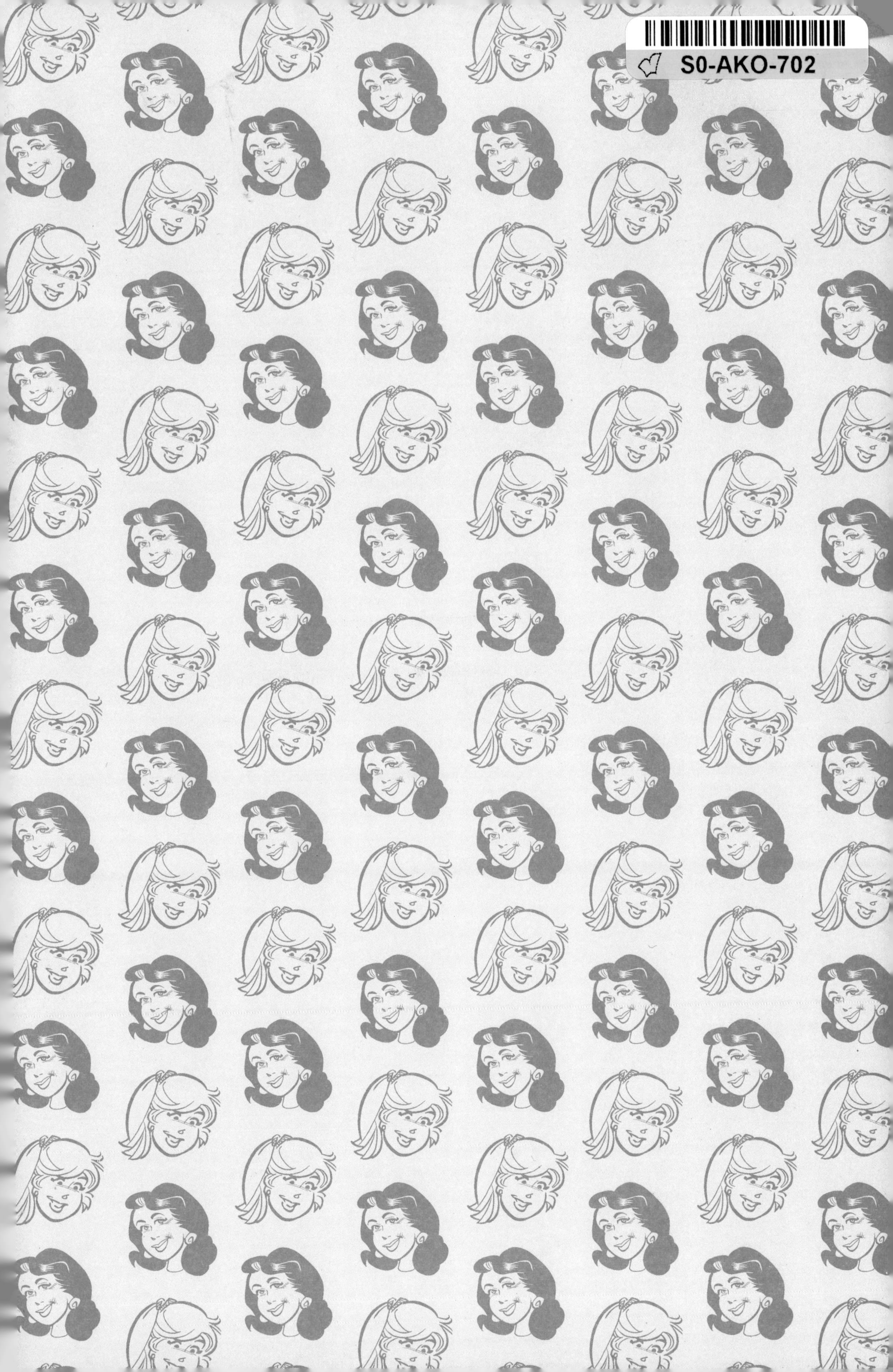

Archie Marries...

Archie Marries...

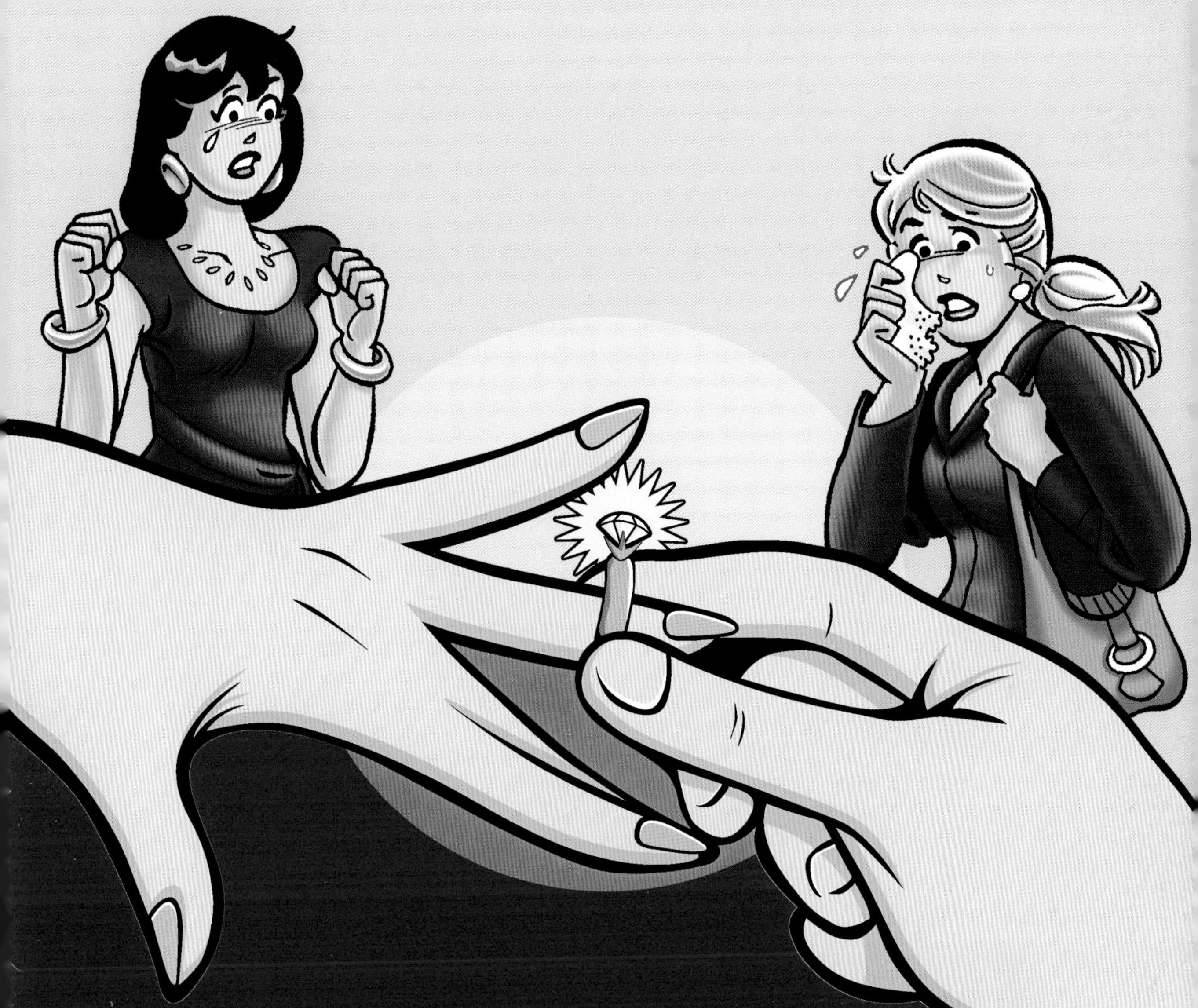

By Michael Uslan
Illustrated by Stan Goldberg & Bob Smith
Lettering by Jack Morelli
Coloring by Glenn Whitmore

Introduction by Danica McKellar

Abrams ComicArts, New York

To the ones who led me to the road less traveled . . .
Lil and Joe, and Paul; Nancy, David, and Sarah.
And *they* have made all the difference.
—M. U.

To Pauline, Stephen, Bennett, and Heidi.
—S. G.

Editor: Sofia Gutiérrez
Project Manager: Charles Kochman
Design: Neil Egan with Francis Coy
Production Manager: Ankur Ghosh

Library of Congress Cataloging-in-Publication Data
Uslan, Michael, 1951–
    [Archie. Selections]
    Archie marries—/ Michael Uslan ; illustrated by Stan Goldberg and
Bob Smith.
        p. cm.
    Issues 600–606.
    ISBN 978-0-8109-9620-5 (alk. paper)
    1. Comic books, strips, etc. I. Goldberg, Stan. II. Smith, Bob (Bob A.),
1951– III. Title.

    PN6728.A72U85 2010
    741.5′973—dc22
                        2010010558

Danica McKellar photograph on page 7: Dana Patrick
Stan Goldberg photograph on page 208: Pauline Goldberg
Glenn Whitmore photograph on page 208: Deb Rehling

Introduction copyright © 2010 Danica McKellar

Cover coloring by Neil Egan with Francis Coy

Printed and bound in China
10 9 8 7 6 5 4 3 2

Abrams books are available at special discounts when purchased
in quantity for premiums and promotions as well as fundraising or
educational use. Special editions can also be created to specification.
For details, contact specialmarkets@abramsbooks.com or the
address below.

ABRAMS
THE ART OF BOOKS SINCE 1949
115 West 18th Street
New York, NY 10011
www.abramsbooks.com

Acknowledgments

My personal thanks go out to Golden Agers John Goldwater, Bob
Montana, Dan DeCarlo, Vic Bloom, Harry Shorten, Louis Silberkleit,
Maurice Coyne, and all the great artists and writers from "The Greatest
Generation" who bequeathed Archie to the world. And for making this
historic series possible, Victor Gorelick, Jon Goldwater, Fred Mausser,
Nancy Silberkleit, the legendary and great Stan Goldberg, Bob Smith,
Jack Morelli, Glenn Whitmore, Mike Pellerito, Rik Offenberger, Paul
Castiglia, Ellen Leonforte, Joe Pepitone, Tito Peña, Carlos Antunes,
Stephen Oswald, Paul Kaminski, Joe Morciglio, Suzannah Rowntree,
and Duncan McLachlan. For their familial support, Nancy, David, Sarah,
and Paul Uslan. To my own three real-life Jugheads (or was I *their*
Jughead?), Bobby Klein, Barry Milberg, and Marc Caplan. And to the
two girls in high school who were my own Betty & Veronica (you know
who you are)!
—M. U.

Thanks to Henry Scarpelli, Dan DeCarlo, Bob Montana, Al Hartley, and
Bob Oksner; and to my editors, Stan Lee and Victor Gorelick.
—S. G.

Abrams ComicArts would like to thank the creative team: Michael
Uslan, Stan Goldberg, Bob Smith, Jack Morelli, and Glenn Whitmore.
This book would not have been possible without the tremendous
efforts of everyone at Archie, Inc., in particular Jon Goldwater, Victor
Gorelick, Mike Pellerito, and Stephen Oswald. We would also like
to thank Danica McKellar for her amazing introduction, and Laura
Nolan for her assistance. Thanks also to Charles Kochman and Sofia
Gutiérrez (editorial); Neil Egan, Francis Coy, and Michelle Ishay-Cohen
(design); Ankur Ghosh and Anet Sirna-Bruder (production); Kristina
Tully and Tammi Guthrie (legal); Jack Copley (digital archivist); and
Jonathan Bennett (coloring).

You are invited

Program

Introduction

Who among us hasn't wished we could look into the future and see how one pivotal decision would change our lives forever? A crystal ball, perhaps, to tell us the future and lead us to the "right" decision? The great poet Robert Frost once wrote of a path diverging in the woods, and that choosing the path less traveled made "all the difference." We all must make choices without the benefit of a crystal ball—but wouldn't it be nice to see into the future? Wouldn't it be nice to be . . . Archie?

For seven decades, and with more than 1.5 billion copies sold, Archie Comics has brought joy and entertainment to kids and adults alike. Archie, the lovable, goofy, redheaded hero, stumbles through high school with his buddies, almost constantly getting into trouble of one sort or another. The main source of his troubles? The fact that he can never make up his mind between his two girlfriends, Veronica Lodge and Betty Cooper!

Now, in the spirit of Robert Frost's diverging path, Archie brings us something new: a walk up Memory Lane. That's right—*up*. We'll get to see into Archie's future—two paths hinging on a single decision: Should he ask Veronica or Betty to marry him? And we'll get to live vicariously through Archie as he watches his two futures unfold. Which girl is right for Archie? Veronica embodies the unreachable fantasy girl—rich, spoiled, beautiful, and probably too good for Archie. Betty is the adorable, wholesome girl next door. She's sweet, endearing, and probably way too understanding of Archie's antics.

As a child actress, I played the role of another such Ms. Cooper: Kevin Arnold's quintessential girl next door, Winnie Cooper, on a TV show called *The Wonder Years*. In fact, I met Michael Uslan, the writer of this Archie book, through friends on that very show! I was delighted when Michael asked me to write this introduction—he saw a parallel between the two childhood sagas, and rightfully so. Much like *Archie,* which is set in the nondescript town of Riverdale, *The Wonder Years* takes place in Anytown, USA, never committing to any particular city or region of the country. And why? Because just like Archie, the adventures and heartaches of growing up—including

on-again, off-again relationships with the girl next door—are about as universal and American as apple pie.

We watch television shows and read comics for entertainment, sure, but also to see our own stories played out, hoping perhaps to catch a glimpse of where our own decisions might lead, especially when faced with a fork in the road. I found myself at a rather large fork shortly after *The Wonder Years* ended. I had just begun college at UCLA, and figured I'd keep acting and attending school simultaneously like I'd always done. Somehow, though, the college professors weren't so understanding when I'd need to, for example, leave for four weeks to shoot a movie in Vancouver and reschedule my final exams. Who knew? So I kept having to drop classes, and I couldn't afford many more Incompletes on my record. At the same time, I had discovered a true, exciting love of mathematics, and I wanted to deepen my studies, even become a math major. The path was diverging . . .

I realized it had become impossible to continue straddling my two loves: acting, the glamorous Veronica of my life, and academics, my levelheaded and profoundly satisfying Betty. And so I came to a big decision: Which do I choose? Do I drop out of college to continue acting? Do I quit acting to focus on math? How I would have loved to walk *up* Memory Lane and see how each choice would pan out.

Maybe because I had already acted all my life and was ready for something new, or maybe because I just had a gut instinct about it, I chose math—the path definitely less traveled! I took my agent to breakfast, broke the news, and traded in my scripts and headshots for math books and a chalkboard (I still have that chalkboard in my condo). As I forged this new path

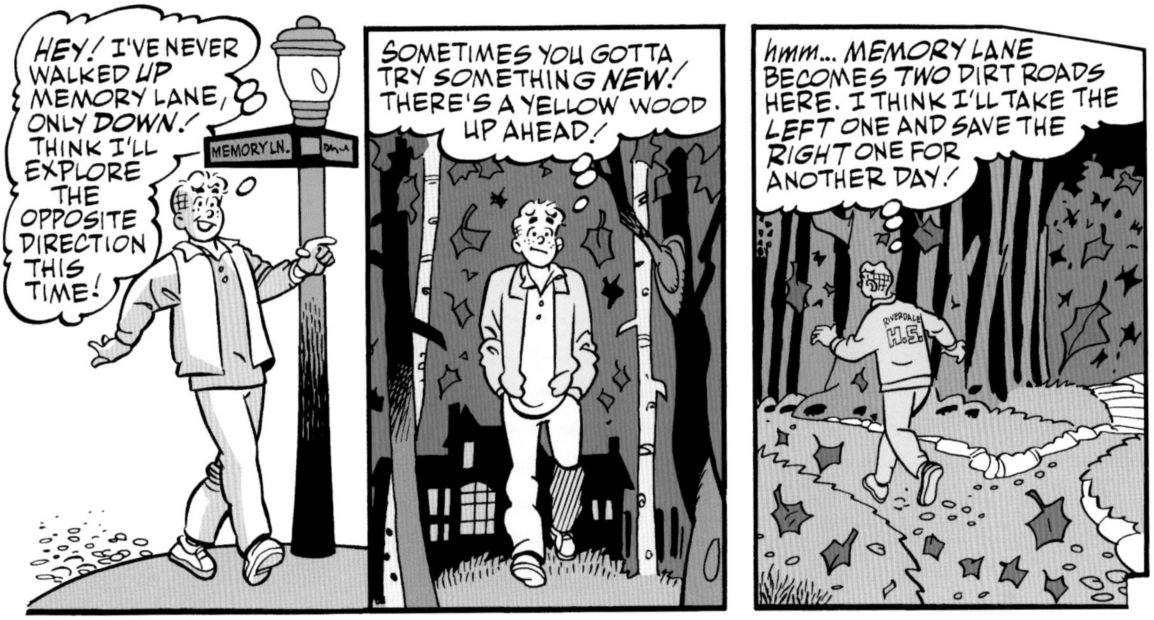
HEY! I'VE NEVER WALKED UP MEMORY LANE, ONLY DOWN! THINK I'LL EXPLORE THE OPPOSITE DIRECTION THIS TIME!
MEMORY LN.
SOMETIMES YOU GOTTA TRY SOMETHING NEW! THERE'S A YELLOW WOOD UP AHEAD!
hmm... MEMORY LANE BECOMES TWO DIRT ROADS HERE. I THINK I'LL TAKE THE LEFT ONE AND SAVE THE RIGHT ONE FOR ANOTHER DAY!
RIVERDALE H.S.

of intellectual discovery, I had no idea it would eventually lead me back to acting, and additionally, into a career of writing humorous math books for teenage girls, an incredibly satisfying combination of academia and entertainment. But one still can't help but wonder where the other path may have led . . .

We are all faced with choices, some big, some small, and all potentially changing our lives in meaningful ways. *Should I get married or break up? Should I quit my job? Should I make that apology? Should . . . ?*

Is there any way for us to join Archie, in a world where we get to see *both* paths?

In quantum physics, the "many worlds" model allows for parallel universes. I'm a math/science junkie myself, so allow me to explain: In this theory, there are an infinite number (or just a very large number) of parallel universes, in which everything that could ever have happened is realized in one of them (that would be a lot of comics). The downside to the parallel-universe theory is that, by definition, those universes can never, ever interact with one another, so we never get to "see" what happens in them. In *Archie Marries . . .*, we get the best of both worlds. Parallel universes, and yes, we get to observe them!

No matter our age or the decade in which we live, we can't ever predict where different paths might lead us—and thank goodness for that. Sure, we all hold the illusion of knowing *anything* about the future, and this keeps us all somewhat sane. But in reality, life has surprises and delights in store that we never could have dreamed of.

And as I write this, four months pregnant with our first child, I know I'll soon be walking down one of life's miraculous and wonderfully irreversible paths, like so many before me. For Archie, and perhaps Archie alone, that path can take two forms simultaneously. He can have his cake and eat it, too: the glamorous Veronica and the girl next door, Betty. So before we return to our own deterministic lives, let's indulge a little fantasy . . .

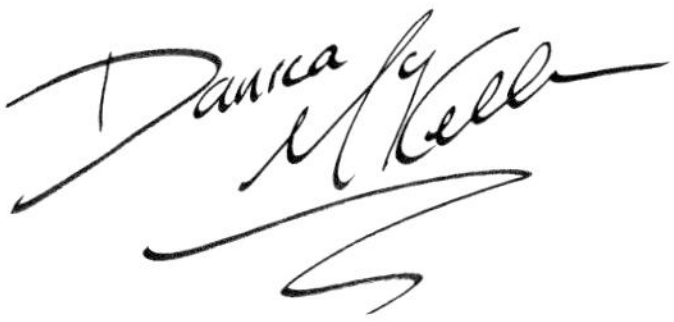

—Danica McKellar, April 2010

Danica McKellar, Winnie Cooper on *The Wonder Years* and Elsie Snuffin on *The West Wing*, is the *New York Times* bestselling author of *Math Doesn't Suck, Kiss My Math*, and *Hot X: Algebra Exposed.*

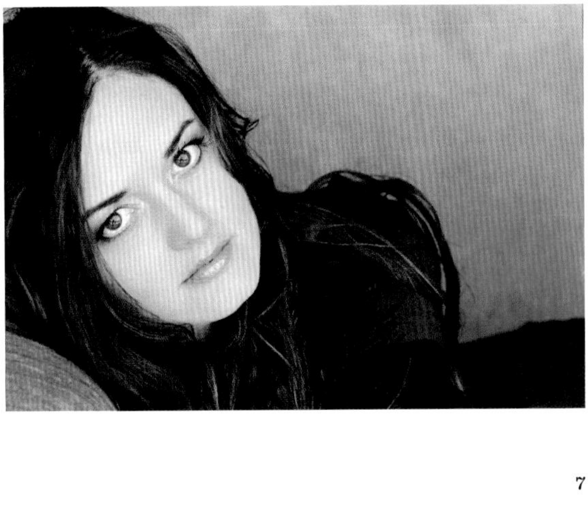

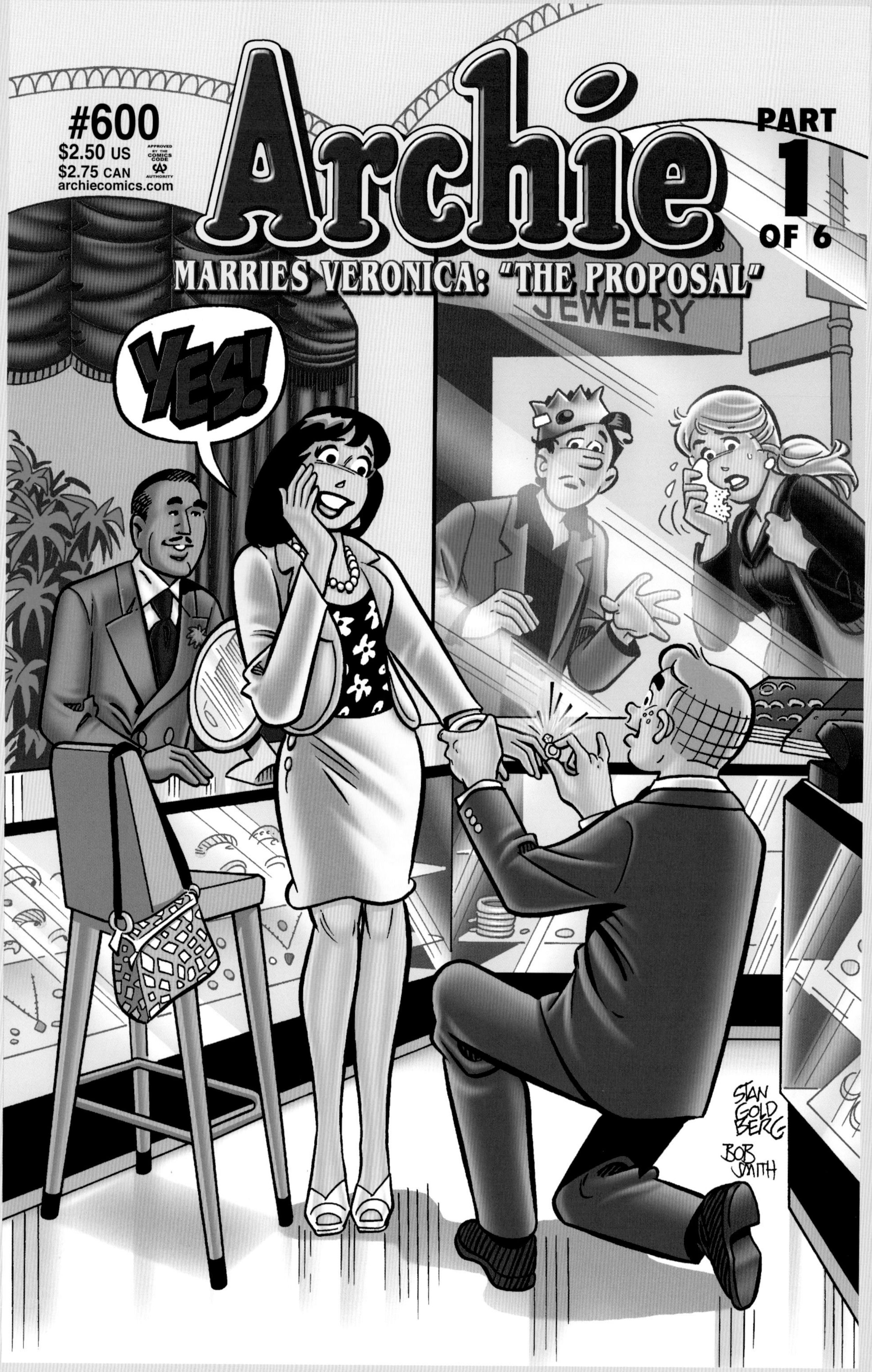
#600
$2.50 US
$2.75 CAN
APPROVED BY THE COMICS CODE AUTHORITY
archiecomics.com
Archie
PART 1 OF 6
MARRIES VERONICA: "THE PROPOSAL"
JEWELRY
YES!
STAN GOLDBERG
BOB SMITH

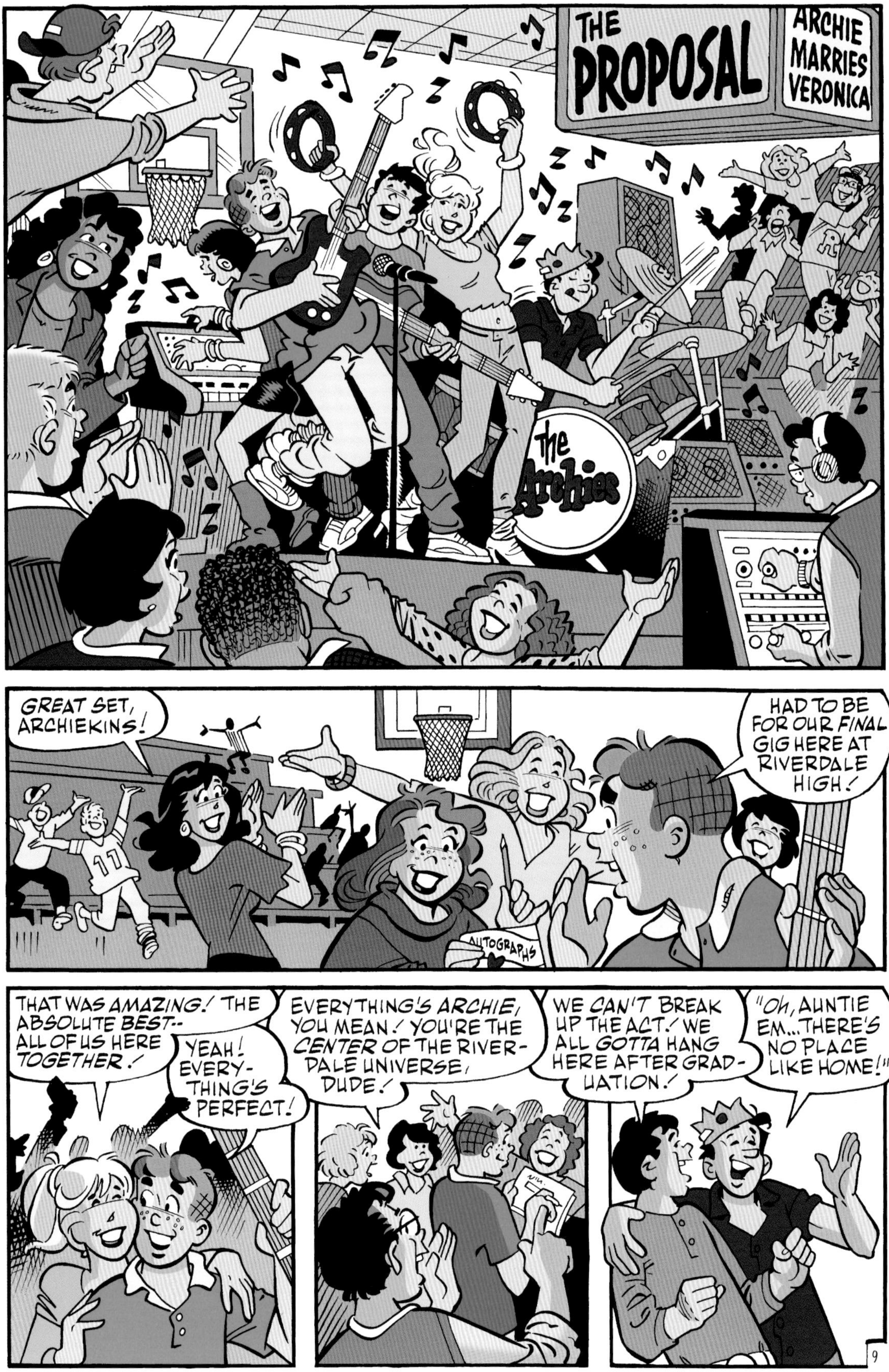
THE PROPOSAL
ARCHIE MARRIES VERONICA
The Archies
GREAT SET, ARCHIEKINS!
HAD TO BE FOR OUR FINAL GIG HERE AT RIVERDALE HIGH!
AUTOGRAPHS
THAT WAS AMAZING! THE ABSOLUTE BEST-- ALL OF US HERE TOGETHER!
YEAH! EVERY-THING'S PERFECT!
EVERYTHING'S ARCHIE, YOU MEAN! YOU'RE THE CENTER OF THE RIVER-DALE UNIVERSE, DUDE!
WE CAN'T BREAK UP THE ACT! WE ALL GOTTA HANG HERE AFTER GRAD-UATION!
"Oh, AUNTIE EM... THERE'S NO PLACE LIKE HOME!"

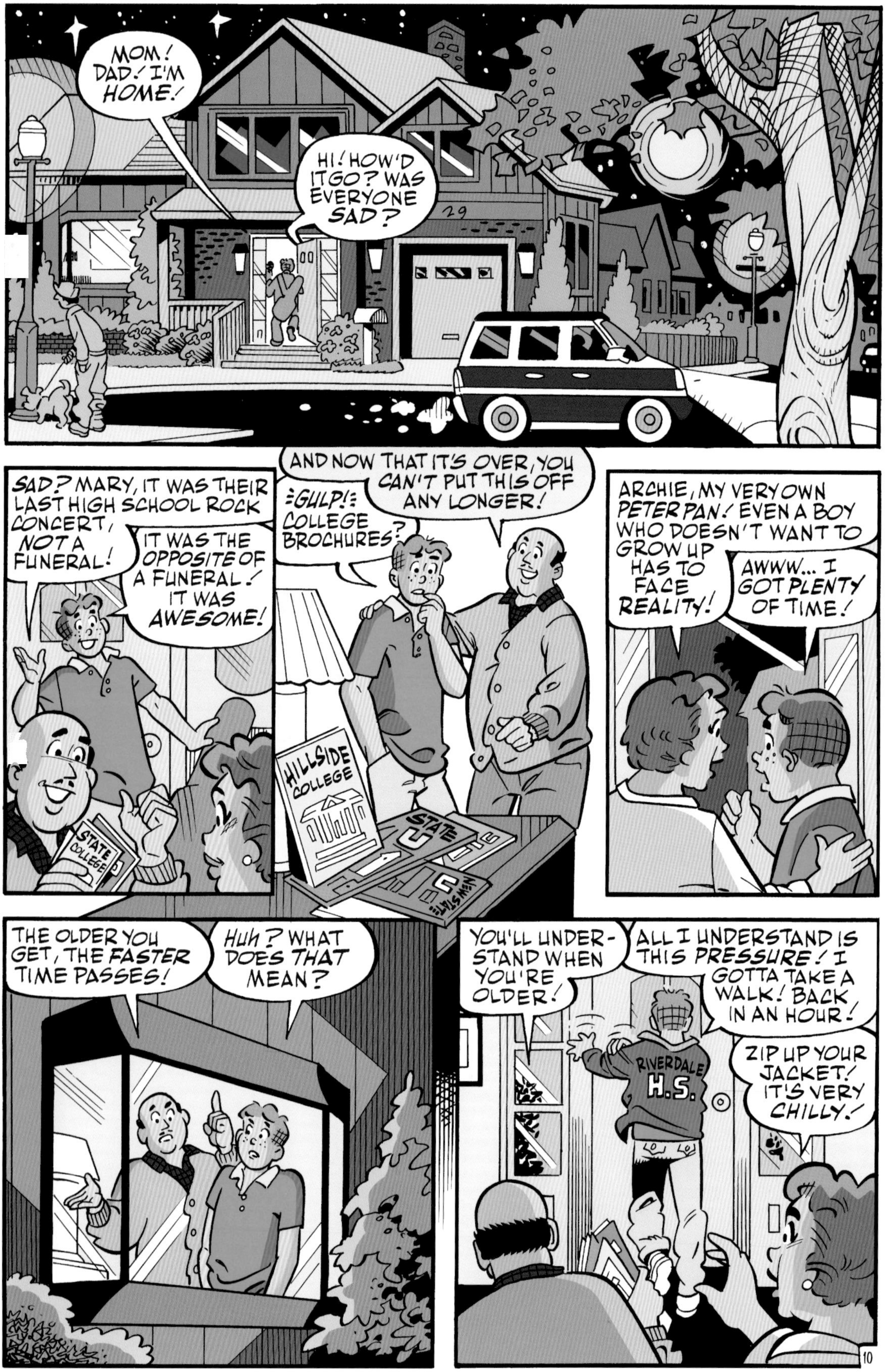
MOM! DAD! I'M HOME!
HI! HOW'D IT GO? WAS EVERYONE SAD?
29
SAD? MARY, IT WAS THEIR LAST HIGH SCHOOL ROCK CONCERT, NOT A FUNERAL!
IT WAS THE OPPOSITE OF A FUNERAL! IT WAS AWESOME!
STATE COLLEGE
AND NOW THAT IT'S OVER, YOU CAN'T PUT THIS OFF ANY LONGER!
GULP! COLLEGE BROCHURES?
HILLSIDE COLLEGE
STATE U
ARCHIE, MY VERY OWN PETER PAN! EVEN A BOY WHO DOESN'T WANT TO GROW UP HAS TO FACE REALITY!
AWWW... I GOT PLENTY OF TIME!
THE OLDER YOU GET, THE FASTER TIME PASSES!
HUH? WHAT DOES THAT MEAN?
YOU'LL UNDERSTAND WHEN YOU'RE OLDER!
ALL I UNDERSTAND IS THIS PRESSURE! I GOTTA TAKE A WALK! BACK IN AN HOUR!
RIVERDALE H.S.
ZIP UP YOUR JACKET! IT'S VERY CHILLY!

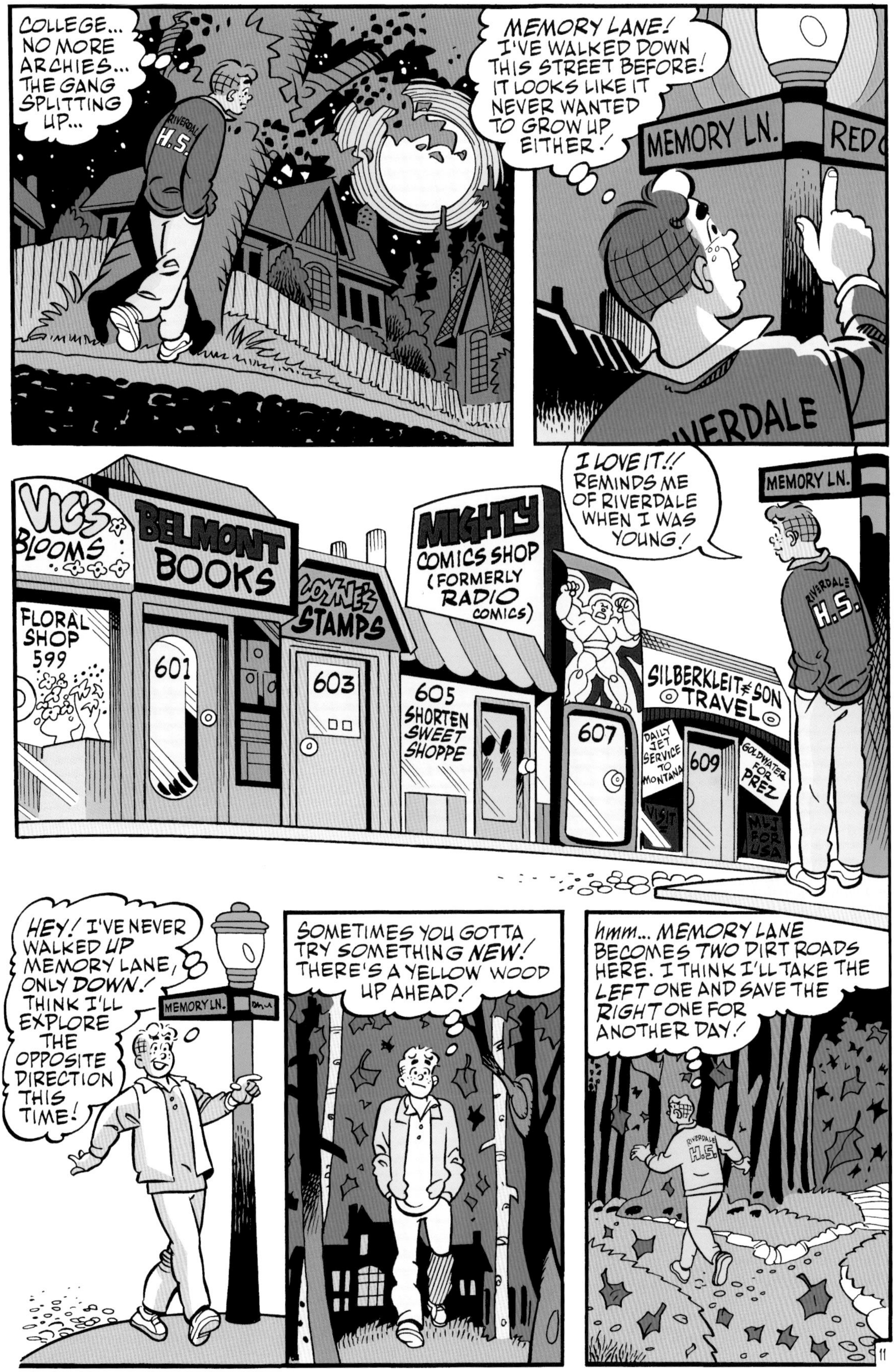
COLLEGE... NO MORE ARCHIES... THE GANG SPLITTING UP...
RIVERDALE H.S.
MEMORY LANE! I'VE WALKED DOWN THIS STREET BEFORE! IT LOOKS LIKE IT NEVER WANTED TO GROW UP EITHER!
MEMORY LN.
RED
RIVERDALE
VIC'S BLOOMS
BELMONT BOOKS
COYNE'S STAMPS
MIGHTY COMICS SHOP (FORMERLY RADIO COMICS)
I LOVE IT!! REMINDS ME OF RIVERDALE WHEN I WAS YOUNG!
MEMORY LN.
FLORAL SHOP 599
601
603
605 SHORTEN SWEET SHOPPE
607
SILBERKLEIT & SON TRAVEL
DAILY JET SERVICE TO MONTANA
609
GOLDWATER FOR PREZ
VISIT
MLJ FOR USA
RIVERDALE H.S.
HEY! I'VE NEVER WALKED UP MEMORY LANE, ONLY DOWN! THINK I'LL EXPLORE THE OPPOSITE DIRECTION THIS TIME!
MEMORY LN.
SOMETIMES YOU GOTTA TRY SOMETHING NEW! THERE'S A YELLOW WOOD UP AHEAD!
hmm... MEMORY LANE BECOMES TWO DIRT ROADS HERE. I THINK I'LL TAKE THE LEFT ONE AND SAVE THE RIGHT ONE FOR ANOTHER DAY!
RIVERDALE H.S.

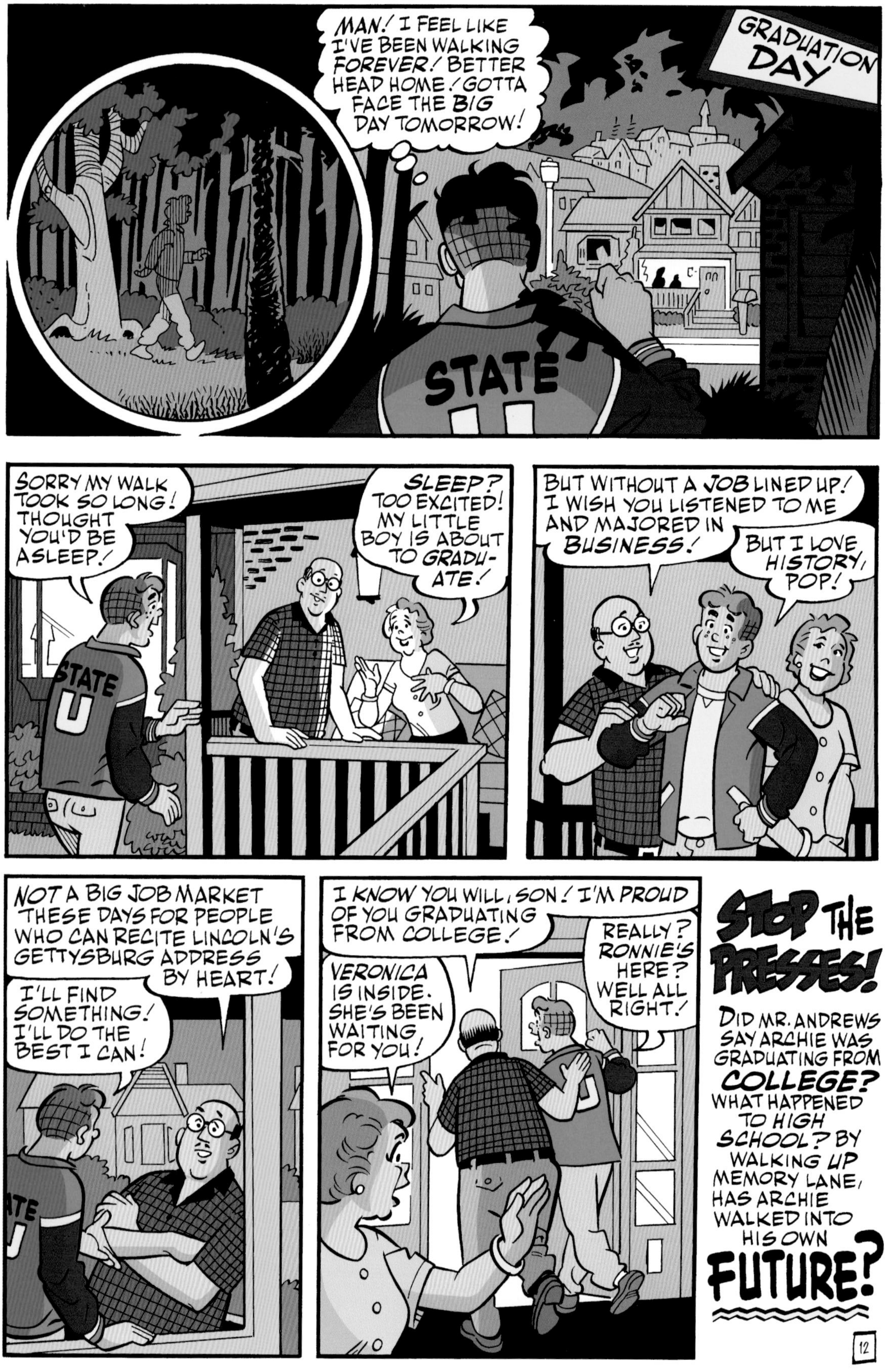
MAN! I FEEL LIKE I'VE BEEN WALKING FOREVER! BETTER HEAD HOME! GOTTA FACE THE BIG DAY TOMORROW!
GRADUATION DAY
STATE U
SORRY MY WALK TOOK SO LONG! THOUGHT YOU'D BE ASLEEP!
SLEEP? TOO EXCITED! MY LITTLE BOY IS ABOUT TO GRADUATE!
BUT WITHOUT A JOB LINED UP! I WISH YOU LISTENED TO ME AND MAJORED IN BUSINESS!
BUT I LOVE HISTORY, POP!
NOT A BIG JOB MARKET THESE DAYS FOR PEOPLE WHO CAN RECITE LINCOLN'S GETTYSBURG ADDRESS BY HEART!
I'LL FIND SOMETHING! I'LL DO THE BEST I CAN!
I KNOW YOU WILL, SON! I'M PROUD OF YOU GRADUATING FROM COLLEGE!
VERONICA IS INSIDE. SHE'S BEEN WAITING FOR YOU!
REALLY? RONNIE'S HERE? WELL ALL RIGHT!
STOP THE PRESSES!
DID MR. ANDREWS SAY ARCHIE WAS GRADUATING FROM COLLEGE? WHAT HAPPENED TO HIGH SCHOOL? BY WALKING UP MEMORY LANE, HAS ARCHIE WALKED INTO HIS OWN FUTURE?

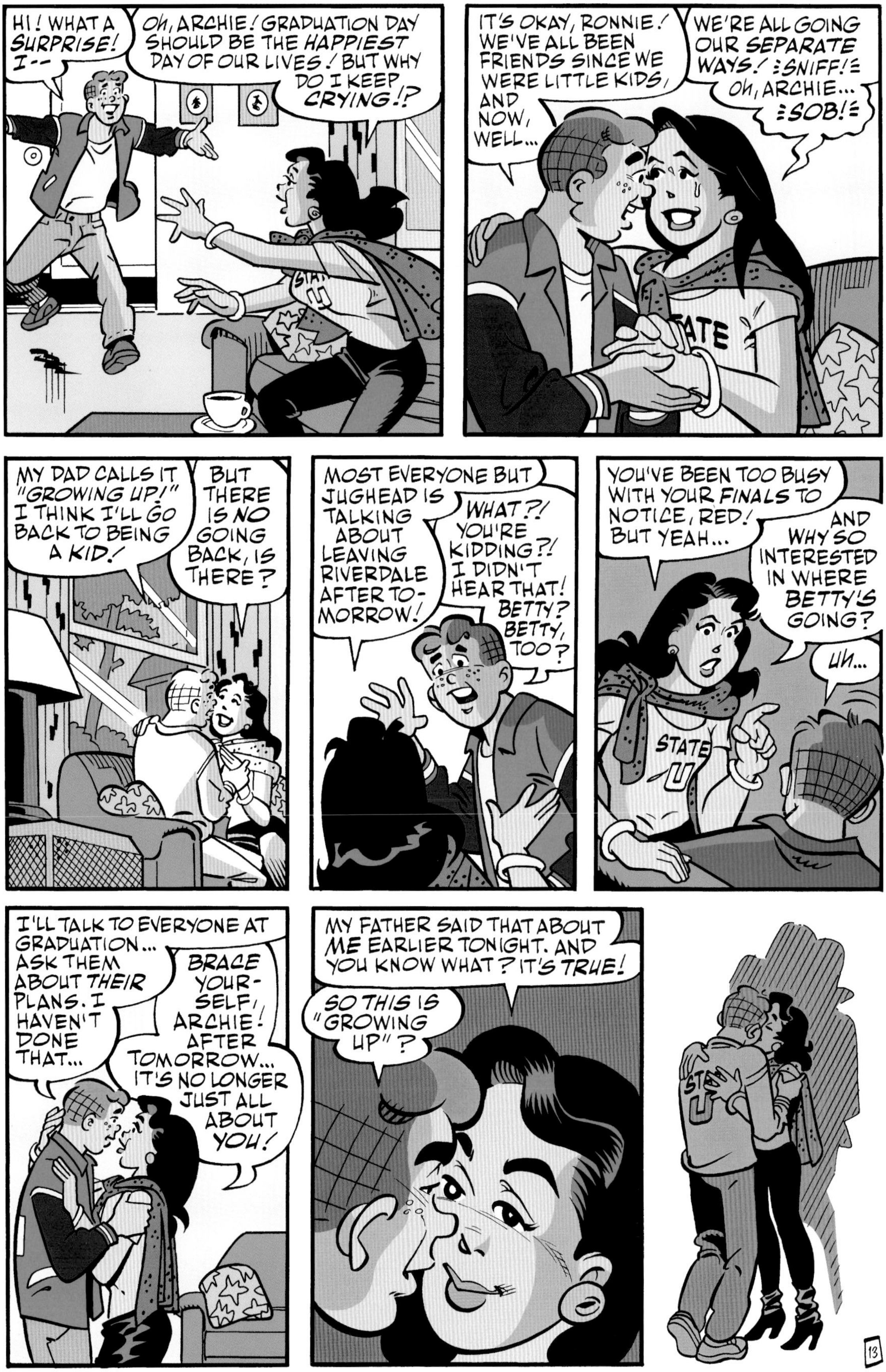
HI! WHAT A SURPRISE! I--
OH, ARCHIE! GRADUATION DAY SHOULD BE THE HAPPIEST DAY OF OUR LIVES! BUT WHY DO I KEEP CRYING!?
IT'S OKAY, RONNIE! WE'VE ALL BEEN FRIENDS SINCE WE WERE LITTLE KIDS, AND NOW, WELL...
WE'RE ALL GOING OUR SEPARATE WAYS! SNIFF! OH, ARCHIE... SOB!
MY DAD CALLS IT "GROWING UP!" I THINK I'LL GO BACK TO BEING A KID!
BUT THERE IS NO GOING BACK, IS THERE?
MOST EVERYONE BUT JUGHEAD IS TALKING ABOUT LEAVING RIVERDALE AFTER TO-MORROW!
WHAT?! YOU'RE KIDDING?! I DIDN'T HEAR THAT! BETTY? BETTY, TOO?
YOU'VE BEEN TOO BUSY WITH YOUR FINALS TO NOTICE, RED! BUT YEAH...
AND WHY SO INTERESTED IN WHERE BETTY'S GOING?
UH...
STATE U
I'LL TALK TO EVERYONE AT GRADUATION... ASK THEM ABOUT THEIR PLANS. I HAVEN'T DONE THAT...
BRACE YOUR-SELF, ARCHIE! AFTER TOMORROW... IT'S NO LONGER JUST ALL ABOUT YOU!
MY FATHER SAID THAT ABOUT ME EARLIER TONIGHT. AND YOU KNOW WHAT? IT'S TRUE!
SO THIS IS "GROWING UP"?

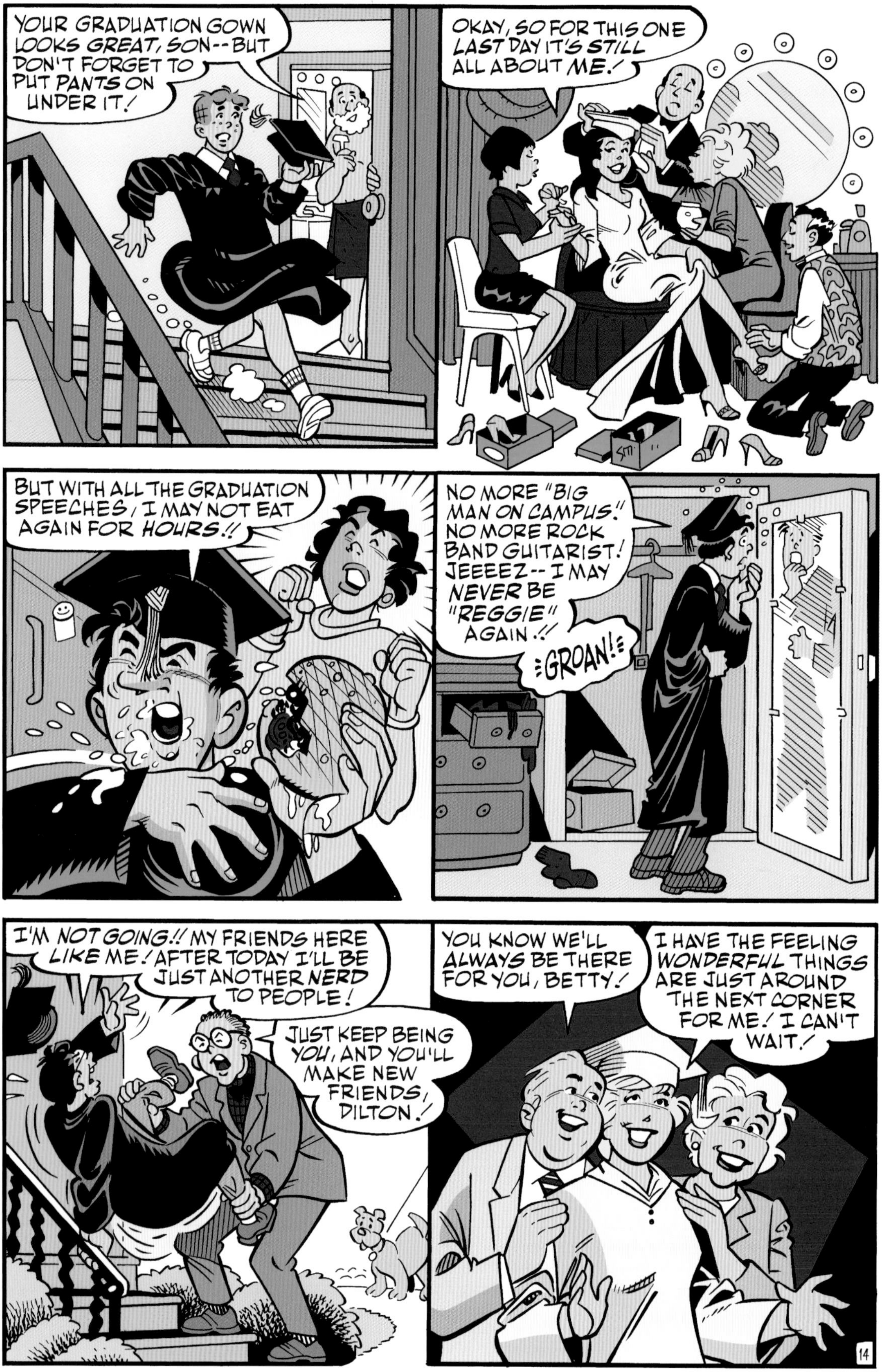
YOUR GRADUATION GOWN LOOKS GREAT, SON--BUT DON'T FORGET TO PUT PANTS ON UNDER IT!
OKAY, SO FOR THIS ONE LAST DAY IT'S STILL ALL ABOUT ME!
BUT WITH ALL THE GRADUATION SPEECHES, I MAY NOT EAT AGAIN FOR HOURS!!
NO MORE "BIG MAN ON CAMPUS!" NO MORE ROCK BAND GUITARIST! JEEEEZ-- I MAY NEVER BE "REGGIE" AGAIN!!
GROAN!
I'M NOT GOING!! MY FRIENDS HERE LIKE ME! AFTER TODAY I'LL BE JUST ANOTHER NERD TO PEOPLE!
JUST KEEP BEING YOU, AND YOU'LL MAKE NEW FRIENDS, DILTON!
YOU KNOW WE'LL ALWAYS BE THERE FOR YOU, BETTY!
I HAVE THE FEELING WONDERFUL THINGS ARE JUST AROUND THE NEXT CORNER FOR ME! I CAN'T WAIT!
14

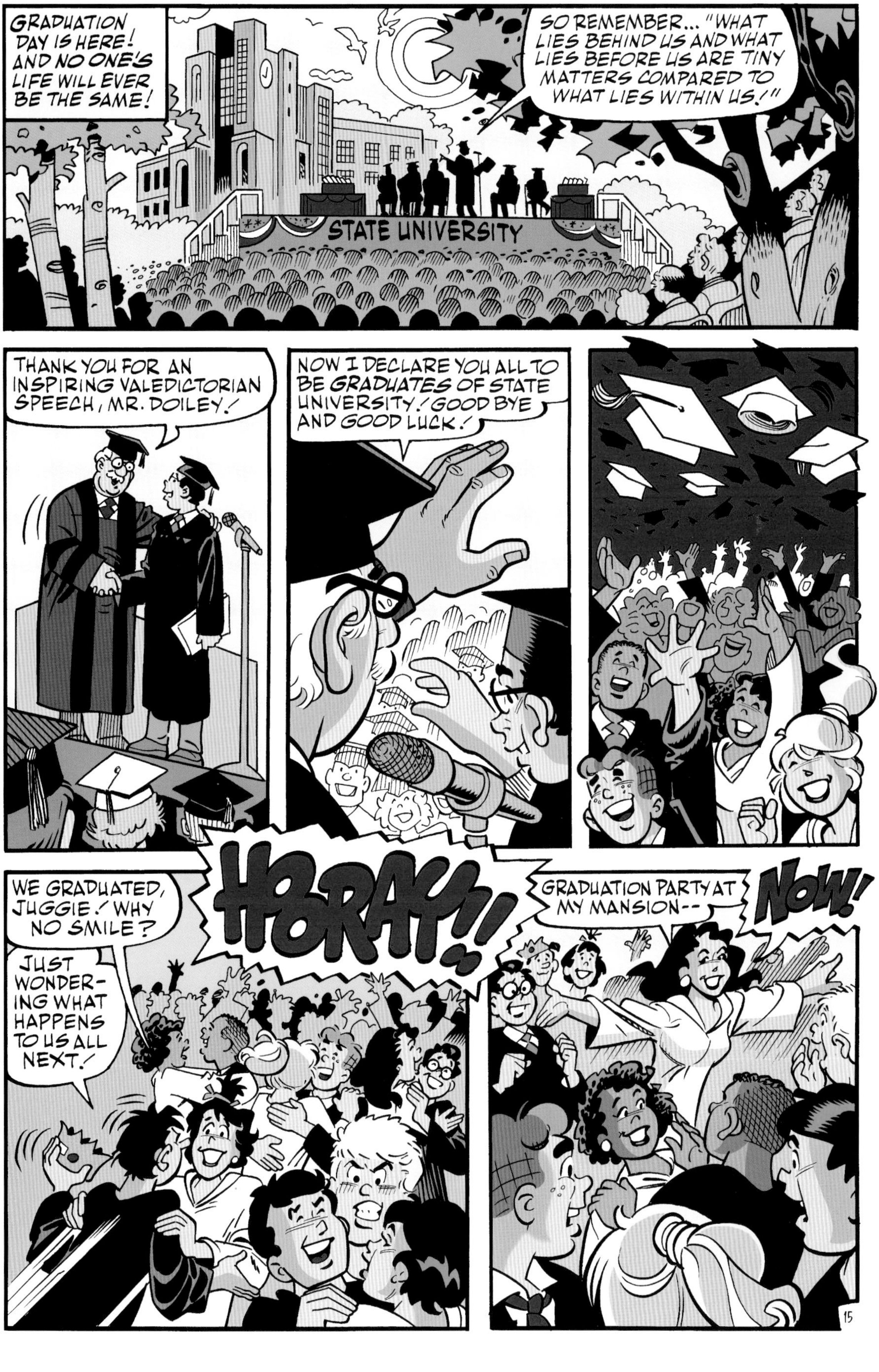
GRADUATION DAY IS HERE! AND NO ONE'S LIFE WILL EVER BE THE SAME!
SO REMEMBER... "WHAT LIES BEHIND US AND WHAT LIES BEFORE US ARE TINY MATTERS COMPARED TO WHAT LIES WITHIN US!"
STATE UNIVERSITY
THANK YOU FOR AN INSPIRING VALEDICTORIAN SPEECH, MR. DOILEY!
NOW I DECLARE YOU ALL TO BE GRADUATES OF STATE UNIVERSITY! GOOD BYE AND GOOD LUCK!
HOORAY!!!
WE GRADUATED, JUGGIE! WHY NO SMILE?
JUST WONDERING WHAT HAPPENS TO US ALL NEXT!
GRADUATION PARTY AT MY MANSION--
NOW!

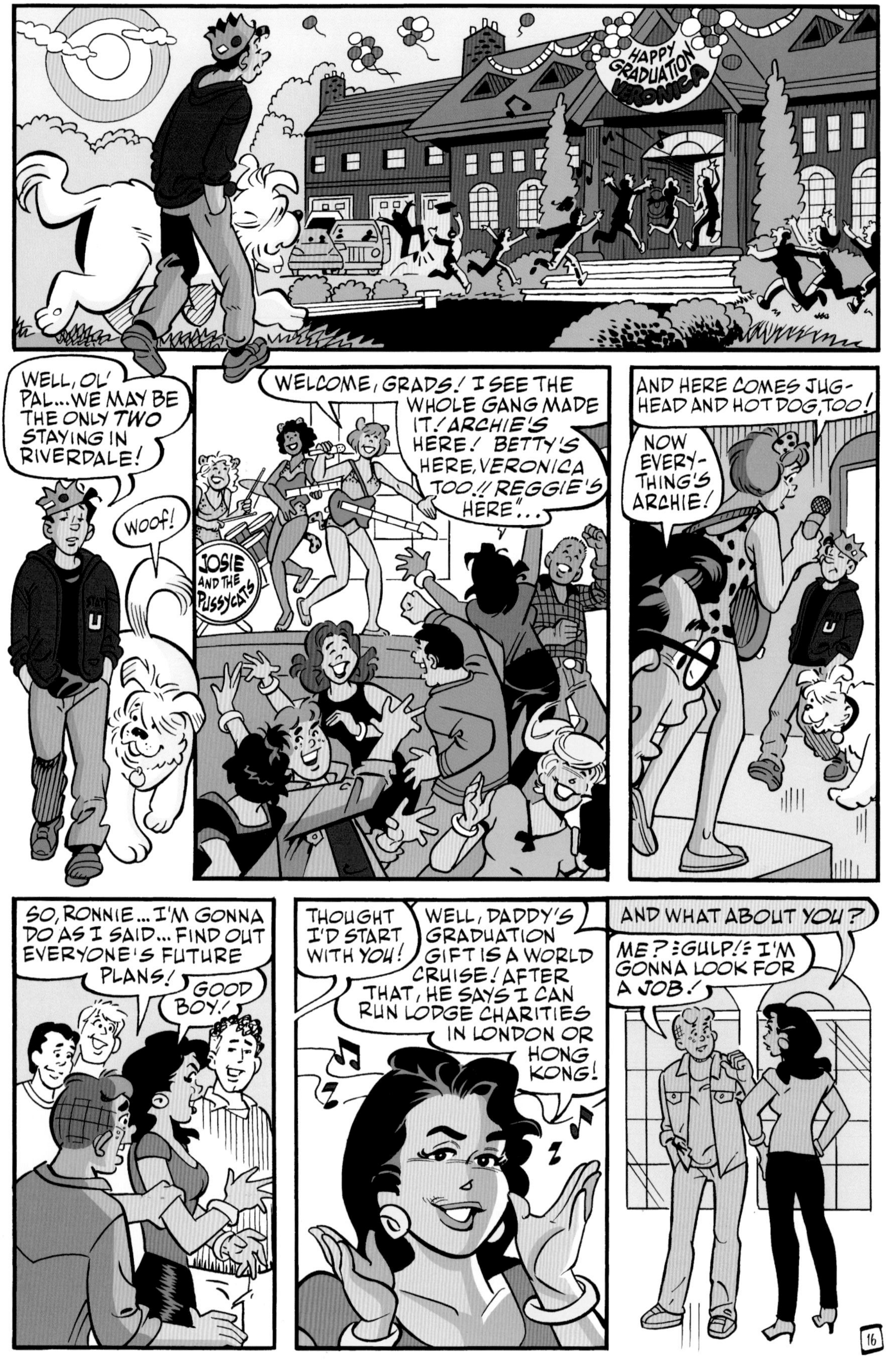
HAPPY GRADUATION VERONICA
WELL, OL' PAL...WE MAY BE THE ONLY TWO STAYING IN RIVERDALE!
WOOF!
WELCOME, GRADS! I SEE THE WHOLE GANG MADE IT! ARCHIE'S HERE! BETTY'S HERE, VERONICA TOO!! REGGIE'S HERE"...
JOSIE AND THE PUSSYCATS
AND HERE COMES JUGHEAD AND HOT DOG, TOO!
NOW EVERYTHING'S ARCHIE!
SO, RONNIE... I'M GONNA DO AS I SAID... FIND OUT EVERYONE'S FUTURE PLANS!
GOOD BOY!
THOUGHT I'D START WITH YOU!
WELL, DADDY'S GRADUATION GIFT IS A WORLD CRUISE! AFTER THAT, HE SAYS I CAN RUN LODGE CHARITIES IN LONDON OR HONG KONG!
AND WHAT ABOUT YOU?
ME? :GULP!: I'M GONNA LOOK FOR A JOB!

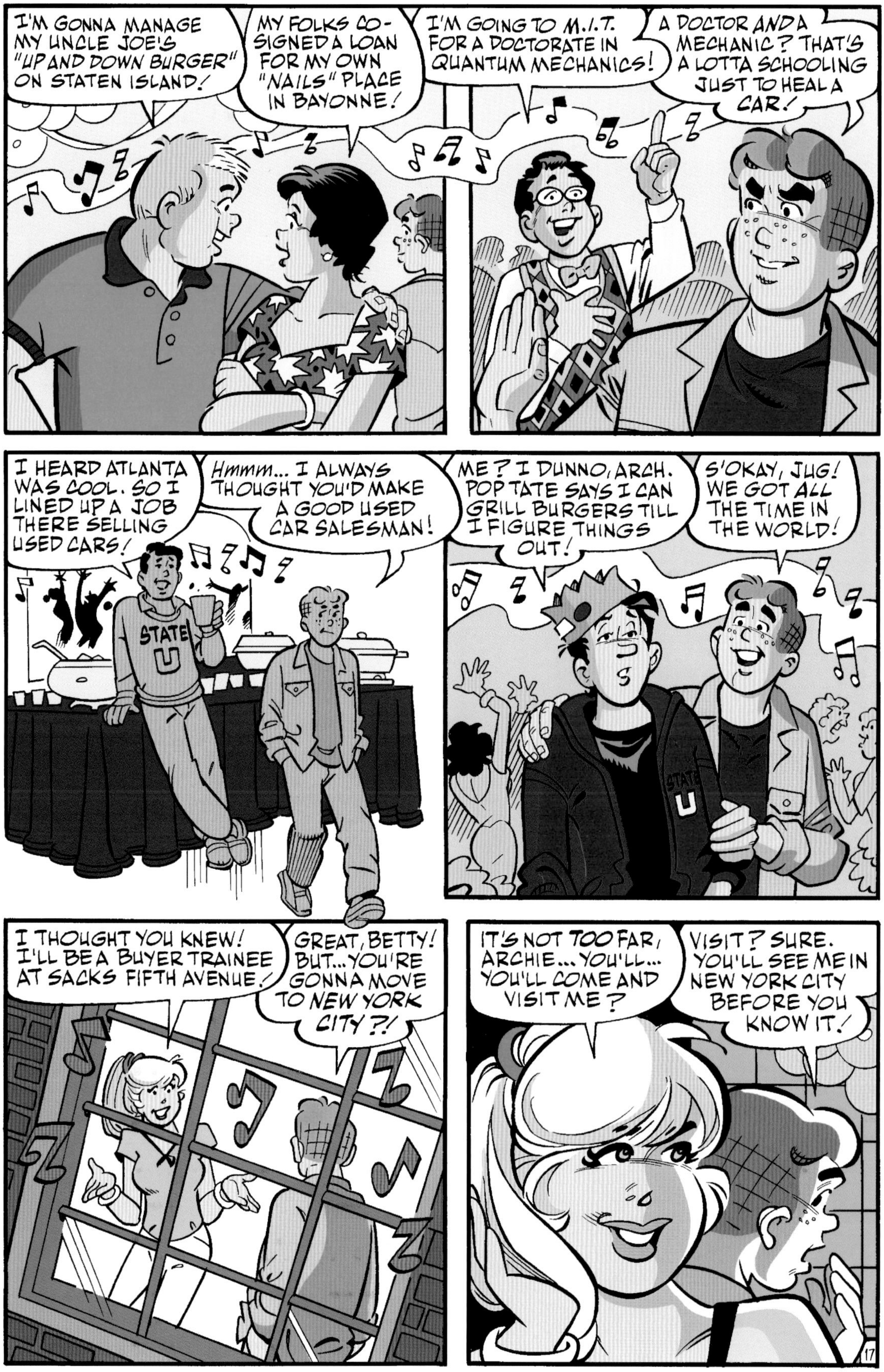
I'M GONNA MANAGE MY UNCLE JOE'S "UP AND DOWN BURGER" ON STATEN ISLAND!
MY FOLKS CO-SIGNED A LOAN FOR MY OWN "NAILS" PLACE IN BAYONNE!
I'M GOING TO M.I.T. FOR A DOCTORATE IN QUANTUM MECHANICS!
A DOCTOR AND A MECHANIC? THAT'S A LOTTA SCHOOLING JUST TO HEAL A CAR!
I HEARD ATLANTA WAS COOL. SO I LINED UP A JOB THERE SELLING USED CARS!
Hmmm... I ALWAYS THOUGHT YOU'D MAKE A GOOD USED CAR SALESMAN!
STATE U
ME? I DUNNO, ARCH. POP TATE SAYS I CAN GRILL BURGERS TILL I FIGURE THINGS OUT!
S'OKAY, JUG! WE GOT ALL THE TIME IN THE WORLD!
STATE U
I THOUGHT YOU KNEW! I'LL BE A BUYER TRAINEE AT SACKS FIFTH AVENUE!
GREAT, BETTY! BUT...YOU'RE GONNA MOVE TO NEW YORK CITY?!
IT'S NOT TOO FAR, ARCHIE... YOU'LL... YOU'LL COME AND VISIT ME?
VISIT? SURE. YOU'LL SEE ME IN NEW YORK CITY BEFORE YOU KNOW IT!

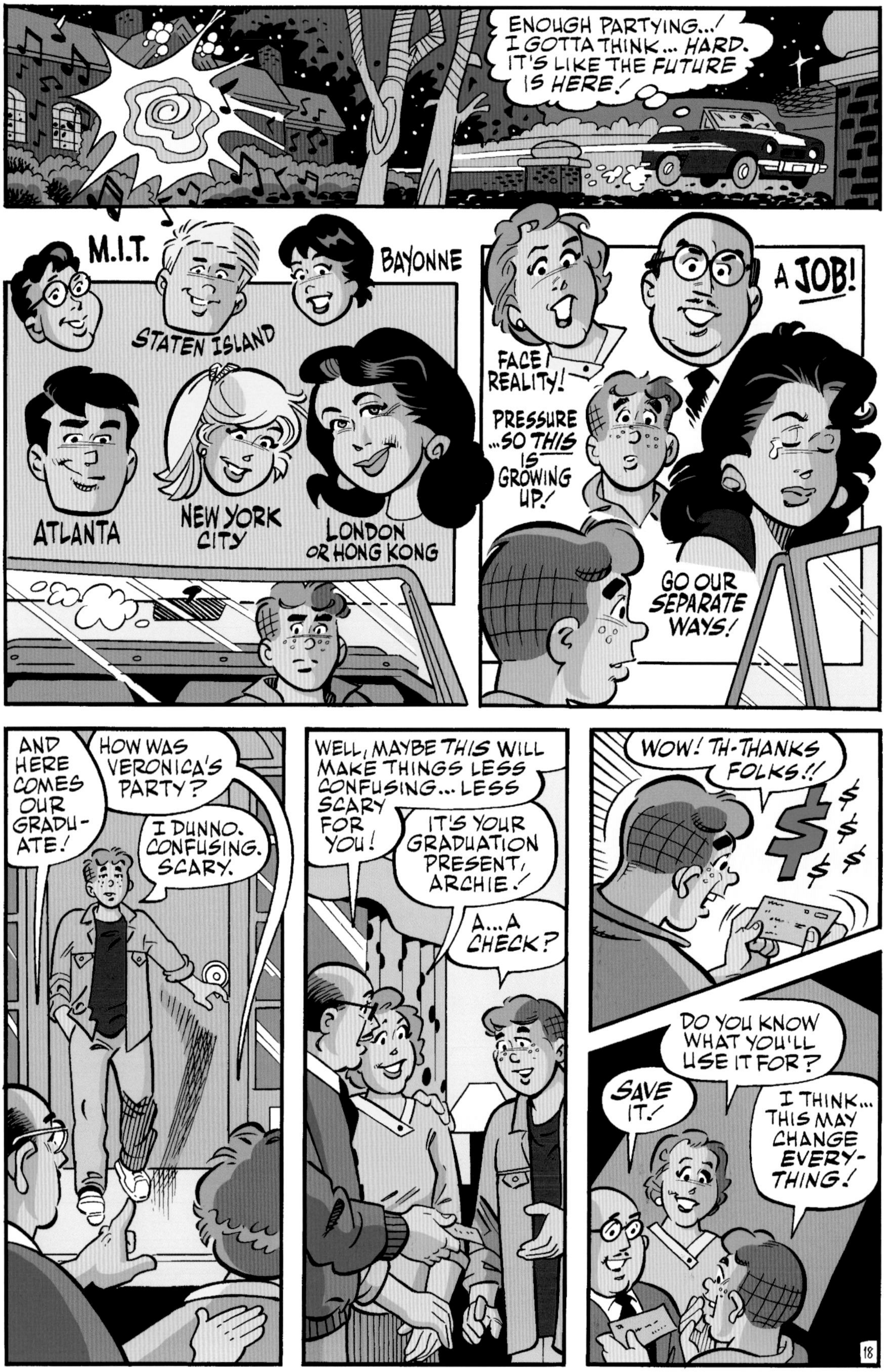
ENOUGH PARTYING...! I GOTTA THINK... HARD. IT'S LIKE THE FUTURE IS HERE!
M.I.T.
STATEN ISLAND
BAYONNE
ATLANTA
NEW YORK CITY
LONDON OR HONG KONG
FACE REALITY!
A JOB!
PRESSURE ...SO THIS IS GROWING UP!
GO OUR SEPARATE WAYS!
AND HERE COMES OUR GRADU-ATE!
HOW WAS VERONICA'S PARTY?
I DUNNO. CONFUSING. SCARY.
WELL, MAYBE THIS WILL MAKE THINGS LESS CONFUSING... LESS SCARY FOR YOU!
IT'S YOUR GRADUATION PRESENT, ARCHIE!
A...A CHECK?
WOW! TH-THANKS FOLKS!!
DO YOU KNOW WHAT YOU'LL USE IT FOR?
SAVE IT!
I THINK... THIS MAY CHANGE EVERY-THING!
18

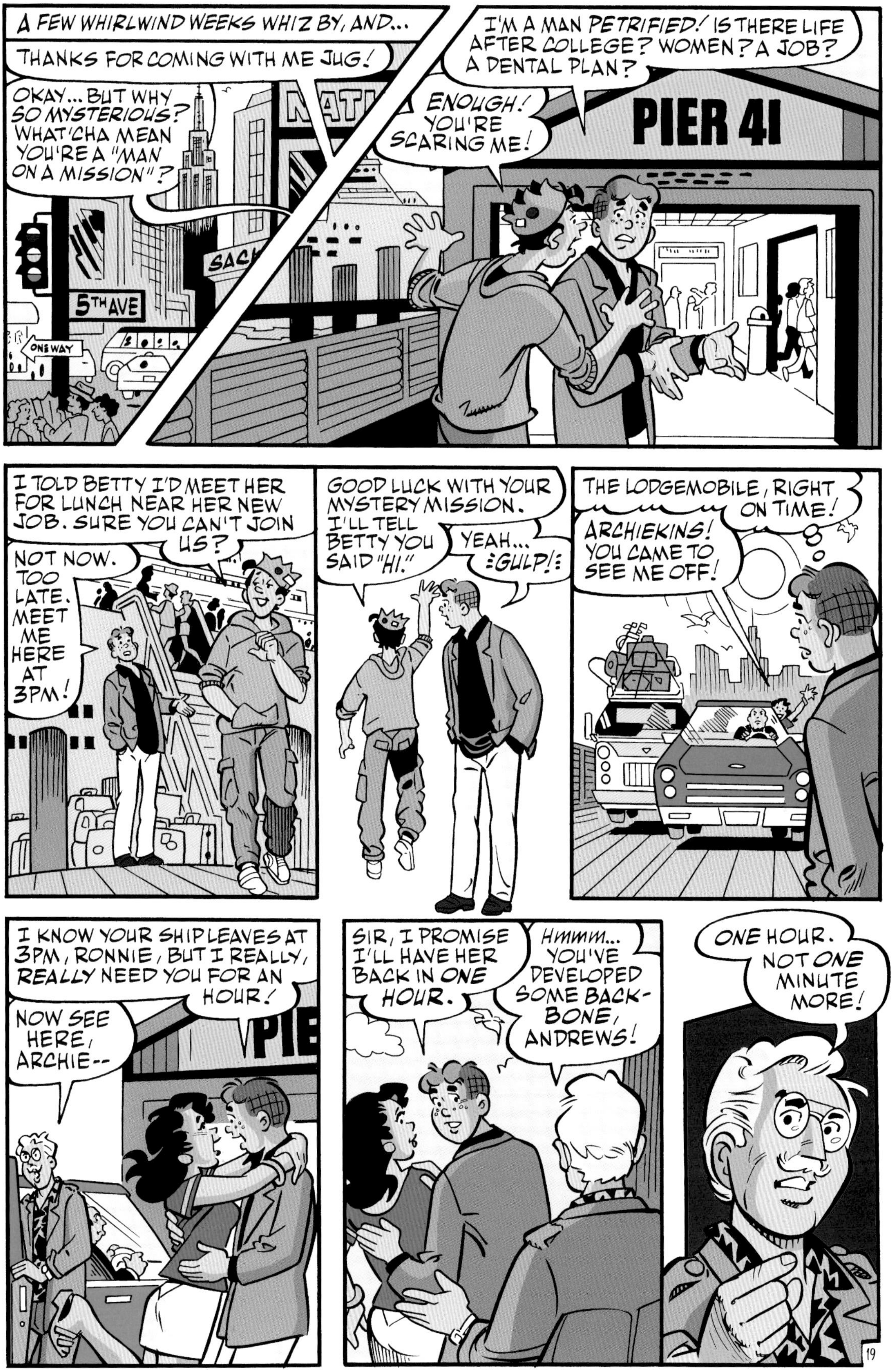
A FEW WHIRLWIND WEEKS WHIZ BY, AND...
THANKS FOR COMING WITH ME JUG!
OKAY... BUT WHY SO MYSTERIOUS? WHAT'CHA MEAN YOU'RE A "MAN ON A MISSION"?
5TH AVE
ONE WAY
I'M A MAN PETRIFIED! IS THERE LIFE AFTER COLLEGE? WOMEN? A JOB? A DENTAL PLAN?
ENOUGH! YOU'RE SCARING ME!
PIER 41
I TOLD BETTY I'D MEET HER FOR LUNCH NEAR HER NEW JOB. SURE YOU CAN'T JOIN US?
NOT NOW. TOO LATE. MEET ME HERE AT 3PM!
GOOD LUCK WITH YOUR MYSTERY MISSION. I'LL TELL BETTY YOU SAID "HI."
YEAH... GULP!
THE LODGEMOBILE, RIGHT ON TIME!
ARCHIEKINS! YOU CAME TO SEE ME OFF!
I KNOW YOUR SHIP LEAVES AT 3PM, RONNIE, BUT I REALLY, REALLY NEED YOU FOR AN HOUR!
NOW SEE HERE, ARCHIE--
SIR, I PROMISE I'LL HAVE HER BACK IN ONE HOUR.
HMMM... YOU'VE DEVELOPED SOME BACKBONE, ANDREWS!
ONE HOUR. NOT ONE MINUTE MORE!

OSTERIA AL ROSEN

GREAT TO SEE YOU, JUGGIE! I THOUGHT ARCHIE--

HE'S BEING VERY SECRETIVE, BUT I THINK HE HAD A BIG JOB INTERVIEW. HE SAYS "HI."

YOU--YOU MEAN HE MIGHT MOVE TO NEW YORK?

DUNNO... YEAH, MAYBE. I GUESS...

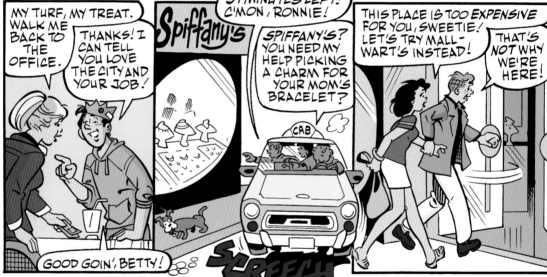

MY TURF, MY TREAT. WALK ME BACK TO THE OFFICE.

THANKS! I CAN TELL YOU LOVE THE CITY AND YOUR JOB!

Spiffany's

39 MINUTES LEFT! C'MON, RONNIE!

SPIFFANY'S? YOU NEED MY HELP PICKING A CHARM FOR YOUR MOM'S BRACELET?

THIS PLACE IS TOO EXPENSIVE FOR YOU, SWEETIE! LET'S TRY MALL-WART'S INSTEAD!

THAT'S NOT WHY WE'RE HERE!

CAB

GOOD GOIN', BETTY!

SCREECH

WELL, THEN WHY ARE WE--

'CAUSE YOU'RE LEAVING TODAY FOR 3 MONTHS AND I HADDA MAKE A BIG CHOICE!

SPIFFANY'S! LET'S LOOK AT THEIR DIAMONDS IN THE WINDOW!

I'D RATHER LOOK AT THE BURGERS IN THE DRIVE-THRU WINDOW AT McDANIEL'S!

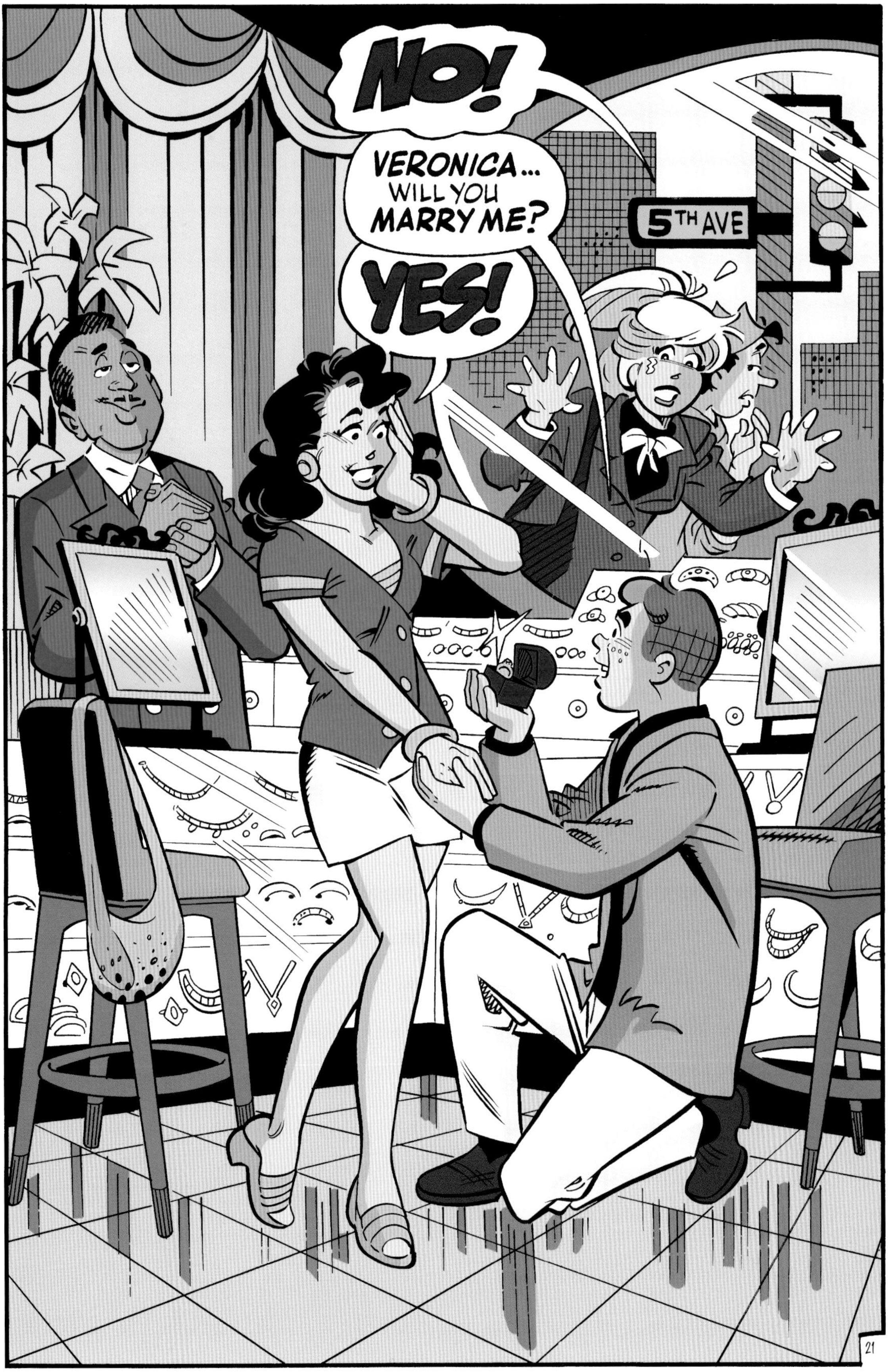

VERONICA... WILL YOU MARRY ME?
YES!
NO!
5TH AVE

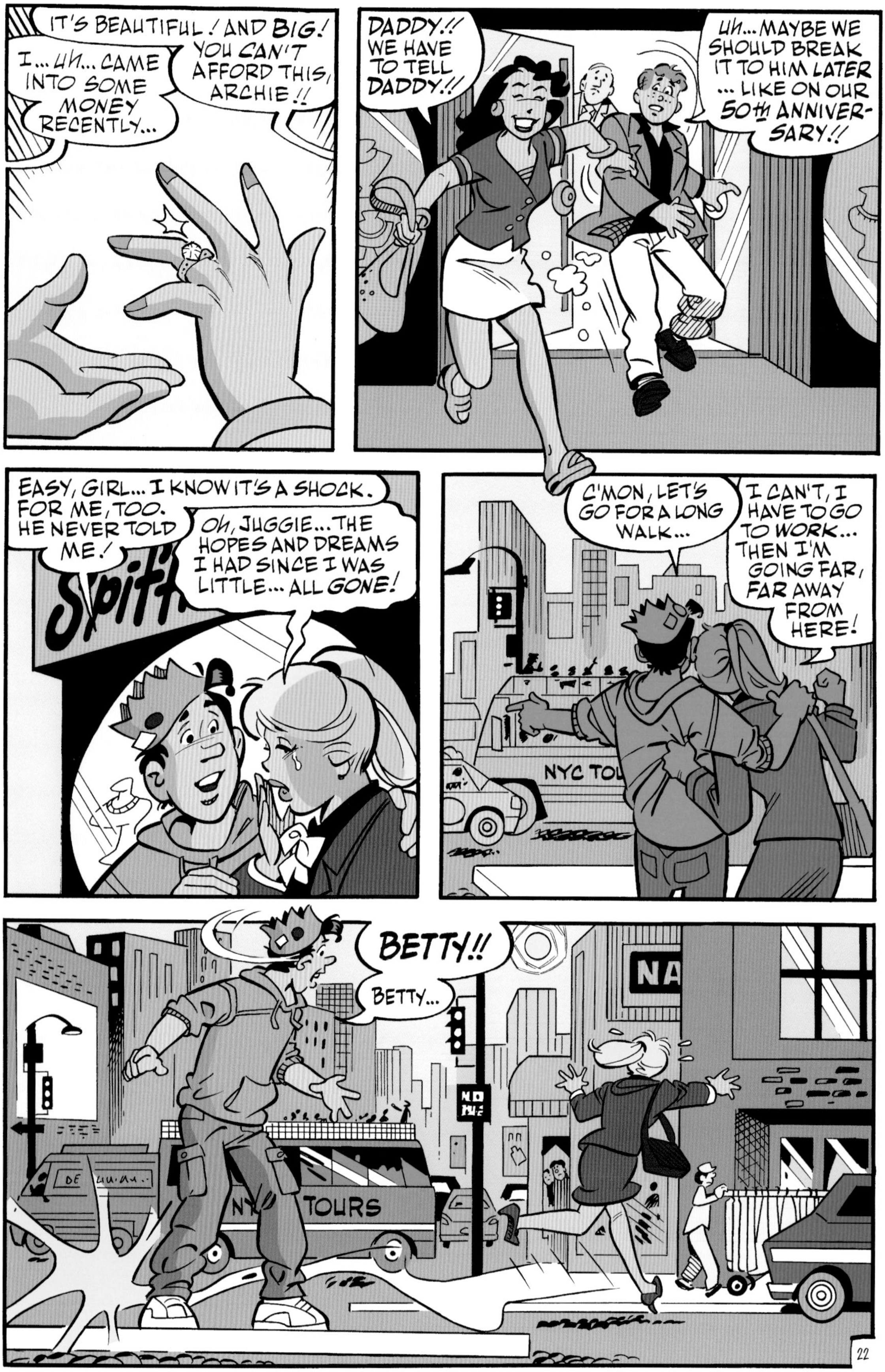

IT'S BEAUTIFUL! AND BIG!
I... UH... CAME INTO SOME MONEY RECENTLY...
YOU CAN'T AFFORD THIS, ARCHIE!!
DADDY!! WE HAVE TO TELL DADDY!!
UH... MAYBE WE SHOULD BREAK IT TO HIM LATER ... LIKE ON OUR 50TH ANNIVERSARY!!
EASY, GIRL... I KNOW IT'S A SHOCK. FOR ME, TOO. HE NEVER TOLD ME!
OH, JUGGIE... THE HOPES AND DREAMS I HAD SINCE I WAS LITTLE... ALL GONE!
C'MON, LET'S GO FOR A LONG WALK...
I CAN'T, I HAVE TO GO TO WORK... THEN I'M GOING FAR, FAR AWAY FROM HERE!
NYC TOURS
BETTY!!
BETTY...
NYC TOURS

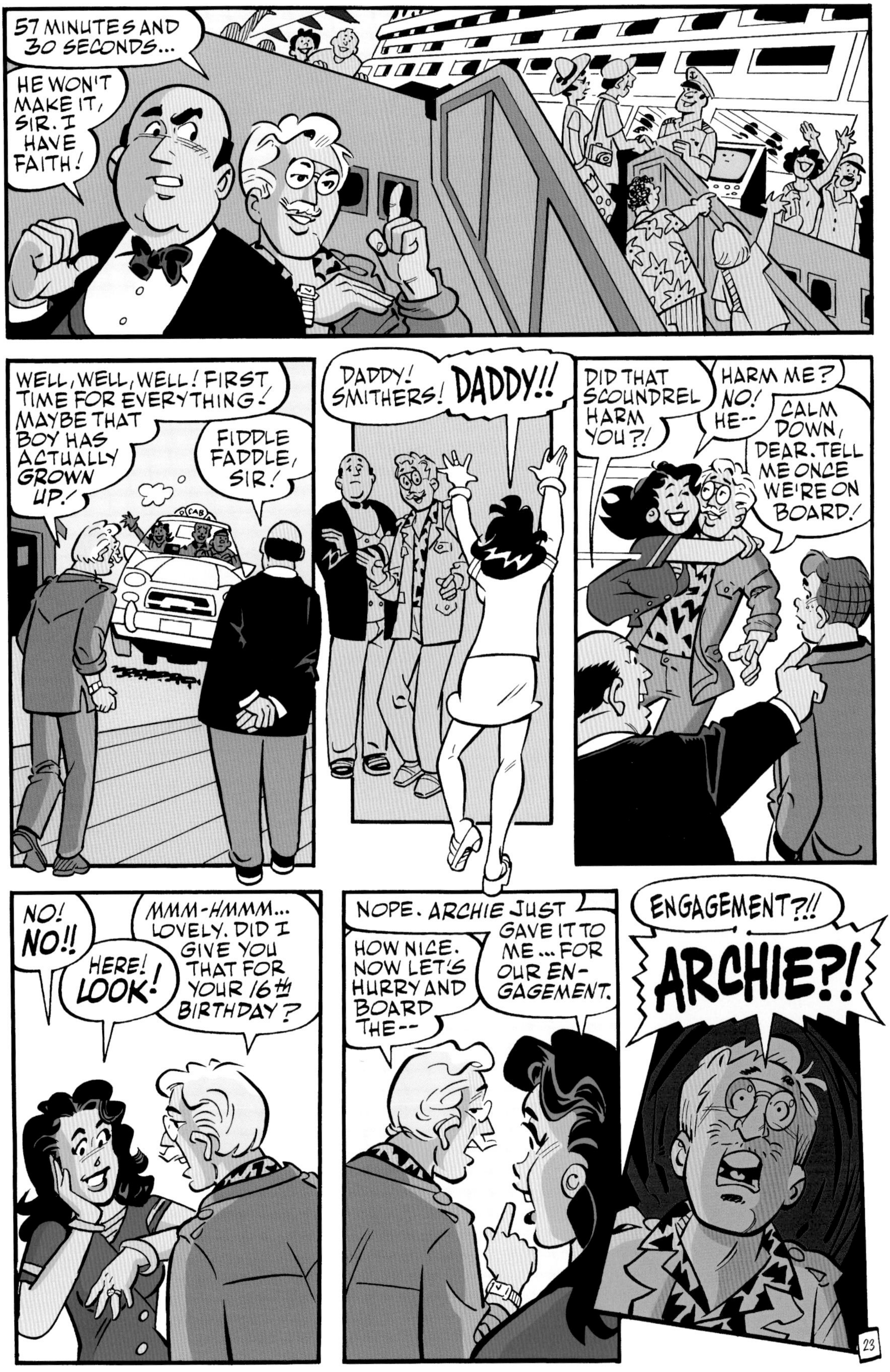
57 MINUTES AND 30 SECONDS...
HE WON'T MAKE IT, SIR. I HAVE FAITH!
WELL, WELL, WELL! FIRST TIME FOR EVERYTHING! MAYBE THAT BOY HAS ACTUALLY GROWN UP!
FIDDLE FADDLE, SIR!
CAB
DADDY! SMITHERS! DADDY!!
DID THAT SCOUNDREL HARM YOU?!
HARM ME? NO! HE--
CALM DOWN, DEAR. TELL ME ONCE WE'RE ON BOARD!
NO! NO!!
HERE! LOOK!
MMM-HMMM... LOVELY. DID I GIVE YOU THAT FOR YOUR 16th BIRTHDAY?
NOPE. ARCHIE JUST GAVE IT TO ME... FOR OUR ENGAGEMENT.
HOW NICE. NOW LET'S HURRY AND BOARD THE--
ENGAGEMENT?!!
ARCHIE?!

VERONICA... HERE'S MY CHECKBOOK. TELL THE CAPTAIN TO DELAY SAILING, AND PAY HIM WHAT HE ASKS!

SMITHERS, TAKE NOTES.

YES, SIR.

AND NOW, MY PROSPECTIVE SON-IN-LAW... WE'RE GOING TO HAVE A LITTLE CHAT!

ARCHIE, DO YOU LOVE MY DAUGHTER?

YES, SIR. I THINK I ALWAYS HAVE.

DO YOU HAVE A JOB?

UH... NO.

AN INCOME?

NO.

A HOUSE?

NO.

A HEALTH PLAN?

NO.

A SAVINGS ACCOUNT?!

NO.

SO IF YOU LOVE HER, THEN HOW DO YOU PLAN TO CARE FOR HER?

I'LL FIND A JOB AND WORK HARD, MR. LODGE!

YOU WILL NOT!

I--I WON'T?

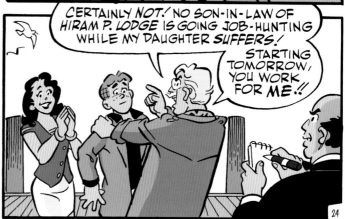

CERTAINLY NOT! NO SON-IN-LAW OF HIRAM P. LODGE IS GOING JOB-HUNTING WHILE MY DAUGHTER SUFFERS!

STARTING TOMORROW, YOU WORK FOR ME!!

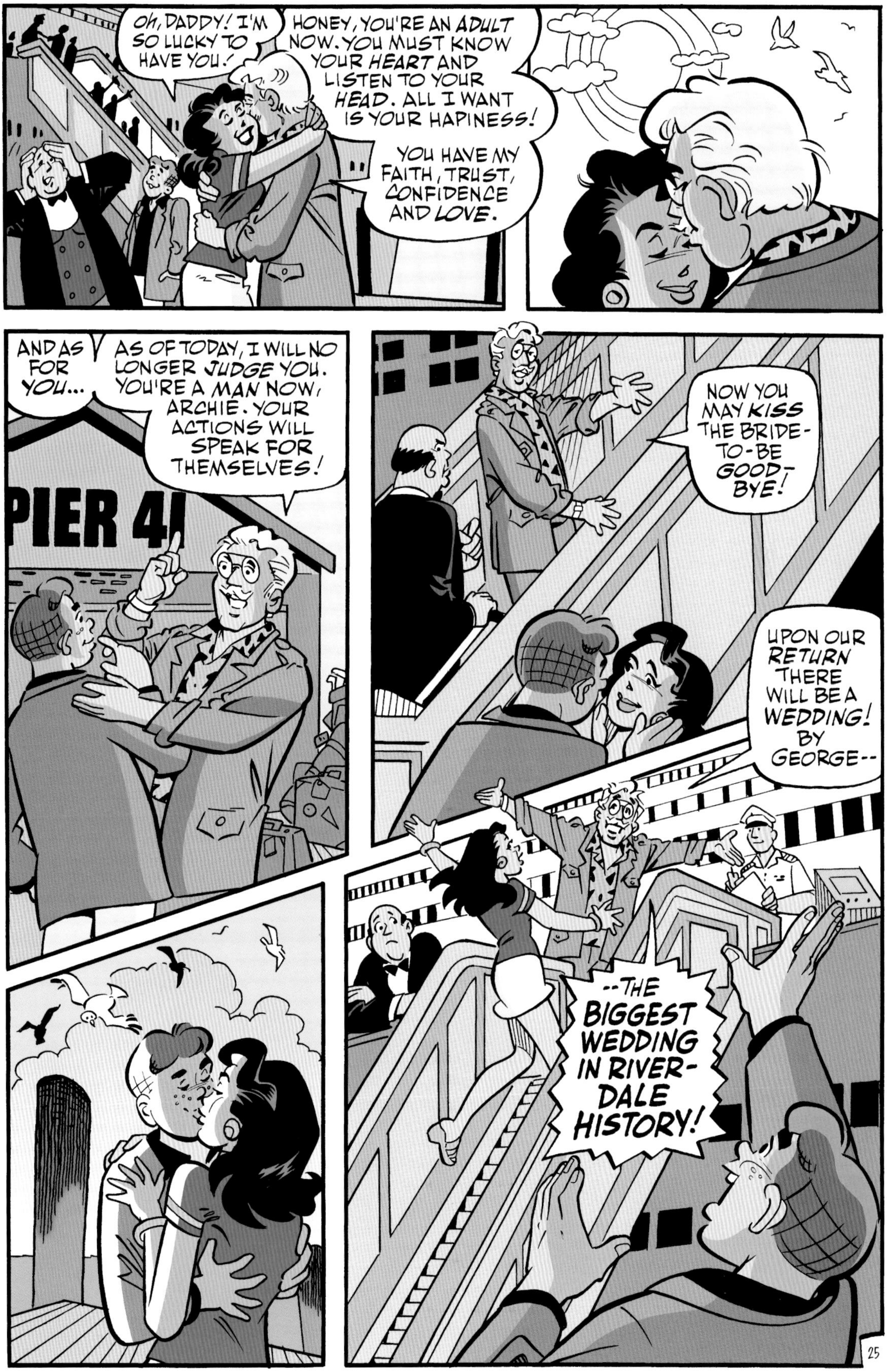
OH, DADDY! I'M SO LUCKY TO HAVE YOU!
HONEY, YOU'RE AN ADULT NOW. YOU MUST KNOW YOUR HEART AND LISTEN TO YOUR HEAD. ALL I WANT IS YOUR HAPINESS!
YOU HAVE MY FAITH, TRUST, CONFIDENCE AND LOVE.
AND AS FOR YOU...
AS OF TODAY, I WILL NO LONGER JUDGE YOU. YOU'RE A MAN NOW, ARCHIE. YOUR ACTIONS WILL SPEAK FOR THEMSELVES!
PIER 4
NOW YOU MAY KISS THE BRIDE-TO-BE GOOD-BYE!
UPON OUR RETURN THERE WILL BE A WEDDING! BY GEORGE--
--THE BIGGEST WEDDING IN RIVER-DALE HISTORY!

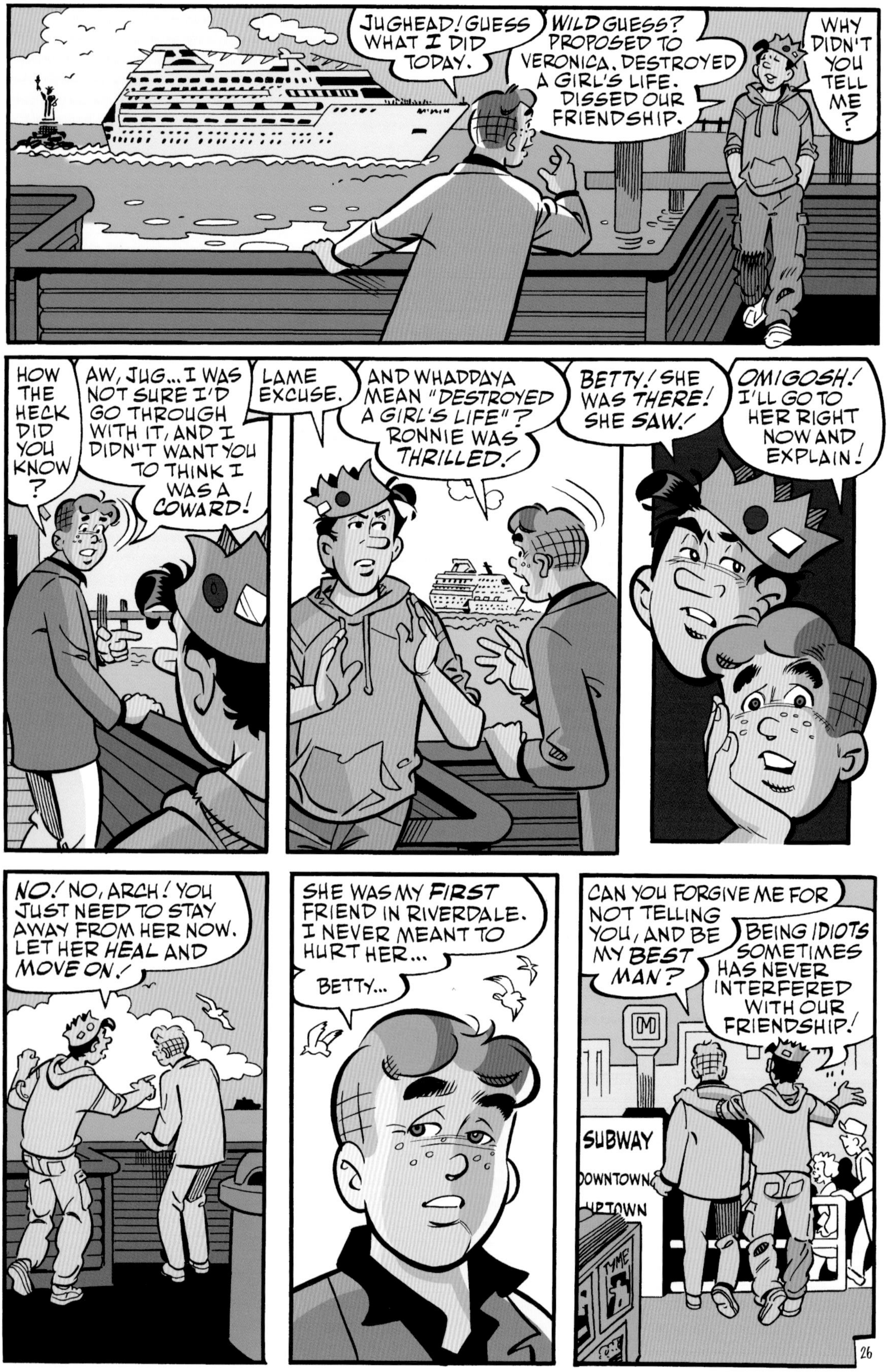
JUGHEAD! GUESS WHAT I DID TODAY.
WILD GUESS? PROPOSED TO VERONICA. DESTROYED A GIRL'S LIFE. DISSED OUR FRIENDSHIP.
WHY DIDN'T YOU TELL ME?
HOW THE HECK DID YOU KNOW?
AW, JUG... I WAS NOT SURE I'D GO THROUGH WITH IT, AND I DIDN'T WANT YOU TO THINK I WAS A COWARD!
LAME EXCUSE.
AND WHADDAYA MEAN "DESTROYED A GIRL'S LIFE"? RONNIE WAS THRILLED!
BETTY! SHE WAS THERE! SHE SAW!
OMIGOSH! I'LL GO TO HER RIGHT NOW AND EXPLAIN!
NO! NO, ARCH! YOU JUST NEED TO STAY AWAY FROM HER NOW. LET HER HEAL AND MOVE ON!
SHE WAS MY FIRST FRIEND IN RIVERDALE. I NEVER MEANT TO HURT HER...
BETTY...
CAN YOU FORGIVE ME FOR NOT TELLING YOU, AND BE MY BEST MAN?
BEING IDIOTS SOMETIMES HAS NEVER INTERFERED WITH OUR FRIENDSHIP!
M
SUBWAY
DOWNTOWN
UPTOWN
TYME

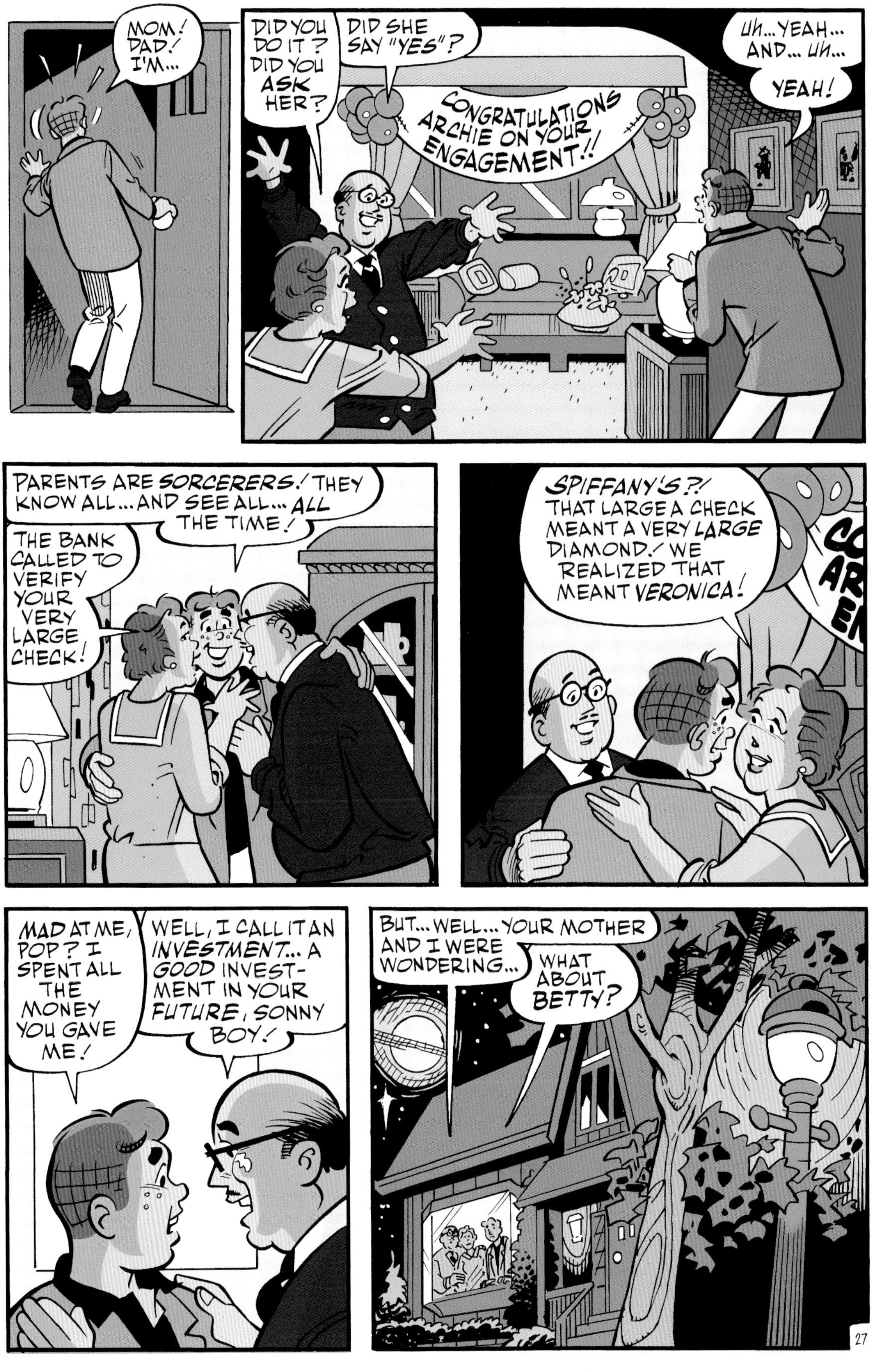
MOM! DAD! I'M...
DID YOU DO IT? DID YOU ASK HER?
DID SHE SAY "YES"?
CONGRATULATIONS ARCHIE ON YOUR ENGAGEMENT!!
UH... YEAH... AND... UH...
YEAH!
PARENTS ARE SORCERERS! THEY KNOW ALL... AND SEE ALL... ALL THE TIME!
THE BANK CALLED TO VERIFY YOUR VERY LARGE CHECK!
SPIFFANY'S?! THAT LARGE A CHECK MEANT A VERY LARGE DIAMOND! WE REALIZED THAT MEANT VERONICA!
MAD AT ME, POP? I SPENT ALL THE MONEY YOU GAVE ME!
WELL, I CALL IT AN INVESTMENT... A GOOD INVESTMENT IN YOUR FUTURE, SONNY BOY!
BUT... WELL... YOUR MOTHER AND I WERE WONDERING...
WHAT ABOUT BETTY?

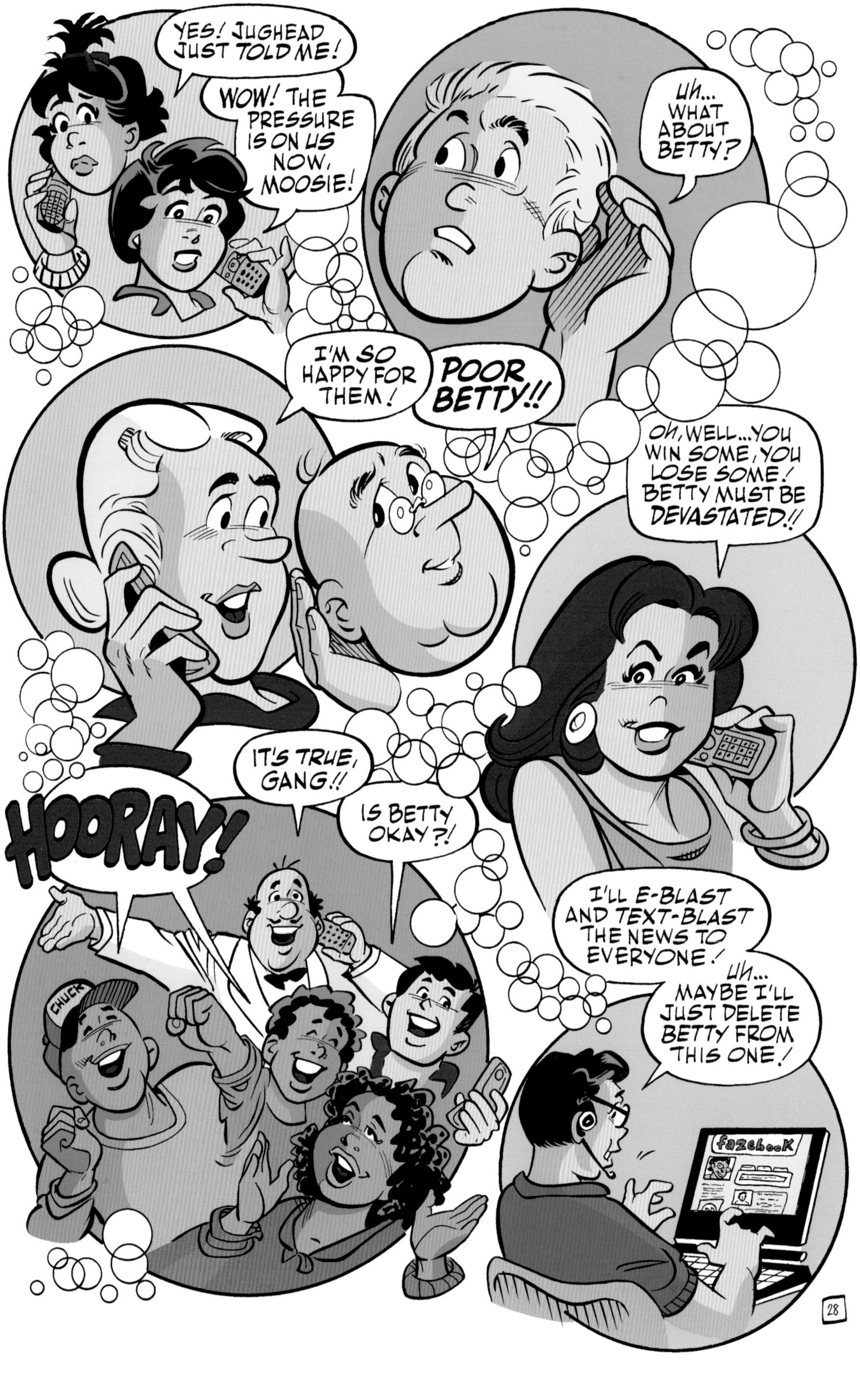
YES! JUGHEAD JUST TOLD ME!
WOW! THE PRESSURE IS ON US NOW, MOOSIE!
UH... WHAT ABOUT BETTY?
I'M SO HAPPY FOR THEM!
POOR BETTY!!
OH, WELL... YOU WIN SOME, YOU LOSE SOME! BETTY MUST BE DEVASTATED!!
HOORAY!
IT'S TRUE, GANG!!
IS BETTY OKAY?!
CHUCK
I'LL E-BLAST AND TEXT-BLAST THE NEWS TO EVERYONE!
UH... MAYBE I'LL JUST DELETE BETTY FROM THIS ONE!
fazebook

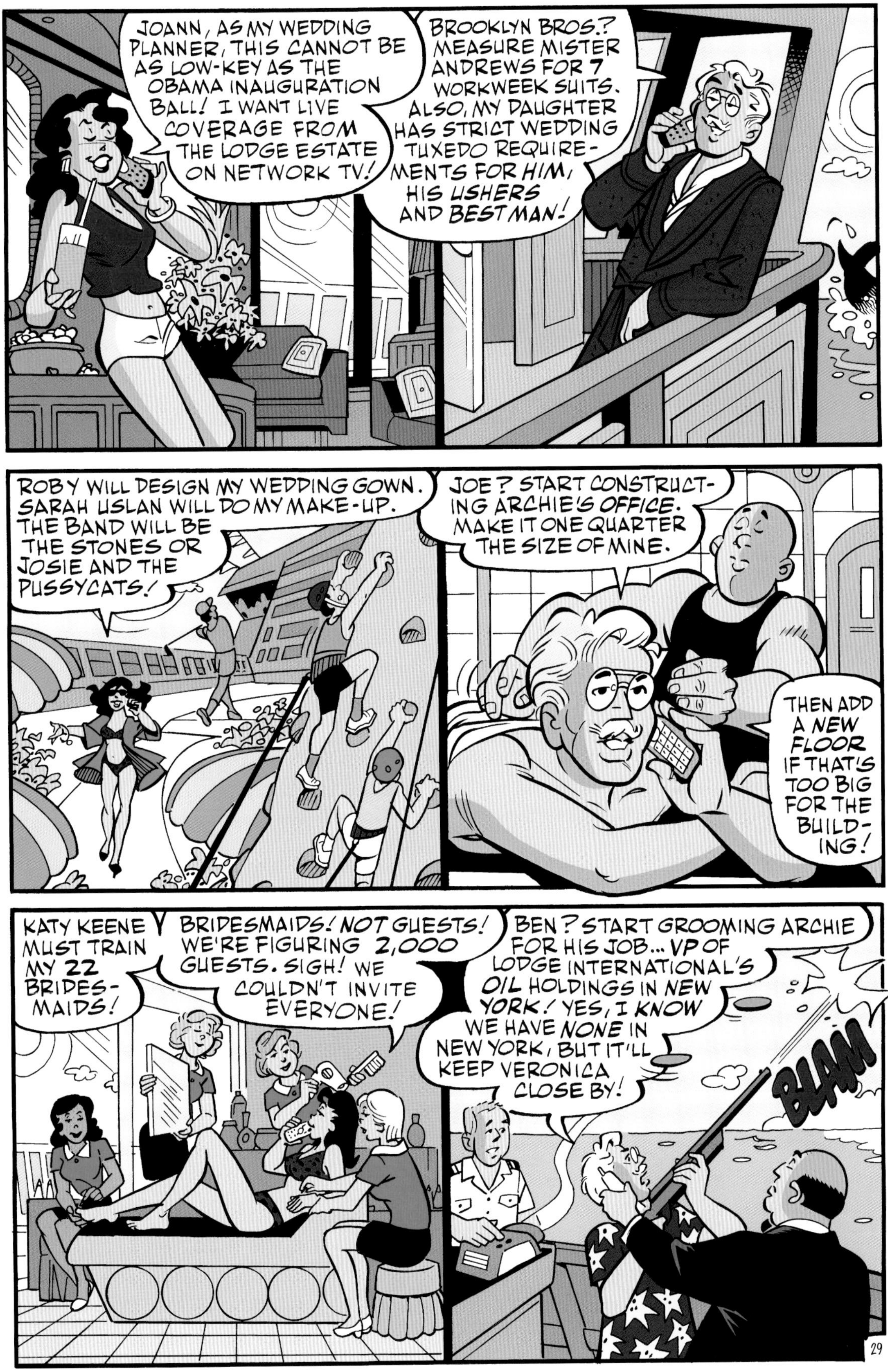
JOANN, AS MY WEDDING PLANNER, THIS CANNOT BE AS LOW-KEY AS THE OBAMA INAUGURATION BALL! I WANT LIVE COVERAGE FROM THE LODGE ESTATE ON NETWORK TV!
BROOKLYN BROS.? MEASURE MISTER ANDREWS FOR 7 WORKWEEK SUITS. ALSO, MY DAUGHTER HAS STRICT WEDDING TUXEDO REQUIREMENTS FOR HIM, HIS USHERS AND BEST MAN!
ROBY WILL DESIGN MY WEDDING GOWN. SARAH USLAN WILL DO MY MAKE-UP. THE BAND WILL BE THE STONES OR JOSIE AND THE PUSSYCATS!
JOE? START CONSTRUCTING ARCHIE'S OFFICE. MAKE IT ONE QUARTER THE SIZE OF MINE.
THEN ADD A NEW FLOOR IF THAT'S TOO BIG FOR THE BUILDING!
KATY KEENE MUST TRAIN MY 22 BRIDESMAIDS!
BRIDESMAIDS! NOT GUESTS! WE'RE FIGURING 2,000 GUESTS. SIGH! WE COULDN'T INVITE EVERYONE!
BEN? START GROOMING ARCHIE FOR HIS JOB... VP OF LODGE INTERNATIONAL'S OIL HOLDINGS IN NEW YORK! YES, I KNOW WE HAVE NONE IN NEW YORK, BUT IT'LL KEEP VERONICA CLOSE BY!
BLAM

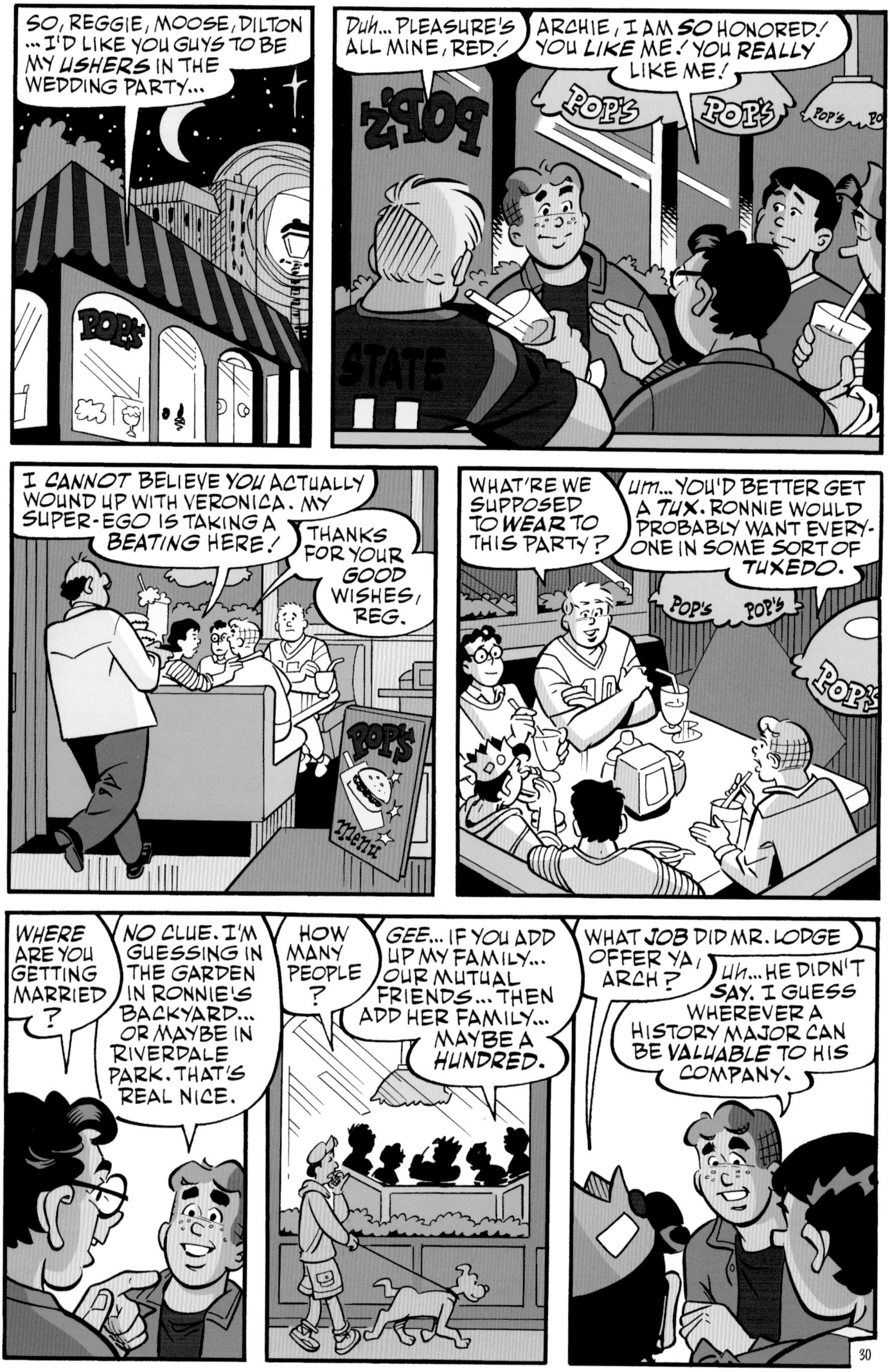
SO, REGGIE, MOOSE, DILTON ... I'D LIKE YOU GUYS TO BE MY USHERS IN THE WEDDING PARTY...
POP'S
DUH... PLEASURE'S ALL MINE, RED!
ARCHIE, I AM SO HONORED! YOU LIKE ME! YOU REALLY LIKE ME!
POP'S
STATE
I CANNOT BELIEVE YOU ACTUALLY WOUND UP WITH VERONICA. MY SUPER-EGO IS TAKING A BEATING HERE!
THANKS FOR YOUR GOOD WISHES, REG.
POP'S
MENU
WHAT'RE WE SUPPOSED TO WEAR TO THIS PARTY?
UM... YOU'D BETTER GET A TUX. RONNIE WOULD PROBABLY WANT EVERYONE IN SOME SORT OF TUXEDO.
WHERE ARE YOU GETTING MARRIED?
NO CLUE. I'M GUESSING IN THE GARDEN IN RONNIE'S BACKYARD... OR MAYBE IN RIVERDALE PARK. THAT'S REAL NICE.
HOW MANY PEOPLE?
GEE... IF YOU ADD UP MY FAMILY... OUR MUTUAL FRIENDS... THEN ADD HER FAMILY... MAYBE A HUNDRED.
WHAT JOB DID MR. LODGE OFFER YA, ARCH?
UH... HE DIDN'T SAY. I GUESS WHEREVER A HISTORY MAJOR CAN BE VALUABLE TO HIS COMPANY.

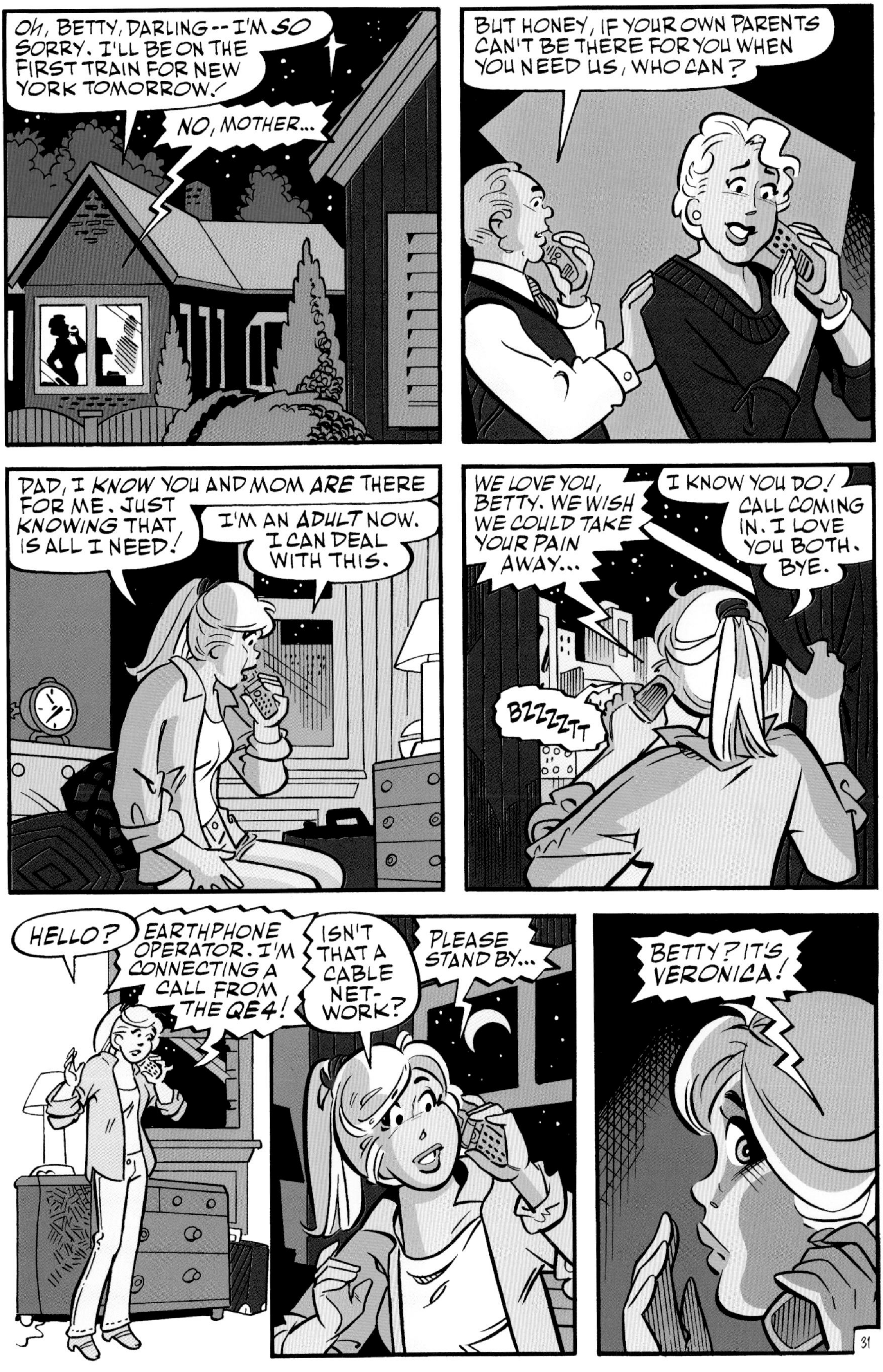
Oh, BETTY, DARLING -- I'M SO SORRY. I'LL BE ON THE FIRST TRAIN FOR NEW YORK TOMORROW!
NO, MOTHER...
BUT HONEY, IF YOUR OWN PARENTS CAN'T BE THERE FOR YOU WHEN YOU NEED US, WHO CAN?
DAD, I KNOW YOU AND MOM ARE THERE FOR ME. JUST KNOWING THAT IS ALL I NEED!
I'M AN ADULT NOW. I CAN DEAL WITH THIS.
WE LOVE YOU, BETTY. WE WISH WE COULD TAKE YOUR PAIN AWAY...
I KNOW YOU DO! CALL COMING IN. I LOVE YOU BOTH. BYE.
BZZZZTT
HELLO?
EARTHPHONE OPERATOR. I'M CONNECTING A CALL FROM THE QE4!
ISN'T THAT A CABLE NET-WORK?
PLEASE STAND BY...
BETTY? IT'S VERONICA!

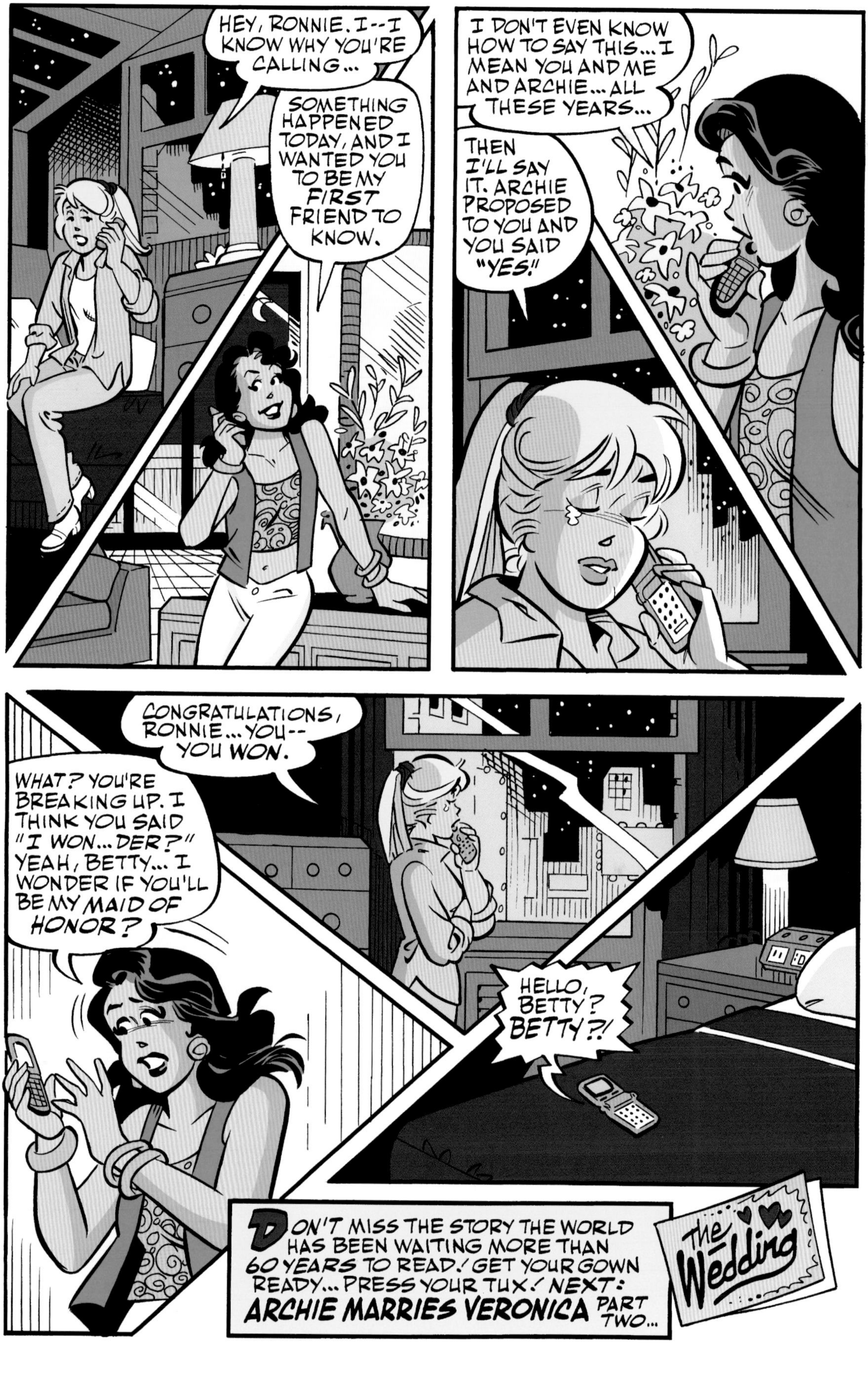
HEY, RONNIE. I--I KNOW WHY YOU'RE CALLING...
SOMETHING HAPPENED TODAY, AND I WANTED YOU TO BE MY FIRST FRIEND TO KNOW.
I DON'T EVEN KNOW HOW TO SAY THIS... I MEAN YOU AND ME AND ARCHIE... ALL THESE YEARS...
THEN I'LL SAY IT. ARCHIE PROPOSED TO YOU AND YOU SAID "YES!"
CONGRATULATIONS, RONNIE... YOU-- YOU WON.
WHAT? YOU'RE BREAKING UP. I THINK YOU SAID "I WON...DER?" YEAH, BETTY... I WONDER IF YOU'LL BE MY MAID OF HONOR?
HELLO, BETTY? BETTY?!
DON'T MISS THE STORY THE WORLD HAS BEEN WAITING MORE THAN 60 YEARS TO READ! GET YOUR GOWN READY... PRESS YOUR TUX! NEXT: ARCHIE MARRIES VERONICA PART TWO...
The Wedding

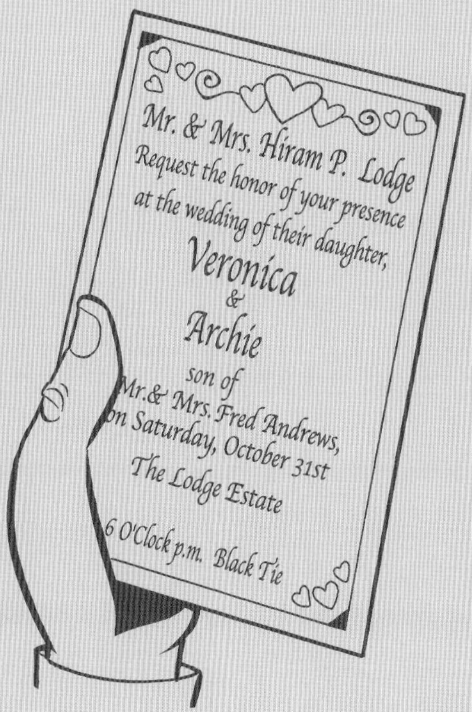
Mr. & Mrs. Hiram P. Lodge
Request the honor of your presence
at the wedding of their daughter,
Veronica
&
Archie
son of
Mr.& Mrs. Fred Andrews,
on Saturday, October 31st
The Lodge Estate
6 O'Clock p.m. Black Tie

#601
$2.50 US
$2.75 CAN
archiecomics.com
Archie
PART 2 OF 6
MARRIES VERONICA: "THE WEDDING"
I DO!
DO I EVER!
STAN GOLDBERG
BOB SMITH

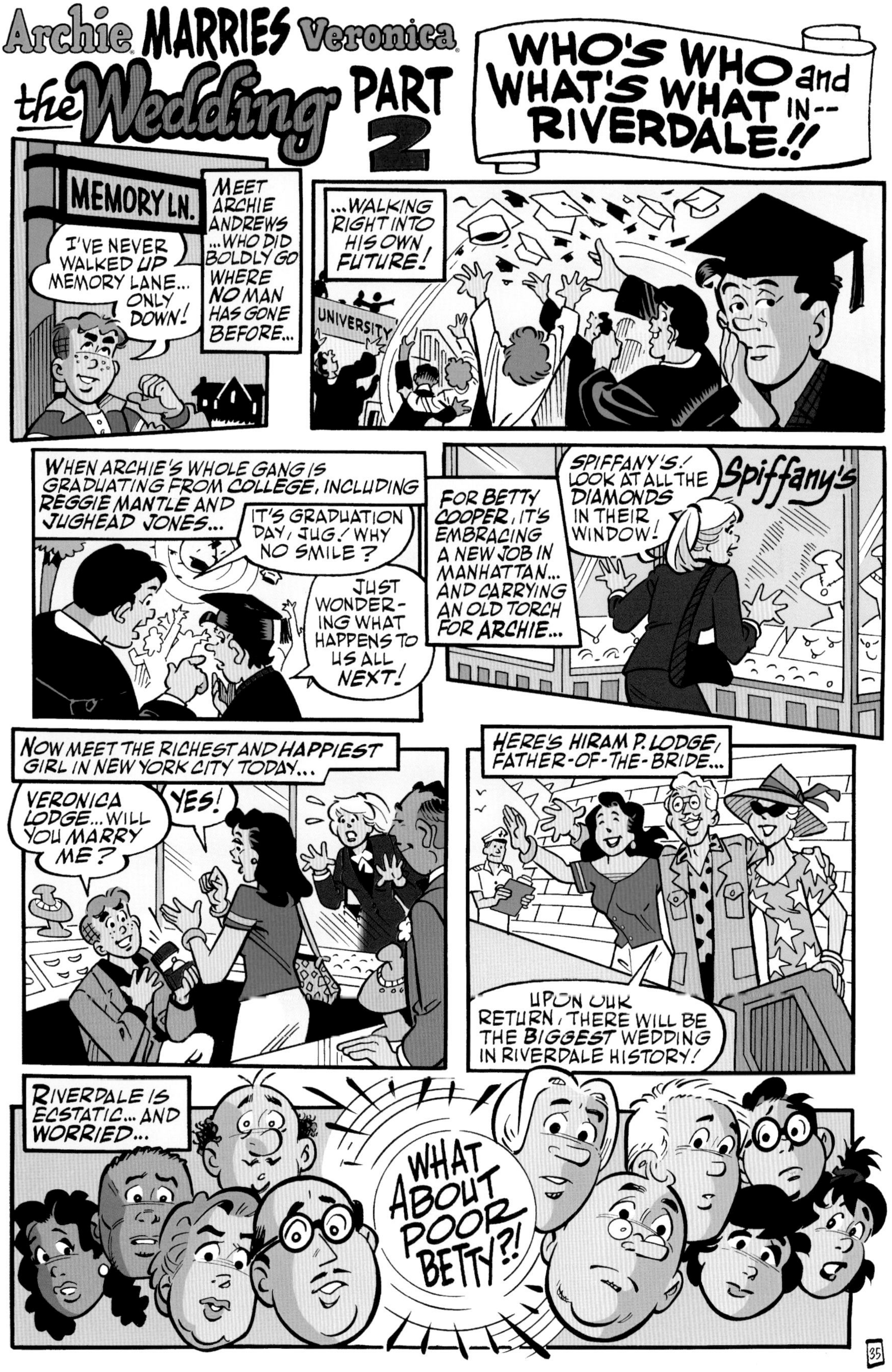
Archie MARRIES Veronica
the Wedding PART 2
WHO'S WHO and WHAT'S WHAT IN-- RIVERDALE!!
MEMORY LN.
I'VE NEVER WALKED UP MEMORY LANE... ONLY DOWN!
MEET ARCHIE ANDREWS ...WHO DID BOLDLY GO WHERE NO MAN HAS GONE BEFORE...
...WALKING RIGHT INTO HIS OWN FUTURE!
UNIVERSITY
WHEN ARCHIE'S WHOLE GANG IS GRADUATING FROM COLLEGE, INCLUDING REGGIE MANTLE AND JUGHEAD JONES...
IT'S GRADUATION DAY, JUG! WHY NO SMILE?
JUST WONDERING WHAT HAPPENS TO US ALL NEXT!
FOR BETTY COOPER, IT'S EMBRACING A NEW JOB IN MANHATTAN... AND CARRYING AN OLD TORCH FOR ARCHIE...
SPIFFANY'S! LOOK AT ALL THE DIAMONDS IN THEIR WINDOW!
Spiffany's
NOW MEET THE RICHEST AND HAPPIEST GIRL IN NEW YORK CITY TODAY...
VERONICA LODGE... WILL YOU MARRY ME?
YES!
HERE'S HIRAM P. LODGE, FATHER-OF-THE-BRIDE...
UPON OUR RETURN, THERE WILL BE THE BIGGEST WEDDING IN RIVERDALE HISTORY!
RIVERDALE IS ECSTATIC... AND WORRIED...
WHAT ABOUT POOR BETTY?!

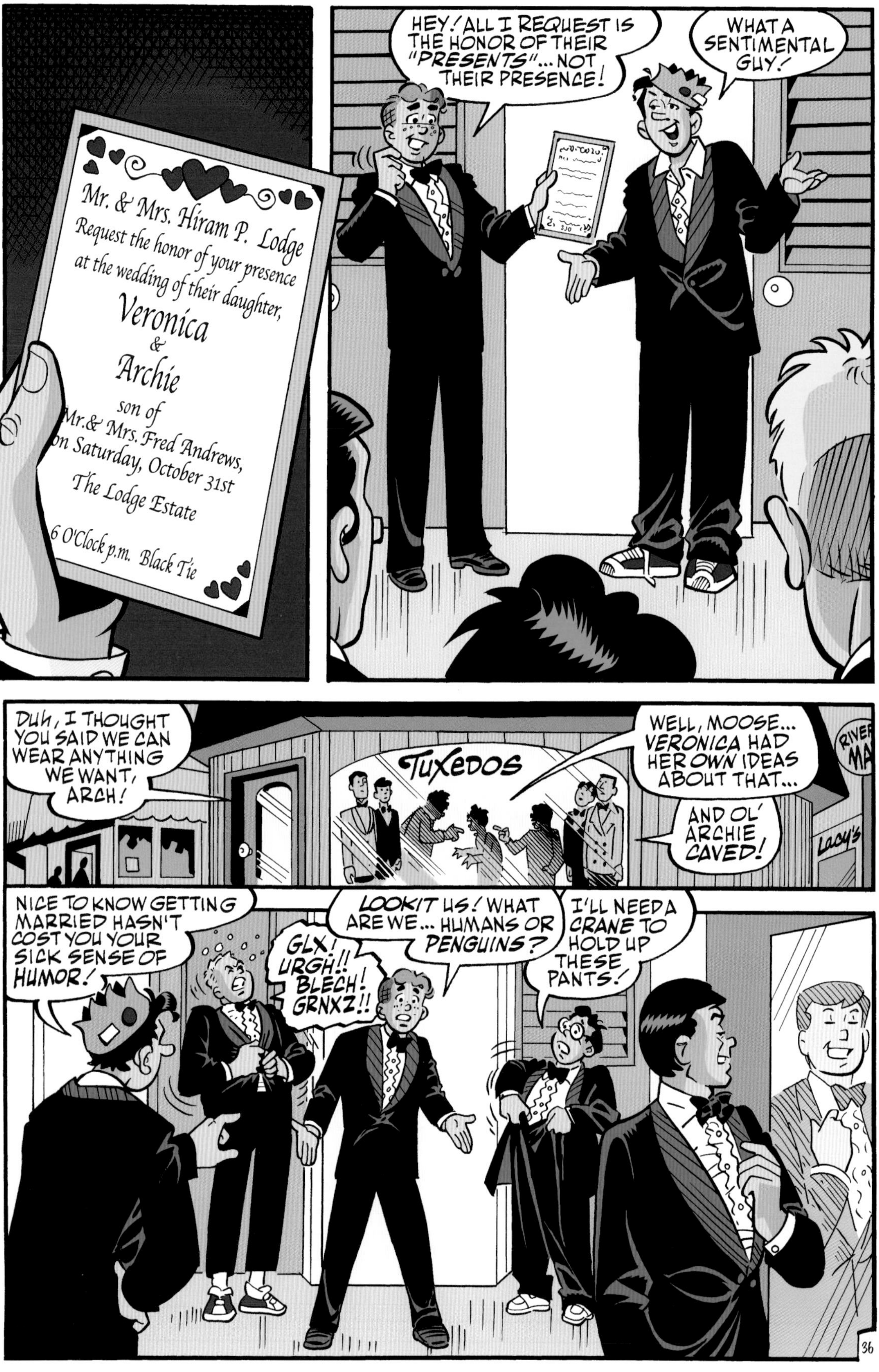
Mr. & Mrs. Hiram P. Lodge
Request the honor of your presence
at the wedding of their daughter,
Veronica
&
Archie
son of
Mr.& Mrs. Fred Andrews,
on Saturday, October 31st
The Lodge Estate
6 O'Clock p.m. Black Tie
HEY! ALL I REQUEST IS THE HONOR OF THEIR "PRESENTS"... NOT THEIR PRESENCE!
WHAT A SENTIMENTAL GUY!
DUH, I THOUGHT YOU SAID WE CAN WEAR ANYTHING WE WANT, ARCH!
TUXEDOS
WELL, MOOSE... VERONICA HAD HER OWN IDEAS ABOUT THAT...
AND OL' ARCHIE CAVED!
LACY'S
NICE TO KNOW GETTING MARRIED HASN'T COST YOU YOUR SICK SENSE OF HUMOR!
GLX! URGH!! BLECH! GRNXZ!!
LOOKIT US! WHAT ARE WE... HUMANS OR PENGUINS?
I'LL NEED A CRANE TO HOLD UP THESE PANTS!

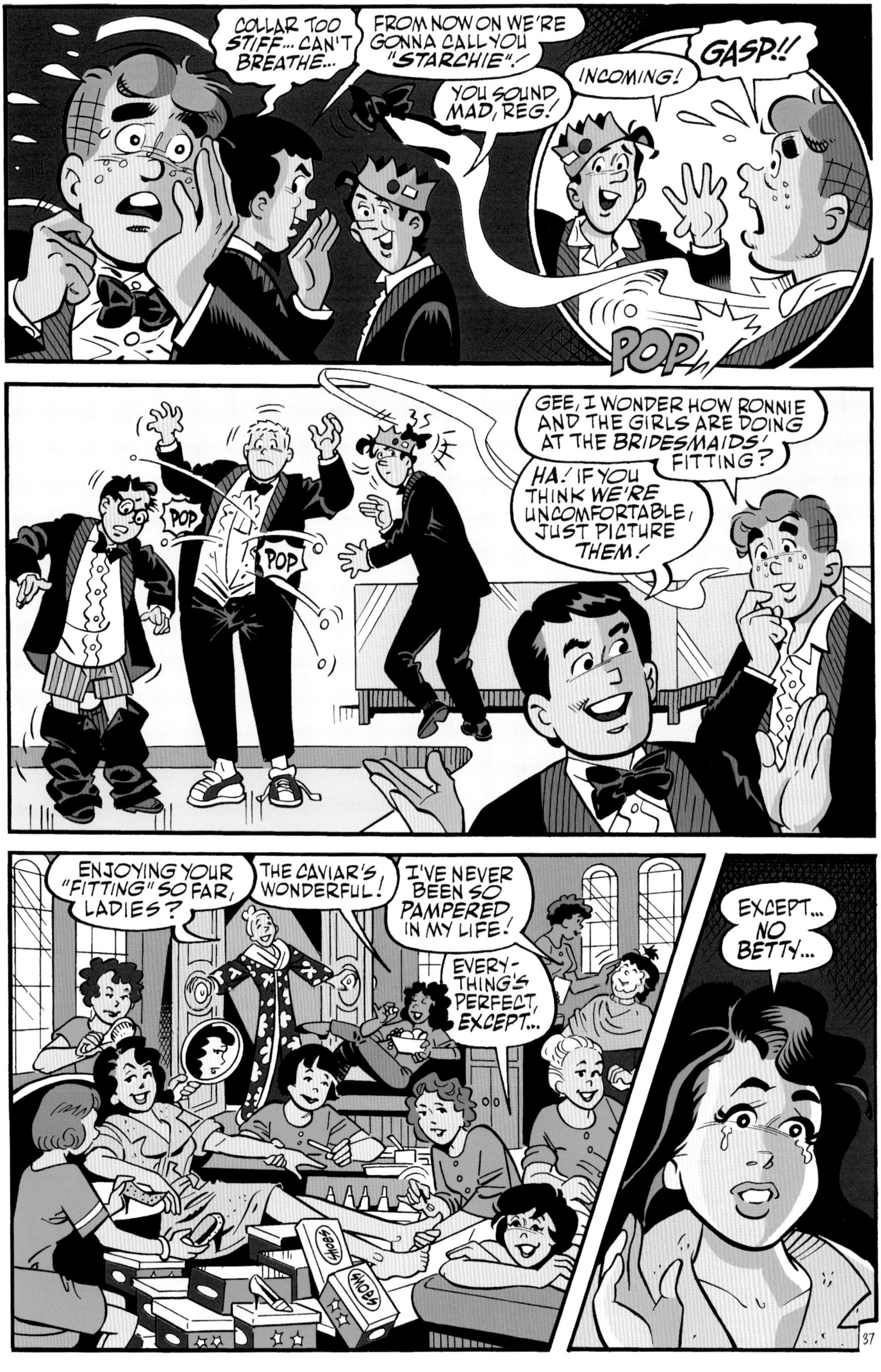
COLLAR TOO STIFF... CAN'T BREATHE...
FROM NOW ON WE'RE GONNA CALL YOU "STARCHIE"!
YOU SOUND MAD, REG!
INCOMING!
GASP!!
POP
GEE, I WONDER HOW RONNIE AND THE GIRLS ARE DOING AT THE BRIDESMAIDS' FITTING?
HA! IF YOU THINK WE'RE UNCOMFORTABLE, JUST PICTURE THEM!
POP
POP
ENJOYING YOUR "FITTING" SO FAR, LADIES?
THE CAVIAR'S WONDERFUL!
I'VE NEVER BEEN SO PAMPERED IN MY LIFE!
EVERY-THING'S PERFECT, EXCEPT...
SHOES
SHOES
EXCEPT... NO BETTY...

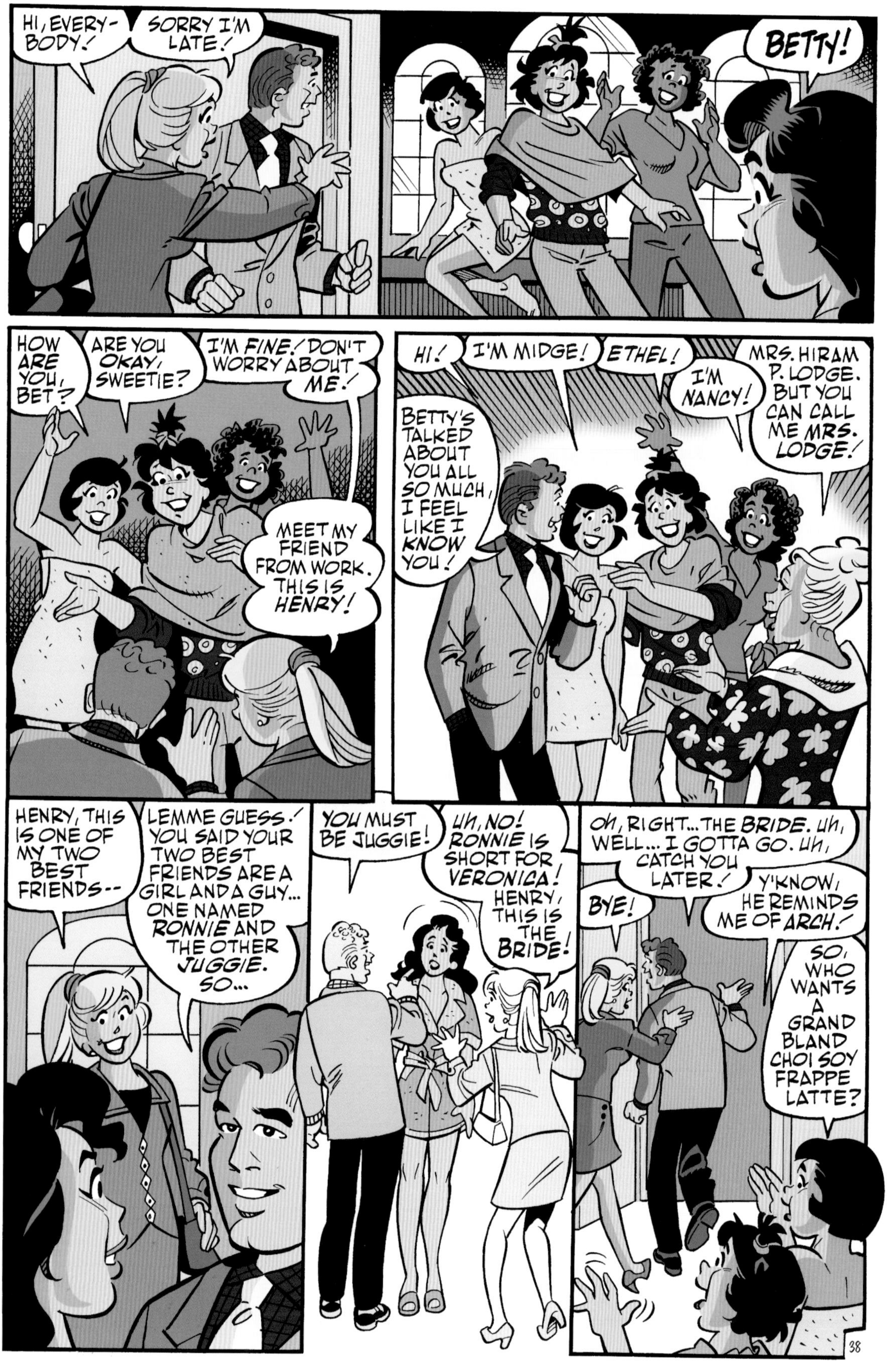
HI, EVERY-BODY!
SORRY I'M LATE!
BETTY!
HOW ARE YOU, BET?
ARE YOU OKAY, SWEETIE?
I'M FINE! DON'T WORRY ABOUT ME!
MEET MY FRIEND FROM WORK. THIS IS HENRY!
HI!
I'M MIDGE!
ETHEL!
I'M NANCY!
MRS. HIRAM P. LODGE. BUT YOU CAN CALL ME MRS. LODGE!
BETTY'S TALKED ABOUT YOU ALL SO MUCH, I FEEL LIKE I KNOW YOU!
HENRY, THIS IS ONE OF MY TWO BEST FRIENDS--
LEMME GUESS! YOU SAID YOUR TWO BEST FRIENDS ARE A GIRL AND A GUY... ONE NAMED RONNIE AND THE OTHER JUGGIE. SO...
YOU MUST BE JUGGIE!
UH, NO! RONNIE IS SHORT FOR VERONICA! HENRY, THIS IS THE BRIDE!
OH, RIGHT... THE BRIDE. UH, WELL... I GOTTA GO. UH, CATCH YOU LATER!
BYE!
Y'KNOW, HE REMINDS ME OF ARCH!
SO, WHO WANTS A GRAND BLAND CHOI SOY FRAPPE LATTE?

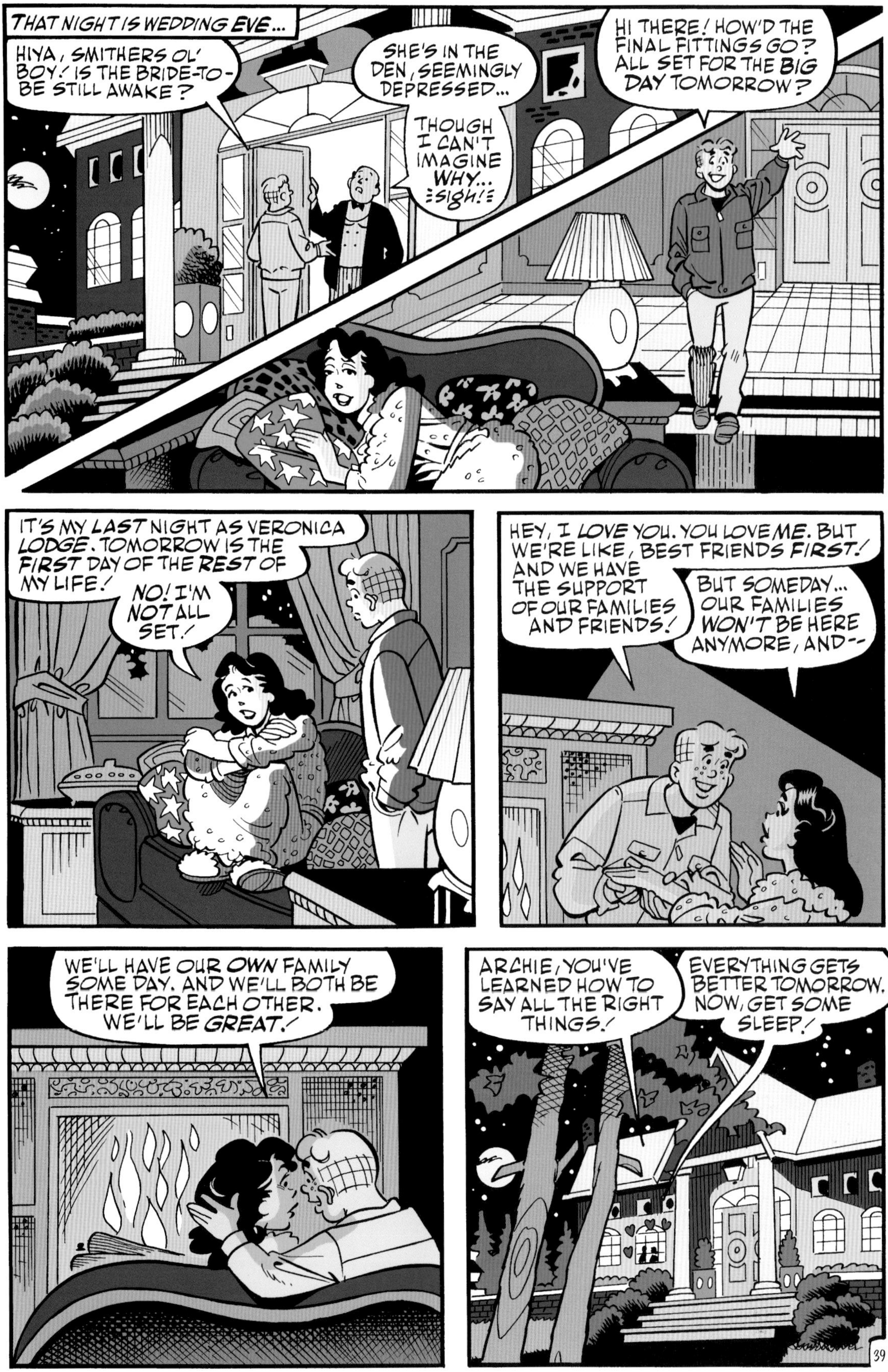

THAT NIGHT IS WEDDING EVE...
HIYA, SMITHERS OL' BOY! IS THE BRIDE-TO-BE STILL AWAKE?
SHE'S IN THE DEN, SEEMINGLY DEPRESSED...
THOUGH I CAN'T IMAGINE WHY... sigh!
HI THERE! HOW'D THE FINAL FITTINGS GO? ALL SET FOR THE BIG DAY TOMORROW?
IT'S MY LAST NIGHT AS VERONICA LODGE. TOMORROW IS THE FIRST DAY OF THE REST OF MY LIFE!
NO! I'M NOT ALL SET!
HEY, I LOVE YOU. YOU LOVE ME. BUT WE'RE LIKE, BEST FRIENDS FIRST!
AND WE HAVE THE SUPPORT OF OUR FAMILIES AND FRIENDS!
BUT SOMEDAY... OUR FAMILIES WON'T BE HERE ANYMORE, AND--
WE'LL HAVE OUR OWN FAMILY SOME DAY. AND WE'LL BOTH BE THERE FOR EACH OTHER. WE'LL BE GREAT!
ARCHIE, YOU'VE LEARNED HOW TO SAY ALL THE RIGHT THINGS!
EVERYTHING GETS BETTER TOMORROW. NOW, GET SOME SLEEP!

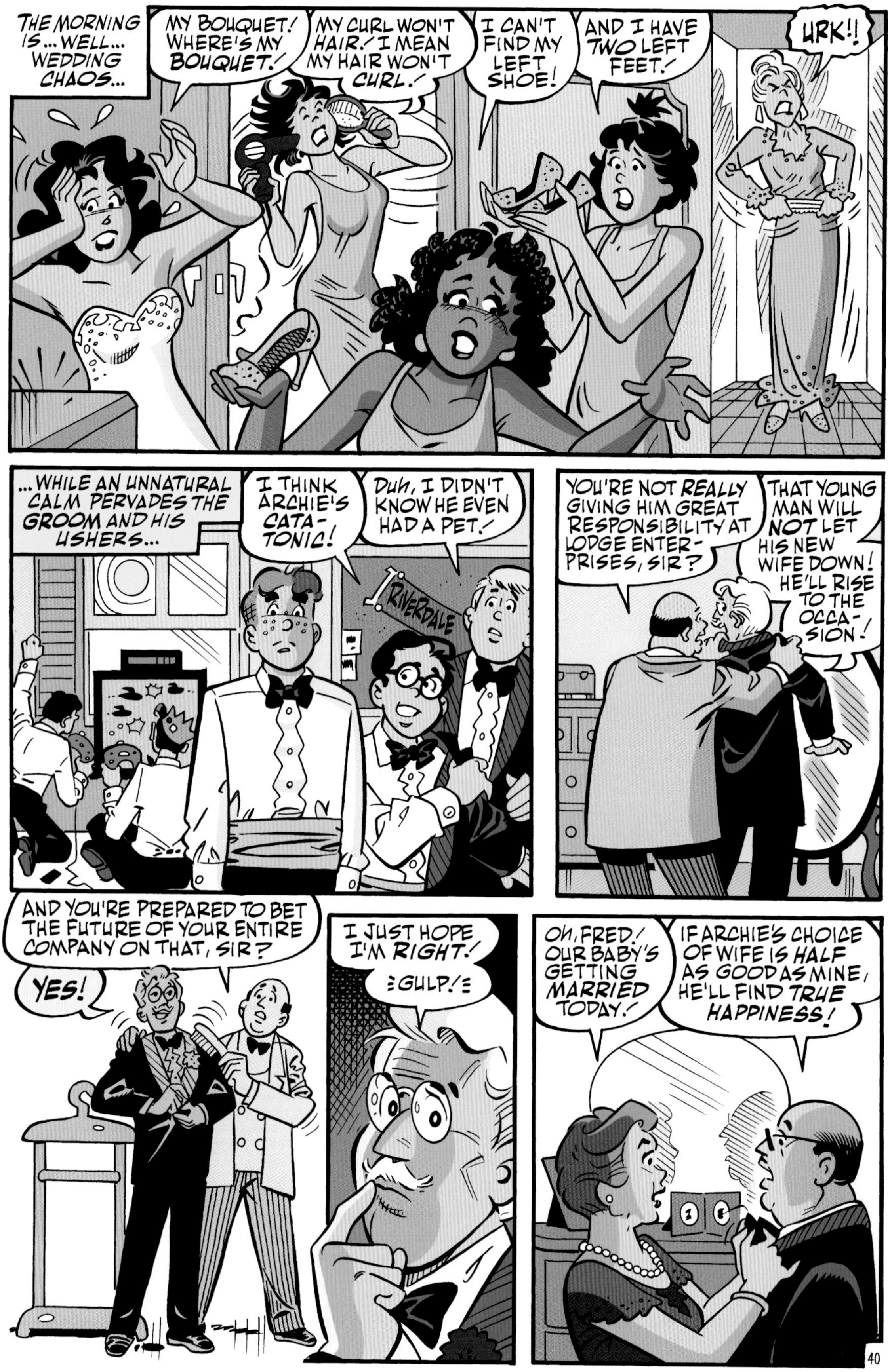
THE MORNING IS... WELL... WEDDING CHAOS...
MY BOUQUET! WHERE'S MY BOUQUET!
MY CURL WON'T HAIR! I MEAN MY HAIR WON'T CURL!
I CAN'T FIND MY LEFT SHOE!
AND I HAVE TWO LEFT FEET!
URK!!
...WHILE AN UNNATURAL CALM PERVADES THE GROOM AND HIS USHERS...
I THINK ARCHIE'S CATA-TONIC!
DUH, I DIDN'T KNOW HE EVEN HAD A PET!
RIVERDALE
YOU'RE NOT REALLY GIVING HIM GREAT RESPONSIBILITY AT LODGE ENTER-PRISES, SIR?
THAT YOUNG MAN WILL NOT LET HIS NEW WIFE DOWN! HE'LL RISE TO THE OCCA-SION!
AND YOU'RE PREPARED TO BET THE FUTURE OF YOUR ENTIRE COMPANY ON THAT, SIR?
YES!
I JUST HOPE I'M RIGHT!
GULP!
OH, FRED! OUR BABY'S GETTING MARRIED TODAY!
IF ARCHIE'S CHOICE OF WIFE IS HALF AS GOOD AS MINE, HE'LL FIND TRUE HAPPINESS!

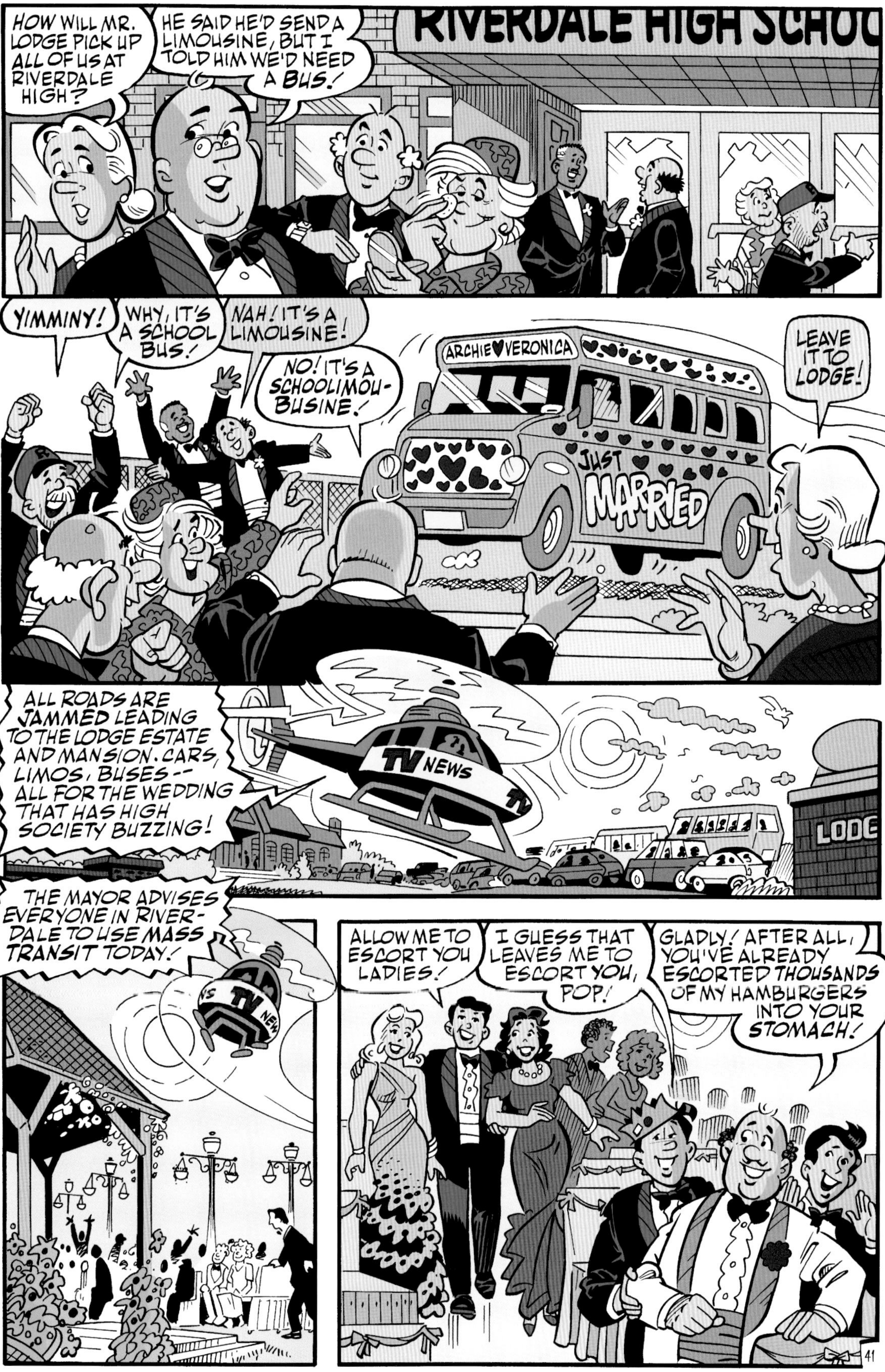

RIVERDALE HIGH SCHOO
HOW WILL MR. LODGE PICK UP ALL OF US AT RIVERDALE HIGH?
HE SAID HE'D SEND A LIMOUSINE, BUT I TOLD HIM WE'D NEED A BUS!
YIMMINY!
WHY, IT'S A SCHOOL BUS!
NAH! IT'S A LIMOUSINE!
NO! IT'S A SCHOOLIMOU-BUSINE!
ARCHIE♥VERONICA
JUST MARRIED
LEAVE IT TO LODGE!
ALL ROADS ARE JAMMED LEADING TO THE LODGE ESTATE AND MANSION. CARS, LIMOS, BUSES -- ALL FOR THE WEDDING THAT HAS HIGH SOCIETY BUZZING!
TV NEWS
LODGE
THE MAYOR ADVISES EVERYONE IN RIVER-DALE TO USE MASS TRANSIT TODAY!
ALLOW ME TO ESCORT YOU LADIES!
I GUESS THAT LEAVES ME TO ESCORT YOU, POP!
GLADLY! AFTER ALL, YOU'VE ALREADY ESCORTED THOUSANDS OF MY HAMBURGERS INTO YOUR STOMACH!

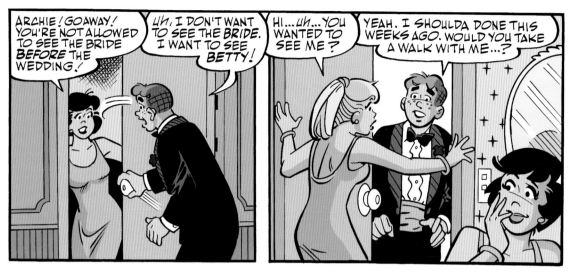

ARCHIE! GO AWAY! YOU'RE NOT ALLOWED TO SEE THE BRIDE *BEFORE* THE WEDDING!

Uh, I DON'T WANT TO SEE THE BRIDE. I WANT TO SEE *BETTY!*

HI...*uh*...YOU WANTED TO SEE ME?

YEAH. I SHOULDA DONE THIS WEEKS AGO. WOULD YOU TAKE A WALK WITH ME...?

BETTY...YOU WERE MY *FIRST FRIEND* WHEN I MOVED TO RIVERDALE. WE WERE KIDS.

I'LL *NEVER* FORGET THAT DAY. I THOUGHT YOU WERE FUNNY. AND VERY CUTE!

AND WHENEVER WE DATED, I HAD THE *GREATEST* TIME. BUT... BUT...

VERONICA CAME ALONG. I KNOW, ARCHIE...

NO, BETTY. WHEN I FINALLY GREW UP, I REALIZED I LOVED YOU UNLIKE ANY *OTHER* GIRL! YOU WERE...*ARE*...TO ME, THE *SISTER* I NEVER HAD!

"SISTER"?

BETTY...WE'LL *ALWAYS* BE FRIENDS, YOU AND ME. BOY-FRIENDS AND GIRLFRIENDS COME AND GO, BUT *FRIENDS* ARE *FOREVER.*

I LOVE YOU, BETTY COOPER. DO YOU AGREE TO BE MY *FRIEND* FOR THE *REST* OF MY LIFE?

I LOVE YOU TOO, ARCHIE ANDREWS. AND... I DO.

42

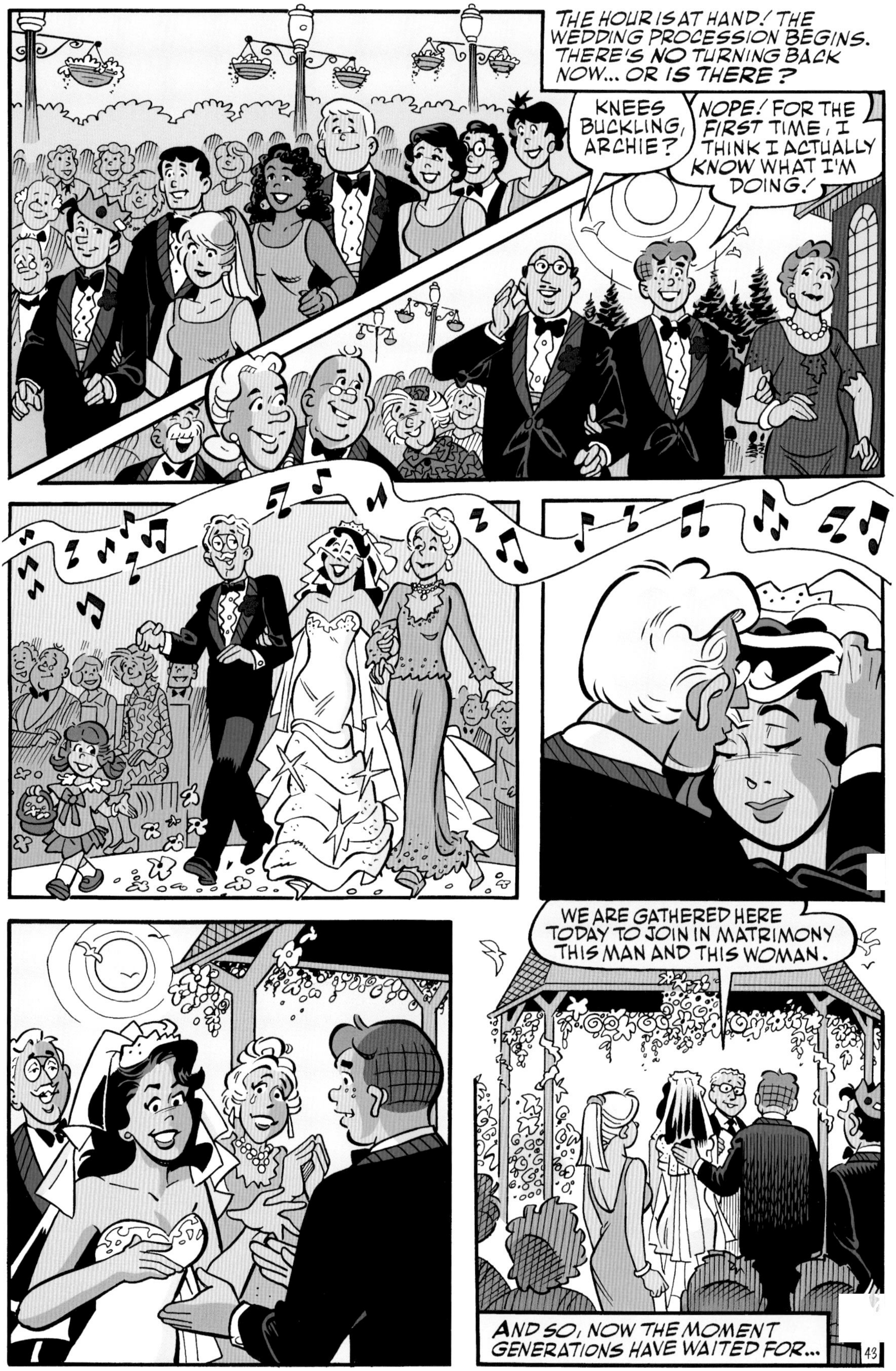
THE HOUR IS AT HAND! THE WEDDING PROCESSION BEGINS. THERE'S NO TURNING BACK NOW... OR IS THERE?
KNEES BUCKLING, ARCHIE?
NOPE! FOR THE FIRST TIME, I THINK I ACTUALLY KNOW WHAT I'M DOING!
WE ARE GATHERED HERE TODAY TO JOIN IN MATRIMONY THIS MAN AND THIS WOMAN.
AND SO, NOW THE MOMENT GENERATIONS HAVE WAITED FOR...

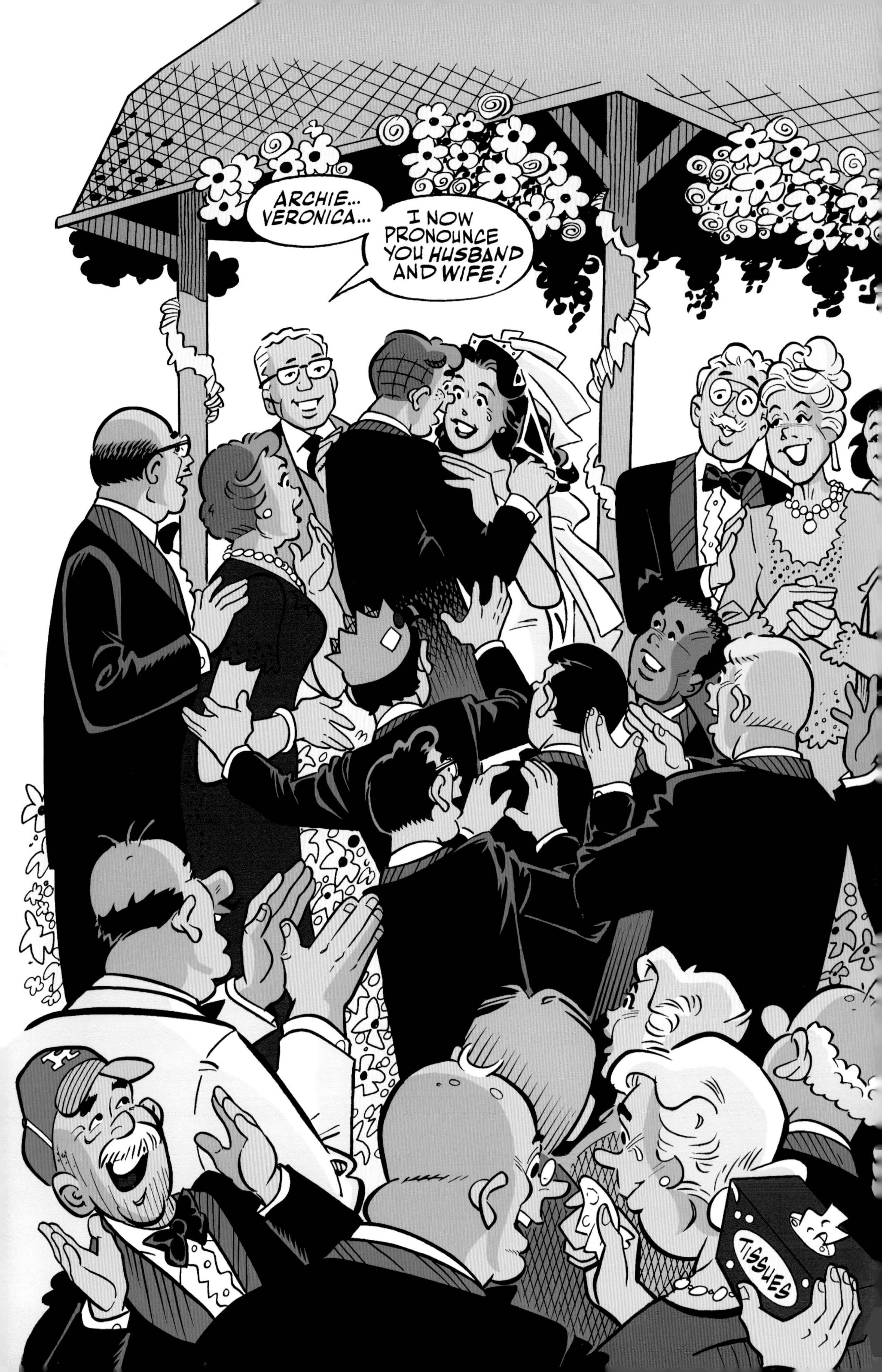
ARCHIE... VERONICA...
I NOW PRONOUNCE YOU HUSBAND AND WIFE!
TISSUES

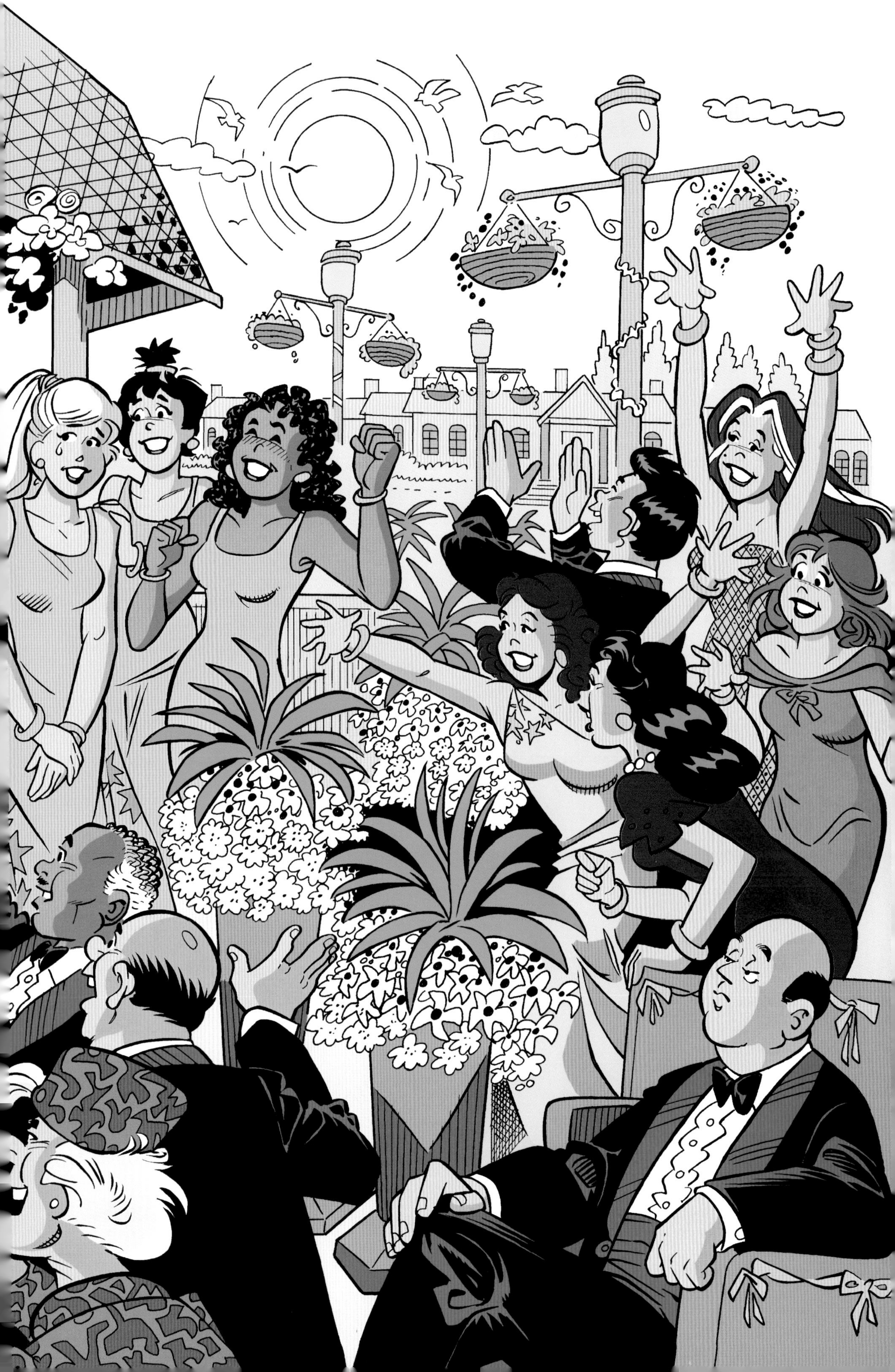

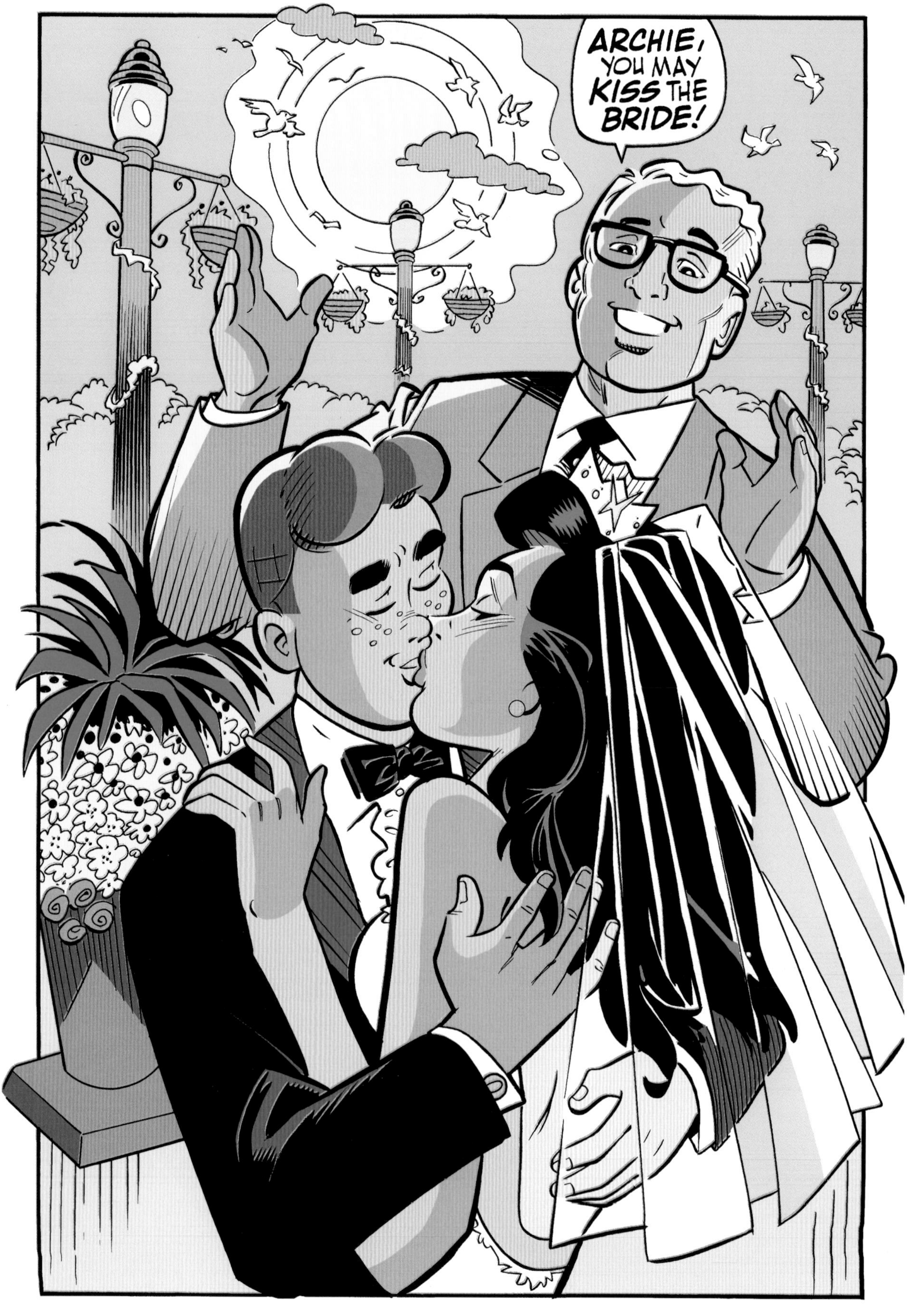
ARCHIE, YOU MAY KISS THE BRIDE!

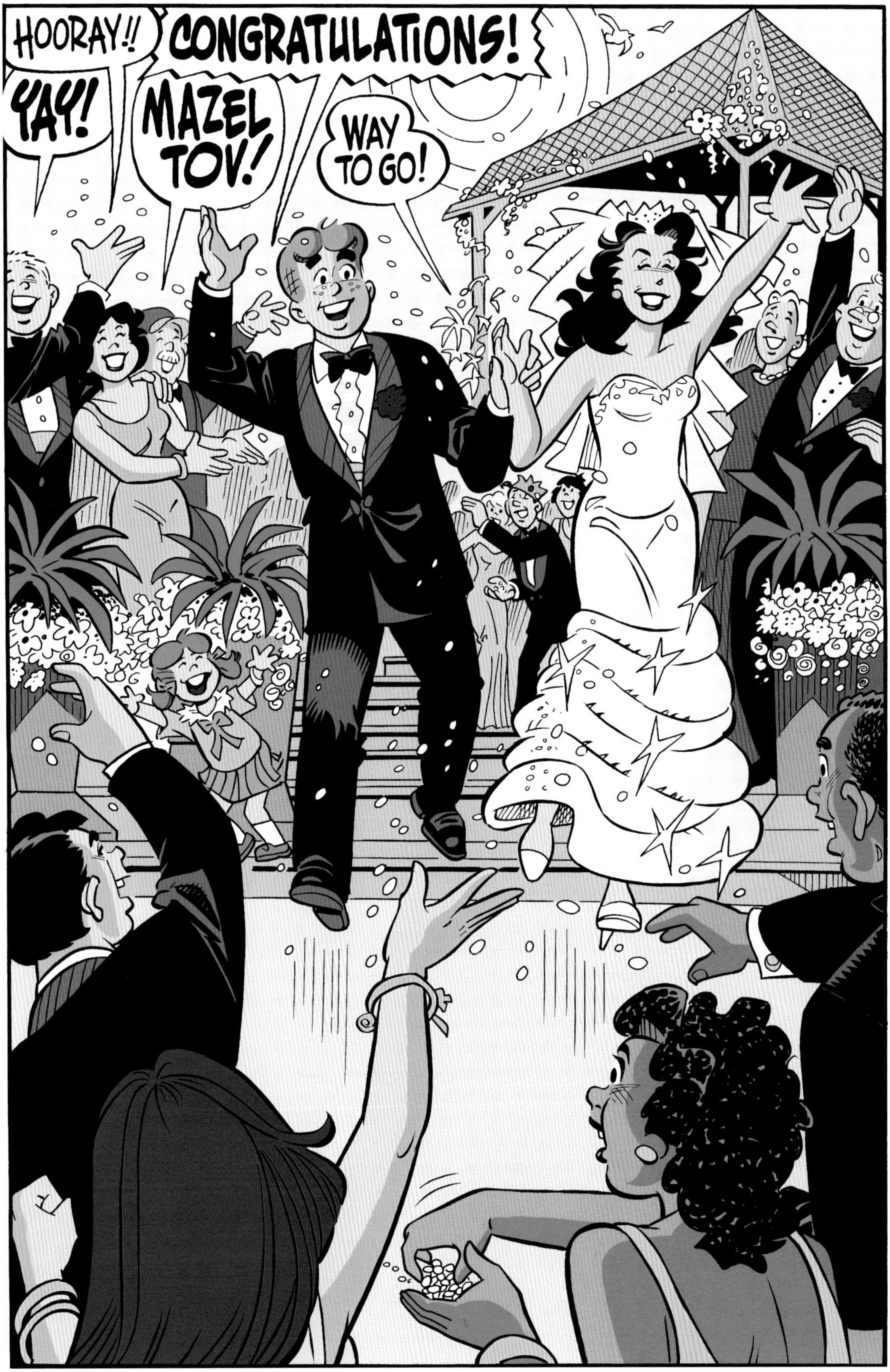
HOORAY!!
CONGRATULATIONS!
YAY!
MAZEL TOV!
WAY TO GO!

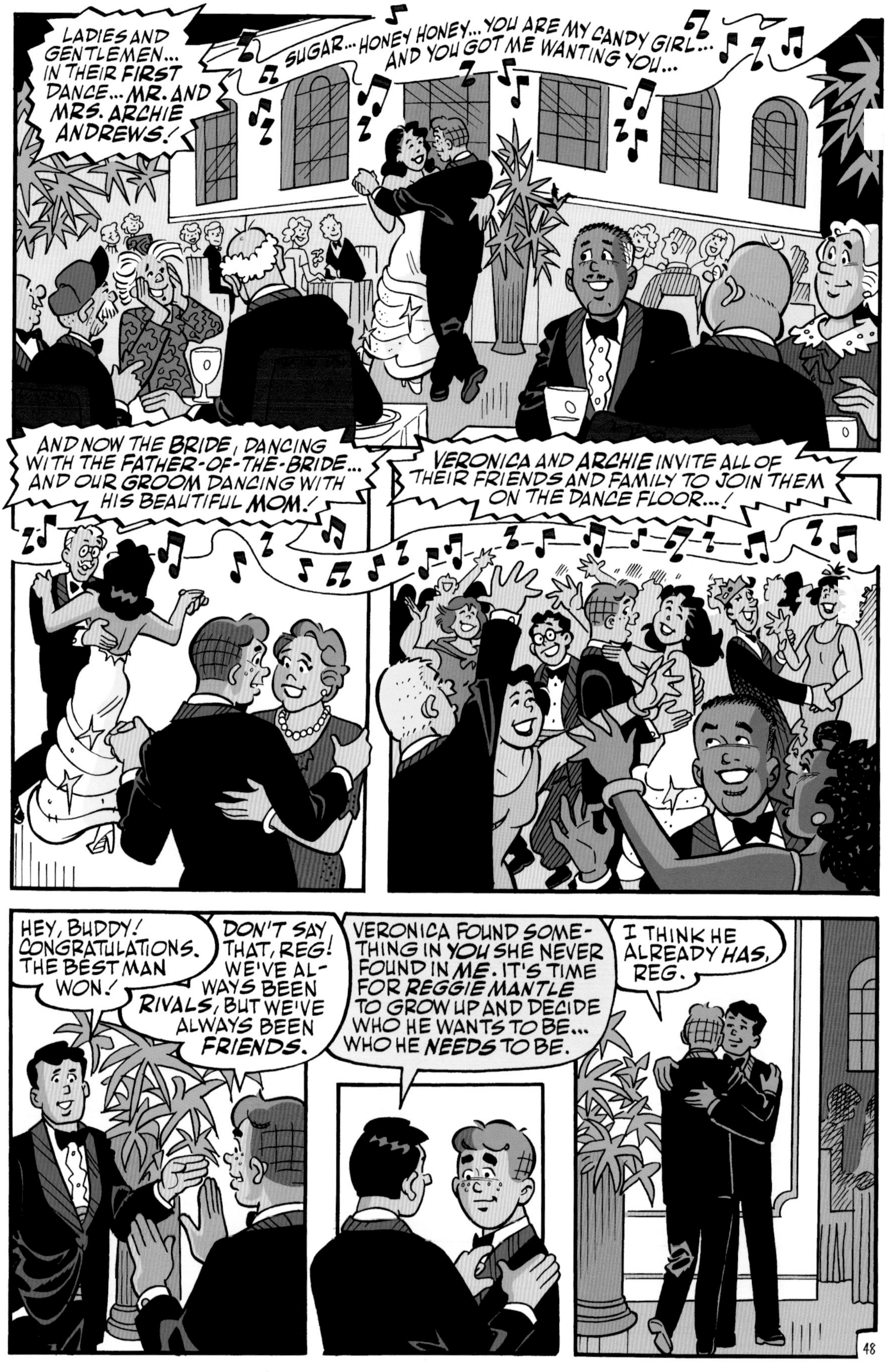
LADIES AND GENTLEMEN... IN THEIR FIRST DANCE... MR. AND MRS. ARCHIE ANDREWS!
SUGAR... HONEY HONEY... YOU ARE MY CANDY GIRL... AND YOU GOT ME WANTING YOU...
AND NOW THE BRIDE, DANCING WITH THE FATHER-OF-THE-BRIDE... AND OUR GROOM DANCING WITH HIS BEAUTIFUL MOM!
VERONICA AND ARCHIE INVITE ALL OF THEIR FRIENDS AND FAMILY TO JOIN THEM ON THE DANCE FLOOR...!
HEY, BUDDY! CONGRATULATIONS. THE BEST MAN WON!
DON'T SAY THAT, REG! WE'VE ALWAYS BEEN RIVALS, BUT WE'VE ALWAYS BEEN FRIENDS.
VERONICA FOUND SOMETHING IN YOU SHE NEVER FOUND IN ME. IT'S TIME FOR REGGIE MANTLE TO GROW UP AND DECIDE WHO HE WANTS TO BE... WHO HE NEEDS TO BE.
I THINK HE ALREADY HAS, REG.

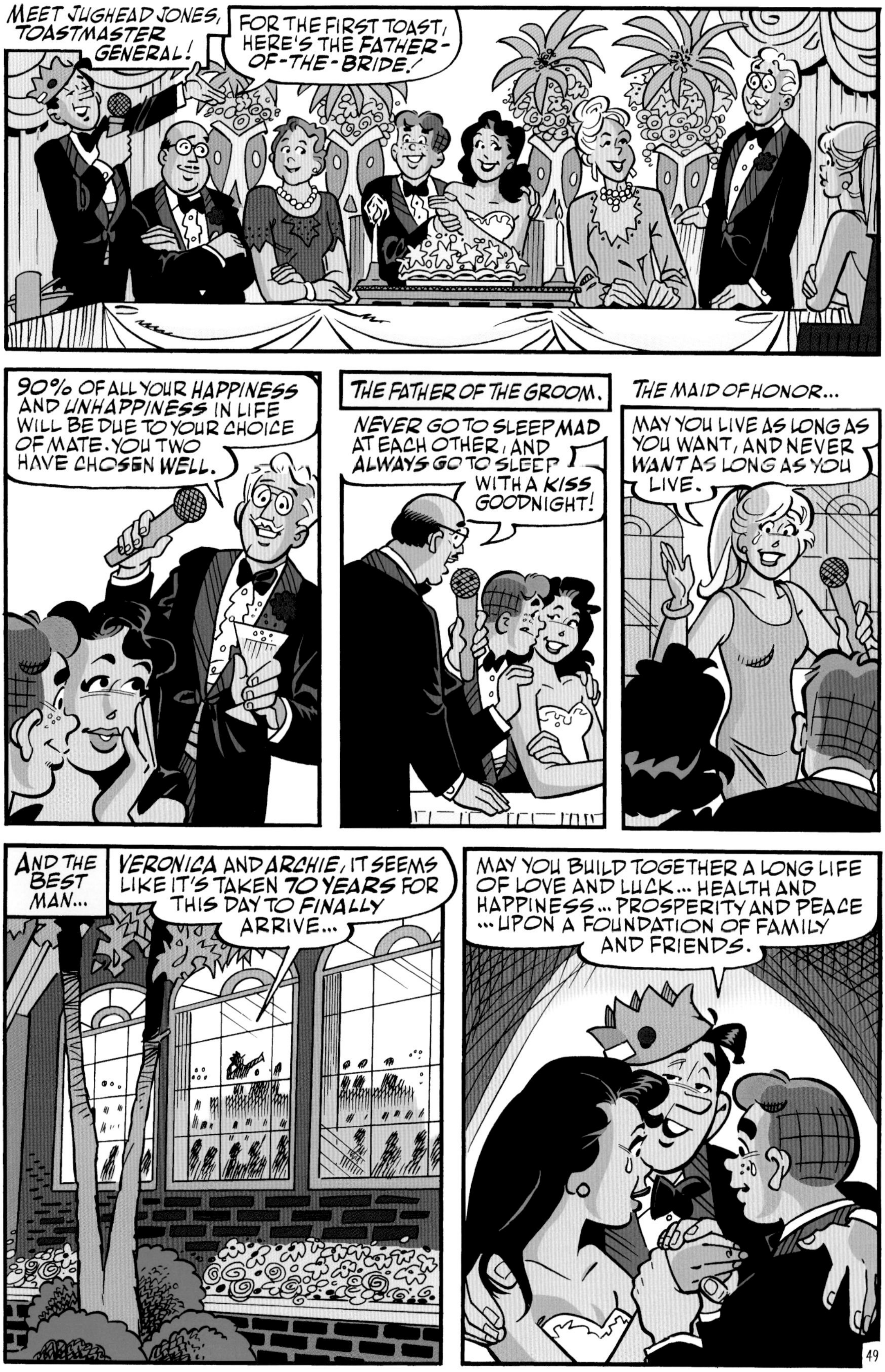
MEET JUGHEAD JONES, TOASTMASTER GENERAL!
FOR THE FIRST TOAST, HERE'S THE FATHER-OF-THE-BRIDE!
90% OF ALL YOUR HAPPINESS AND UNHAPPINESS IN LIFE WILL BE DUE TO YOUR CHOICE OF MATE. YOU TWO HAVE CHOSEN WELL.
THE FATHER OF THE GROOM.
NEVER GO TO SLEEP MAD AT EACH OTHER, AND ALWAYS GO TO SLEEP
WITH A KISS GOODNIGHT!
THE MAID OF HONOR...
MAY YOU LIVE AS LONG AS YOU WANT, AND NEVER WANT AS LONG AS YOU LIVE.
AND THE BEST MAN...
VERONICA AND ARCHIE, IT SEEMS LIKE IT'S TAKEN 70 YEARS FOR THIS DAY TO FINALLY ARRIVE...
MAY YOU BUILD TOGETHER A LONG LIFE OF LOVE AND LUCK... HEALTH AND HAPPINESS... PROSPERITY AND PEACE ...UPON A FOUNDATION OF FAMILY AND FRIENDS.

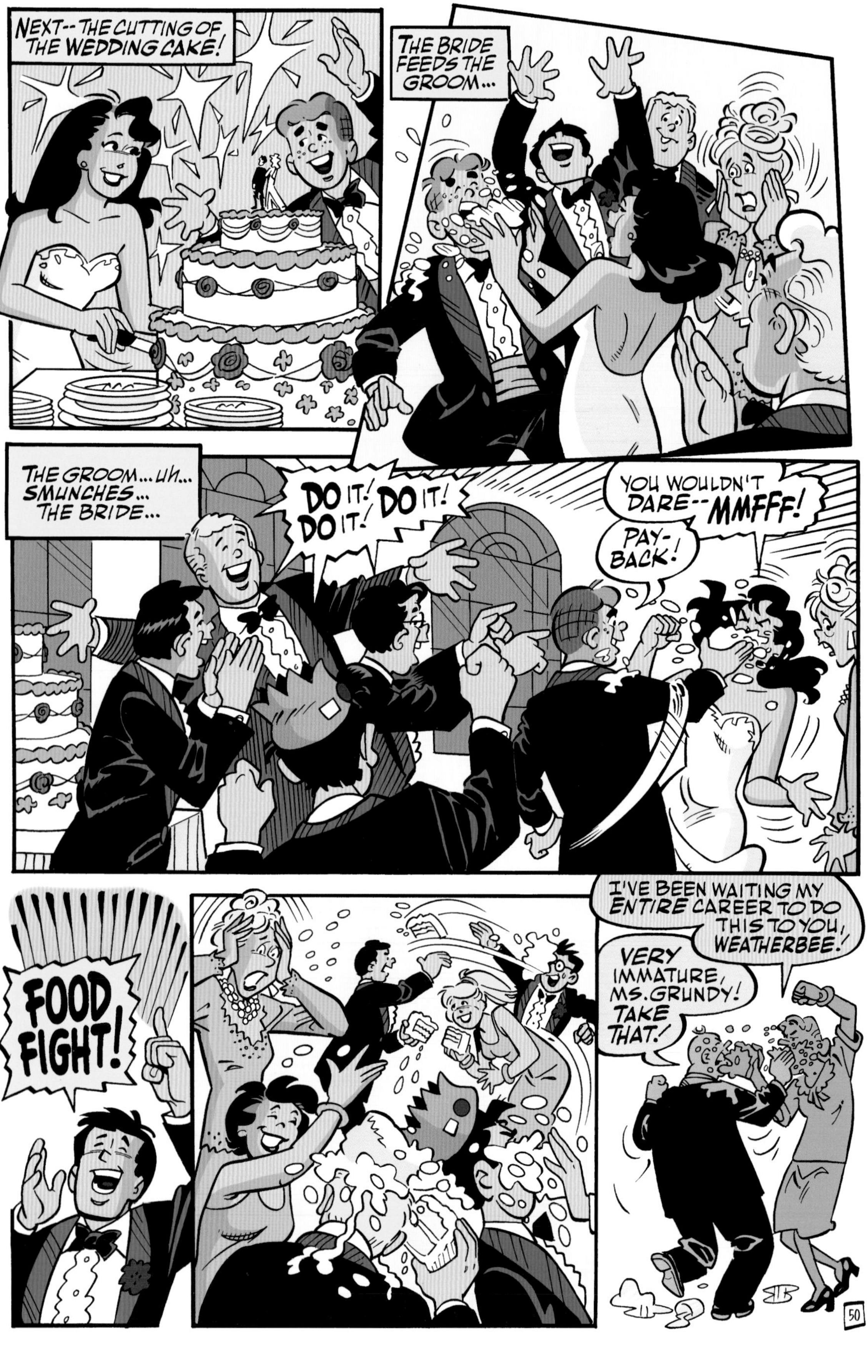
NEXT-- THE CUTTING OF THE WEDDING CAKE!
THE BRIDE FEEDS THE GROOM...
THE GROOM... uh... SMUNCHES... THE BRIDE...
DO IT! DO IT! DO IT!
YOU WOULDN'T DARE-- MMFFF!
PAY-BACK!
FOOD FIGHT!
I'VE BEEN WAITING MY ENTIRE CAREER TO DO THIS TO YOU, WEATHERBEE!
VERY IMMATURE, MS. GRUNDY! TAKE THAT!

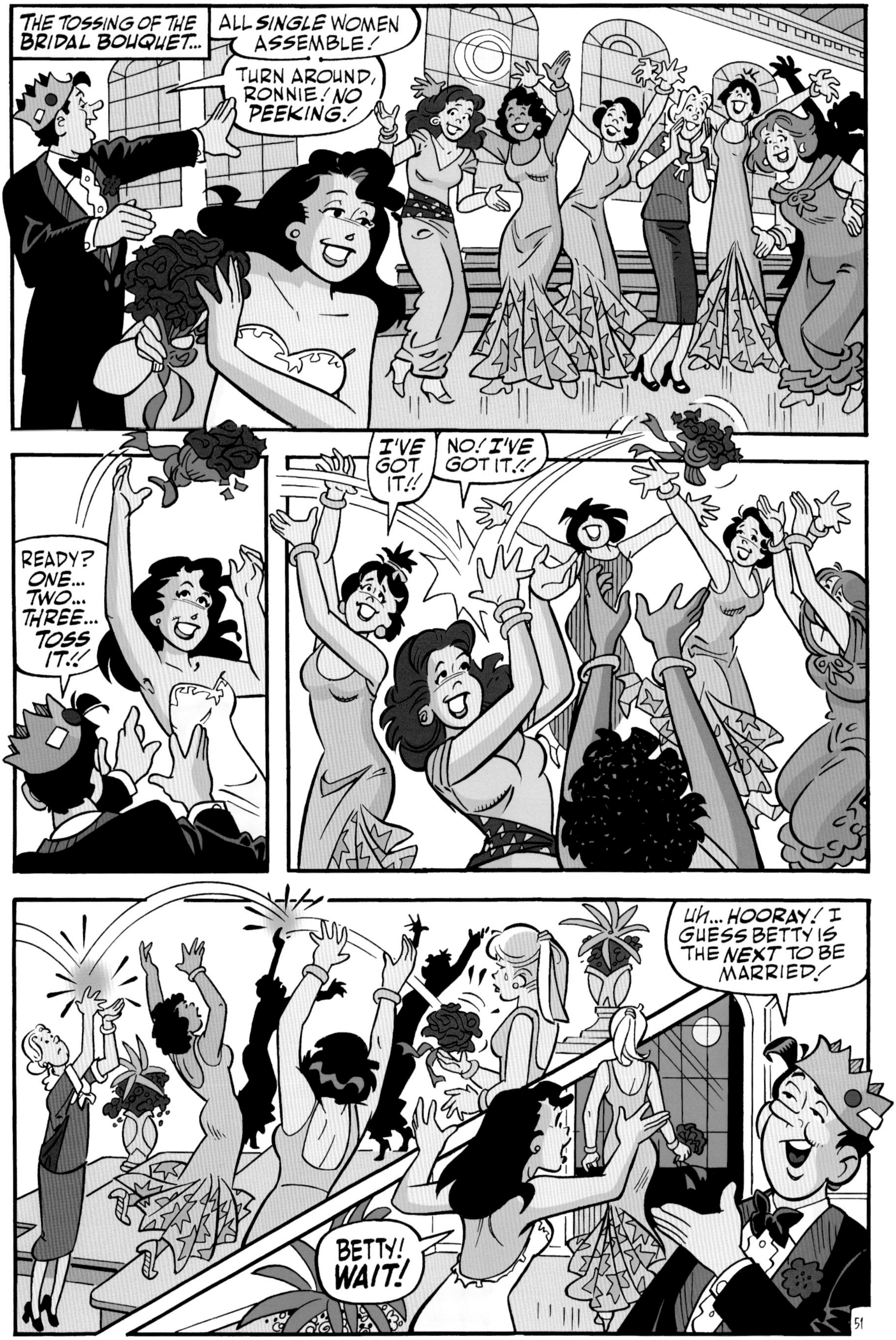
THE TOSSING OF THE BRIDAL BOUQUET...
ALL SINGLE WOMEN ASSEMBLE!
TURN AROUND, RONNIE! NO PEEKING!
READY? ONE... TWO... THREE... TOSS IT!!
I'VE GOT IT!!
NO! I'VE GOT IT!!
UH... HOORAY! I GUESS BETTY IS THE NEXT TO BE MARRIED!
BETTY! WAIT!

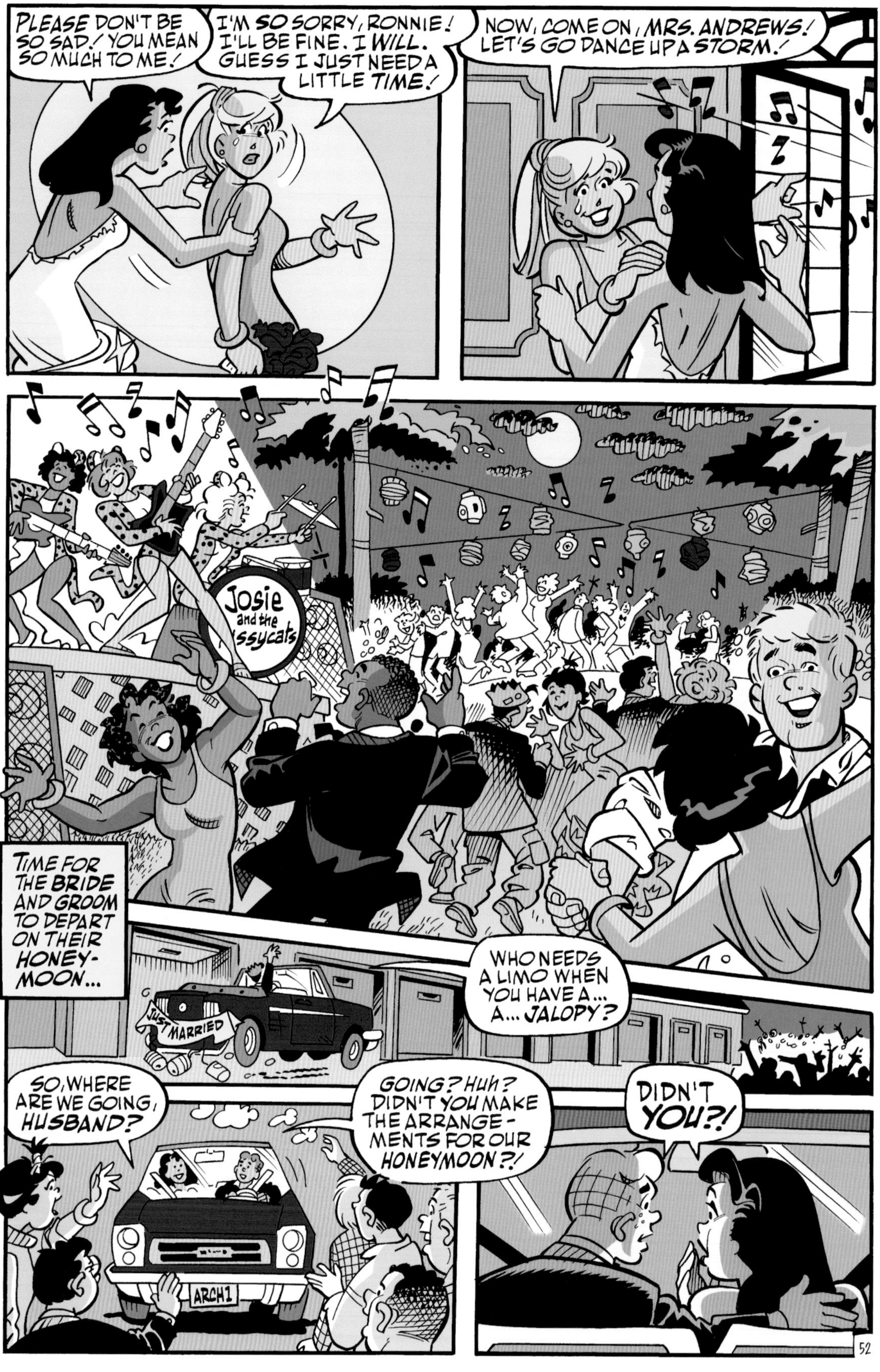
PLEASE DON'T BE SO SAD! YOU MEAN SO MUCH TO ME!
I'M SO SORRY, RONNIE! I'LL BE FINE. I WILL. GUESS I JUST NEED A LITTLE TIME!
NOW, COME ON, MRS. ANDREWS! LET'S GO DANCE UP A STORM!
Josie and the Pussycats
TIME FOR THE BRIDE AND GROOM TO DEPART ON THEIR HONEYMOON...
JUST MARRIED
WHO NEEDS A LIMO WHEN YOU HAVE A... A... JALOPY?
SO, WHERE ARE WE GOING, HUSBAND?
GOING? Huh? DIDN'T YOU MAKE THE ARRANGEMENTS FOR OUR HONEYMOON?!
ARCH1
DIDN'T YOU?!

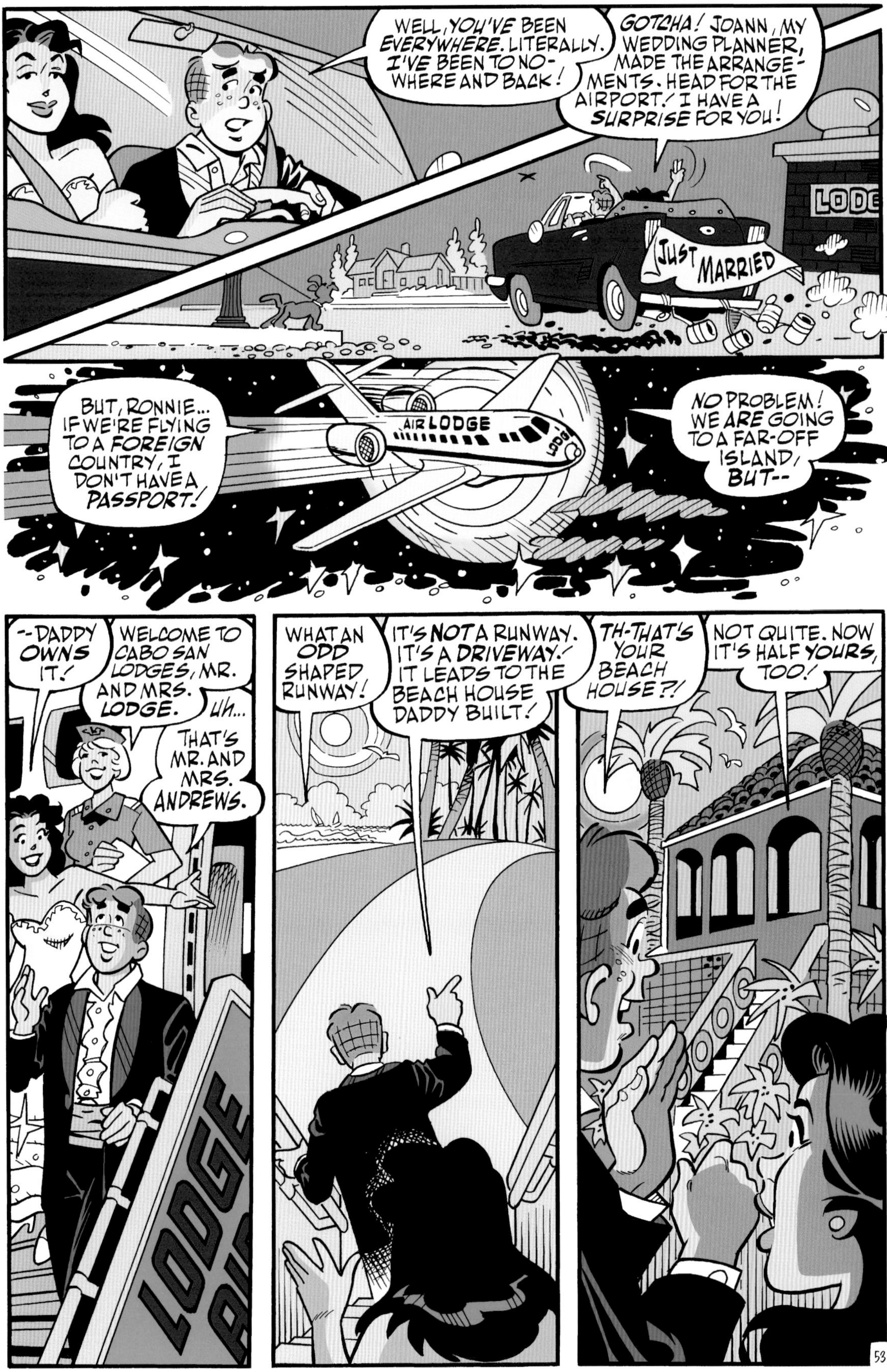
WELL, YOU'VE BEEN EVERYWHERE. LITERALLY. I'VE BEEN TO NO-WHERE AND BACK!
GOTCHA! JOANN, MY WEDDING PLANNER, MADE THE ARRANGE-MENTS. HEAD FOR THE AIRPORT! I HAVE A SURPRISE FOR YOU!
LODGE
JUST MARRIED
BUT, RONNIE... IF WE'RE FLYING TO A FOREIGN COUNTRY, I DON'T HAVE A PASSPORT!
AIR LODGE
NO PROBLEM! WE ARE GOING TO A FAR-OFF ISLAND, BUT--
--DADDY OWNS IT!
WELCOME TO CABO SAN LODGES, MR. AND MRS. LODGE.
UH... THAT'S MR. AND MRS. ANDREWS.
LODGE
WHAT AN ODD SHAPED RUNWAY!
IT'S NOT A RUNWAY. IT'S A DRIVEWAY! IT LEADS TO THE BEACH HOUSE DADDY BUILT!
TH-THAT'S YOUR BEACH HOUSE?!
NOT QUITE. NOW IT'S HALF YOURS, TOO!

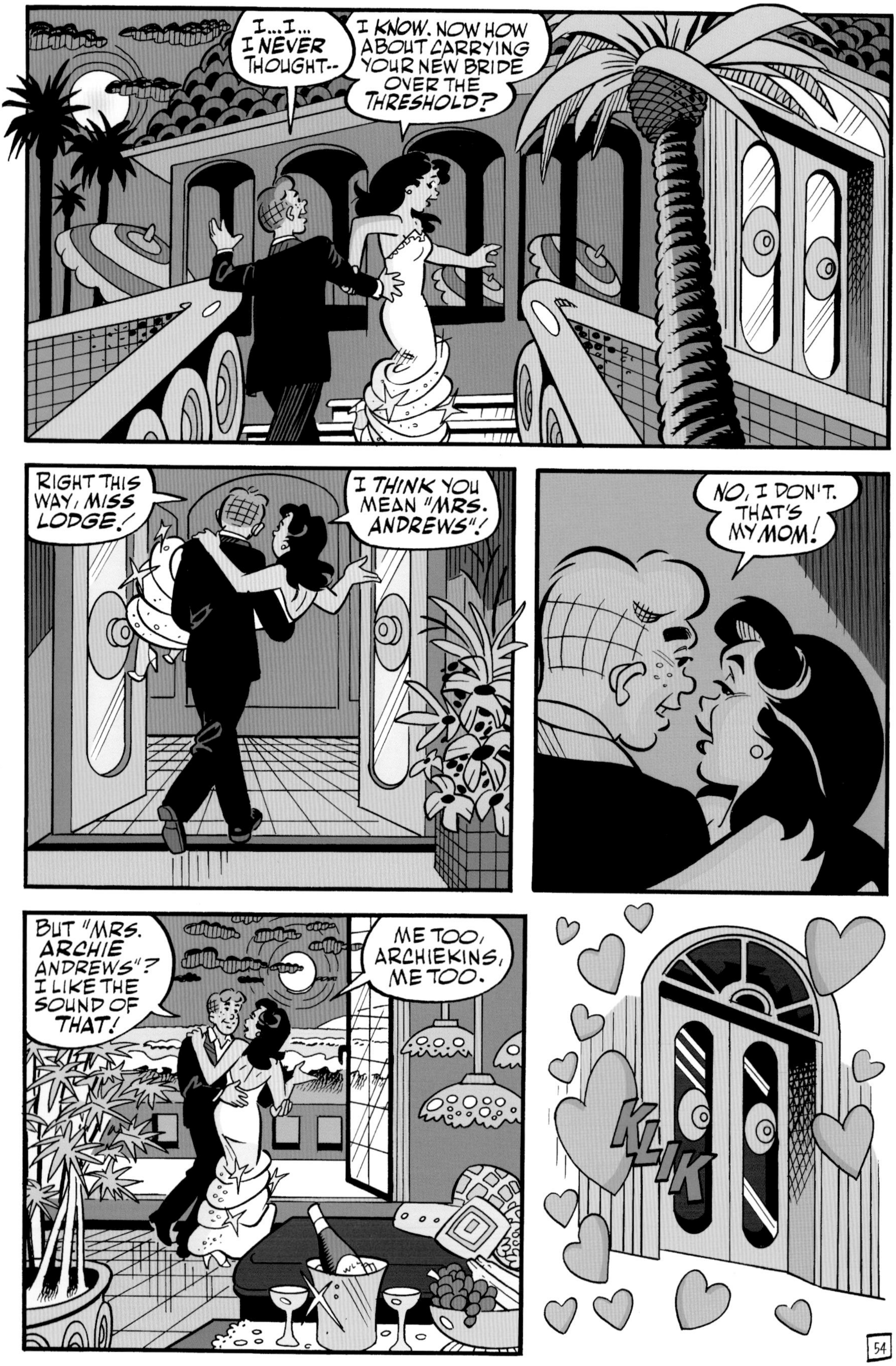
I... I... I NEVER THOUGHT--
I KNOW. NOW HOW ABOUT CARRYING YOUR NEW BRIDE OVER THE THRESHOLD?
RIGHT THIS WAY, MISS LODGE!
I THINK YOU MEAN "MRS. ANDREWS"!
NO, I DON'T. THAT'S MY MOM!
BUT "MRS. ARCHIE ANDREWS"? I LIKE THE SOUND OF THAT!
ME TOO, ARCHIEKINS, ME TOO.
KLIK

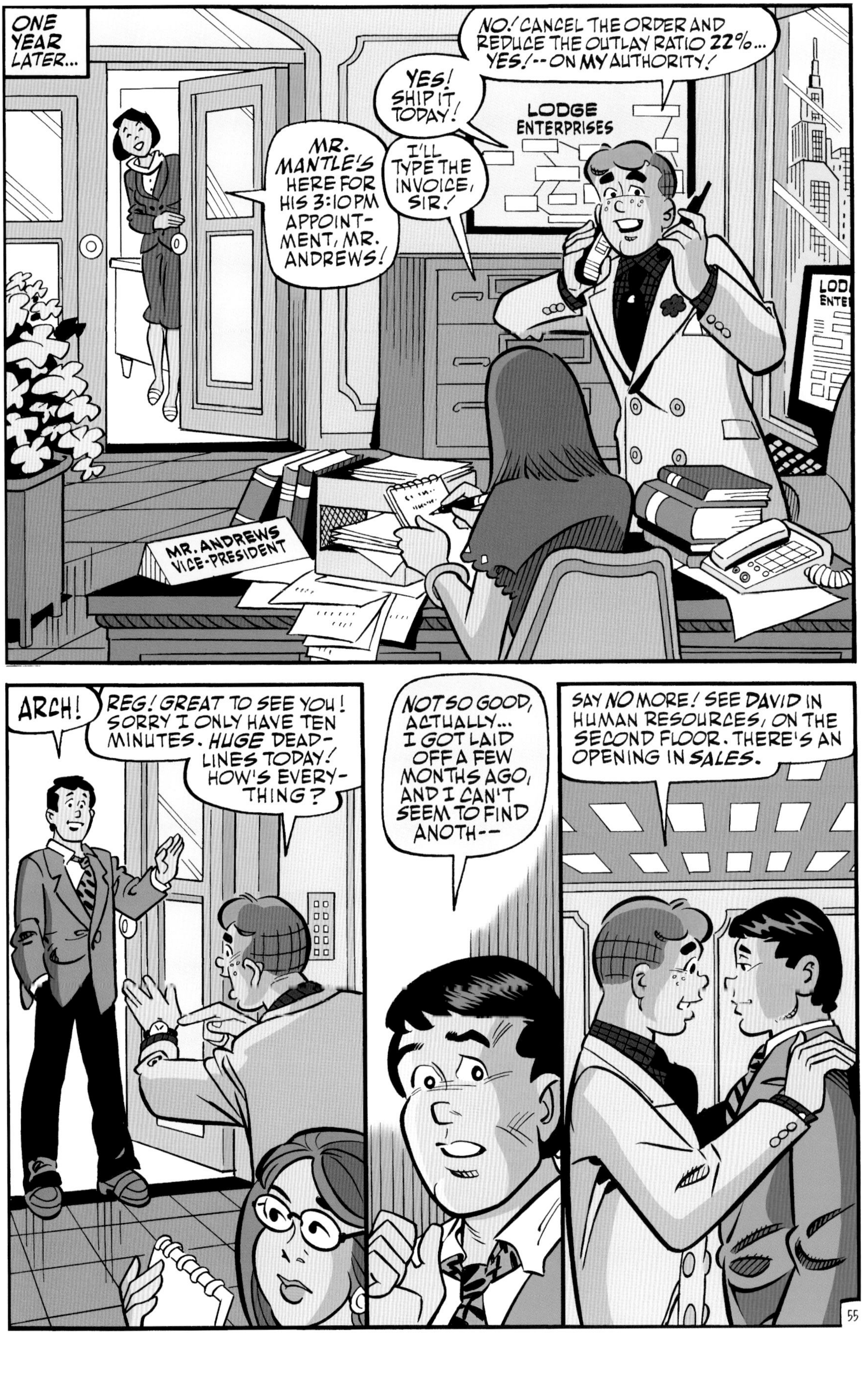
ONE YEAR LATER...
MR. MANTLE'S HERE FOR HIS 3:10 PM APPOINTMENT, MR. ANDREWS!
YES! SHIP IT TODAY!
I'LL TYPE THE INVOICE, SIR!
NO! CANCEL THE ORDER AND REDUCE THE OUTLAY RATIO 22%... YES!--ON MY AUTHORITY!
LODGE ENTERPRISES
MR. ANDREWS VICE-PRESIDENT
ARCH!
REG! GREAT TO SEE YOU! SORRY I ONLY HAVE TEN MINUTES. HUGE DEADLINES TODAY! HOW'S EVERYTHING?
NOT SO GOOD, ACTUALLY... I GOT LAID OFF A FEW MONTHS AGO, AND I CAN'T SEEM TO FIND ANOTH--
SAY NO MORE! SEE DAVID IN HUMAN RESOURCES, ON THE SECOND FLOOR. THERE'S AN OPENING IN SALES.

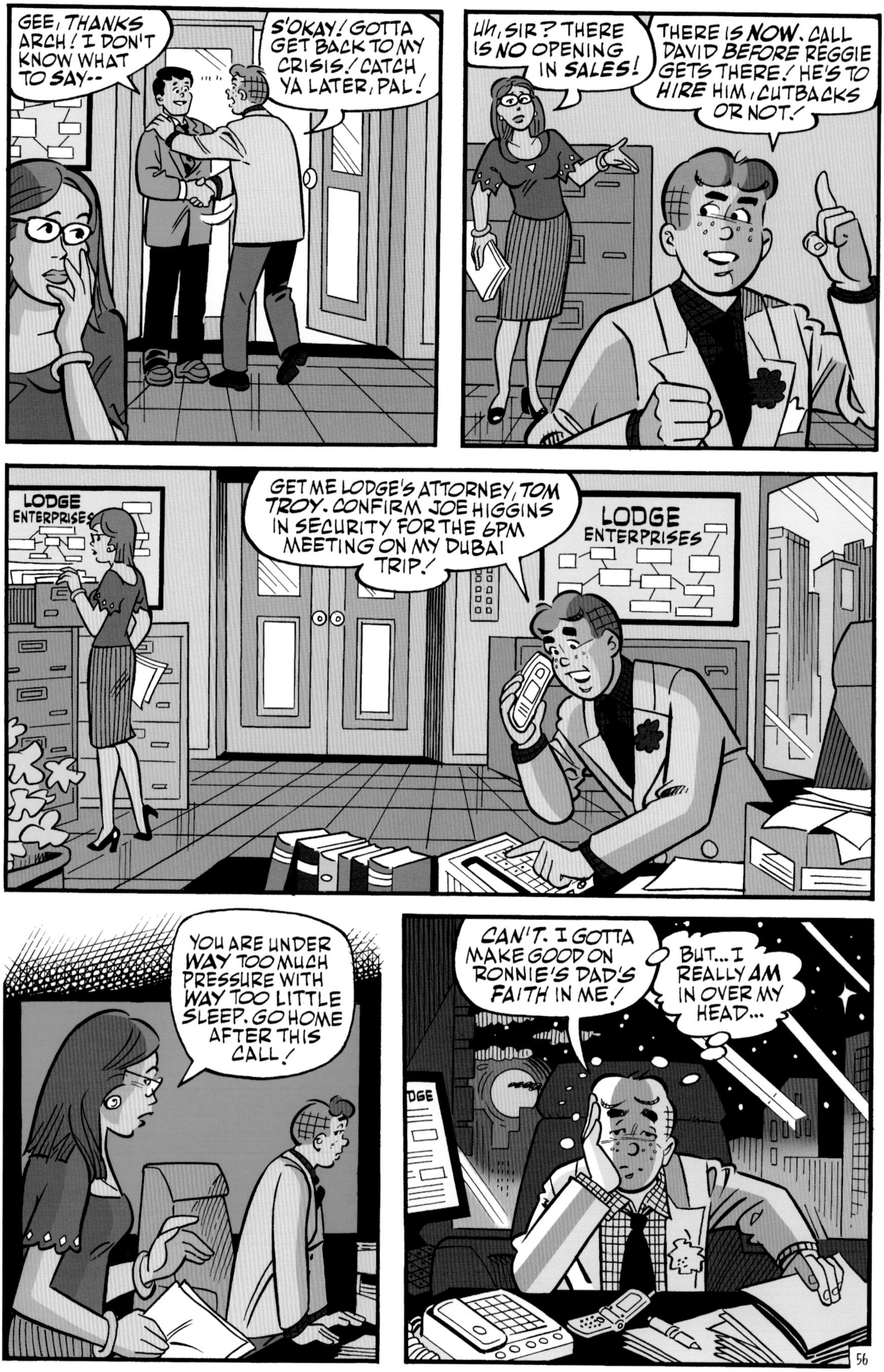

GEE, THANKS ARCH! I DON'T KNOW WHAT TO SAY--
S'OKAY! GOTTA GET BACK TO MY CRISIS! CATCH YA LATER, PAL!
UH, SIR? THERE IS NO OPENING IN SALES!
THERE IS NOW. CALL DAVID BEFORE REGGIE GETS THERE! HE'S TO HIRE HIM, CUTBACKS OR NOT!
LODGE ENTERPRISES
GET ME LODGE'S ATTORNEY, TOM TROY. CONFIRM JOE HIGGINS IN SECURITY FOR THE 6PM MEETING ON MY DUBAI TRIP!
LODGE ENTERPRISES
YOU ARE UNDER WAY TOO MUCH PRESSURE WITH WAY TOO LITTLE SLEEP. GO HOME AFTER THIS CALL!
CAN'T. I GOTTA MAKE GOOD ON RONNIE'S DAD'S FAITH IN ME!
BUT... I REALLY AM IN OVER MY HEAD...

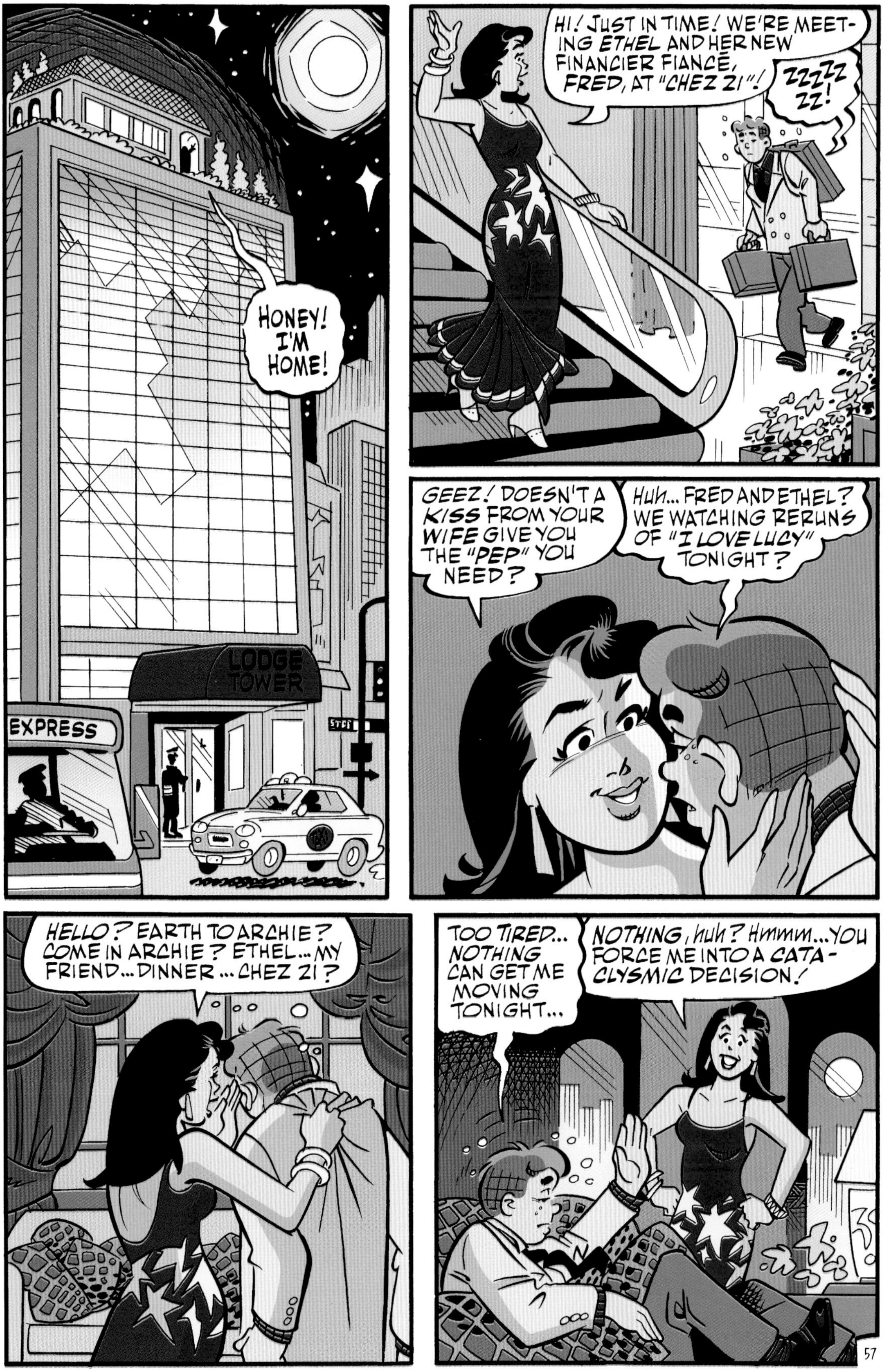
HONEY! I'M HOME!
LODGE TOWER
EXPRESS
HI! JUST IN TIME! WE'RE MEETING ETHEL AND HER NEW FINANCIER FIANCÉ, FRED, AT "CHEZ ZI"!
ZZZZZ ZZ!
GEEZ! DOESN'T A KISS FROM YOUR WIFE GIVE YOU THE "PEP" YOU NEED?
HUH... FRED AND ETHEL? WE WATCHING RERUNS OF "I LOVE LUCY" TONIGHT?
HELLO? EARTH TO ARCHIE? COME IN ARCHIE? ETHEL... MY FRIEND... DINNER... CHEZ ZI?
TOO TIRED... NOTHING CAN GET ME MOVING TONIGHT...
NOTHING, HUH? HMMM... YOU FORCE ME INTO A CATACLYSMIC DECISION!

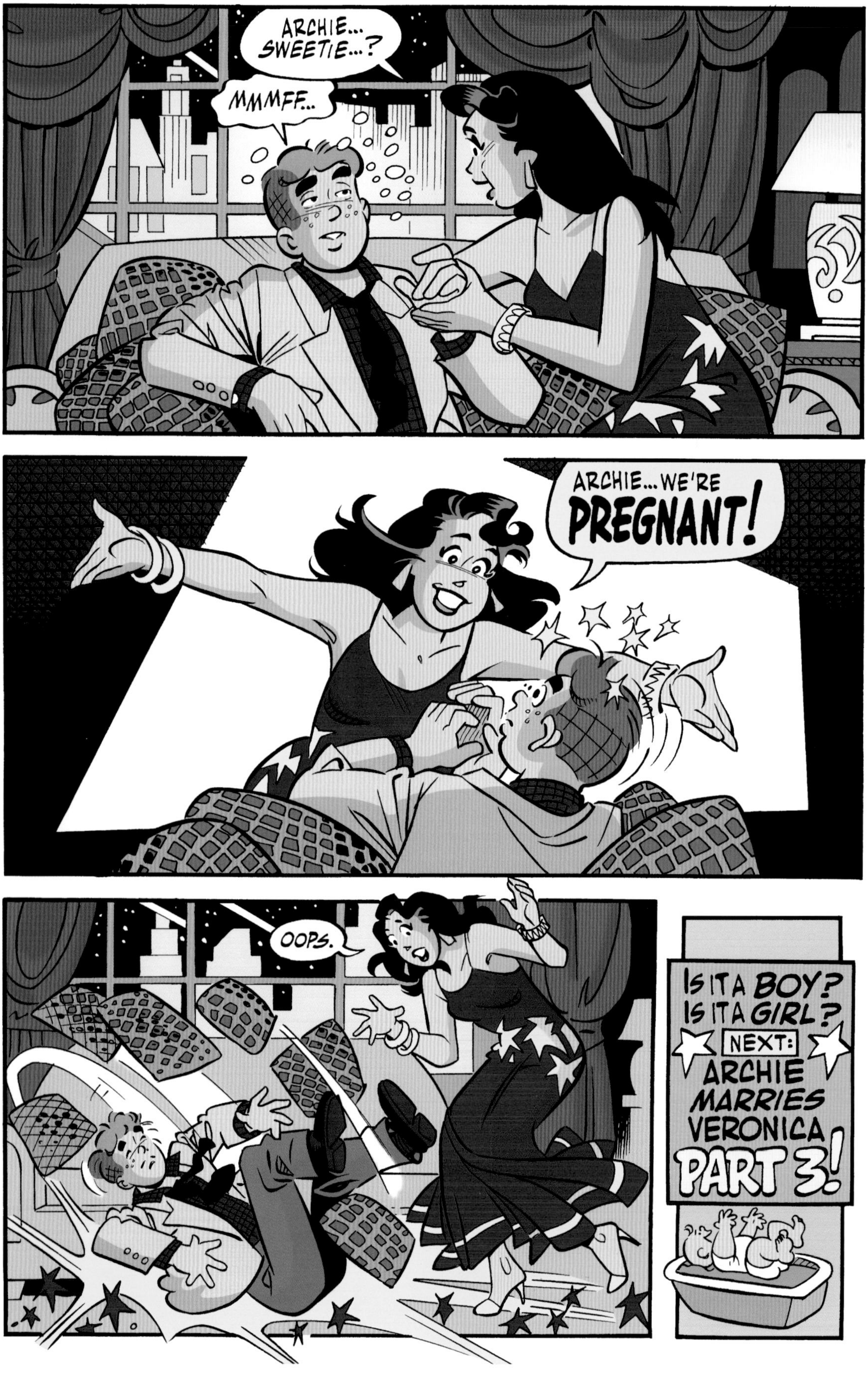
ARCHIE... SWEETIE...?
MMMFF...
ARCHIE... WE'RE PREGNANT!
OOPS.
IS IT A BOY? IS IT A GIRL?
NEXT:
ARCHIE MARRIES VERONICA PART 3!

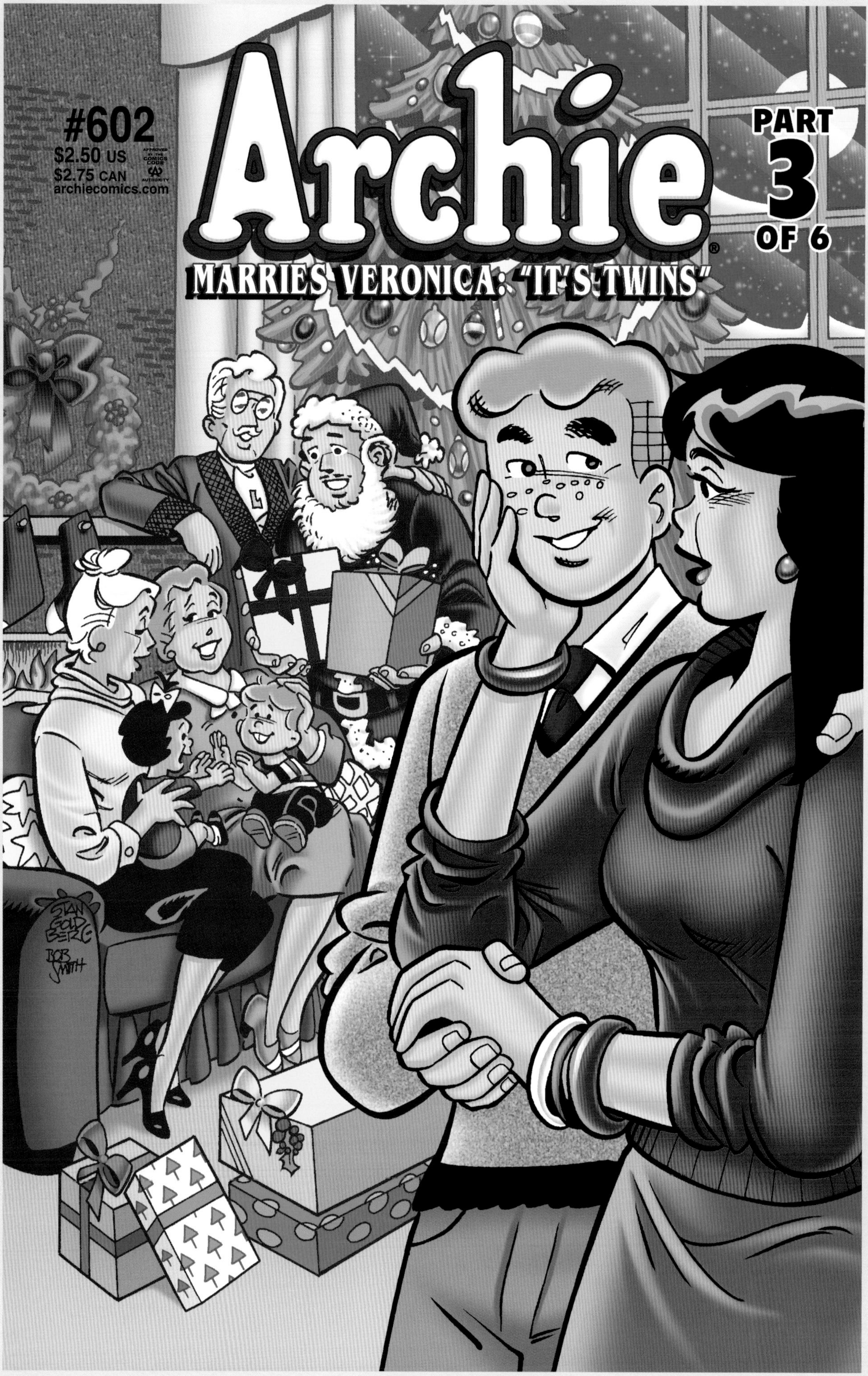

#602
$2.50 US
$2.75 CAN
archiecomics.com
Archie
MARRIES VERONICA: "IT'S TWINS"
PART 3 OF 6
STAN GOLDBERG
BOB SMITH

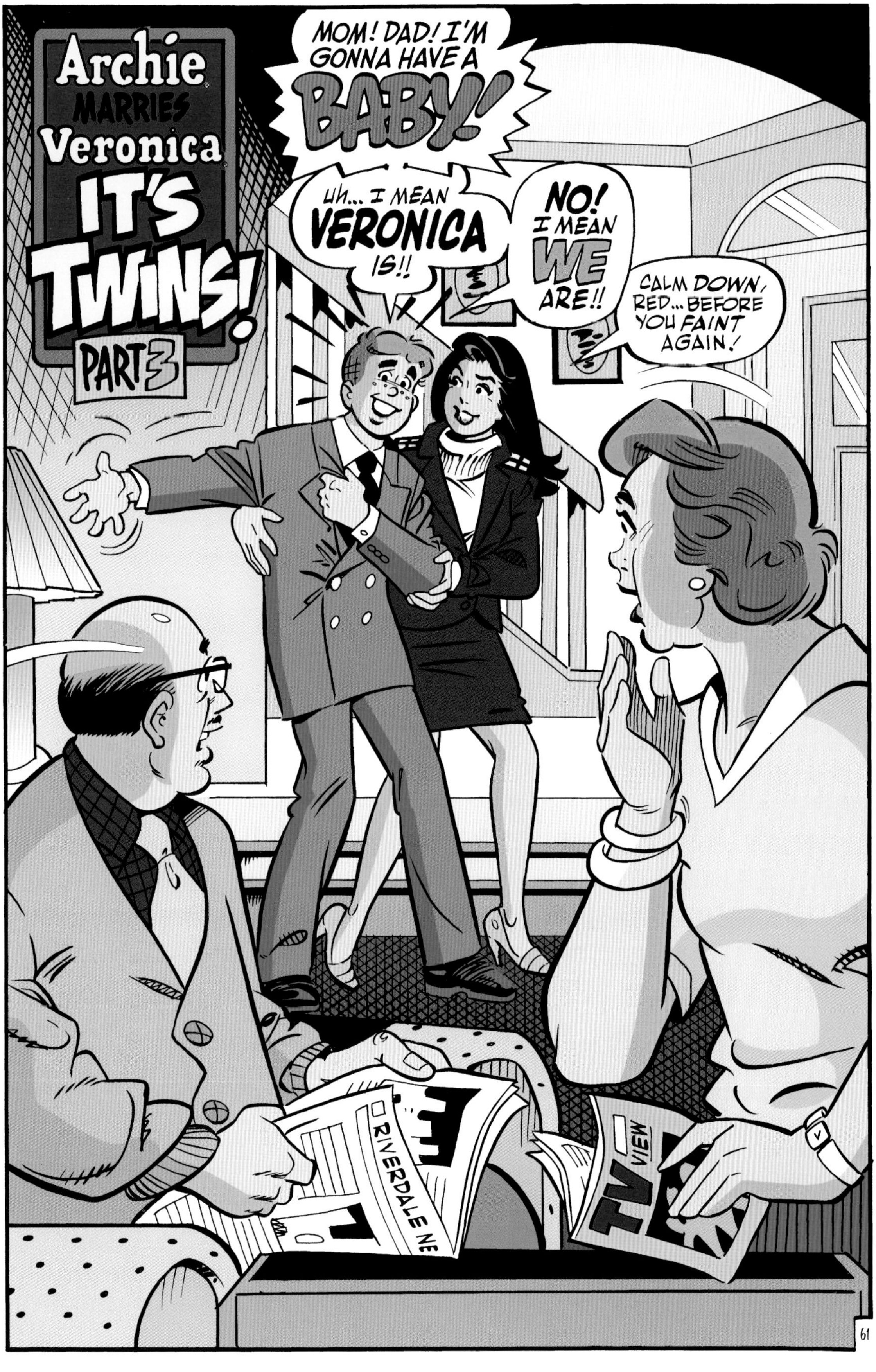
Archie MARRIES Veronica
IT'S TWINS!
PART 3
MOM! DAD! I'M GONNA HAVE A BABY!
UH... I MEAN VERONICA IS!!
NO! I MEAN WE ARE!!
CALM DOWN, RED... BEFORE YOU FAINT AGAIN!
RIVERDALE NE
TV VIEW

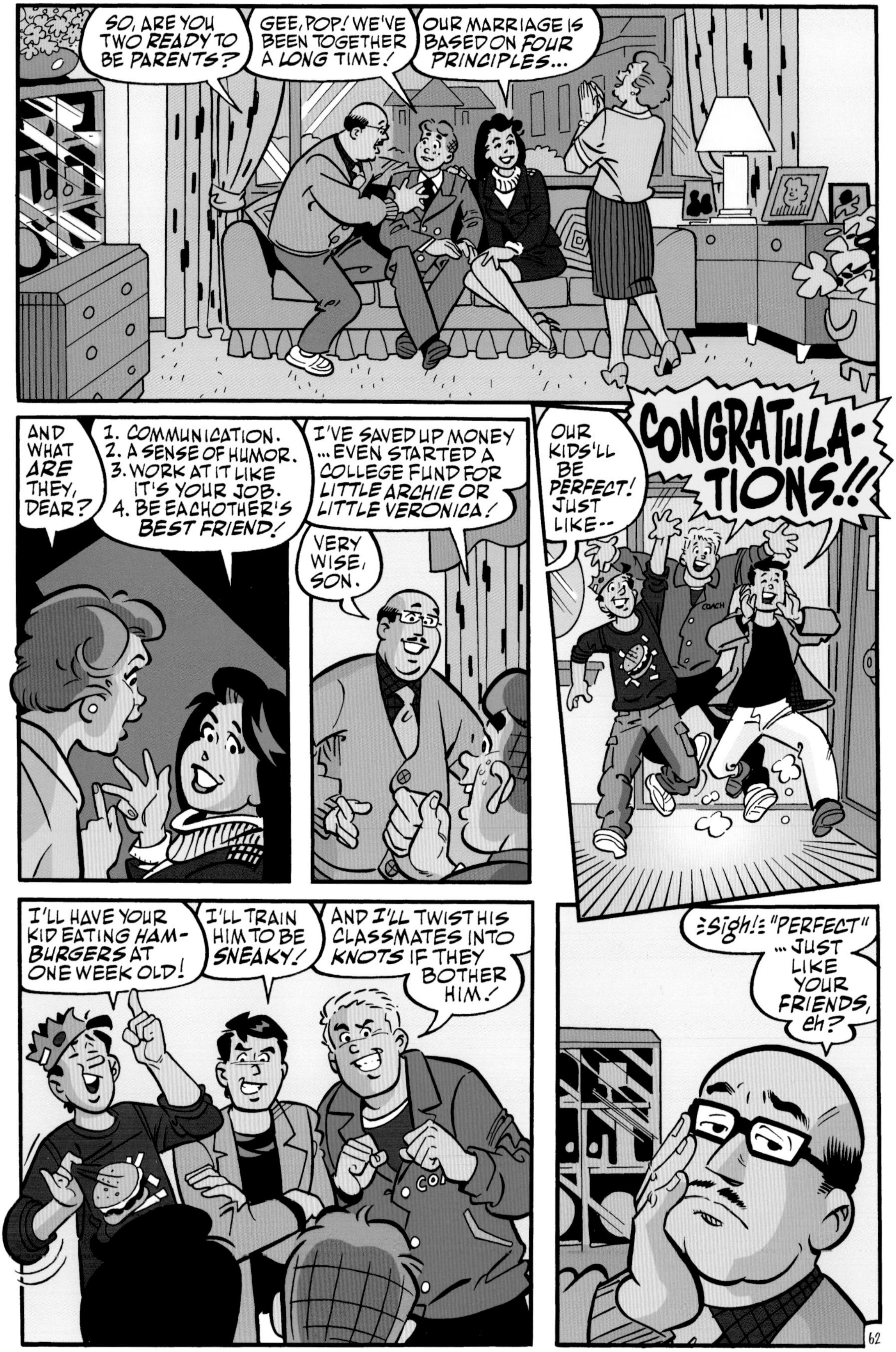
SO, ARE YOU TWO READY TO BE PARENTS?
GEE, POP! WE'VE BEEN TOGETHER A LONG TIME!
OUR MARRIAGE IS BASED ON FOUR PRINCIPLES...
AND WHAT ARE THEY, DEAR?
1. COMMUNICATION. 2. A SENSE OF HUMOR. 3. WORK AT IT LIKE IT'S YOUR JOB. 4. BE EACHOTHER'S BEST FRIEND!
I'VE SAVED UP MONEY ...EVEN STARTED A COLLEGE FUND FOR LITTLE ARCHIE OR LITTLE VERONICA!
VERY WISE, SON.
OUR KIDS'LL BE PERFECT! JUST LIKE--
CONGRATULATIONS!!
COACH
I'LL HAVE YOUR KID EATING HAMBURGERS AT ONE WEEK OLD!
I'LL TRAIN HIM TO BE SNEAKY!
AND I'LL TWIST HIS CLASSMATES INTO KNOTS IF THEY BOTHER HIM!
sigh! "PERFECT" ...JUST LIKE YOUR FRIENDS, eh?

C'MON, ARCHIEKINS! WE HAVE TO BREAK THE NEWS TO *DADDY* BEFORE MY FLIGHT!

OKAY. ARE YOU SURE YOU DON'T WANT ME TO GO WITH YOU?

NOPE. I HAVE TO DO THIS ALONE.

I UNDER-STAND.

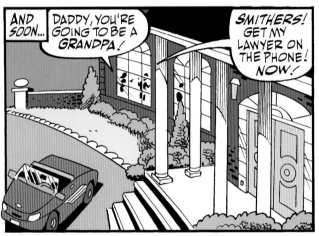

AND SOON...

DADDY, YOU'RE GOING TO BE A GRANDPA!

SMITHERS! GET MY LAWYER ON THE PHONE! NOW!

UH... ARE YOU GOING TO *SUE* ME FOR THIS?

MR. LOOPHOLE, I WANT MY WILL TO BE *CHANGED* -- LEAVING MY MOST *PRIZED* POSSESSION TO MY *GRANDCHILD!*

Whew!

ARE YOU *CERTAIN,* SIR? YOUR MOST *PRIZED* POSSESSION? YOUR STOCKS AND BONDS? REAL ESTATE? OIL WELLS? GOLD?

NO! MY CHILD-HOOD *SLED,* "ROSE-BUDDY"! =SNIFF!=

ROSEBUDDY

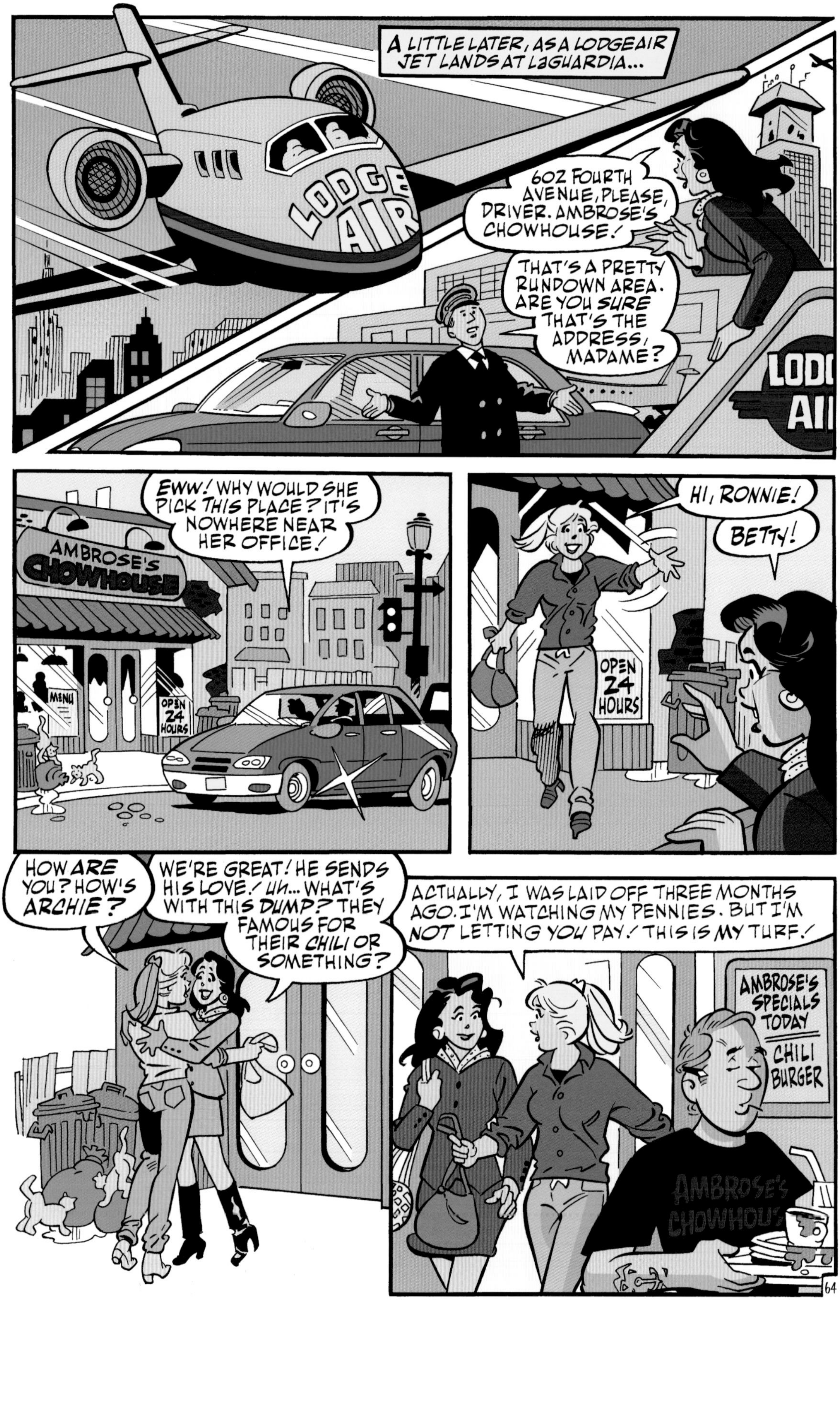
A LITTLE LATER, AS A LODGEAIR JET LANDS AT LAGUARDIA...
LODGE AIR
602 FOURTH AVENUE, PLEASE, DRIVER. AMBROSE'S CHOWHOUSE!
THAT'S A PRETTY RUNDOWN AREA. ARE YOU SURE THAT'S THE ADDRESS, MADAME?
EWW! WHY WOULD SHE PICK THIS PLACE? IT'S NOWHERE NEAR HER OFFICE!
AMBROSE'S CHOWHOUSE
MENU
OPEN 24 HOURS
HI, RONNIE!
BETTY!
OPEN 24 HOURS
HOW ARE YOU? HOW'S ARCHIE?
WE'RE GREAT! HE SENDS HIS LOVE! UH... WHAT'S WITH THIS DUMP? THEY FAMOUS FOR THEIR CHILI OR SOMETHING?
ACTUALLY, I WAS LAID OFF THREE MONTHS AGO. I'M WATCHING MY PENNIES. BUT I'M NOT LETTING YOU PAY! THIS IS MY TURF!
AMBROSE'S SPECIALS TODAY
CHILI BURGER
AMBROSE'S CHOWHOUS

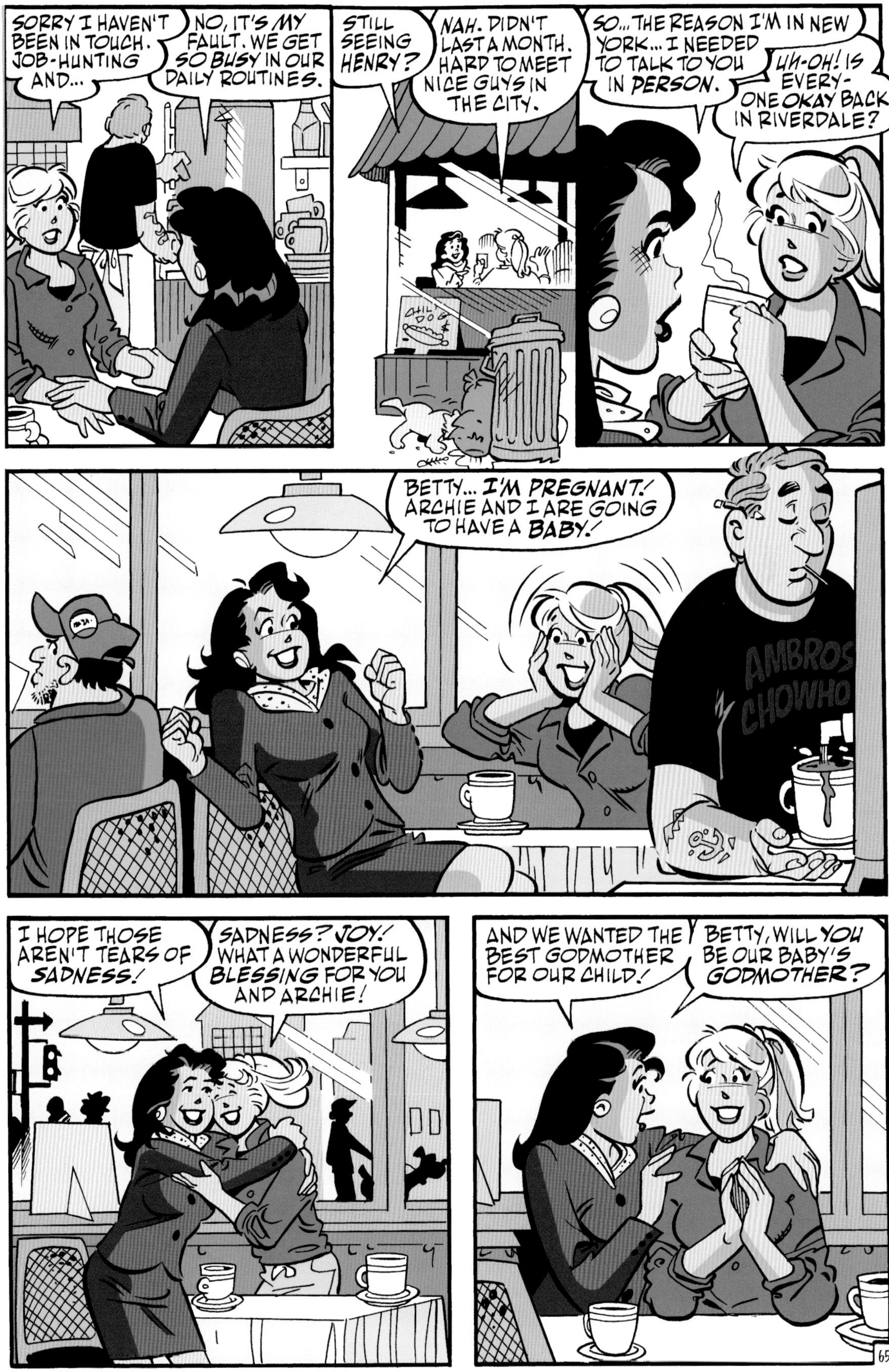
SORRY I HAVEN'T BEEN IN TOUCH. JOB-HUNTING AND...
NO, IT'S MY FAULT. WE GET SO BUSY IN OUR DAILY ROUTINES.
STILL SEEING HENRY?
NAH. DIDN'T LAST A MONTH. HARD TO MEET NICE GUYS IN THE CITY.
CHILI DOG $
SO... THE REASON I'M IN NEW YORK... I NEEDED TO TALK TO YOU IN PERSON.
UH-OH! IS EVERYONE OKAY BACK IN RIVERDALE?
BETTY... I'M PREGNANT! ARCHIE AND I ARE GOING TO HAVE A BABY!
AMBROS CHOWHO
I HOPE THOSE AREN'T TEARS OF SADNESS!
SADNESS? JOY! WHAT A WONDERFUL BLESSING FOR YOU AND ARCHIE!
AND WE WANTED THE BEST GODMOTHER FOR OUR CHILD!
BETTY, WILL YOU BE OUR BABY'S GODMOTHER?

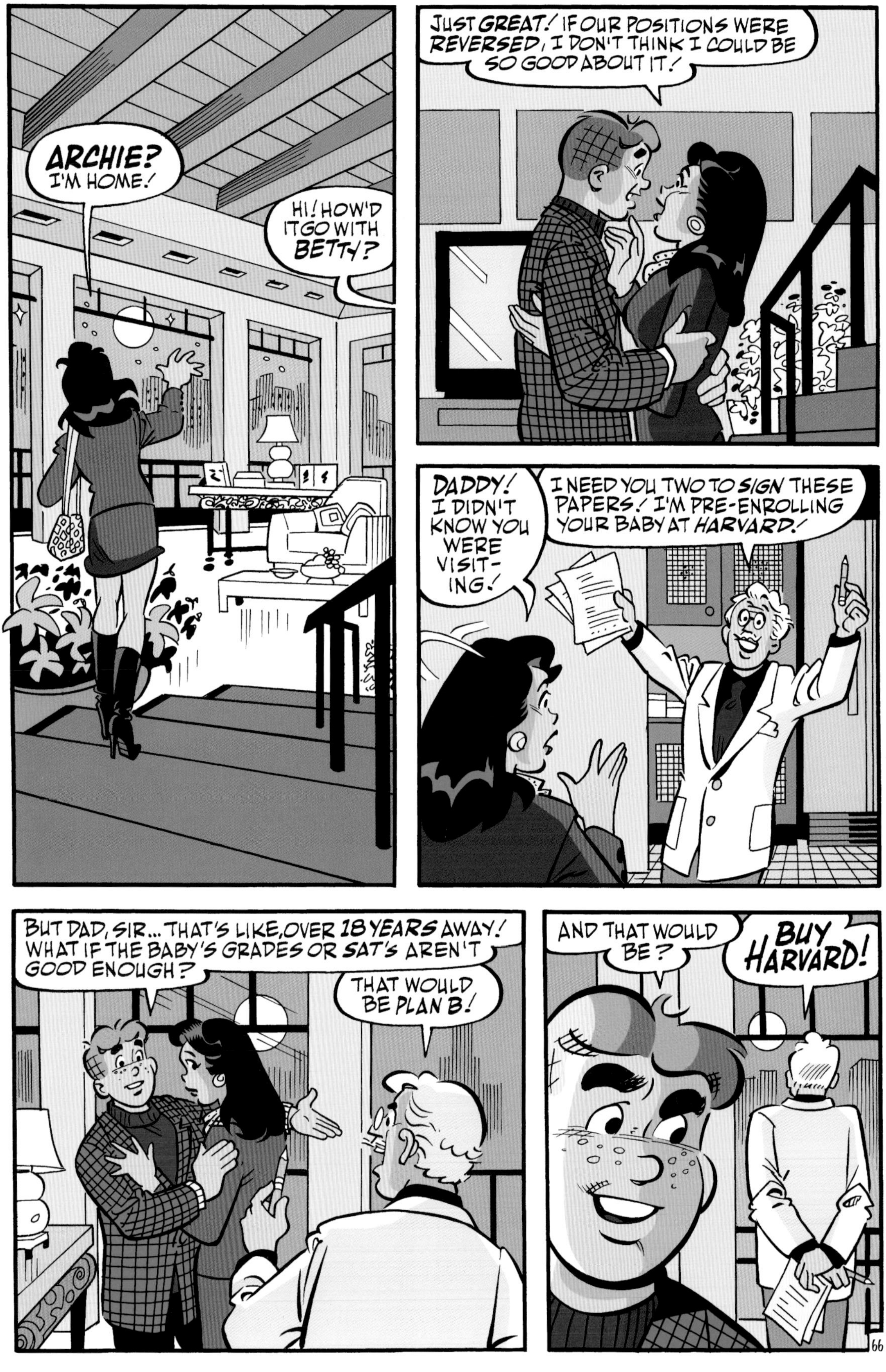
ARCHIE? I'M HOME!
HI! HOW'D IT GO WITH BETTY?
JUST GREAT! IF OUR POSITIONS WERE REVERSED, I DON'T THINK I COULD BE SO GOOD ABOUT IT!
DADDY! I DIDN'T KNOW YOU WERE VISIT-ING!
I NEED YOU TWO TO SIGN THESE PAPERS! I'M PRE-ENROLLING YOUR BABY AT HARVARD!
BUT DAD, SIR... THAT'S LIKE, OVER 18 YEARS AWAY! WHAT IF THE BABY'S GRADES OR SAT's AREN'T GOOD ENOUGH?
THAT WOULD BE PLAN B!
AND THAT WOULD BE?
BUY HARVARD!

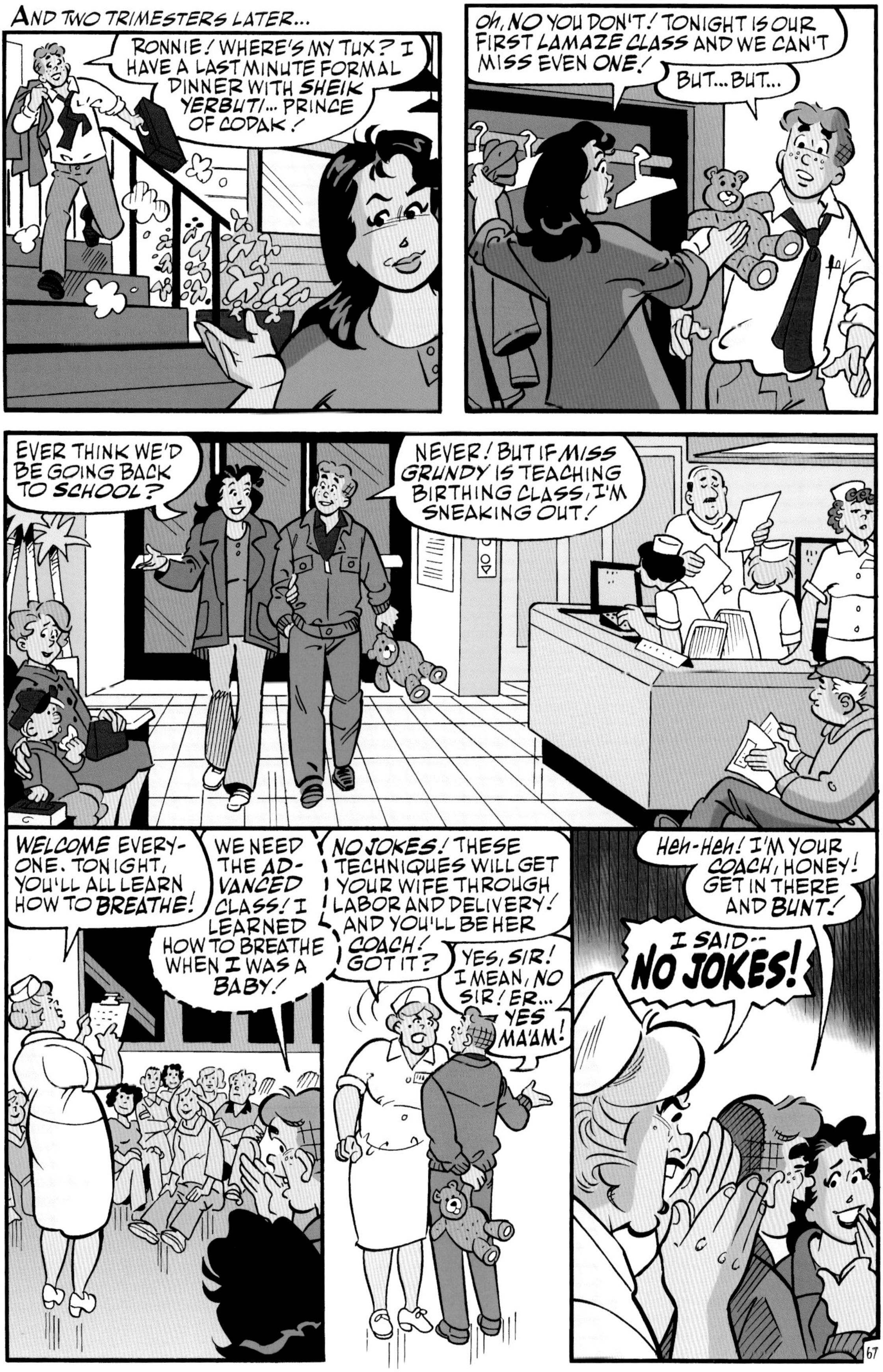
AND TWO TRIMESTERS LATER...
RONNIE! WHERE'S MY TUX? I HAVE A LAST MINUTE FORMAL DINNER WITH SHEIK YERBUTI... PRINCE OF CODAK!
OH, NO YOU DON'T! TONIGHT IS OUR FIRST LAMAZE CLASS AND WE CAN'T MISS EVEN ONE!
BUT...BUT...
EVER THINK WE'D BE GOING BACK TO SCHOOL?
NEVER! BUT IF MISS GRUNDY IS TEACHING BIRTHING CLASS, I'M SNEAKING OUT!
WELCOME EVERY-ONE. TONIGHT, YOU'LL ALL LEARN HOW TO BREATHE!
WE NEED THE AD-VANCED CLASS! I LEARNED HOW TO BREATHE WHEN I WAS A BABY!
NO JOKES! THESE TECHNIQUES WILL GET YOUR WIFE THROUGH LABOR AND DELIVERY! AND YOU'LL BE HER COACH! GOT IT?
YES, SIR! I MEAN, NO SIR! ER... YES MA'AM!
HEH-HEH! I'M YOUR COACH, HONEY! GET IN THERE AND BUNT!
I SAID-- NO JOKES!

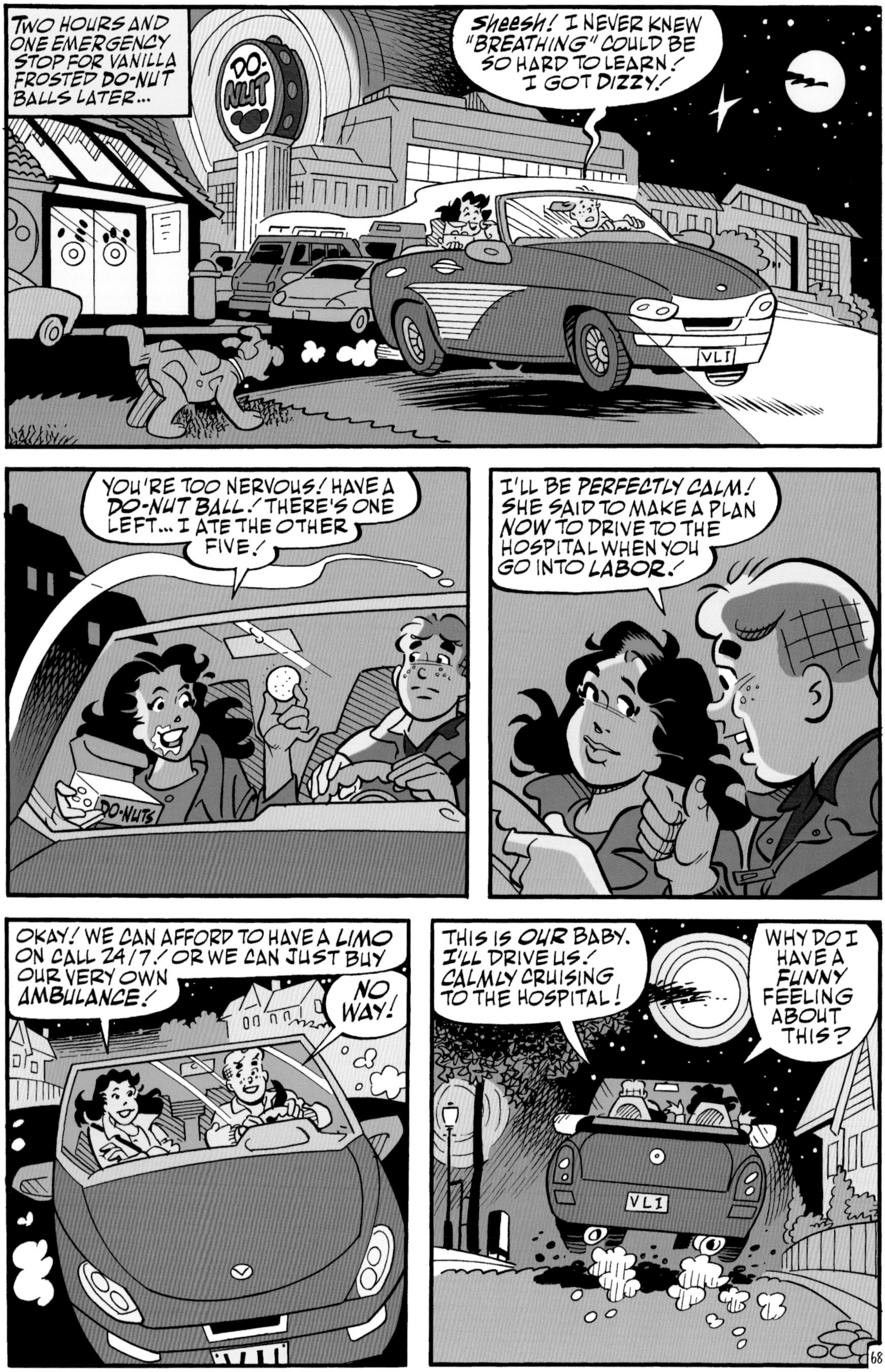
TWO HOURS AND ONE EMERGENCY STOP FOR VANILLA FROSTED DO-NUT BALLS LATER...
DO-NUT
SHEESH! I NEVER KNEW "BREATHING" COULD BE SO HARD TO LEARN! I GOT DIZZY!
VL1
YOU'RE TOO NERVOUS! HAVE A DO-NUT BALL! THERE'S ONE LEFT... I ATE THE OTHER FIVE!
DO-NUTS
I'LL BE PERFECTLY CALM! SHE SAID TO MAKE A PLAN NOW TO DRIVE TO THE HOSPITAL WHEN YOU GO INTO LABOR!
OKAY! WE CAN AFFORD TO HAVE A LIMO ON CALL 24/7! OR WE CAN JUST BUY OUR VERY OWN AMBULANCE!
NO WAY!
THIS IS OUR BABY. I'LL DRIVE US! CALMLY CRUISING TO THE HOSPITAL!
WHY DO I HAVE A FUNNY FEELING ABOUT THIS?
VL1

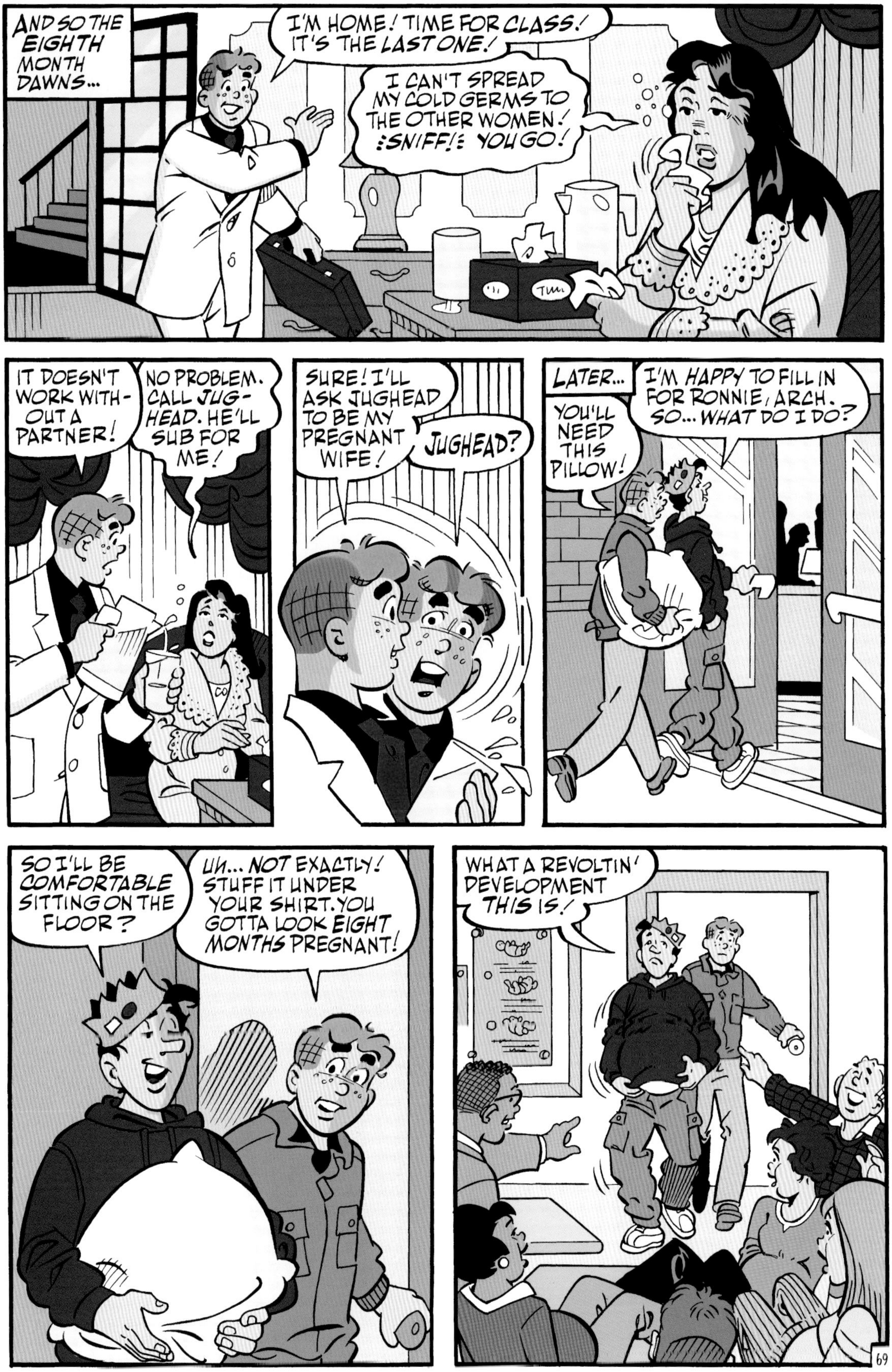
AND SO THE EIGHTH MONTH DAWNS...
I'M HOME! TIME FOR CLASS! IT'S THE LAST ONE!
I CAN'T SPREAD MY COLD GERMS TO THE OTHER WOMEN! :SNIFF!: YOU GO!
IT DOESN'T WORK WITH-OUT A PARTNER!
NO PROBLEM. CALL JUG-HEAD. HE'LL SUB FOR ME!
SURE! I'LL ASK JUGHEAD TO BE MY PREGNANT WIFE!
JUGHEAD?
LATER...
I'M HAPPY TO FILL IN FOR RONNIE, ARCH. SO... WHAT DO I DO?
YOU'LL NEED THIS PILLOW!
SO I'LL BE COMFORTABLE SITTING ON THE FLOOR?
UH... NOT EXACTLY! STUFF IT UNDER YOUR SHIRT. YOU GOTTA LOOK EIGHT MONTHS PREGNANT!
WHAT A REVOLTIN' DEVELOPMENT THIS IS!

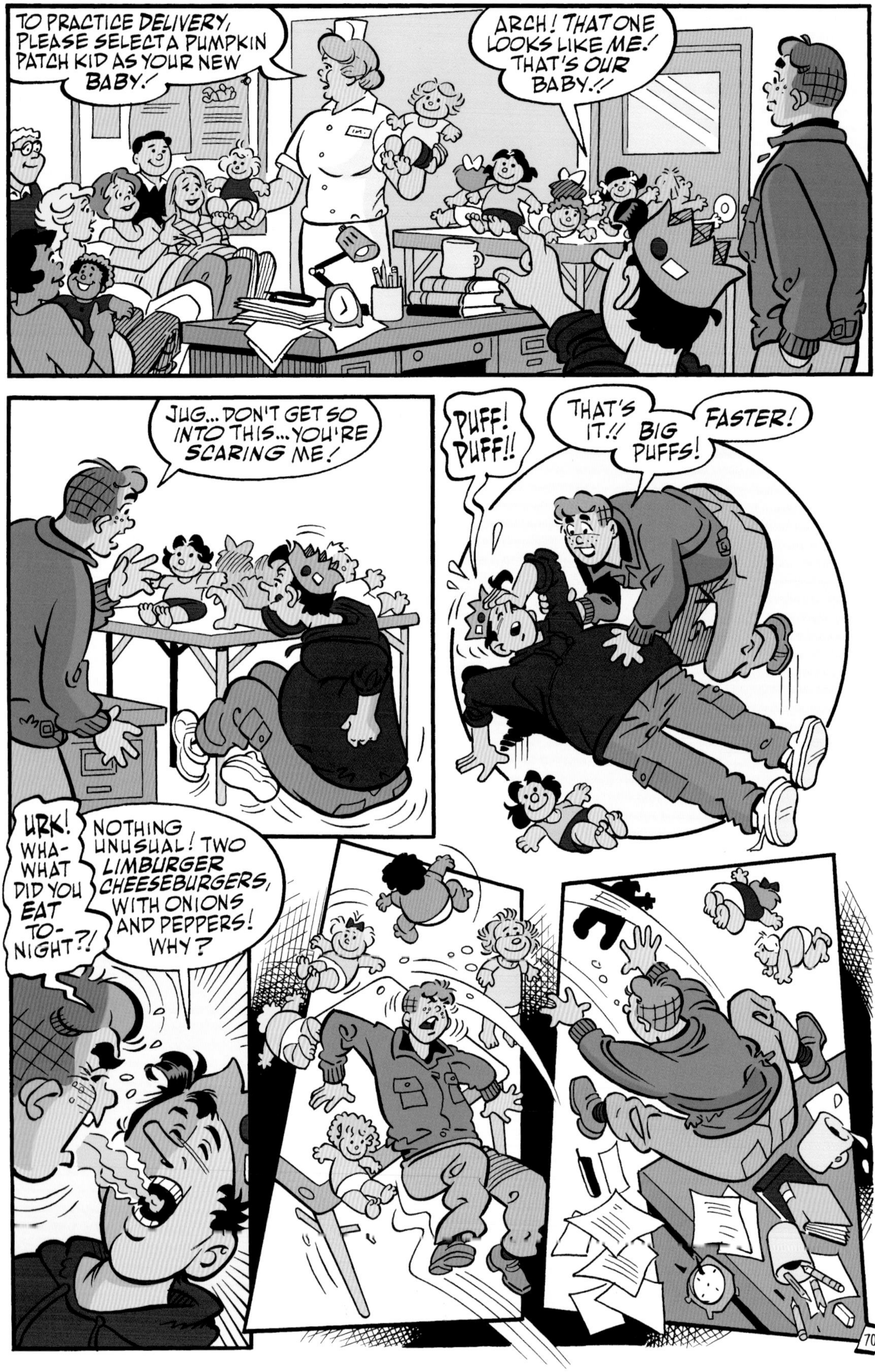
TO PRACTICE DELIVERY, PLEASE SELECT A PUMPKIN PATCH KID AS YOUR NEW BABY!
ARCH! THAT ONE LOOKS LIKE ME! THAT'S OUR BABY!!
JUG... DON'T GET SO INTO THIS... YOU'RE SCARING ME!
PUFF! PUFF!!
THAT'S IT!!
BIG PUFFS!
FASTER!
URK! WHA-WHAT DID YOU EAT TO-NIGHT?!
NOTHING UNUSUAL! TWO LIMBURGER CHEESEBURGERS, WITH ONIONS AND PEPPERS! WHY?

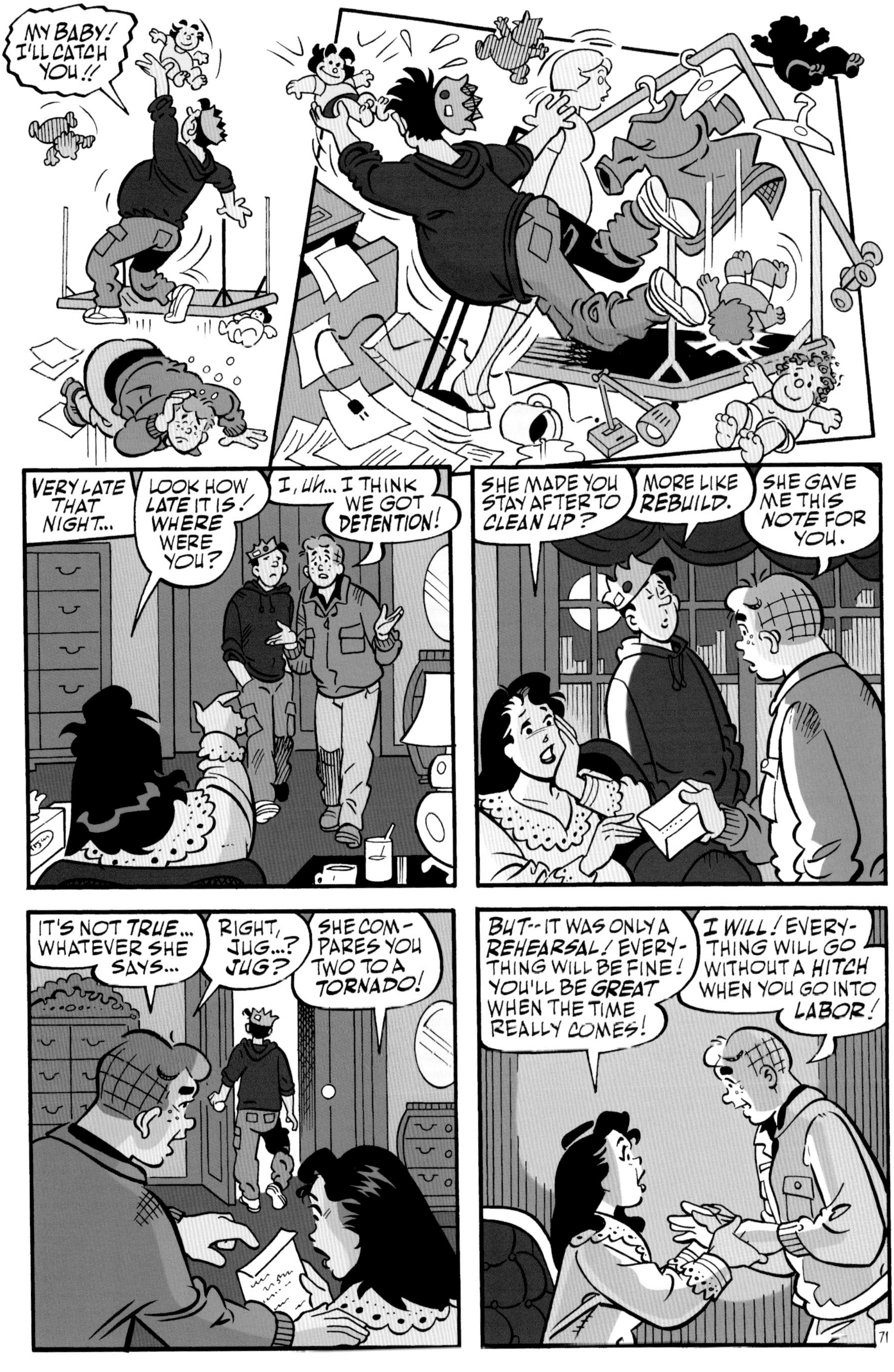
MY BABY! I'LL CATCH YOU!!
VERY LATE THAT NIGHT...
LOOK HOW LATE IT IS! WHERE WERE YOU?
I, uh... I THINK WE GOT DETENTION!
SHE MADE YOU STAY AFTER TO CLEAN UP?
MORE LIKE REBUILD.
SHE GAVE ME THIS NOTE FOR YOU.
IT'S NOT TRUE... WHATEVER SHE SAYS...
RIGHT, JUG...? JUG?
SHE COMPARES YOU TWO TO A TORNADO!
BUT-- IT WAS ONLY A REHEARSAL! EVERYTHING WILL BE FINE! YOU'LL BE GREAT WHEN THE TIME REALLY COMES!
I WILL! EVERYTHING WILL GO WITHOUT A HITCH WHEN YOU GO INTO LABOR!

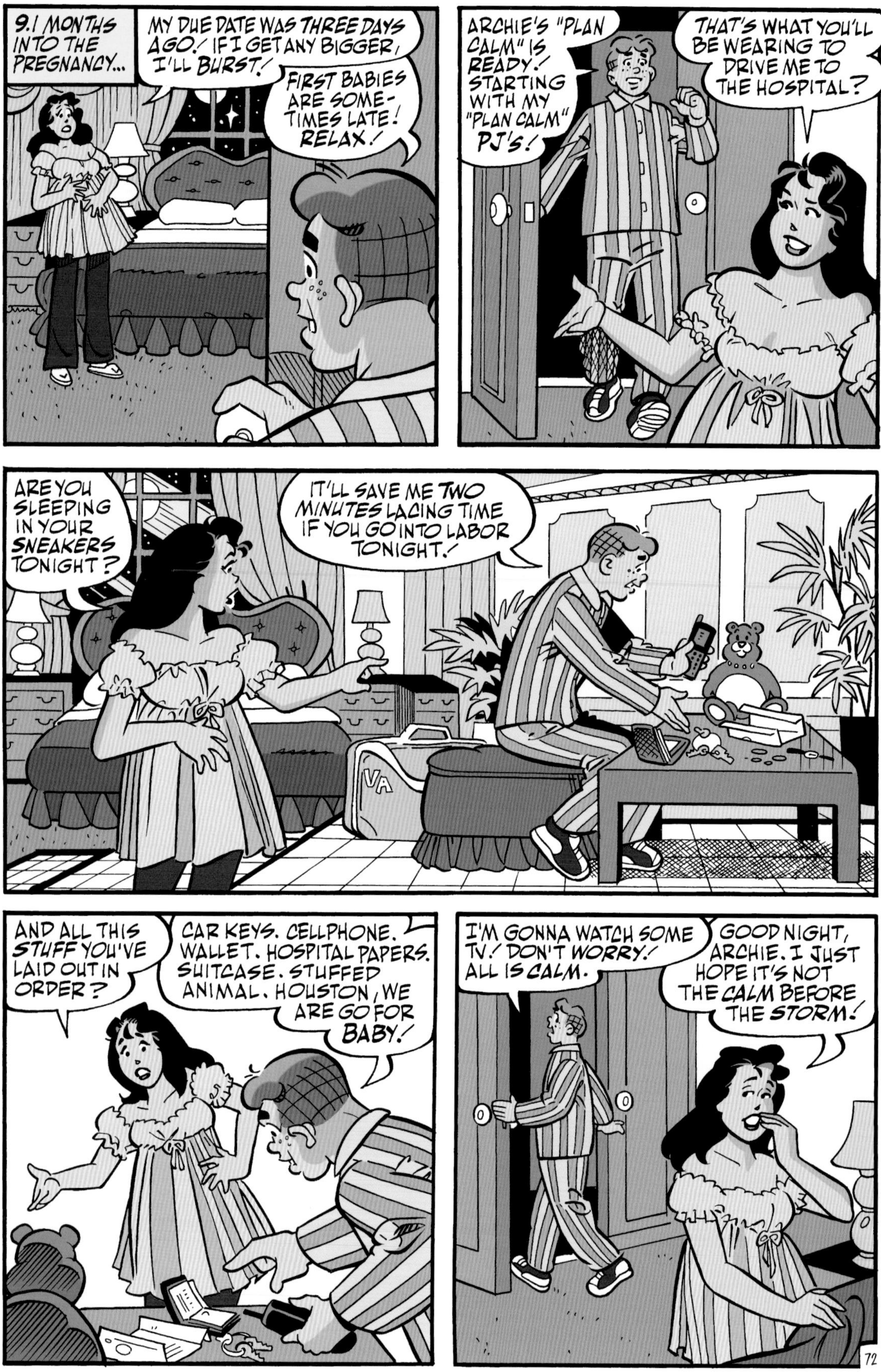
9.1 MONTHS INTO THE PREGNANCY...
MY DUE DATE WAS THREE DAYS AGO! IF I GET ANY BIGGER, I'LL BURST!
FIRST BABIES ARE SOME-TIMES LATE! RELAX!
ARCHIE'S "PLAN CALM" IS READY! STARTING WITH MY "PLAN CALM" PJ'S!
THAT'S WHAT YOU'LL BE WEARING TO DRIVE ME TO THE HOSPITAL?
ARE YOU SLEEPING IN YOUR SNEAKERS TONIGHT?
IT'LL SAVE ME TWO MINUTES LACING TIME IF YOU GO INTO LABOR TONIGHT!
VA
AND ALL THIS STUFF YOU'VE LAID OUT IN ORDER?
CAR KEYS. CELLPHONE. WALLET. HOSPITAL PAPERS. SUITCASE. STUFFED ANIMAL. HOUSTON, WE ARE GO FOR BABY!
I'M GONNA WATCH SOME TV! DON'T WORRY! ALL IS CALM.
GOOD NIGHT, ARCHIE. I JUST HOPE IT'S NOT THE CALM BEFORE THE STORM!

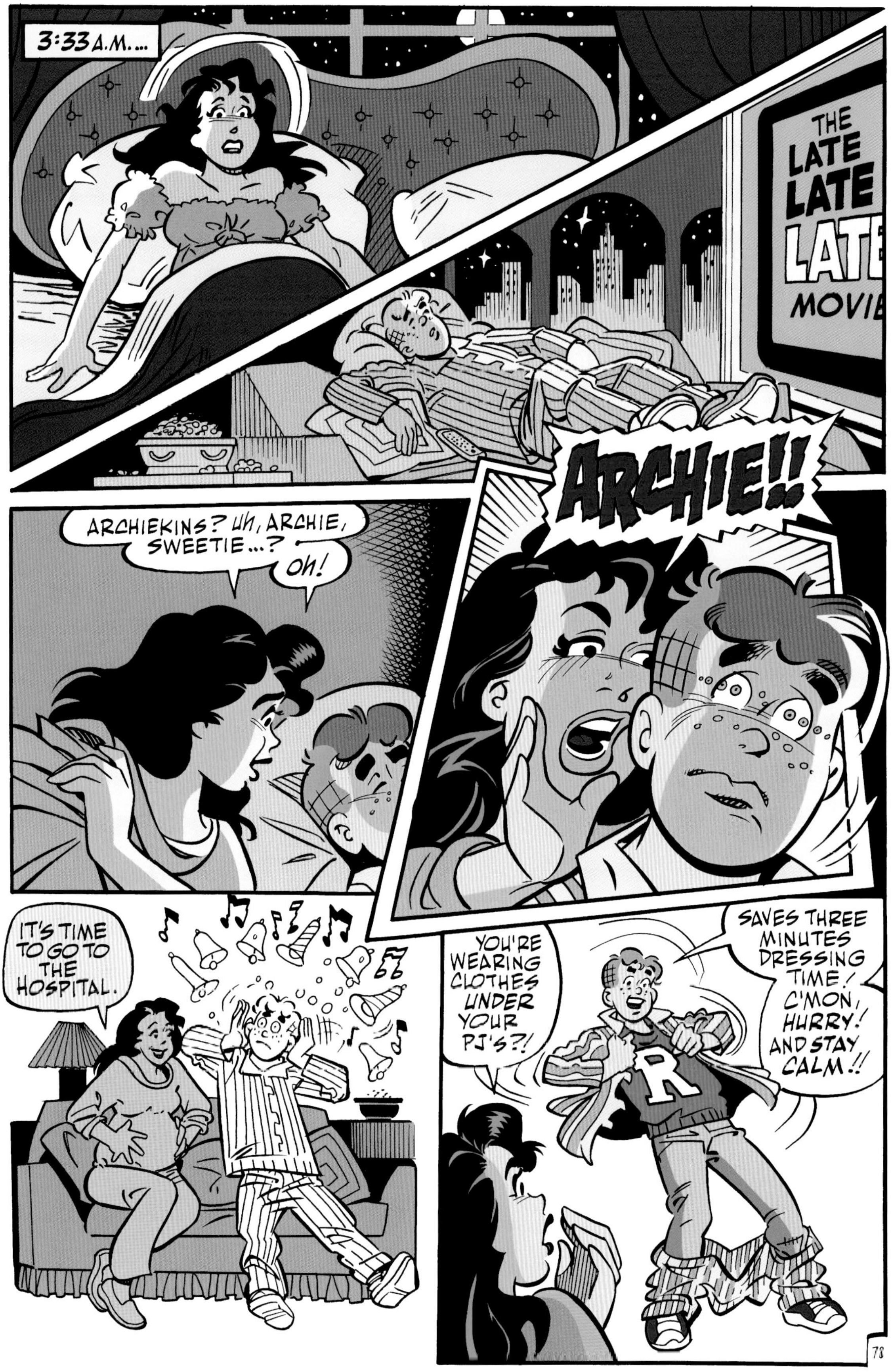
3:33 A.M. ...
THE LATE LATE LATE MOVIE
ARCHIE!!
ARCHIEKINS? UH, ARCHIE, SWEETIE...?
OH!
IT'S TIME TO GO TO THE HOSPITAL.
YOU'RE WEARING CLOTHES UNDER YOUR PJ'S?!
SAVES THREE MINUTES DRESSING TIME! C'MON, HURRY! AND STAY CALM!!

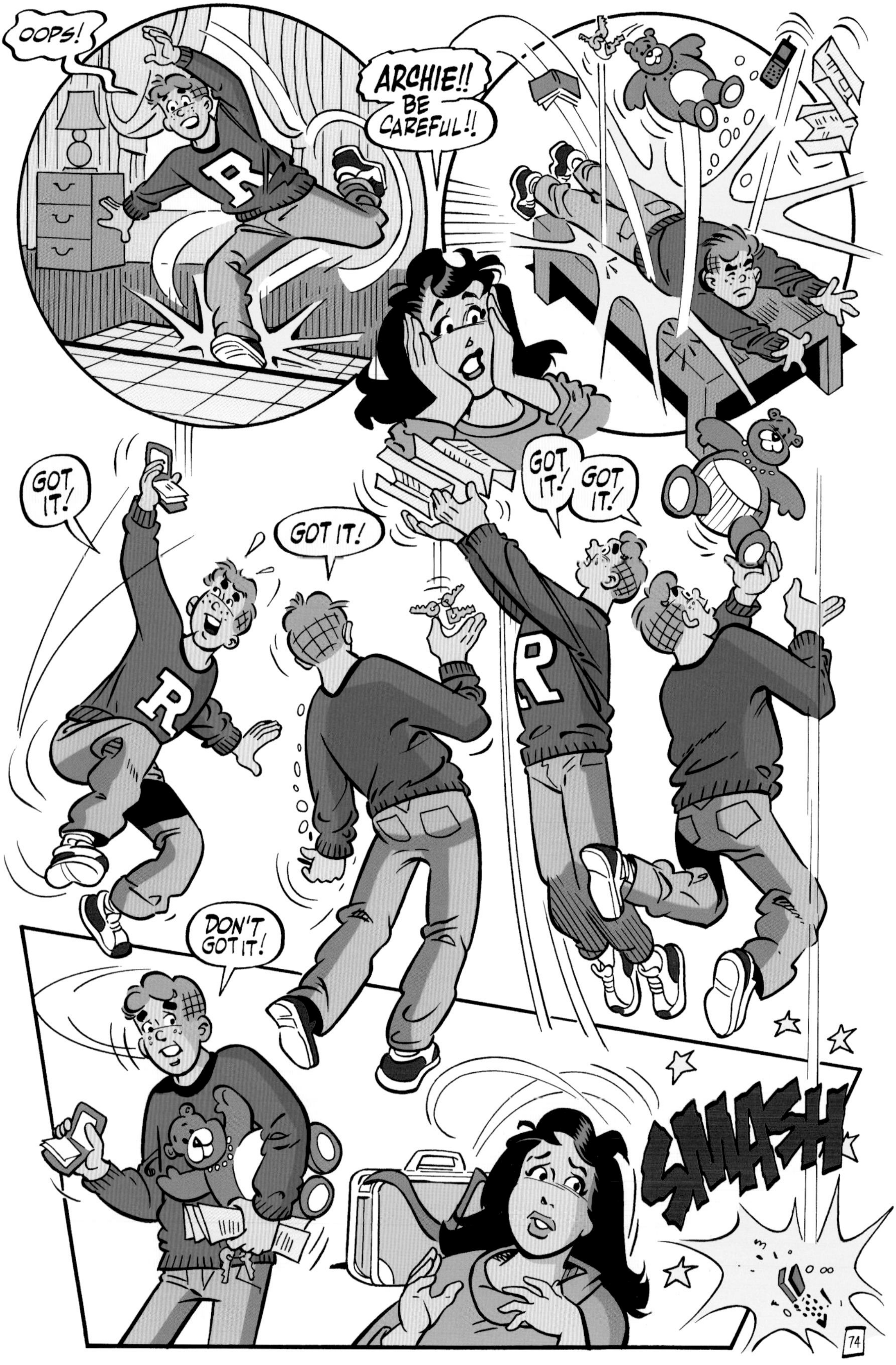

OOPS!
ARCHIE!! BE CAREFUL!!
GOT IT!
GOT IT!
GOT IT!
GOT IT!
DON'T GOT IT!
SMASH

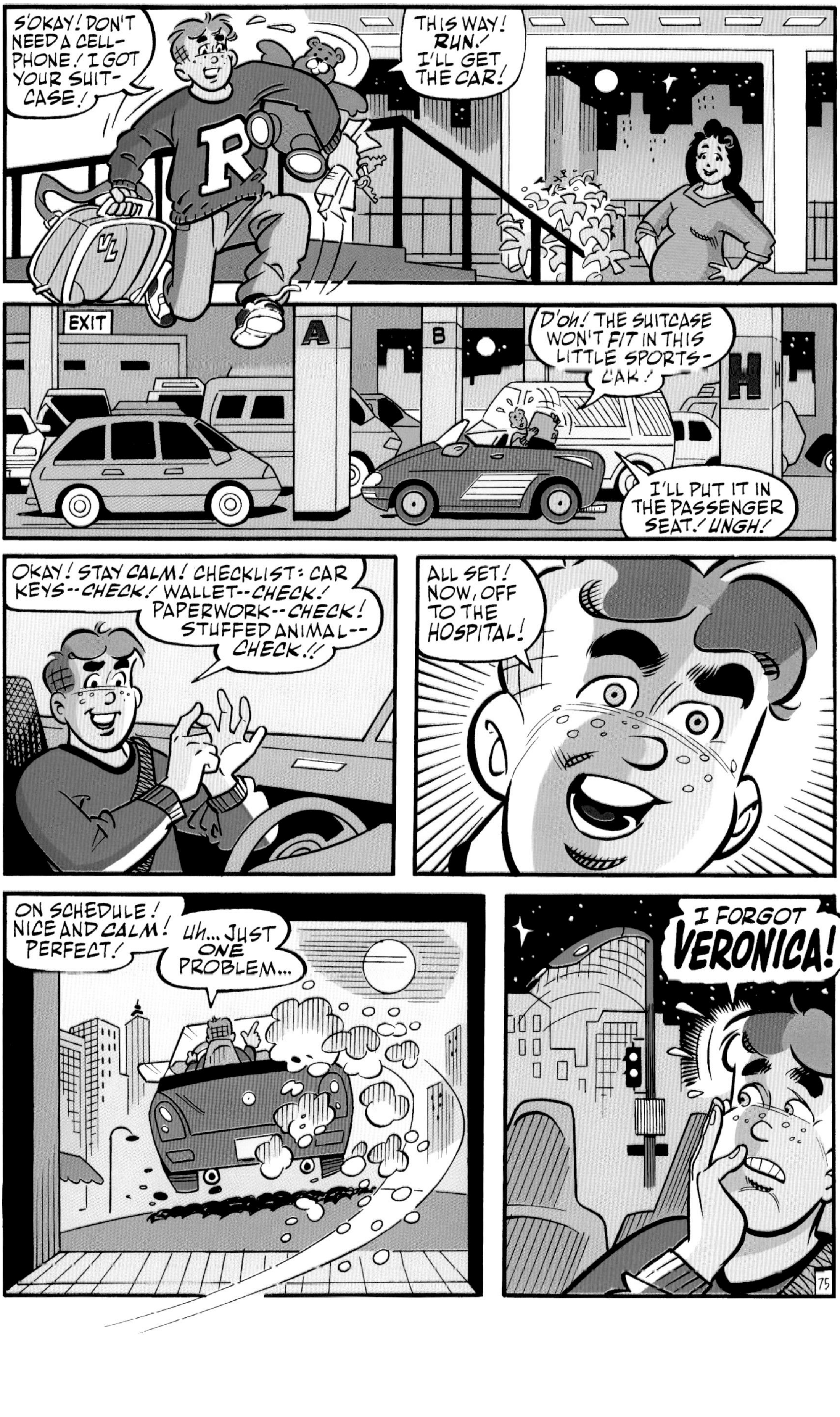
S'OKAY! DON'T NEED A CELL-PHONE! I GOT YOUR SUIT-CASE!
THIS WAY! RUN! I'LL GET THE CAR!
EXIT
A
B
H
D'oh! THE SUITCASE WON'T FIT IN THIS LITTLE SPORTS-CAR!
I'LL PUT IT IN THE PASSENGER SEAT! UNGH!
OKAY! STAY CALM! CHECKLIST: CAR KEYS--CHECK! WALLET--CHECK! PAPERWORK--CHECK! STUFFED ANIMAL--CHECK!!
ALL SET! NOW, OFF TO THE HOSPITAL!
ON SCHEDULE! NICE AND CALM! PERFECT!
Uh... JUST ONE PROBLEM...
I FORGOT VERONICA!
75

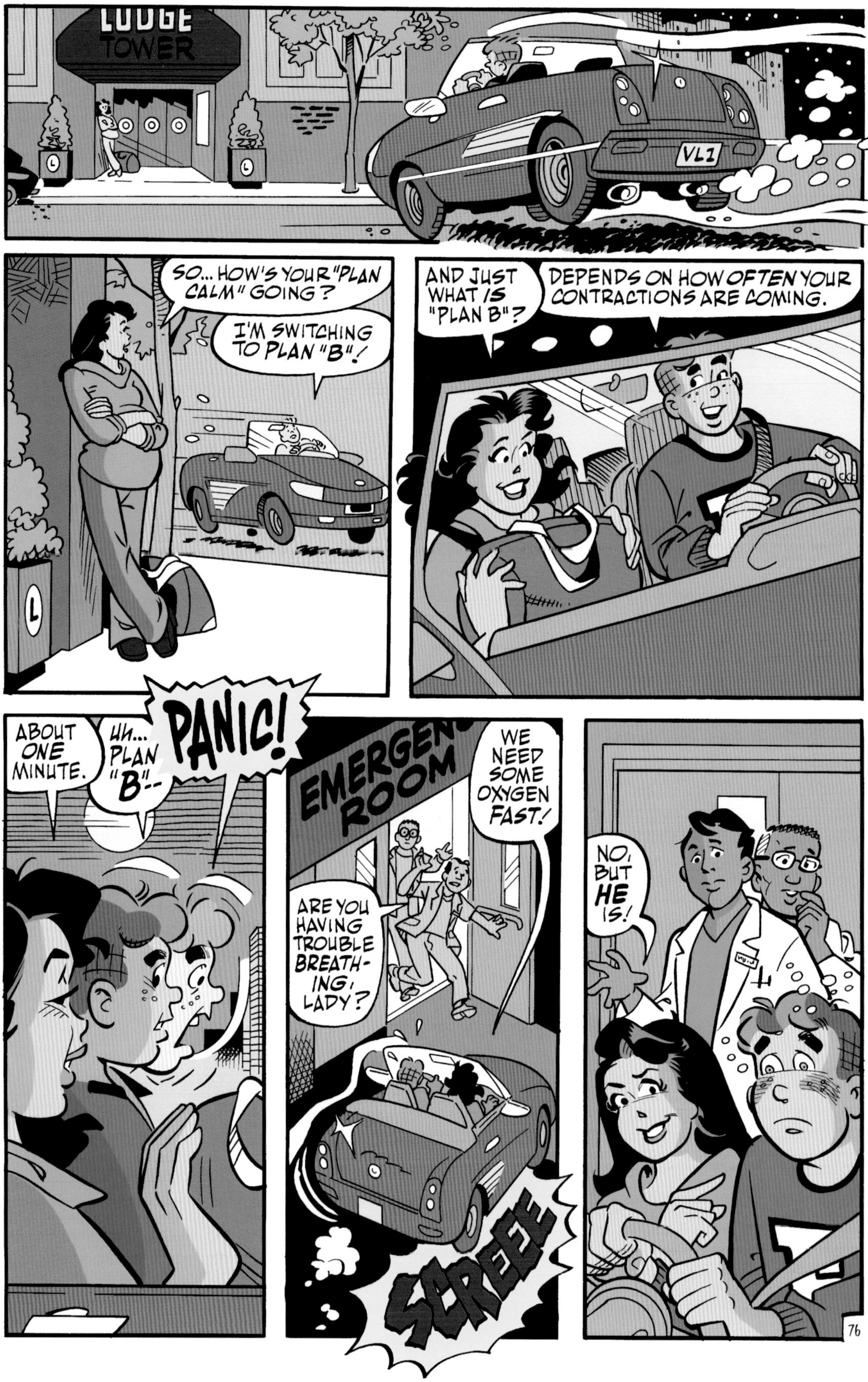
LODGE TOWER
VL1
SO... HOW'S YOUR "PLAN CALM" GOING?
I'M SWITCHING TO PLAN "B"!
AND JUST WHAT IS "PLAN B"?
DEPENDS ON HOW OFTEN YOUR CONTRACTIONS ARE COMING.
ABOUT ONE MINUTE.
UH... PLAN "B"--
PANIC!
EMERGEN ROOM
WE NEED SOME OXYGEN FAST!
ARE YOU HAVING TROUBLE BREATH-ING, LADY?
SCREEE
NO, BUT HE IS!

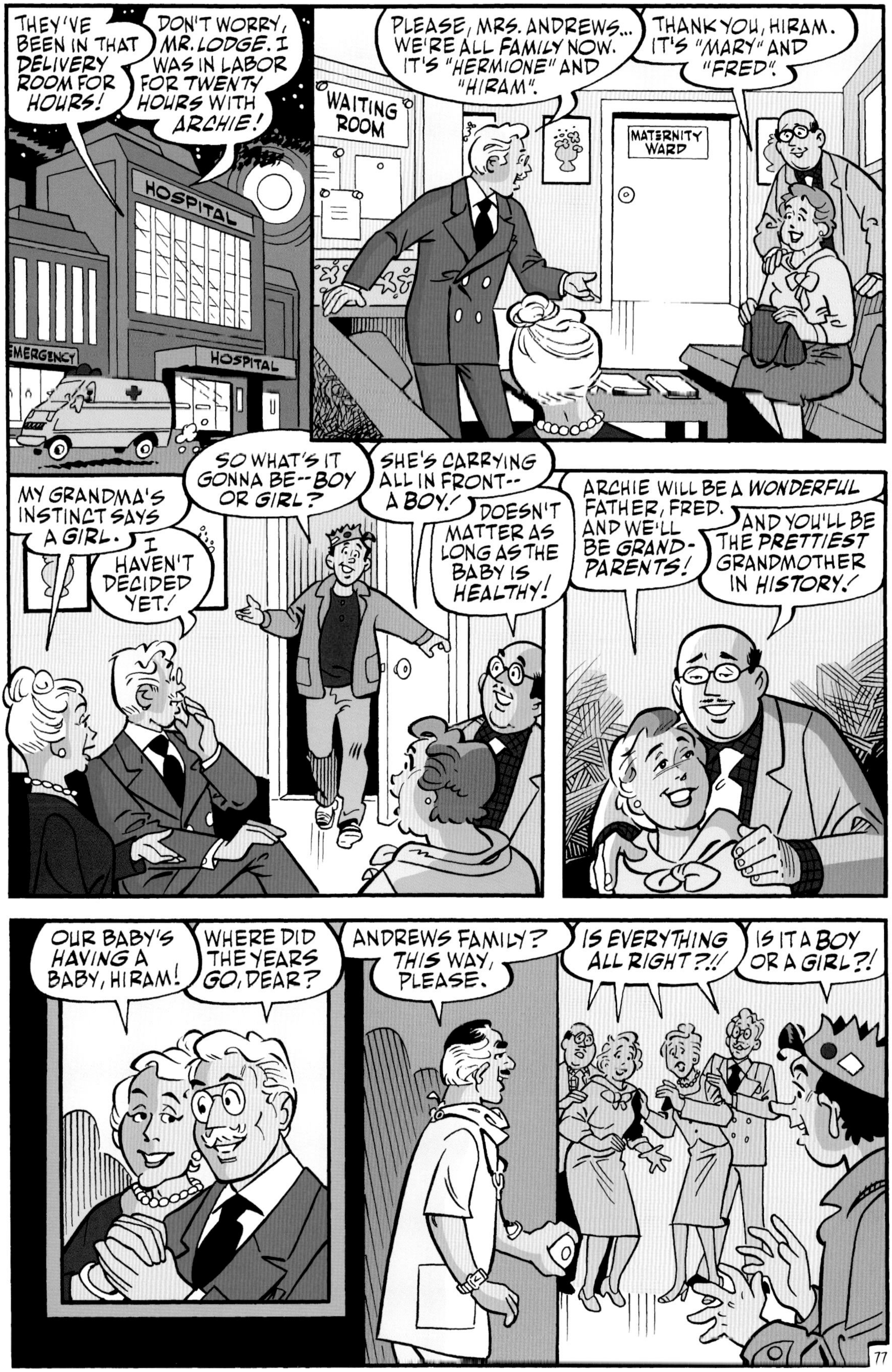
THEY'VE BEEN IN THAT DELIVERY ROOM FOR HOURS!
DON'T WORRY, MR. LODGE. I WAS IN LABOR FOR TWENTY HOURS WITH ARCHIE!
HOSPITAL
EMERGENCY
HOSPITAL
PLEASE, MRS. ANDREWS... WE'RE ALL FAMILY NOW. IT'S "HERMIONE" AND "HIRAM".
THANK YOU, HIRAM. IT'S "MARY" AND "FRED".
WAITING ROOM
MATERNITY WARD
MY GRANDMA'S INSTINCT SAYS A GIRL.
I HAVEN'T DECIDED YET!
SO WHAT'S IT GONNA BE--BOY OR GIRL?
SHE'S CARRYING ALL IN FRONT--A BOY!
DOESN'T MATTER AS LONG AS THE BABY IS HEALTHY!
ARCHIE WILL BE A WONDERFUL FATHER, FRED. AND WE'LL BE GRAND-PARENTS!
AND YOU'LL BE THE PRETTIEST GRANDMOTHER IN HISTORY!
OUR BABY'S HAVING A BABY, HIRAM!
WHERE DID THE YEARS GO, DEAR?
ANDREWS FAMILY? THIS WAY, PLEASE.
IS EVERYTHING ALL RIGHT?!!
IS IT A BOY OR A GIRL?!

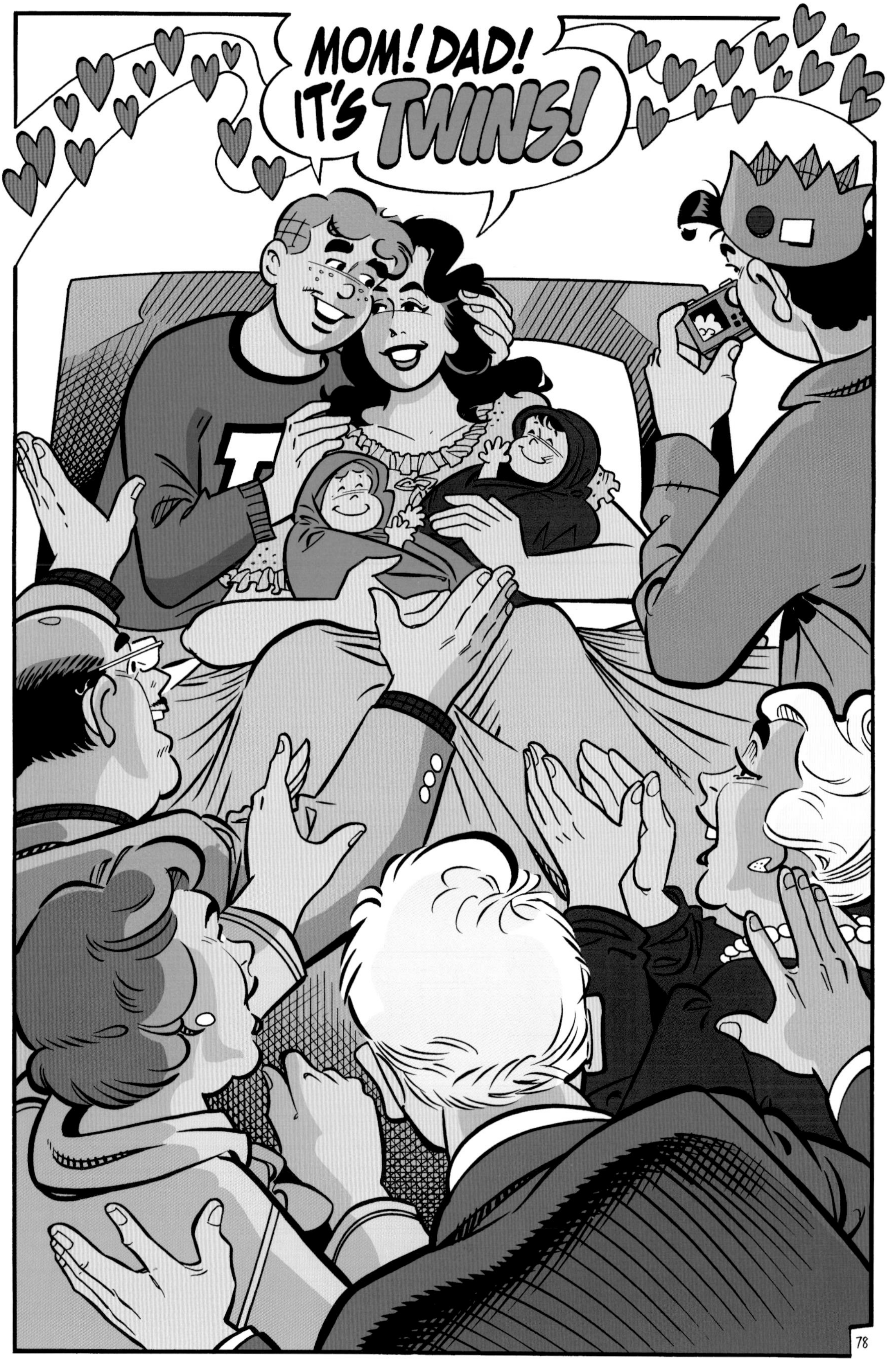
MOM! DAD! IT'S TWINS!

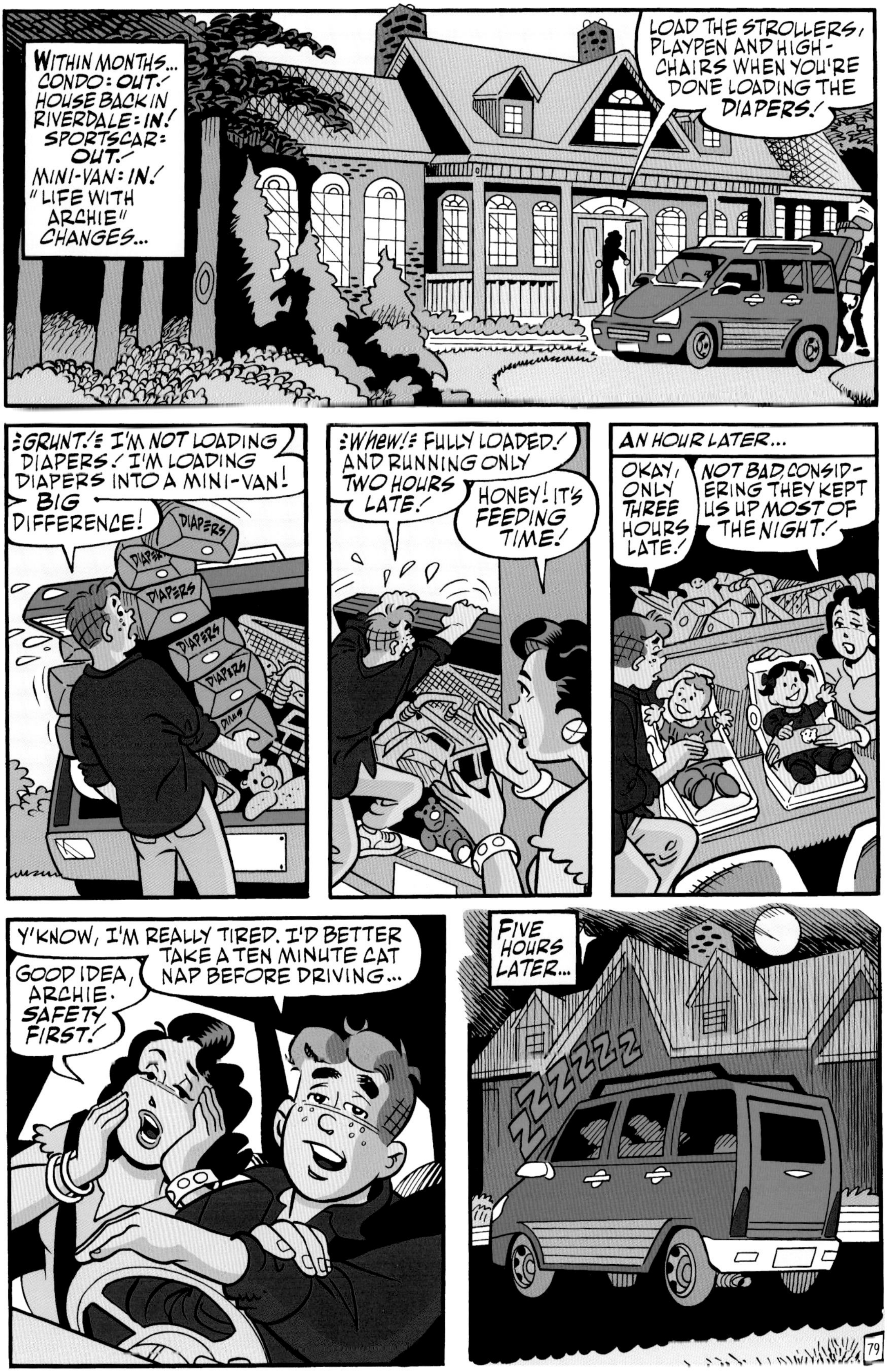
WITHIN MONTHS... CONDO: OUT! HOUSE BACK IN RIVERDALE: IN! SPORTSCAR: OUT! MINI-VAN: IN! "LIFE WITH ARCHIE" CHANGES...
LOAD THE STROLLERS, PLAYPEN AND HIGH-CHAIRS WHEN YOU'RE DONE LOADING THE DIAPERS!
:GRUNT!: I'M NOT LOADING DIAPERS! I'M LOADING DIAPERS INTO A MINI-VAN! BIG DIFFERENCE!
DIAPERS
:WHEW!: FULLY LOADED! AND RUNNING ONLY TWO HOURS LATE!
HONEY! IT'S FEEDING TIME!
AN HOUR LATER...
OKAY, ONLY THREE HOURS LATE!
NOT BAD CONSIDERING THEY KEPT US UP MOST OF THE NIGHT!
Y'KNOW, I'M REALLY TIRED. I'D BETTER TAKE A TEN MINUTE CAT NAP BEFORE DRIVING...
GOOD IDEA, ARCHIE. SAFETY FIRST!
FIVE HOURS LATER...
ZZZZZZ

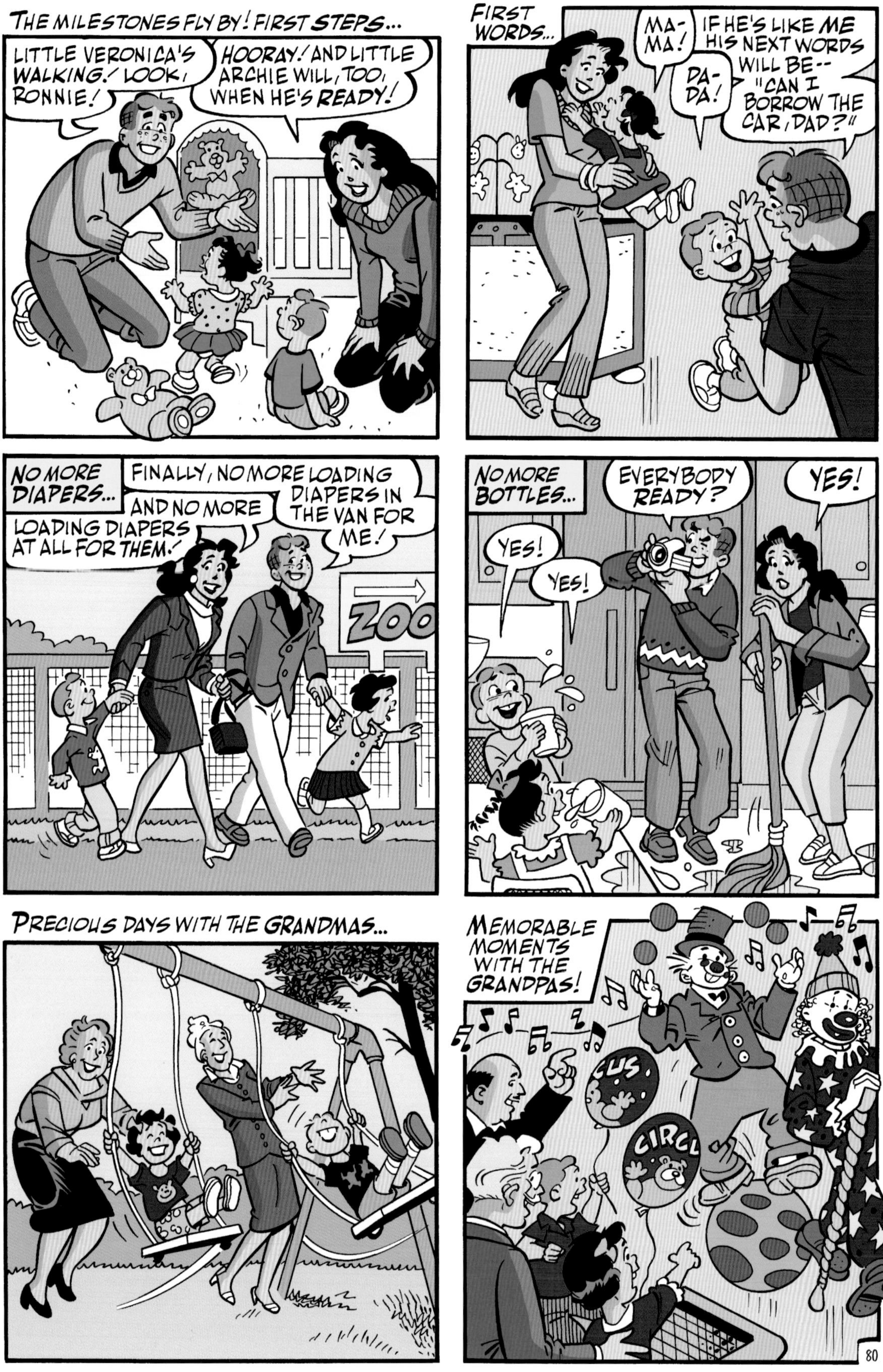
THE MILESTONES FLY BY! FIRST STEPS...
LITTLE VERONICA'S WALKING! LOOK, RONNIE!
HOORAY! AND LITTLE ARCHIE WILL, TOO, WHEN HE'S READY!
FIRST WORDS...
MA-MA!
DA-DA!
IF HE'S LIKE ME HIS NEXT WORDS WILL BE-- "CAN I BORROW THE CAR, DAD?"
NO MORE DIAPERS...
FINALLY, NO MORE LOADING DIAPERS IN THE VAN FOR ME!
AND NO MORE LOADING DIAPERS AT ALL FOR THEM!
ZOO
NO MORE BOTTLES...
EVERYBODY READY?
YES!
YES!
YES!
PRECIOUS DAYS WITH THE GRANDMAS...
MEMORABLE MOMENTS WITH THE GRANDPAS!
CUS
CIRCL

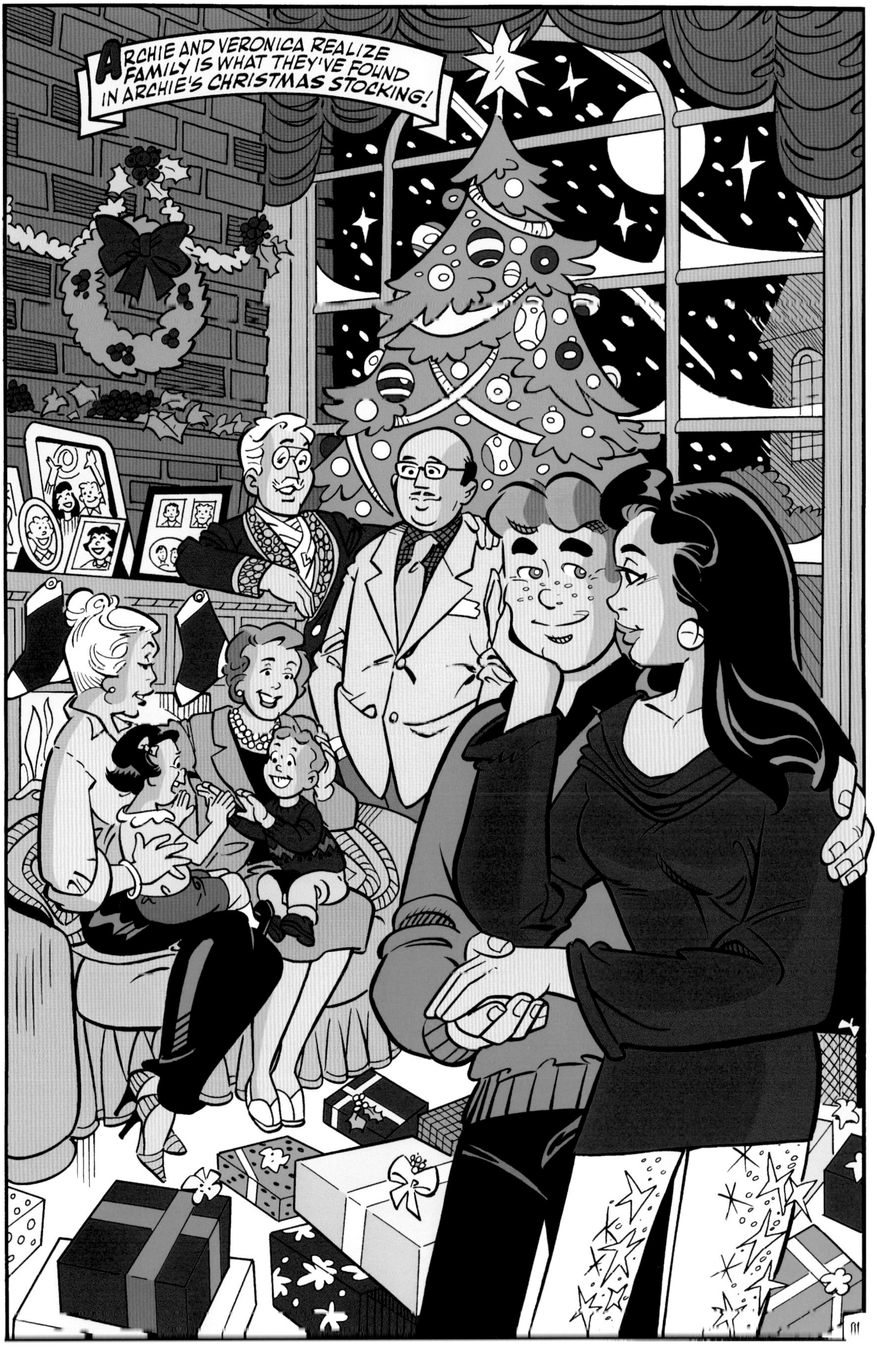
ARCHIE AND VERONICA REALIZE FAMILY IS WHAT THEY'VE FOUND IN ARCHIE'S CHRISTMAS STOCKING!

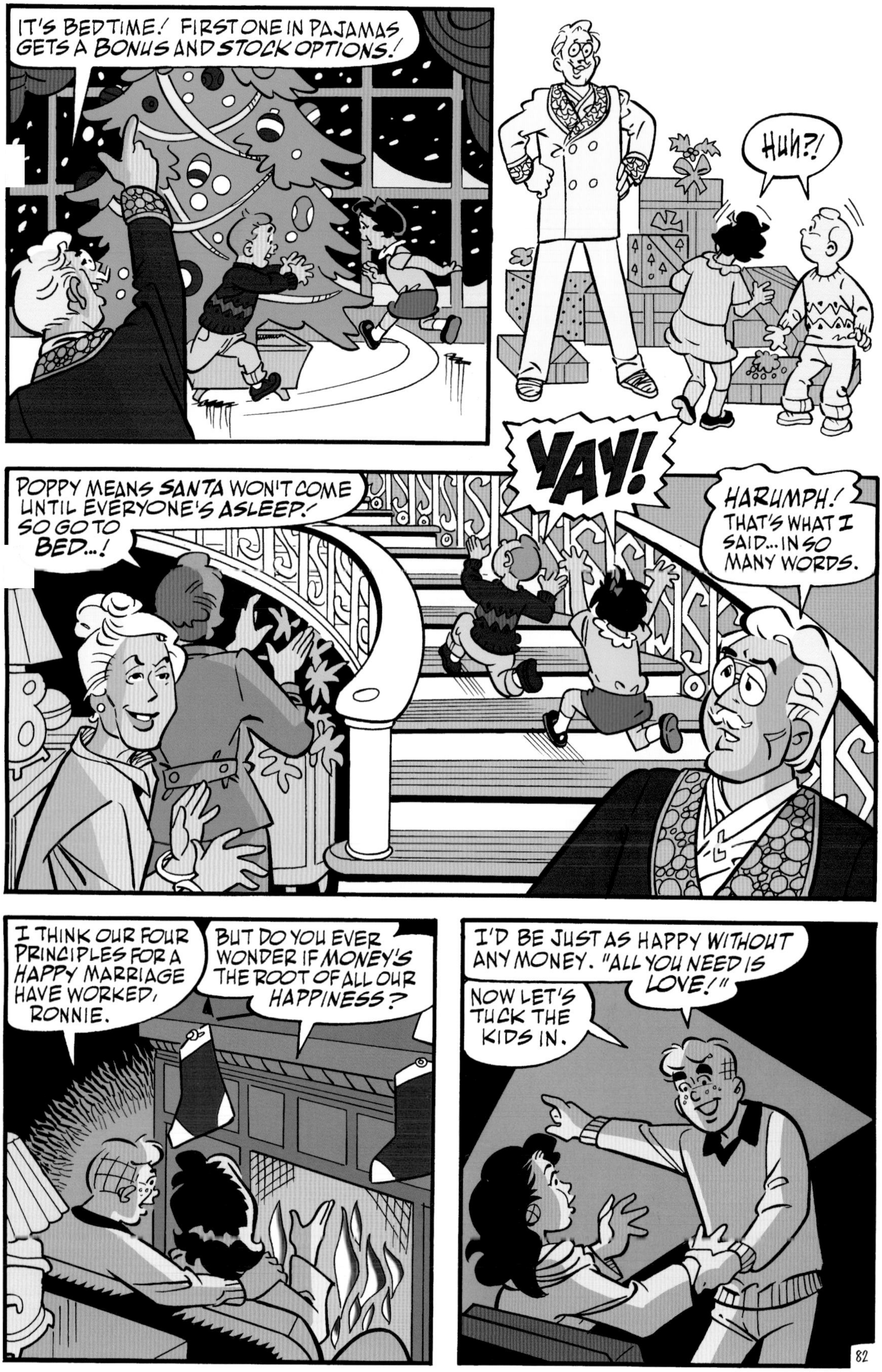
IT'S BEDTIME! FIRST ONE IN PAJAMAS GETS A BONUS AND STOCK OPTIONS!
HUH?!
YAY!
POPPY MEANS SANTA WON'T COME UNTIL EVERYONE'S ASLEEP! SO GO TO BED...!
HARUMPH! THAT'S WHAT I SAID... IN SO MANY WORDS.
I THINK OUR FOUR PRINCIPLES FOR A HAPPY MARRIAGE HAVE WORKED, RONNIE.
BUT DO YOU EVER WONDER IF MONEY'S THE ROOT OF ALL OUR HAPPINESS?
I'D BE JUST AS HAPPY WITHOUT ANY MONEY. "ALL YOU NEED IS LOVE!"
NOW LET'S TUCK THE KIDS IN.

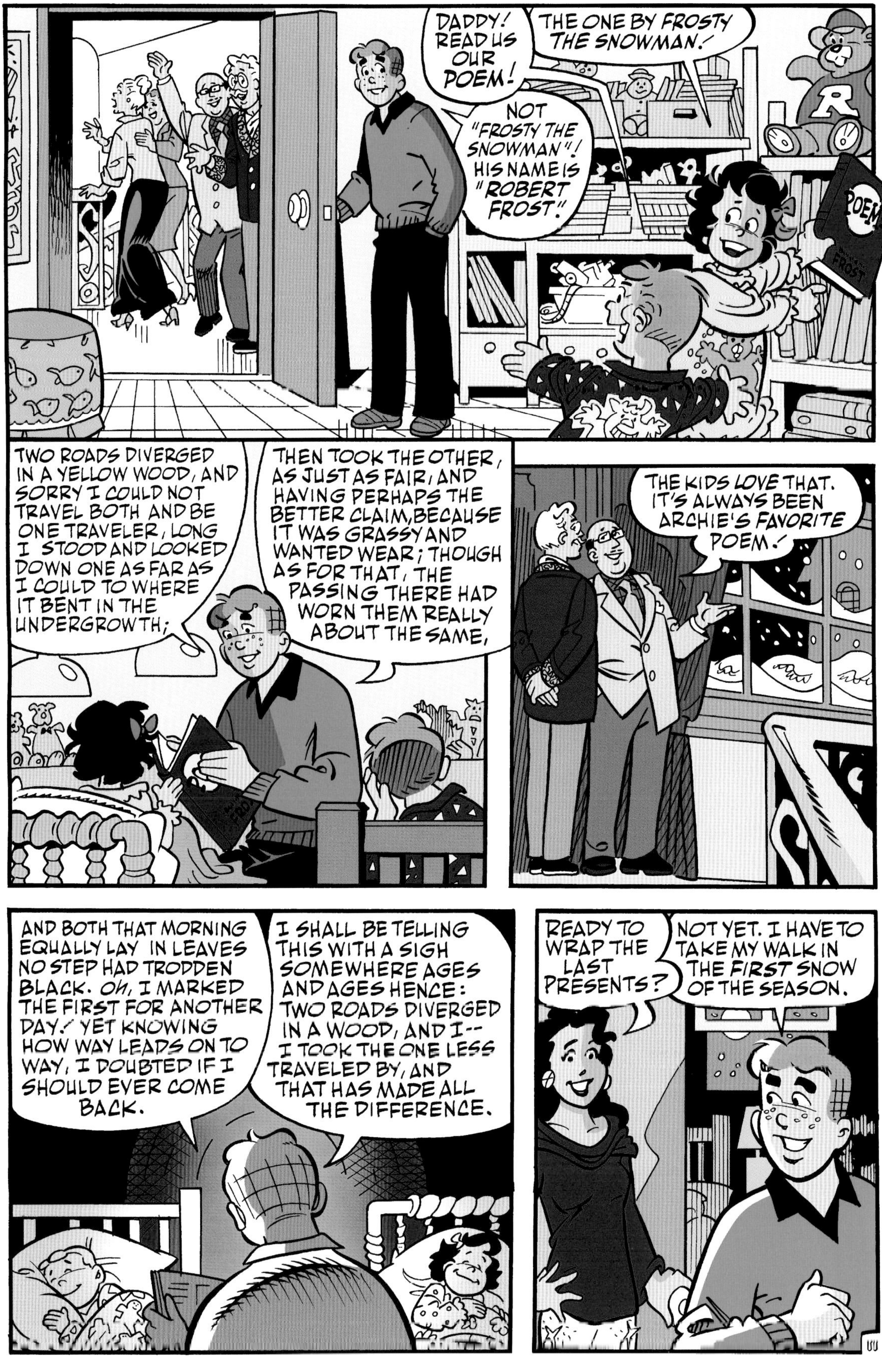
DADDY! READ US OUR POEM!
THE ONE BY FROSTY THE SNOWMAN!
NOT "FROSTY THE SNOWMAN"! HIS NAME IS "ROBERT FROST."
POEMS
FROST
TWO ROADS DIVERGED IN A YELLOW WOOD, AND SORRY I COULD NOT TRAVEL BOTH AND BE ONE TRAVELER, LONG I STOOD AND LOOKED DOWN ONE AS FAR AS I COULD TO WHERE IT BENT IN THE UNDERGROWTH;
THEN TOOK THE OTHER, AS JUST AS FAIR; AND HAVING PERHAPS THE BETTER CLAIM, BECAUSE IT WAS GRASSY AND WANTED WEAR; THOUGH AS FOR THAT, THE PASSING THERE HAD WORN THEM REALLY ABOUT THE SAME,
THE KIDS LOVE THAT. IT'S ALWAYS BEEN ARCHIE'S FAVORITE POEM!
AND BOTH THAT MORNING EQUALLY LAY IN LEAVES NO STEP HAD TRODDEN BLACK. OH, I MARKED THE FIRST FOR ANOTHER DAY! YET KNOWING HOW WAY LEADS ON TO WAY, I DOUBTED IF I SHOULD EVER COME BACK.
I SHALL BE TELLING THIS WITH A SIGH SOMEWHERE AGES AND AGES HENCE: TWO ROADS DIVERGED IN A WOOD, AND I-- I TOOK THE ONE LESS TRAVELED BY, AND THAT HAS MADE ALL THE DIFFERENCE.
READY TO WRAP THE LAST PRESENTS?
NOT YET. I HAVE TO TAKE MY WALK IN THE FIRST SNOW OF THE SEASON.

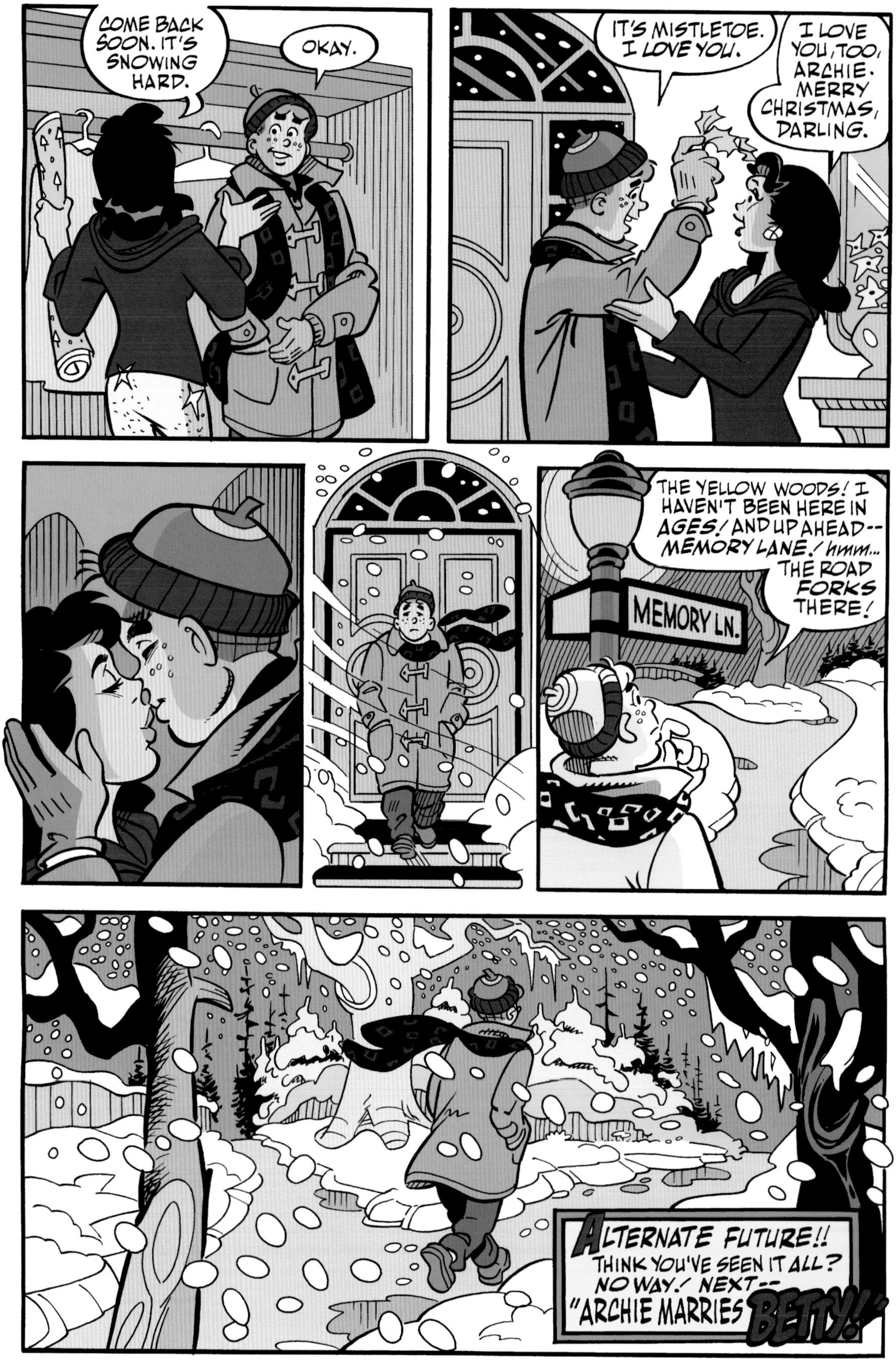
COME BACK SOON. IT'S SNOWING HARD.
OKAY.
IT'S MISTLETOE. I LOVE YOU.
I LOVE YOU, TOO, ARCHIE. MERRY CHRISTMAS, DARLING.
THE YELLOW WOODS! I HAVEN'T BEEN HERE IN AGES! AND UP AHEAD-- MEMORY LANE! hmm... THE ROAD FORKS THERE!
MEMORY LN.
ALTERNATE FUTURE!! THINK YOU'VE SEEN IT ALL? NO WAY! NEXT-- "ARCHIE MARRIES BETTY!"

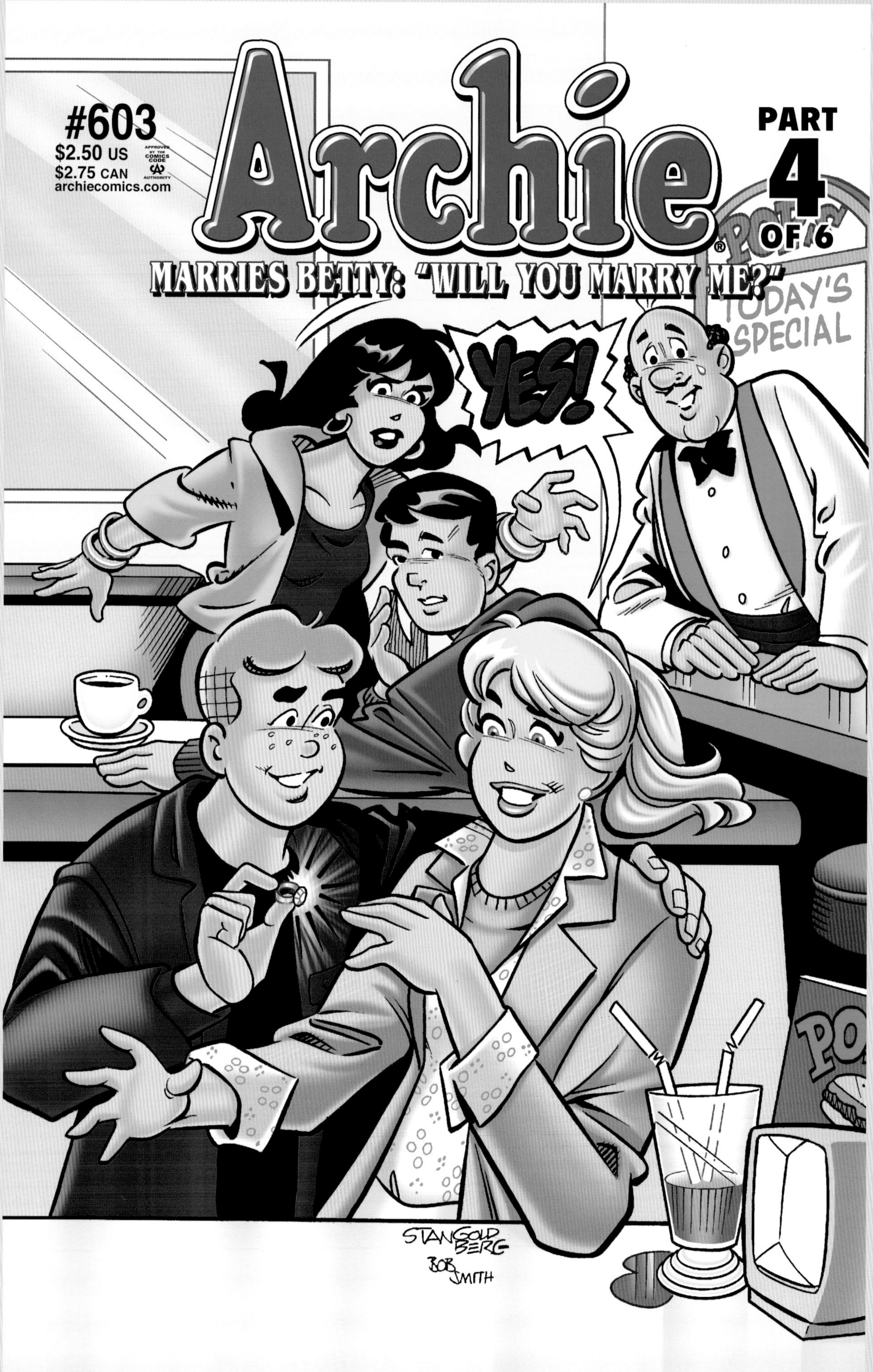
#603
$2.50 US
$2.75 CAN
APPROVED BY THE COMICS CODE AUTHORITY
archiecomics.com
Archie
PART 4 OF 6
MARRIES BETTY: "WILL YOU MARRY ME?"
YES!
TODAY'S SPECIAL
STAN GOLDBERG
BOB SMITH

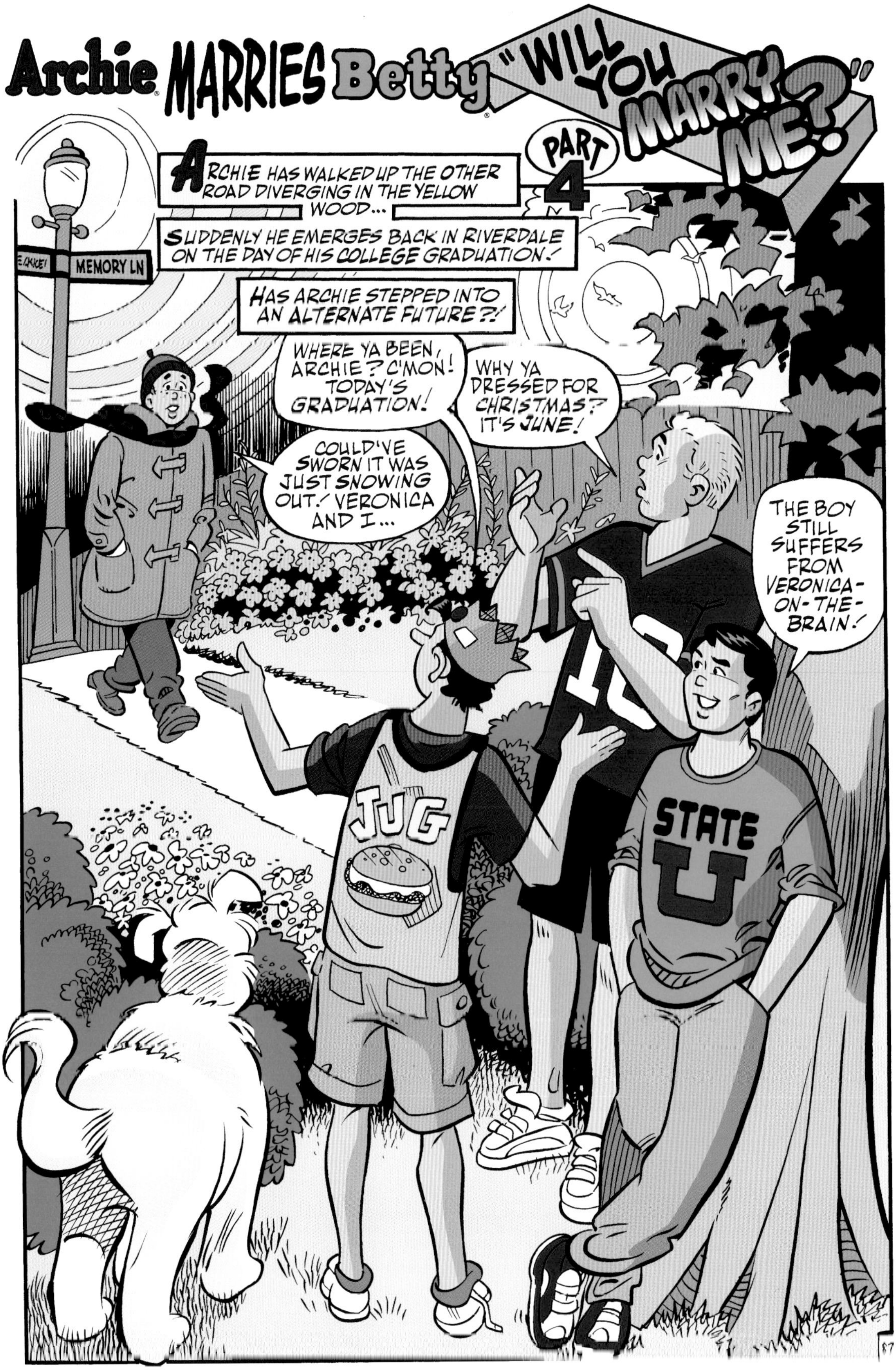
Archie MARRIES Betty "WILL YOU MARRY ME?"
PART 4
ARCHIE HAS WALKED UP THE OTHER ROAD DIVERGING IN THE YELLOW WOOD...
SUDDENLY HE EMERGES BACK IN RIVERDALE ON THE DAY OF HIS COLLEGE GRADUATION!
HAS ARCHIE STEPPED INTO AN ALTERNATE FUTURE?!
MEMORY LN
WHERE YA BEEN, ARCHIE? C'MON! TODAY'S GRADUATION!
WHY YA DRESSED FOR CHRISTMAS? IT'S JUNE!
COULD'VE SWORN IT WAS JUST SNOWING OUT! VERONICA AND I...
THE BOY STILL SUFFERS FROM VERONICA-ON-THE-BRAIN!
JUG
STATE U

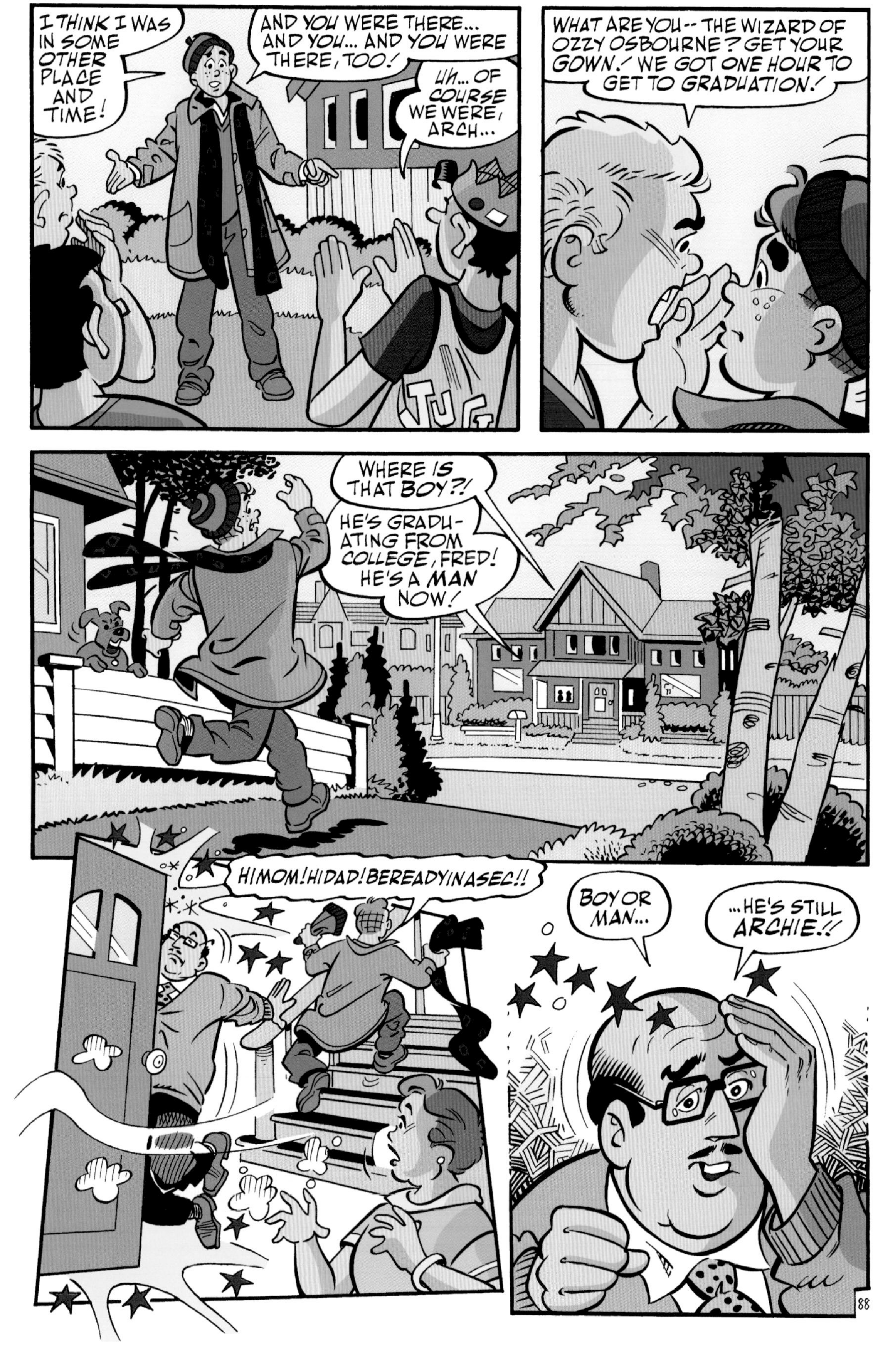
I THINK I WAS IN SOME OTHER PLACE AND TIME!
AND YOU WERE THERE... AND YOU... AND YOU WERE THERE, TOO!
UH... OF COURSE WE WERE, ARCH...
WHAT ARE YOU -- THE WIZARD OF OZZY OSBOURNE? GET YOUR GOWN! WE GOT ONE HOUR TO GET TO GRADUATION!
WHERE IS THAT BOY?!
HE'S GRADUATING FROM COLLEGE, FRED! HE'S A MAN NOW!
HIMOM!HIDAD!BEREADYINASEC!!
BOY OR MAN...
...HE'S STILL ARCHIE!!

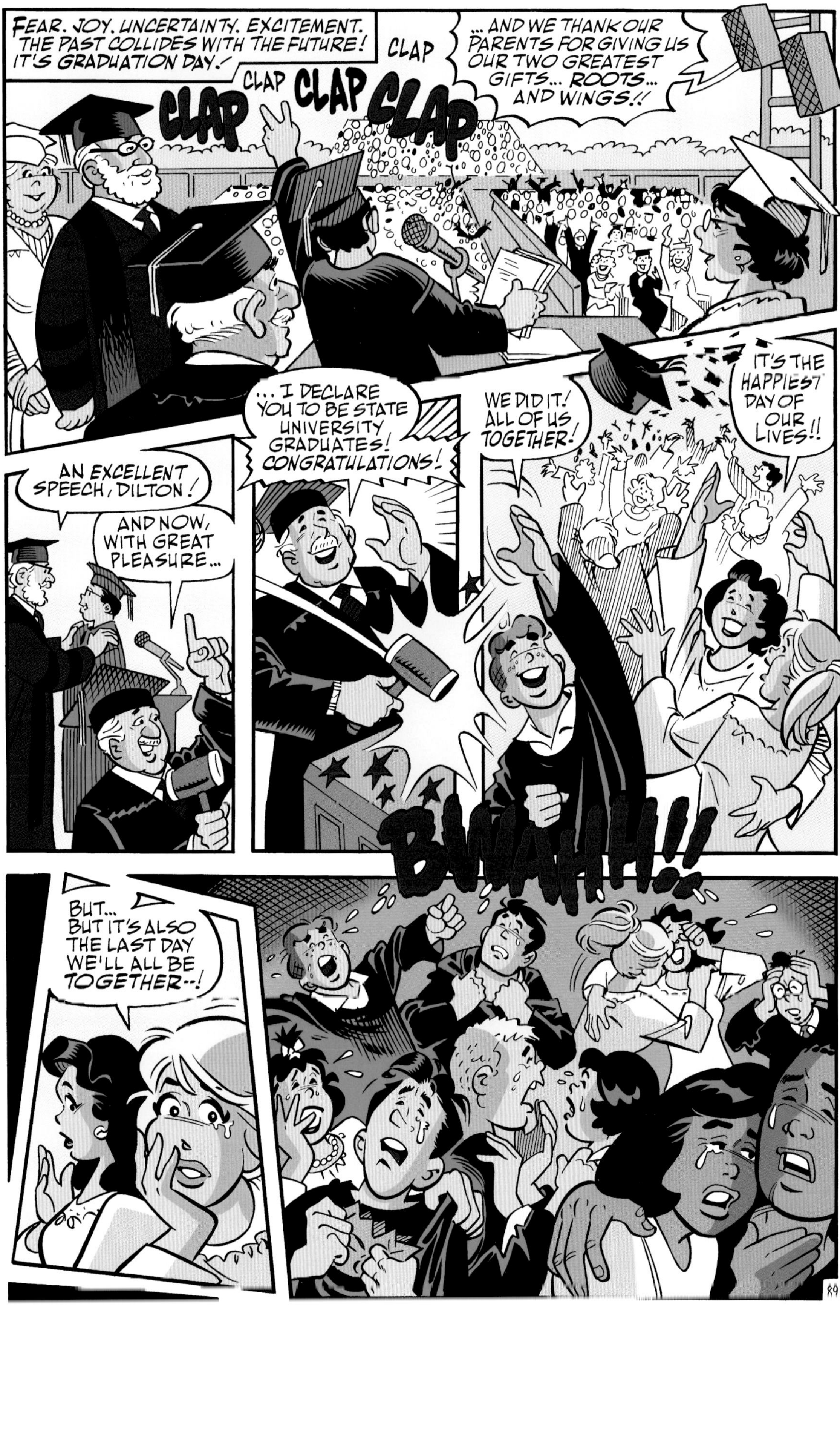
FEAR. JOY. UNCERTAINTY. EXCITEMENT. THE PAST COLLIDES WITH THE FUTURE! IT'S GRADUATION DAY!
CLAP CLAP CLAP CLAP CLAP
...AND WE THANK OUR PARENTS FOR GIVING US OUR TWO GREATEST GIFTS... ROOTS... AND WINGS!!
AN EXCELLENT SPEECH, DILTON!
AND NOW, WITH GREAT PLEASURE...
...I DECLARE YOU TO BE STATE UNIVERSITY GRADUATES! CONGRATULATIONS!
WE DID IT! ALL OF US TOGETHER!
IT'S THE HAPPIEST DAY OF OUR LIVES!!
BWAHH!!
BUT... BUT IT'S ALSO THE LAST DAY WE'LL ALL BE TOGETHER--!

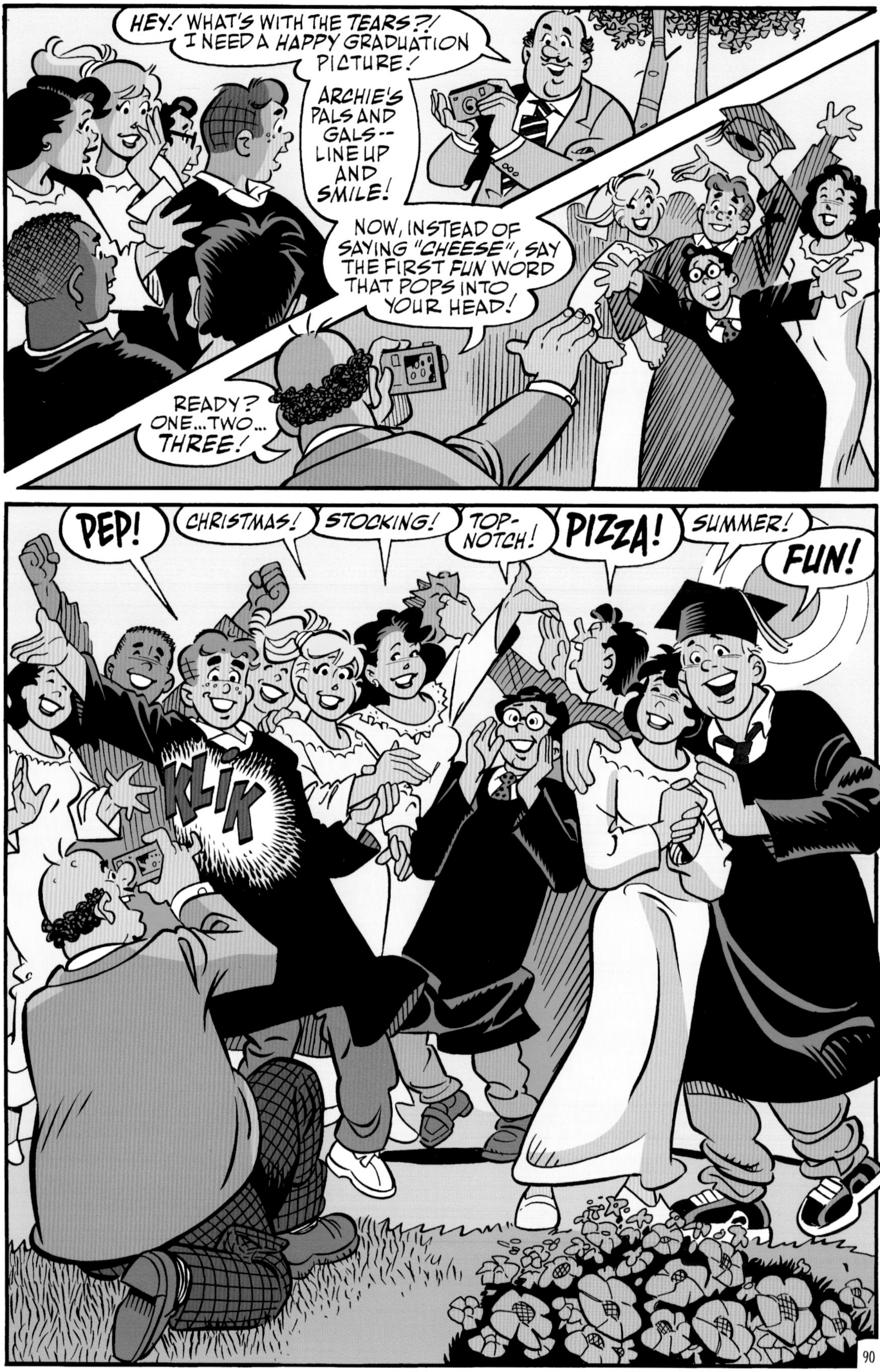
HEY! WHAT'S WITH THE TEARS?! I NEED A HAPPY GRADUATION PICTURE!
ARCHIE'S PALS AND GALS-- LINE UP AND SMILE!
NOW, INSTEAD OF SAYING "CHEESE", SAY THE FIRST FUN WORD THAT POPS INTO YOUR HEAD!
READY? ONE...TWO... THREE!
PEP!
CHRISTMAS!
STOCKING!
TOP-NOTCH!
PIZZA!
SUMMER!
FUN!
KLIK

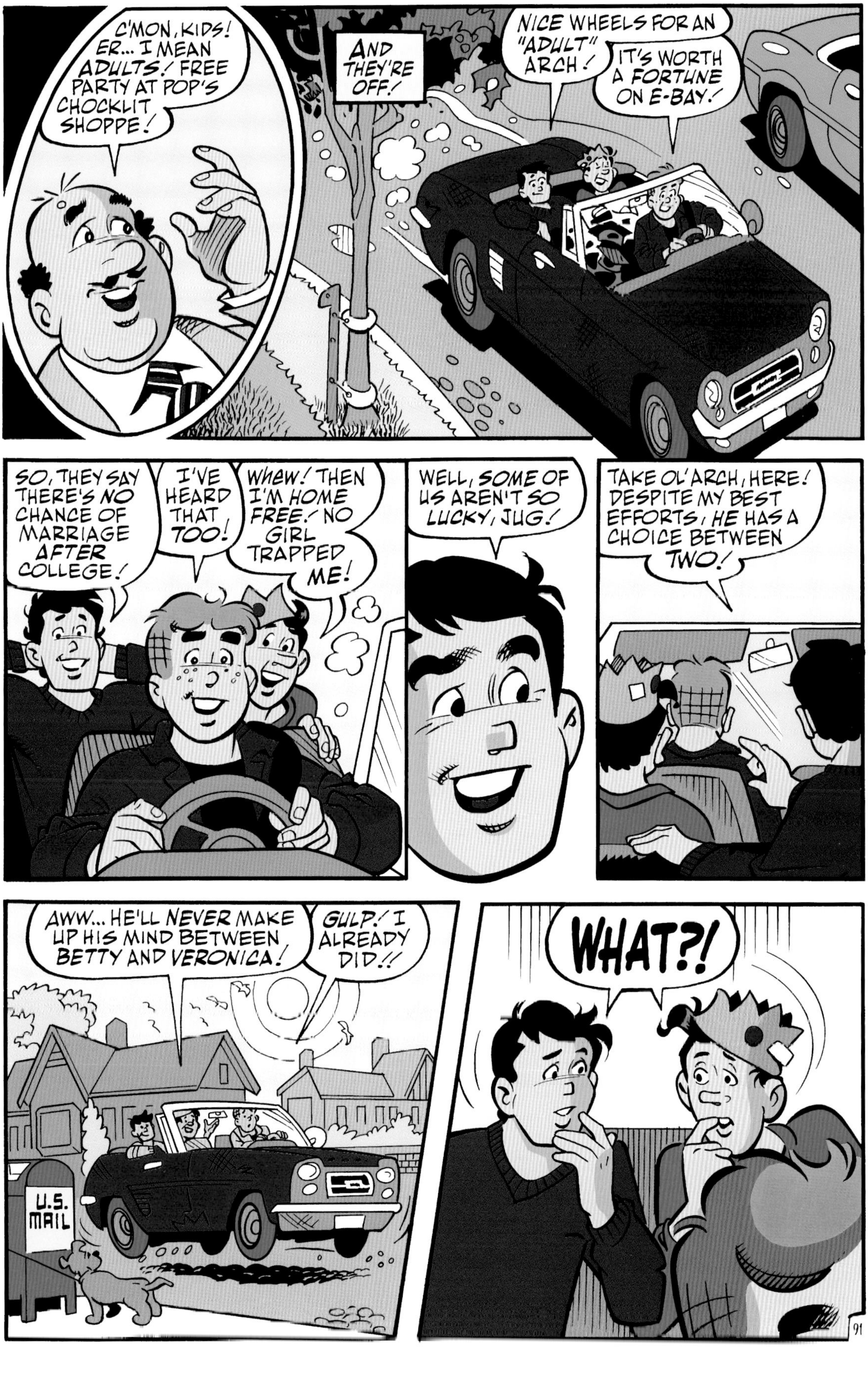
C'MON, KIDS! ER... I MEAN ADULTS! FREE PARTY AT POP'S CHOCKLIT SHOPPE!
AND THEY'RE OFF!
NICE WHEELS FOR AN "ADULT" ARCH!
IT'S WORTH A FORTUNE ON E-BAY!
SO, THEY SAY THERE'S NO CHANCE OF MARRIAGE AFTER COLLEGE!
I'VE HEARD THAT TOO!
WHEW! THEN I'M HOME FREE! NO GIRL TRAPPED ME!
WELL, SOME OF US AREN'T SO LUCKY, JUG!
TAKE OL' ARCH, HERE! DESPITE MY BEST EFFORTS, HE HAS A CHOICE BETWEEN TWO!
AWW... HE'LL NEVER MAKE UP HIS MIND BETWEEN BETTY AND VERONICA!
GULP! I ALREADY DID!!
U.S. MAIL
WHAT?!

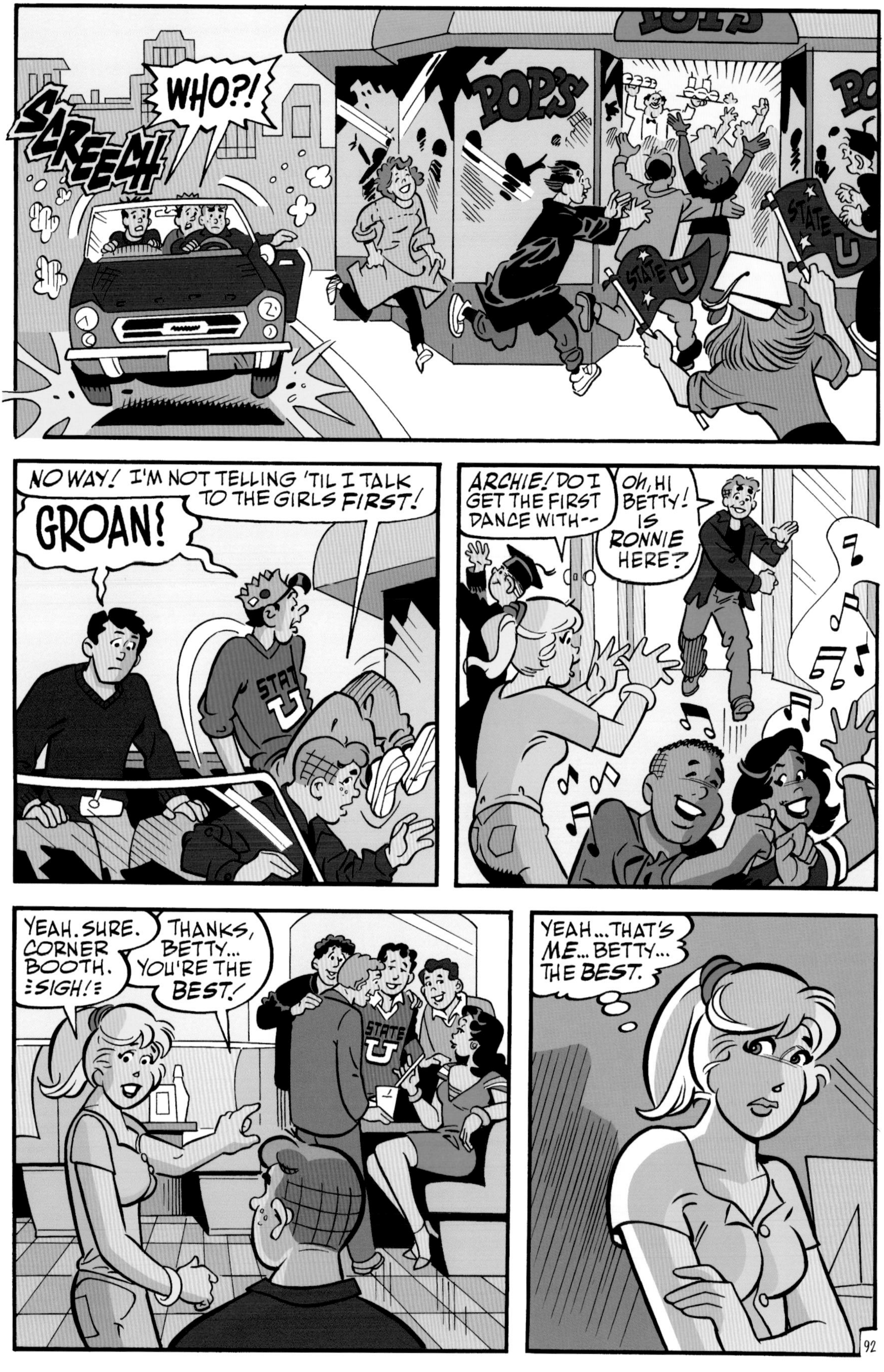
SCREECH
WHO?!
POP'S
STATE U
NO WAY! I'M NOT TELLING 'TIL I TALK TO THE GIRLS FIRST!
GROAN!
STATE U
ARCHIE! DO I GET THE FIRST DANCE WITH--
Oh, HI BETTY! IS RONNIE HERE?
YEAH. SURE. CORNER BOOTH. SIGH!
THANKS, BETTY... YOU'RE THE BEST!
STATE U
YEAH...THAT'S ME... BETTY... THE BEST.

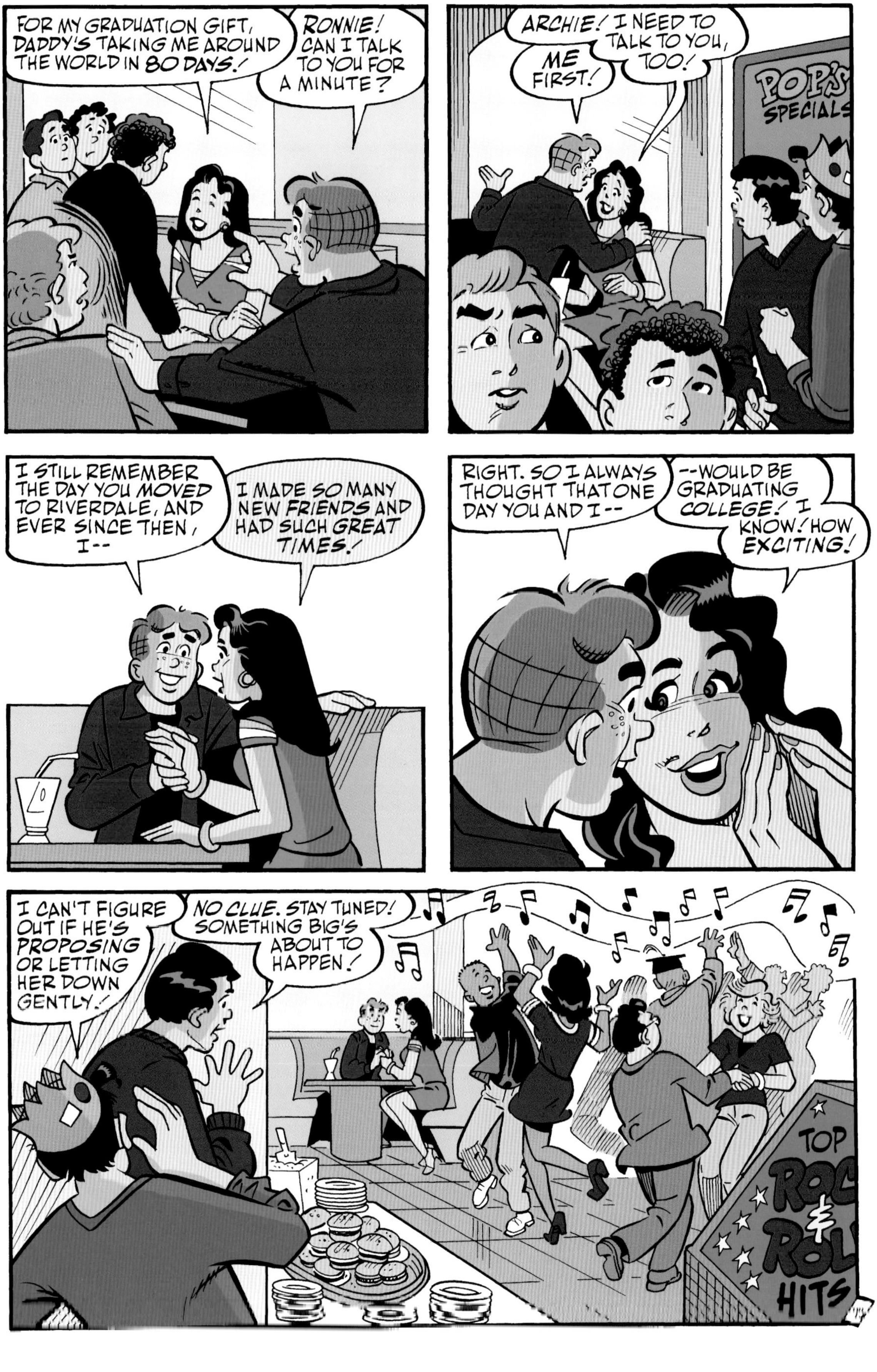
FOR MY GRADUATION GIFT, DADDY'S TAKING ME AROUND THE WORLD IN 80 DAYS!
RONNIE! CAN I TALK TO YOU FOR A MINUTE?
ARCHIE! I NEED TO TALK TO YOU, TOO!
ME FIRST!
POP'S SPECIALS
I STILL REMEMBER THE DAY YOU MOVED TO RIVERDALE, AND EVER SINCE THEN, I--
I MADE SO MANY NEW FRIENDS AND HAD SUCH GREAT TIMES!
RIGHT. SO I ALWAYS THOUGHT THAT ONE DAY YOU AND I--
--WOULD BE GRADUATING COLLEGE! I KNOW! HOW EXCITING!
I CAN'T FIGURE OUT IF HE'S PROPOSING OR LETTING HER DOWN GENTLY!
NO CLUE. STAY TUNED! SOMETHING BIG'S ABOUT TO HAPPEN!
TOP ROC & ROL HITS

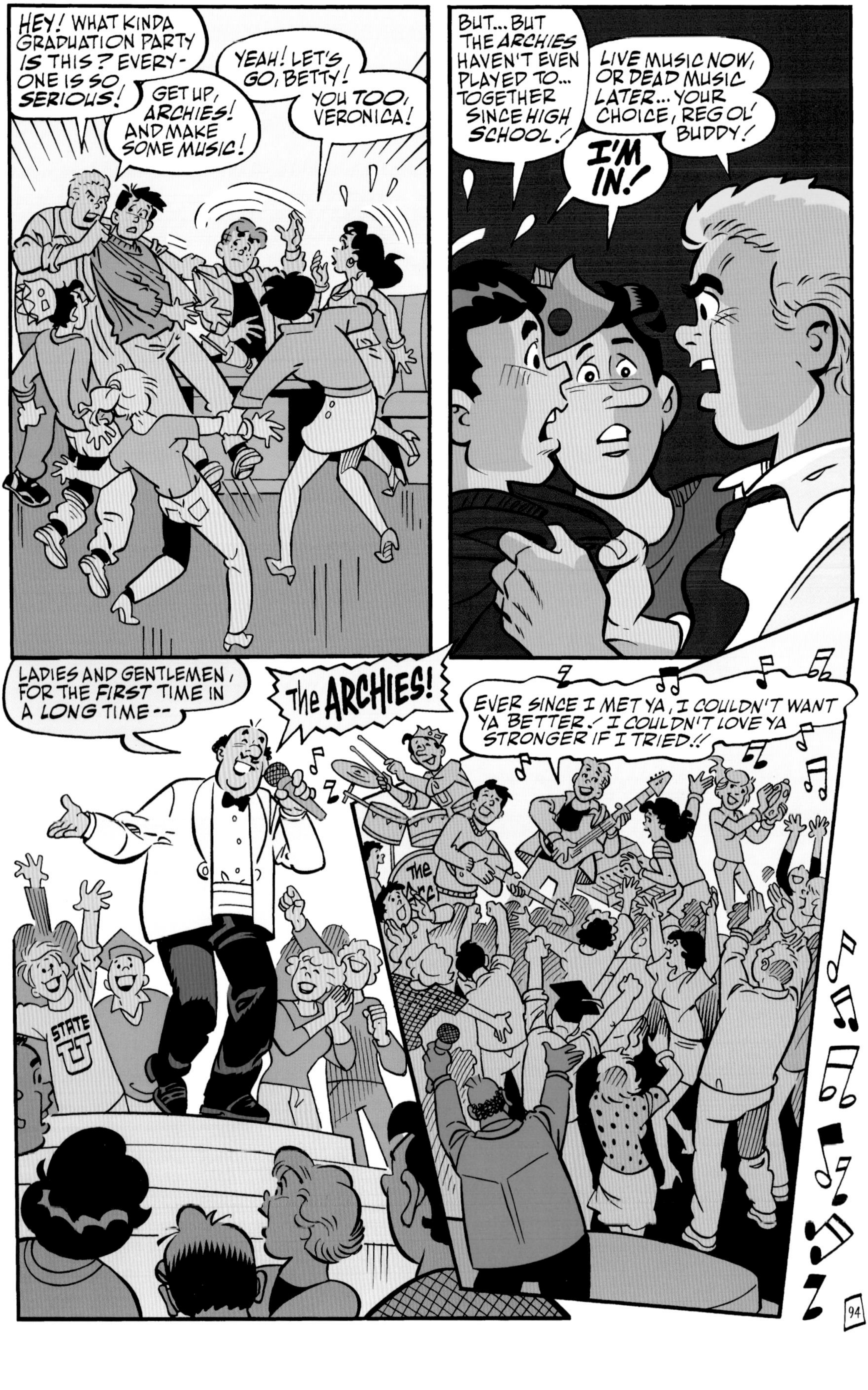
HEY! WHAT KINDA GRADUATION PARTY IS THIS? EVERY-ONE IS SO SERIOUS!
GET UP, ARCHIES! AND MAKE SOME MUSIC!
YEAH! LET'S GO, BETTY!
YOU TOO, VERONICA!
BUT... BUT THE ARCHIES HAVEN'T EVEN PLAYED TO... TOGETHER SINCE HIGH SCHOOL!
LIVE MUSIC NOW, OR DEAD MUSIC LATER... YOUR CHOICE, REG OL' BUDDY!
I'M IN!
LADIES AND GENTLEMEN, FOR THE FIRST TIME IN A LONG TIME--
The ARCHIES!
EVER SINCE I MET YA, I COULDN'T WANT YA BETTER! I COULDN'T LOVE YA STRONGER IF I TRIED!!
STATE U
The Arc

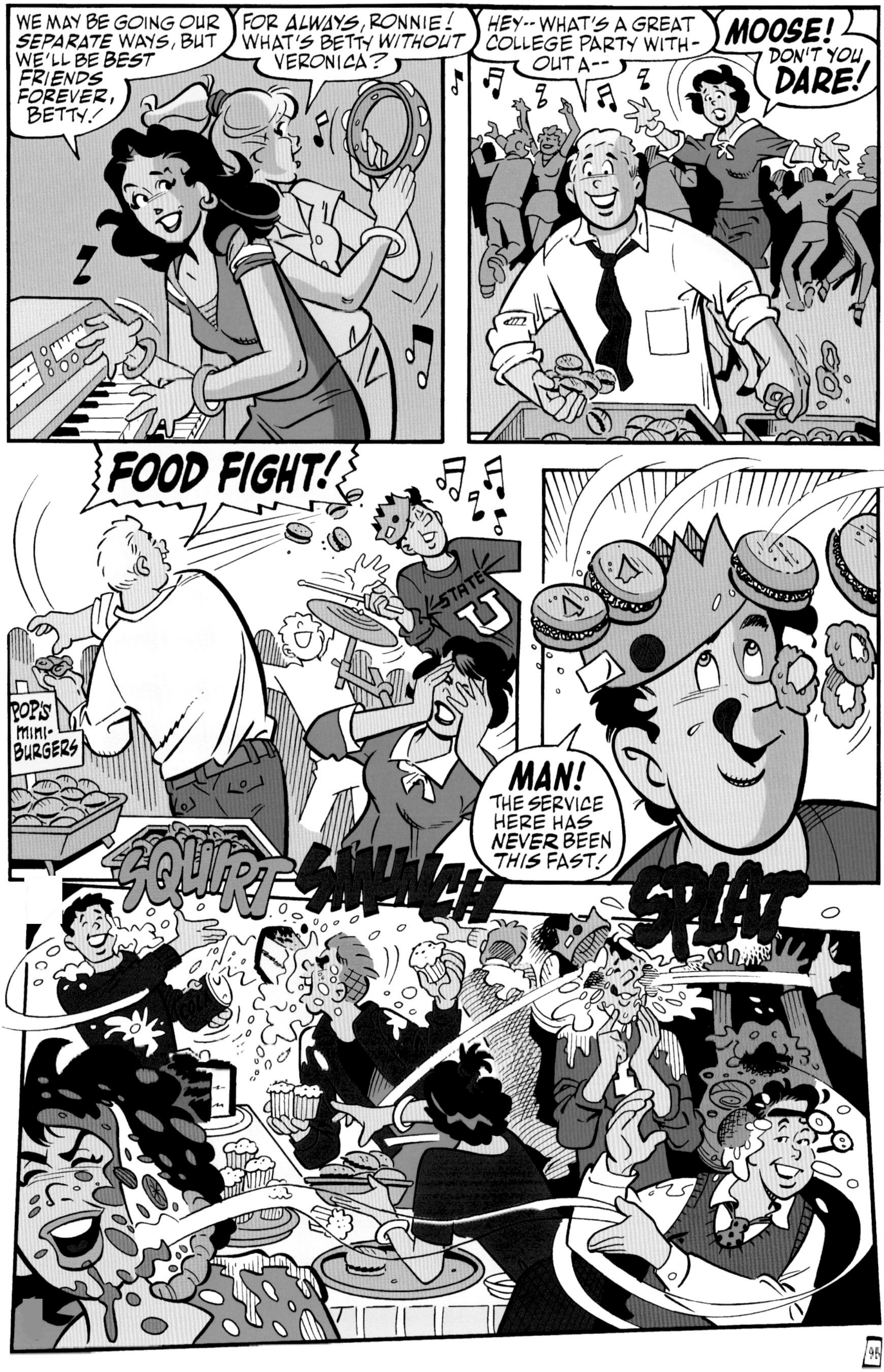
WE MAY BE GOING OUR SEPARATE WAYS, BUT WE'LL BE BEST FRIENDS FOREVER, BETTY!
FOR ALWAYS, RONNIE! WHAT'S BETTY WITHOUT VERONICA?
HEY-- WHAT'S A GREAT COLLEGE PARTY WITH-OUT A--
MOOSE! DON'T YOU DARE!
FOOD FIGHT!
STATE U
POP'S MINI-BURGERS
MAN! THE SERVICE HERE HAS NEVER BEEN THIS FAST!
SQUIRT
SPLAT

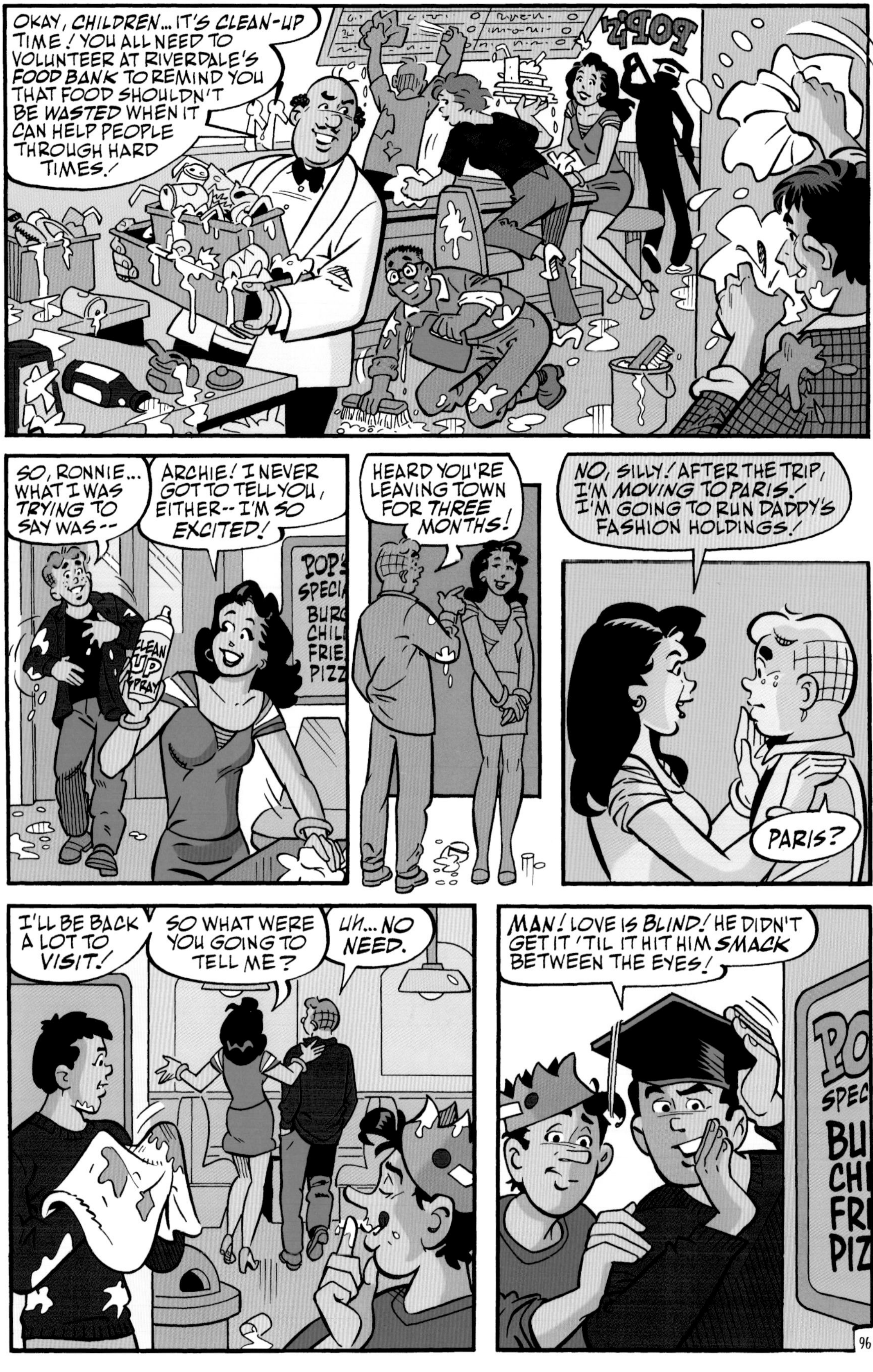
OKAY, CHILDREN... IT'S CLEAN-UP TIME! YOU ALL NEED TO VOLUNTEER AT RIVERDALE'S FOOD BANK TO REMIND YOU THAT FOOD SHOULDN'T BE WASTED WHEN IT CAN HELP PEOPLE THROUGH HARD TIMES!
POP'S
SO, RONNIE... WHAT I WAS TRYING TO SAY WAS--
ARCHIE! I NEVER GOT TO TELL YOU, EITHER-- I'M SO EXCITED!
CLEAN UP SPRAY
HEARD YOU'RE LEAVING TOWN FOR THREE MONTHS!
NO, SILLY! AFTER THE TRIP, I'M MOVING TO PARIS! I'M GOING TO RUN DADDY'S FASHION HOLDINGS!
PARIS?
I'LL BE BACK A LOT TO VISIT!
SO WHAT WERE YOU GOING TO TELL ME?
UH... NO NEED.
MAN! LOVE IS BLIND! HE DIDN'T GET IT 'TIL IT HIT HIM SMACK BETWEEN THE EYES!

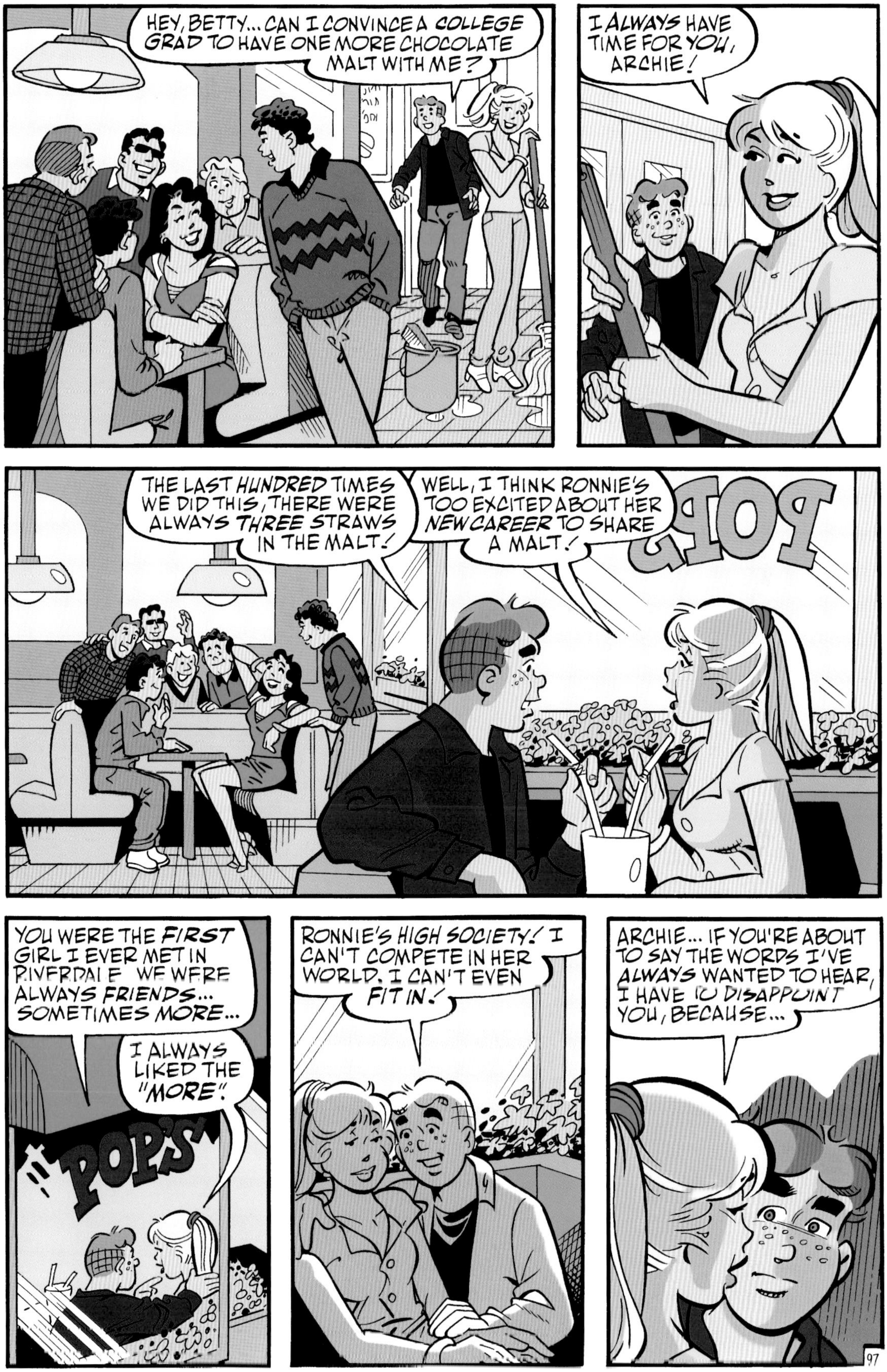
HEY, BETTY... CAN I CONVINCE A COLLEGE GRAD TO HAVE ONE MORE CHOCOLATE MALT WITH ME?
I ALWAYS HAVE TIME FOR YOU, ARCHIE!
THE LAST HUNDRED TIMES WE DID THIS, THERE WERE ALWAYS THREE STRAWS IN THE MALT!
WELL, I THINK RONNIE'S TOO EXCITED ABOUT HER NEW CAREER TO SHARE A MALT!
POPS
YOU WERE THE FIRST GIRL I EVER MET IN RIVERDALE. WE WERE ALWAYS FRIENDS... SOMETIMES MORE...
I ALWAYS LIKED THE "MORE".
POP'S
RONNIE'S HIGH SOCIETY! I CAN'T COMPETE IN HER WORLD. I CAN'T EVEN FIT IN!
ARCHIE... IF YOU'RE ABOUT TO SAY THE WORDS I'VE ALWAYS WANTED TO HEAR, I HAVE TO DISAPPOINT YOU, BECAUSE...

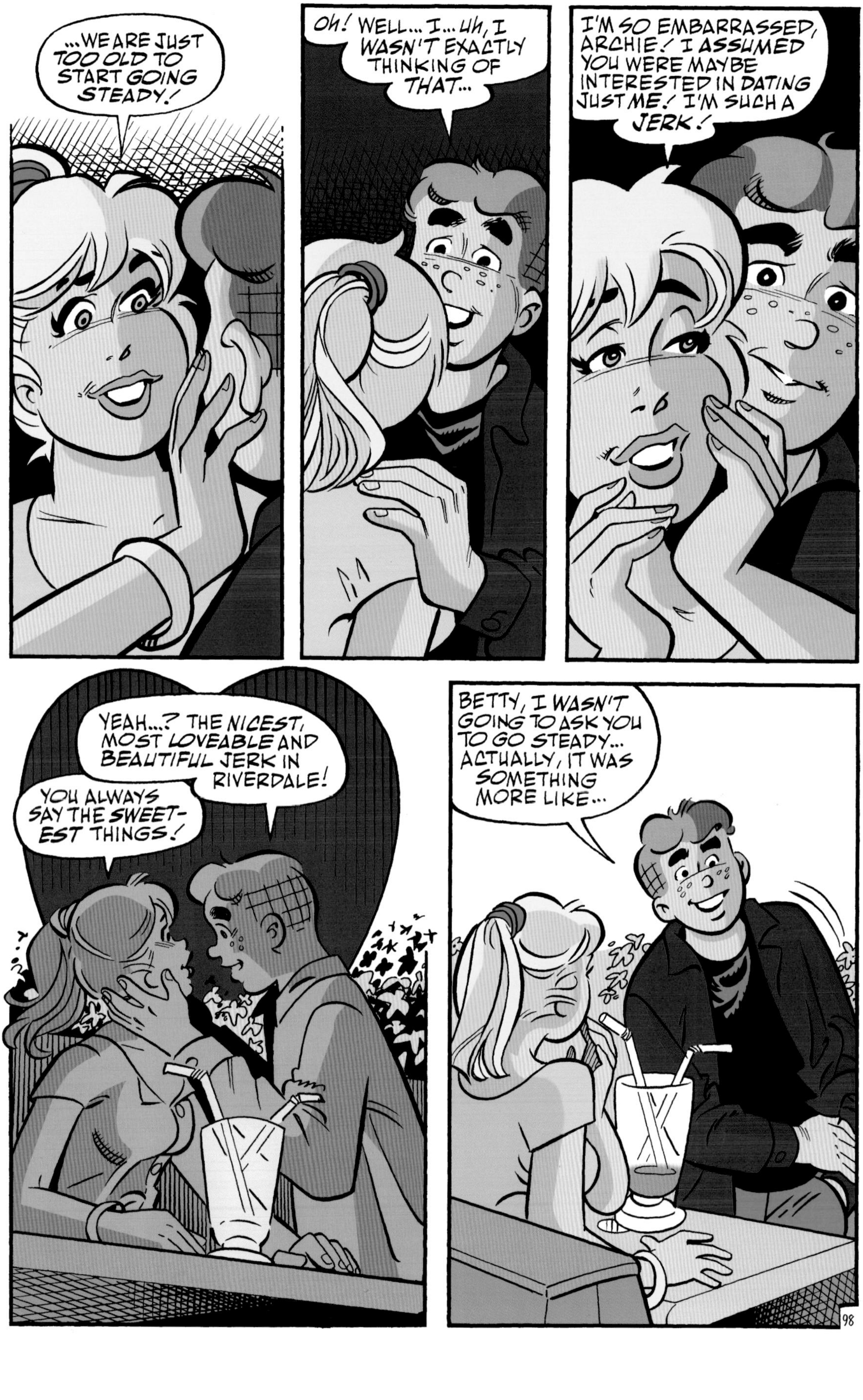
...WE ARE JUST TOO OLD TO START GOING STEADY!
OH! WELL... I... UH, I WASN'T EXACTLY THINKING OF THAT...
I'M SO EMBARRASSED, ARCHIE! I ASSUMED YOU WERE MAYBE INTERESTED IN DATING JUST ME! I'M SUCH A JERK!
YEAH...? THE NICEST, MOST LOVEABLE AND BEAUTIFUL JERK IN RIVERDALE!
YOU ALWAYS SAY THE SWEET-EST THINGS!
BETTY, I WASN'T GOING TO ASK YOU TO GO STEADY... ACTUALLY, IT WAS SOMETHING MORE LIKE...

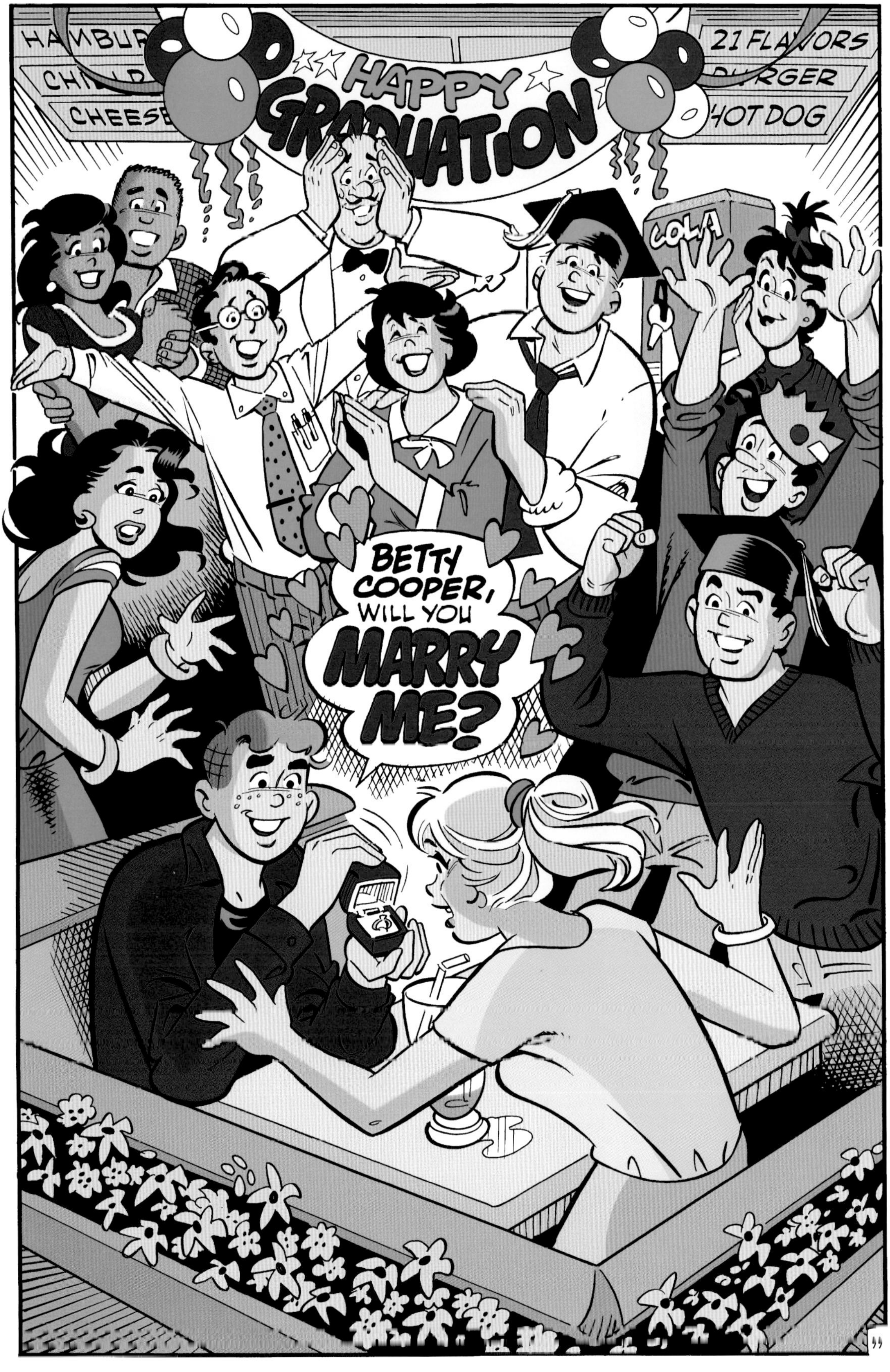
HAPPY GRADUATION
21 FLAVORS
HOT DOG
COLA
BETTY COOPER, WILL YOU MARRY ME?

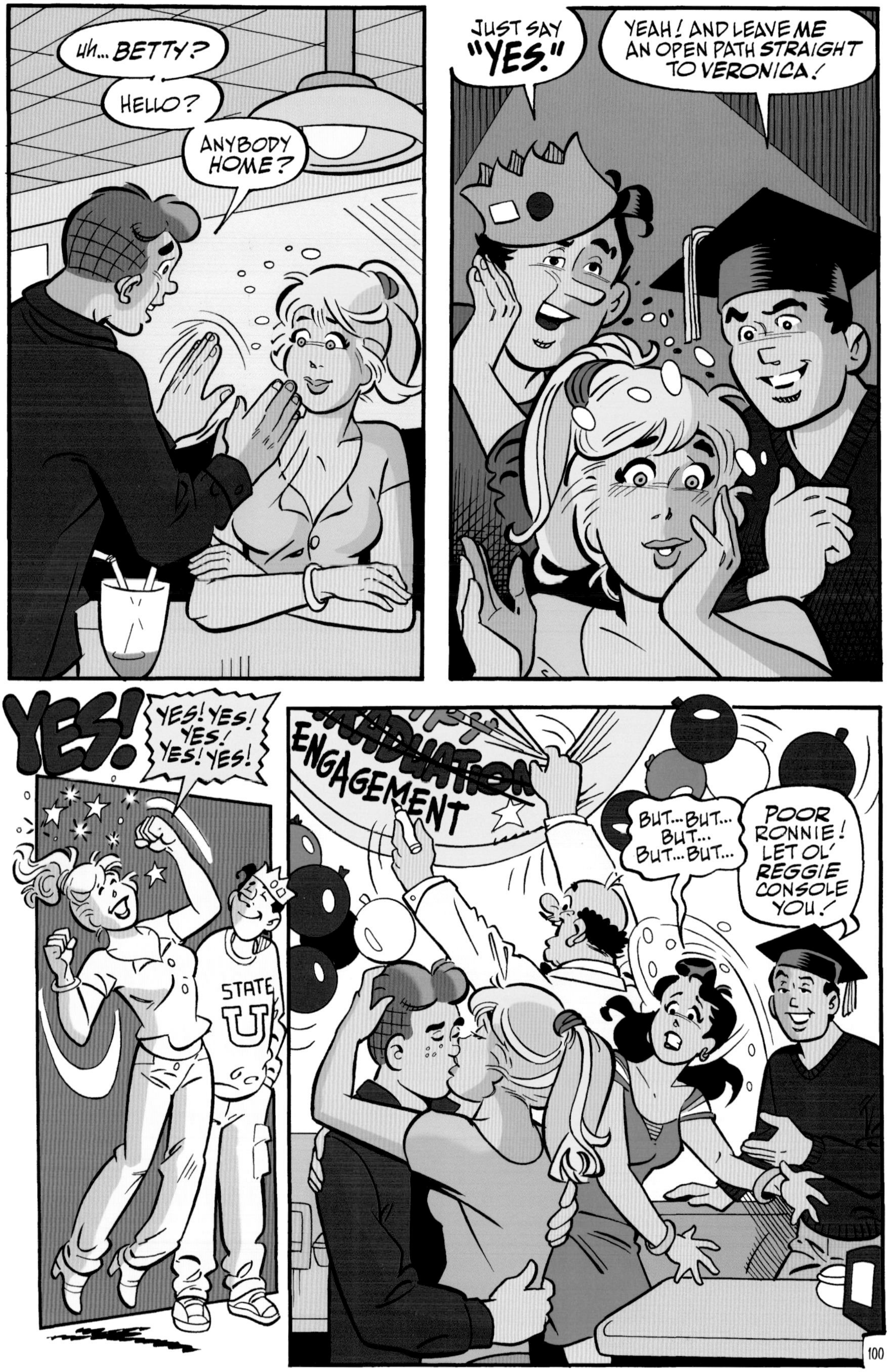

UH... BETTY?
HELLO?
ANYBODY HOME?
JUST SAY "YES."
YEAH! AND LEAVE ME AN OPEN PATH STRAIGHT TO VERONICA!
YES!
YES! YES! YES! YES! YES!
STATE U
GRADUATION
ENGAGEMENT
BUT... BUT... BUT... BUT... BUT...
POOR RONNIE! LET OL' REGGIE CONSOLE YOU!

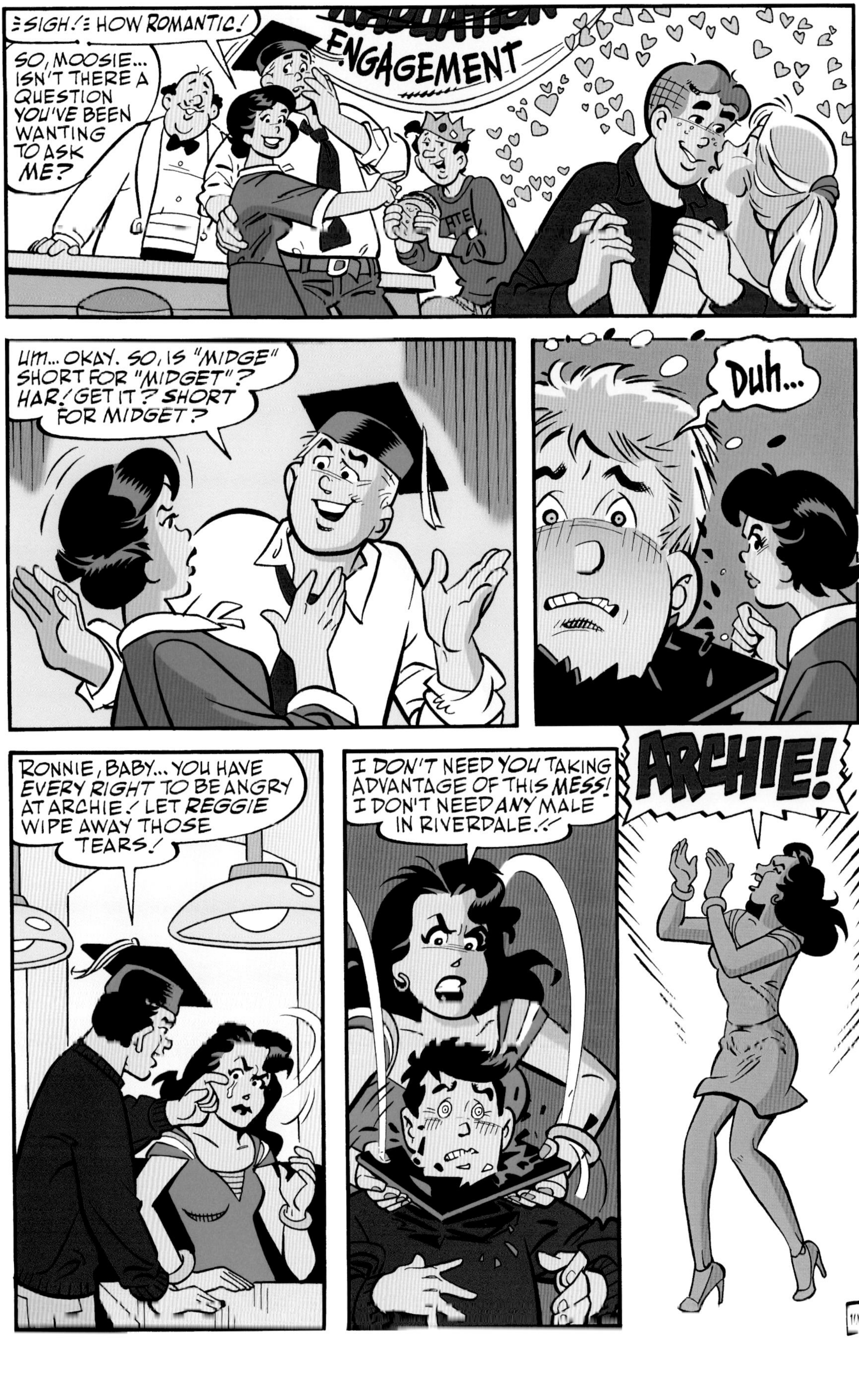
⋮SIGH!⋮ HOW ROMANTIC!
ENGAGEMENT
SO, MOOSIE... ISN'T THERE A QUESTION YOU'VE BEEN WANTING TO ASK ME?
UM... OKAY. SO, IS "MIDGE" SHORT FOR "MIDGET"? HAR! GET IT? SHORT FOR MIDGET?
Duh...
RONNIE, BABY... YOU HAVE EVERY RIGHT TO BE ANGRY AT ARCHIE! LET REGGIE WIPE AWAY THOSE TEARS!
I DON'T NEED YOU TAKING ADVANTAGE OF THIS MESS! I DON'T NEED ANY MALE IN RIVERDALE!
ARCHIE!

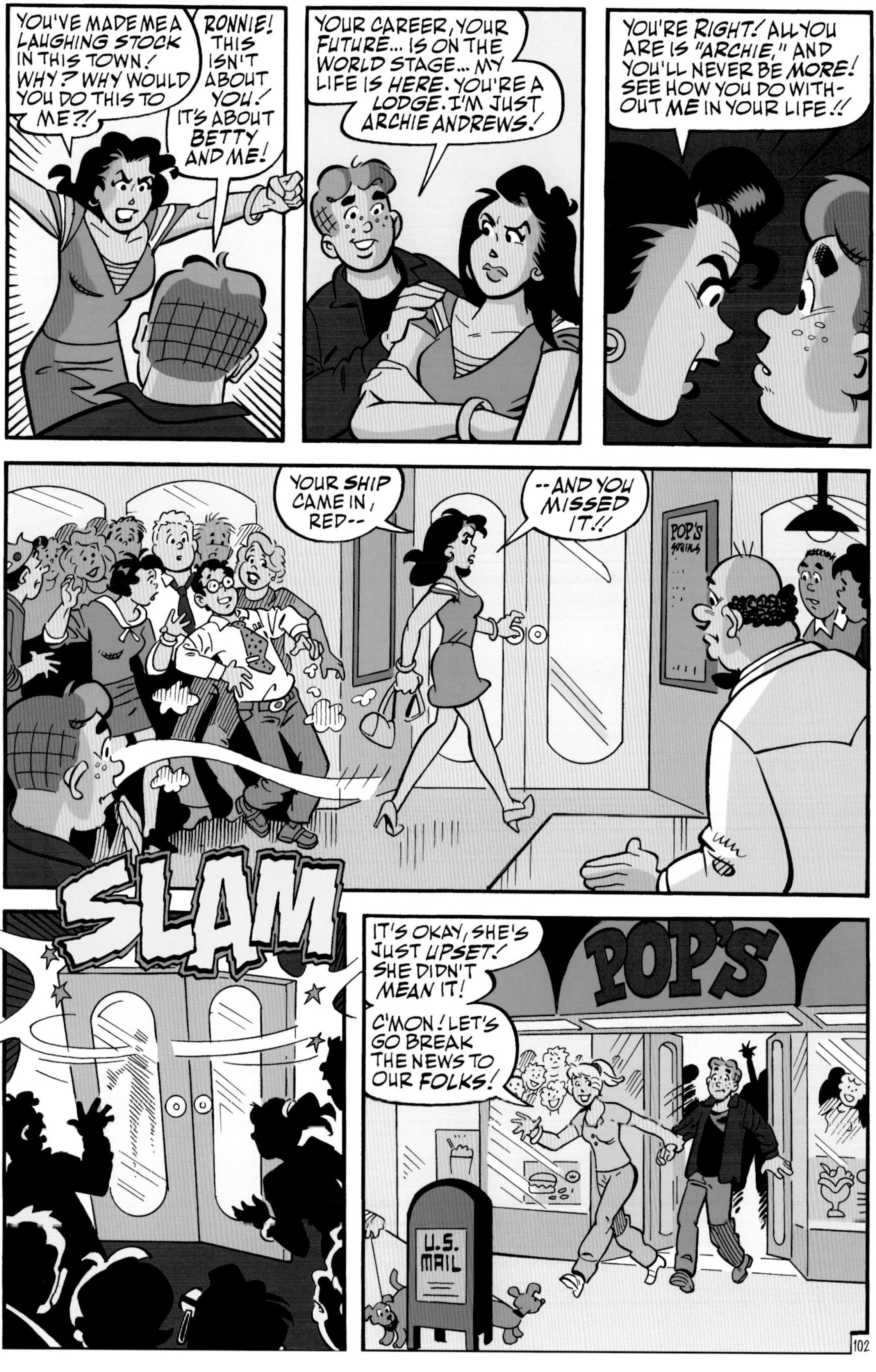
YOU'VE MADE ME A LAUGHING STOCK IN THIS TOWN! WHY? WHY WOULD YOU DO THIS TO ME?!
RONNIE! THIS ISN'T ABOUT YOU! IT'S ABOUT BETTY AND ME!
YOUR CAREER, YOUR FUTURE... IS ON THE WORLD STAGE... MY LIFE IS HERE. YOU'RE A LODGE. I'M JUST ARCHIE ANDREWS!
YOU'RE RIGHT! ALL YOU ARE IS "ARCHIE," AND YOU'LL NEVER BE MORE! SEE HOW YOU DO WITHOUT ME IN YOUR LIFE!!
YOUR SHIP CAME IN, RED--
--AND YOU MISSED IT!!
POP'S
SLAM
POP'S
IT'S OKAY, SHE'S JUST UPSET! SHE DIDN'T MEAN IT!
C'MON! LET'S GO BREAK THE NEWS TO OUR FOLKS!
U.S. MAIL

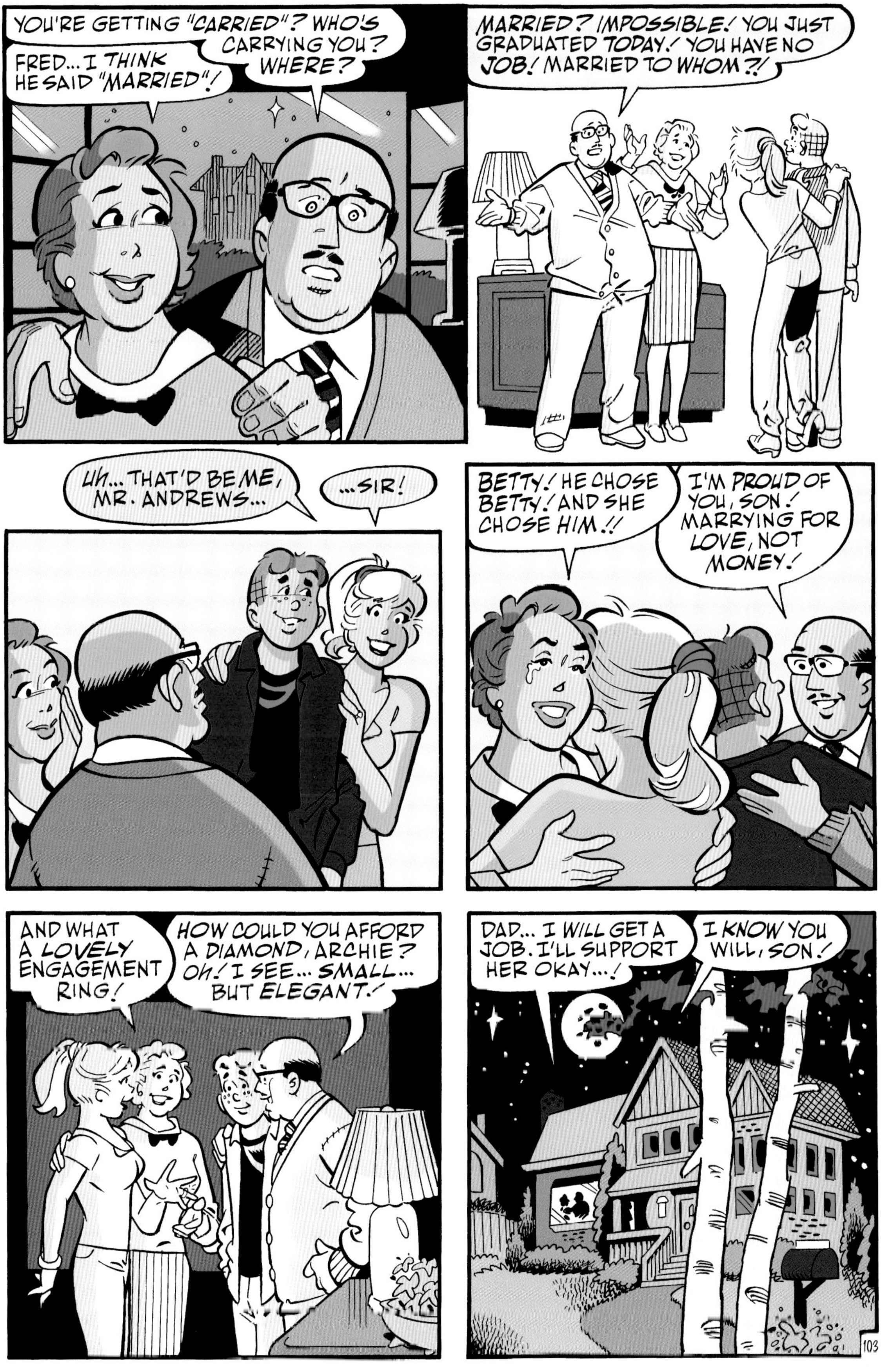
YOU'RE GETTING "CARRIED"? WHO'S CARRYING YOU? WHERE?
FRED... I THINK HE SAID "MARRIED"!
MARRIED? IMPOSSIBLE! YOU JUST GRADUATED TODAY! YOU HAVE NO JOB! MARRIED TO WHOM?!
UH... THAT'D BE ME, MR. ANDREWS...
...SIR!
BETTY! HE CHOSE BETTY! AND SHE CHOSE HIM!!
I'M PROUD OF YOU, SON! MARRYING FOR LOVE, NOT MONEY!
AND WHAT A LOVELY ENGAGEMENT RING!
HOW COULD YOU AFFORD A DIAMOND, ARCHIE? OH! I SEE... SMALL... BUT ELEGANT!
DAD... I WILL GET A JOB. I'LL SUPPORT HER OKAY...!
I KNOW YOU WILL, SON!

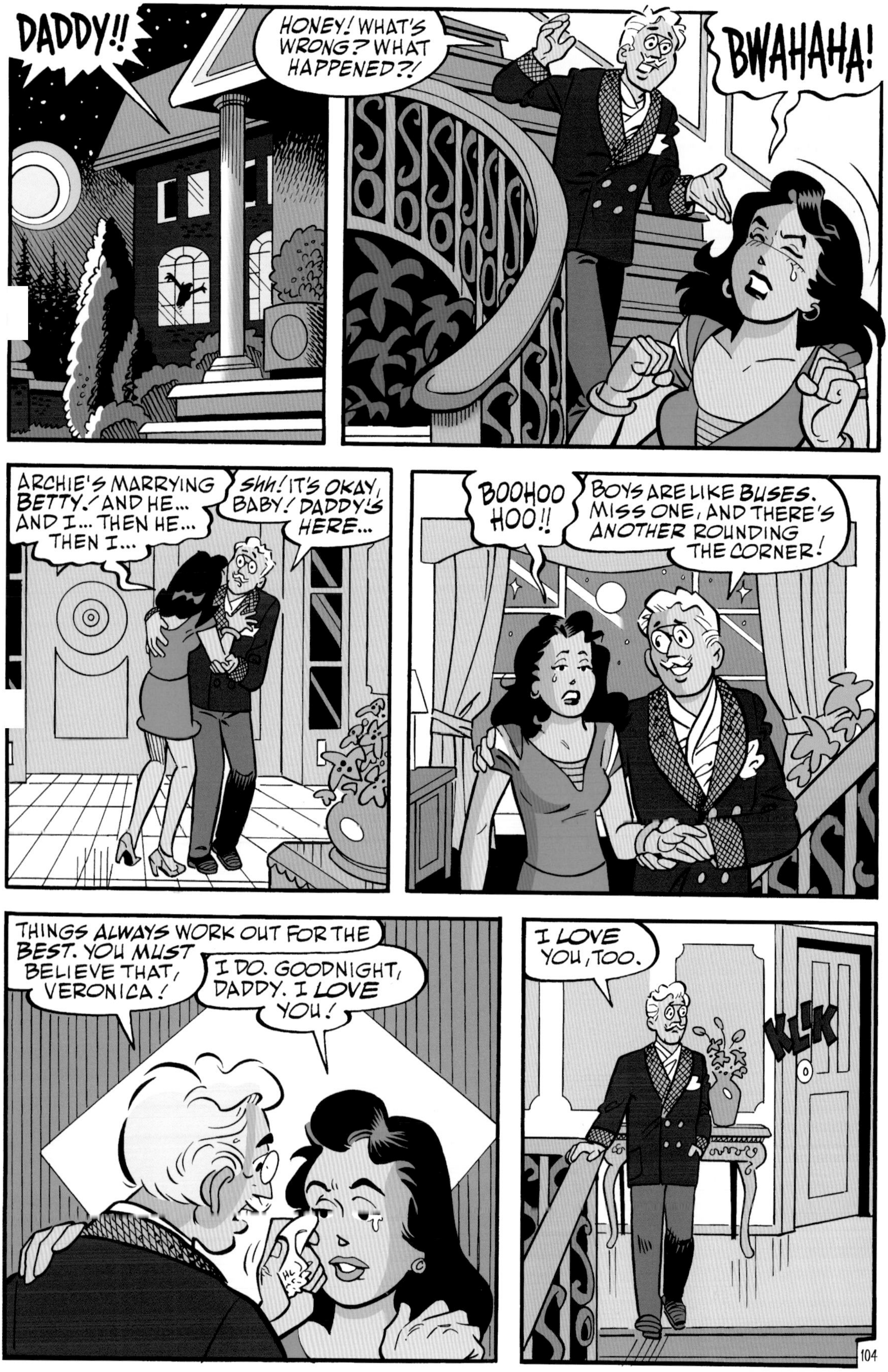
DADDY!!
HONEY! WHAT'S WRONG? WHAT HAPPENED?!
BWAHAHA!
ARCHIE'S MARRYING BETTY! AND HE... AND I... THEN HE... THEN I...
SHH! IT'S OKAY, BABY! DADDY'S HERE...
BOOHOO HOO!!
BOYS ARE LIKE BUSES. MISS ONE, AND THERE'S ANOTHER ROUNDING THE CORNER!
THINGS ALWAYS WORK OUT FOR THE BEST. YOU MUST BELIEVE THAT, VERONICA!
I DO. GOODNIGHT, DADDY. I LOVE YOU!
I LOVE YOU, TOO.
KLIK

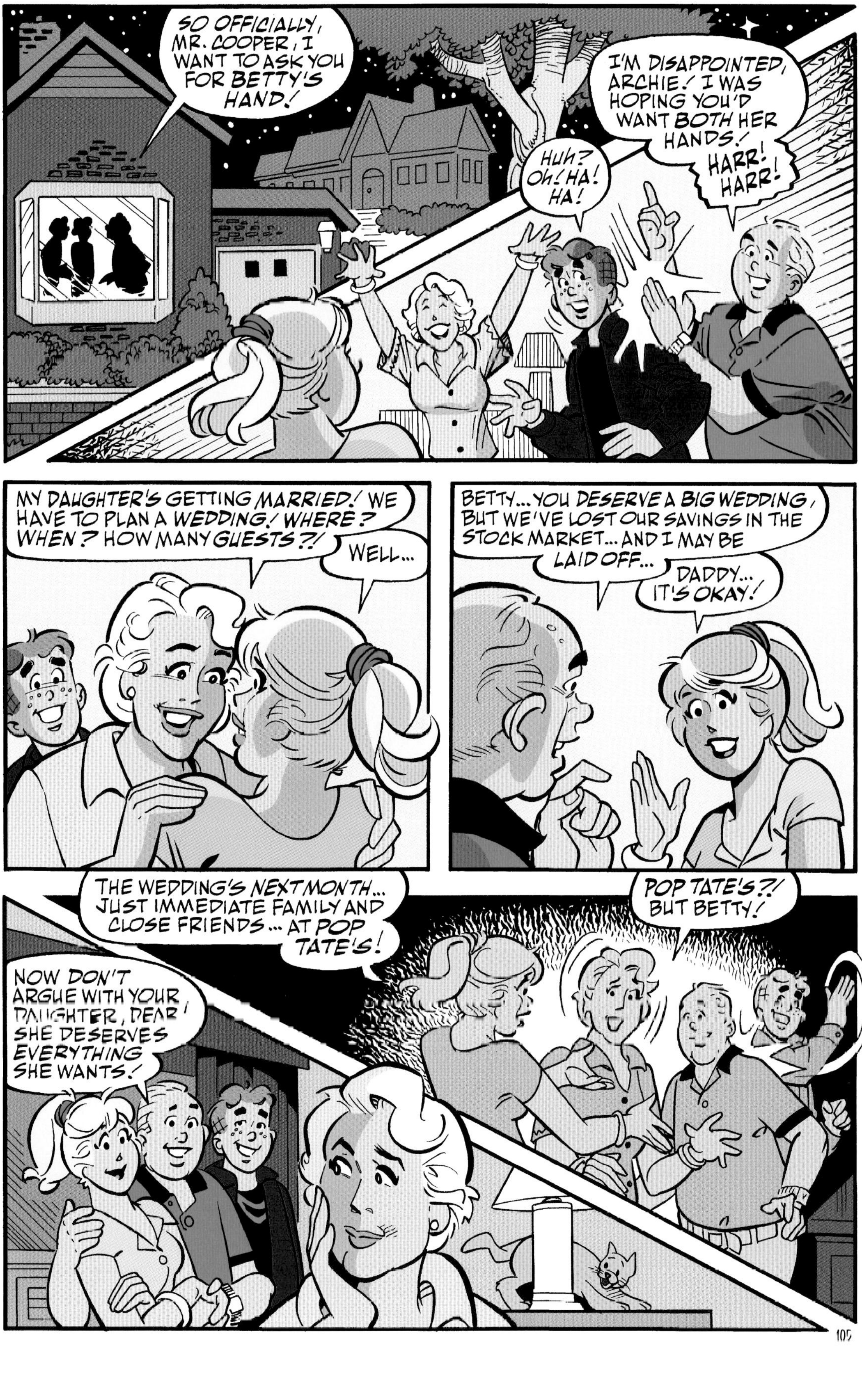

SO OFFICIALLY, MR. COOPER, I WANT TO ASK YOU FOR BETTY'S HAND!
I'M DISAPPOINTED, ARCHIE! I WAS HOPING YOU'D WANT BOTH HER HANDS!
HARR! HARR!
HUH? OH! HA! HA!
MY DAUGHTER'S GETTING MARRIED! WE HAVE TO PLAN A WEDDING! WHERE? WHEN? HOW MANY GUESTS?!
WELL...
BETTY... YOU DESERVE A BIG WEDDING, BUT WE'VE LOST OUR SAVINGS IN THE STOCK MARKET... AND I MAY BE LAID OFF...
DADDY... IT'S OKAY!
THE WEDDING'S NEXT MONTH... JUST IMMEDIATE FAMILY AND CLOSE FRIENDS... AT POP TATE'S!
POP TATE'S?! BUT BETTY!
NOW DON'T ARGUE WITH YOUR DAUGHTER, DEAR! SHE DESERVES EVERYTHING SHE WANTS!

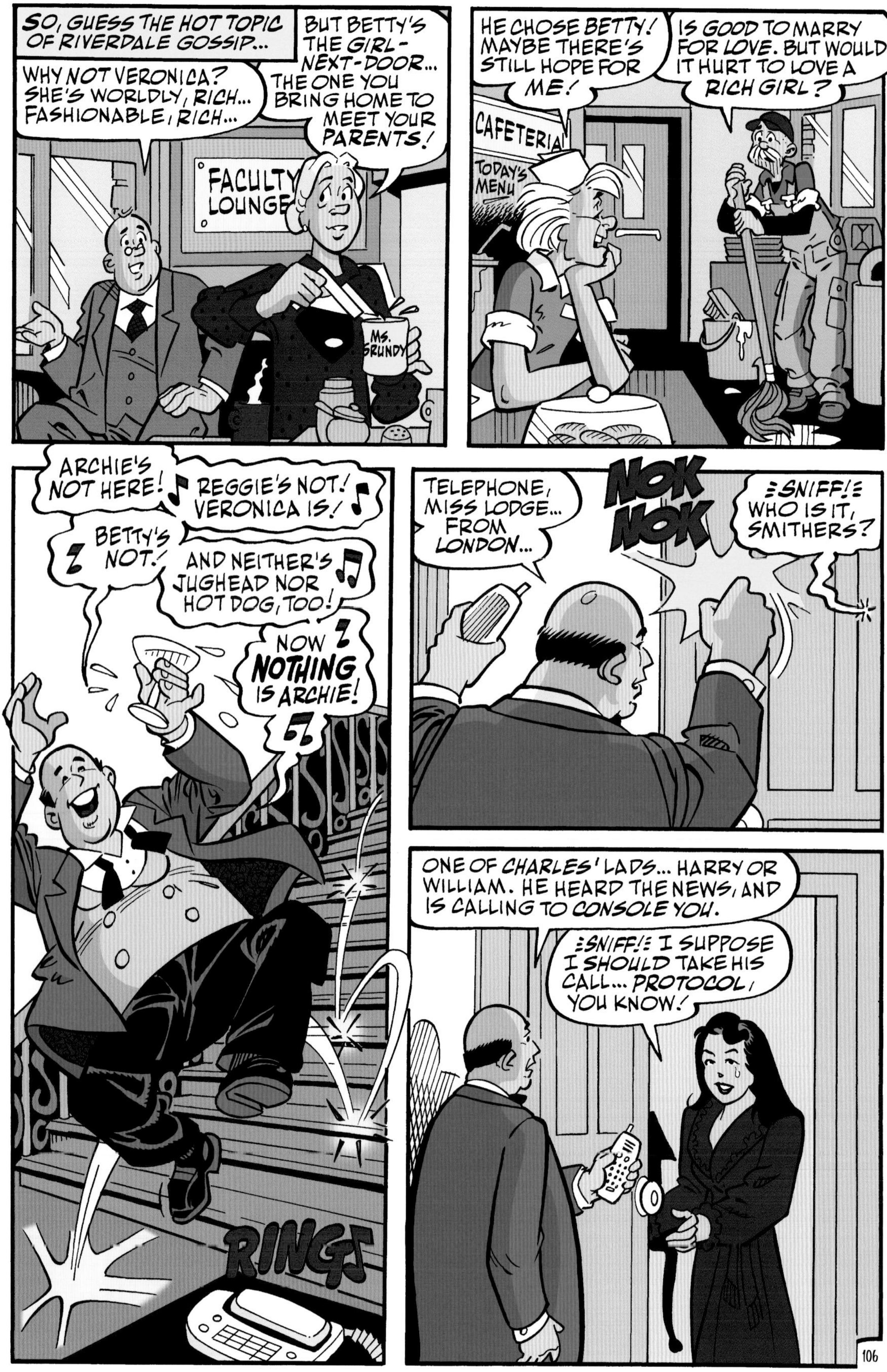
SO, GUESS THE HOT TOPIC OF RIVERDALE GOSSIP...
WHY NOT VERONICA? SHE'S WORLDLY, RICH... FASHIONABLE, RICH...
BUT BETTY'S THE GIRL-NEXT-DOOR... THE ONE YOU BRING HOME TO MEET YOUR PARENTS!
FACULTY LOUNGE
MS. GRUNDY
HE CHOSE BETTY! MAYBE THERE'S STILL HOPE FOR ME!
IS GOOD TO MARRY FOR LOVE. BUT WOULD IT HURT TO LOVE A RICH GIRL?
CAFETERIA
TODAY'S MENU
ARCHIE'S NOT HERE!
REGGIE'S NOT! VERONICA IS!
BETTY'S NOT!
AND NEITHER'S JUGHEAD NOR HOT DOG, TOO!
NOW NOTHING IS ARCHIE!
RING
TELEPHONE, MISS LODGE... FROM LONDON...
NOK NOK
SNIFF! WHO IS IT, SMITHERS?
ONE OF CHARLES' LADS... HARRY OR WILLIAM. HE HEARD THE NEWS, AND IS CALLING TO CONSOLE YOU.
SNIFF! I SUPPOSE I SHOULD TAKE HIS CALL... PROTOCOL, YOU KNOW!

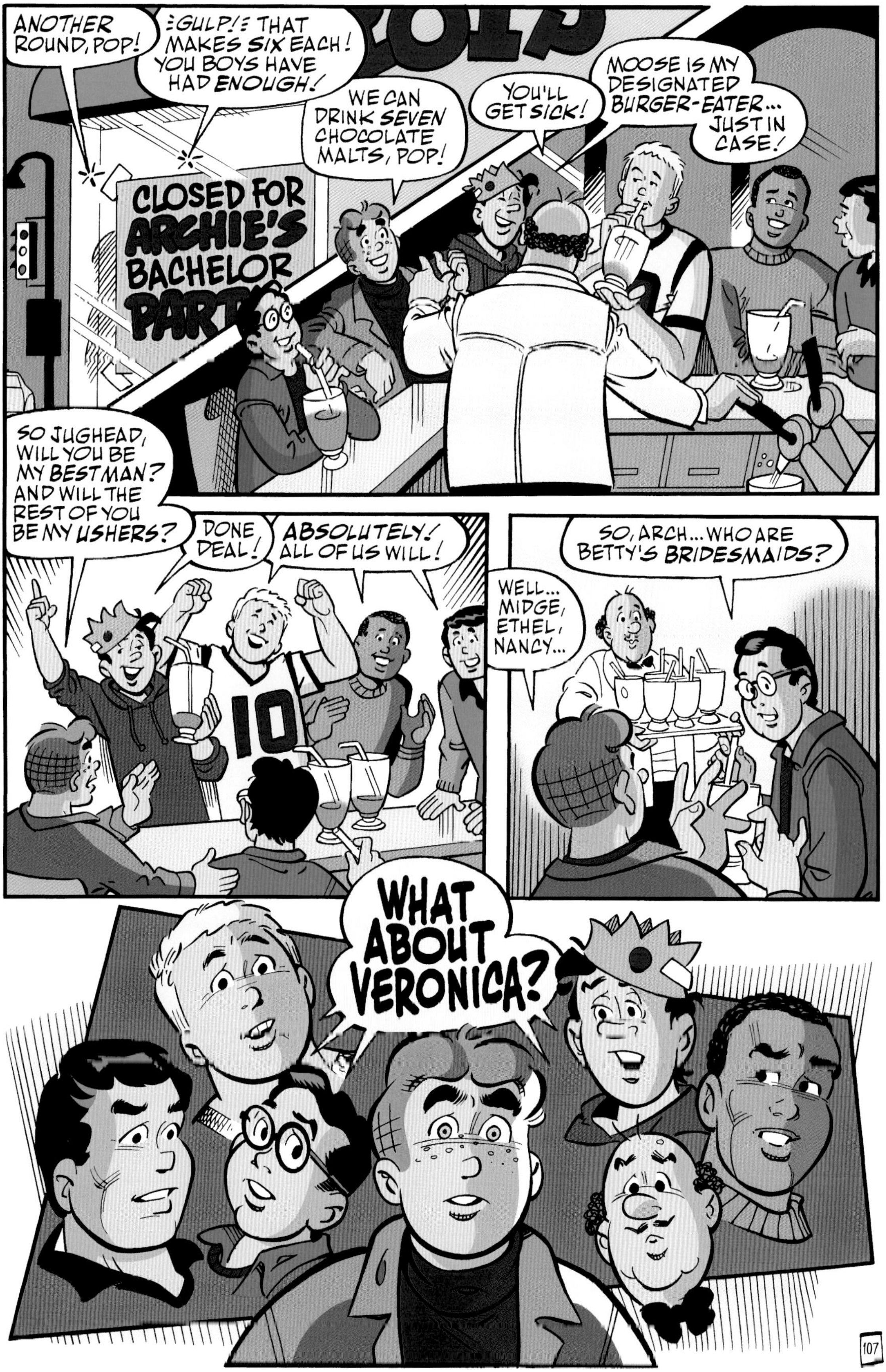
ANOTHER ROUND, POP!
=GULP!= THAT MAKES SIX EACH! YOU BOYS HAVE HAD ENOUGH!
WE CAN DRINK SEVEN CHOCOLATE MALTS, POP!
YOU'LL GET SICK!
MOOSE IS MY DESIGNATED BURGER-EATER... JUST IN CASE!
CLOSED FOR ARCHIE'S BACHELOR PART
SO JUGHEAD, WILL YOU BE MY BEST MAN? AND WILL THE REST OF YOU BE MY USHERS?
DONE DEAL!
ABSOLUTELY! ALL OF US WILL!
10
SO, ARCH... WHO ARE BETTY'S BRIDESMAIDS?
WELL... MIDGE, ETHEL, NANCY...
WHAT ABOUT VERONICA?

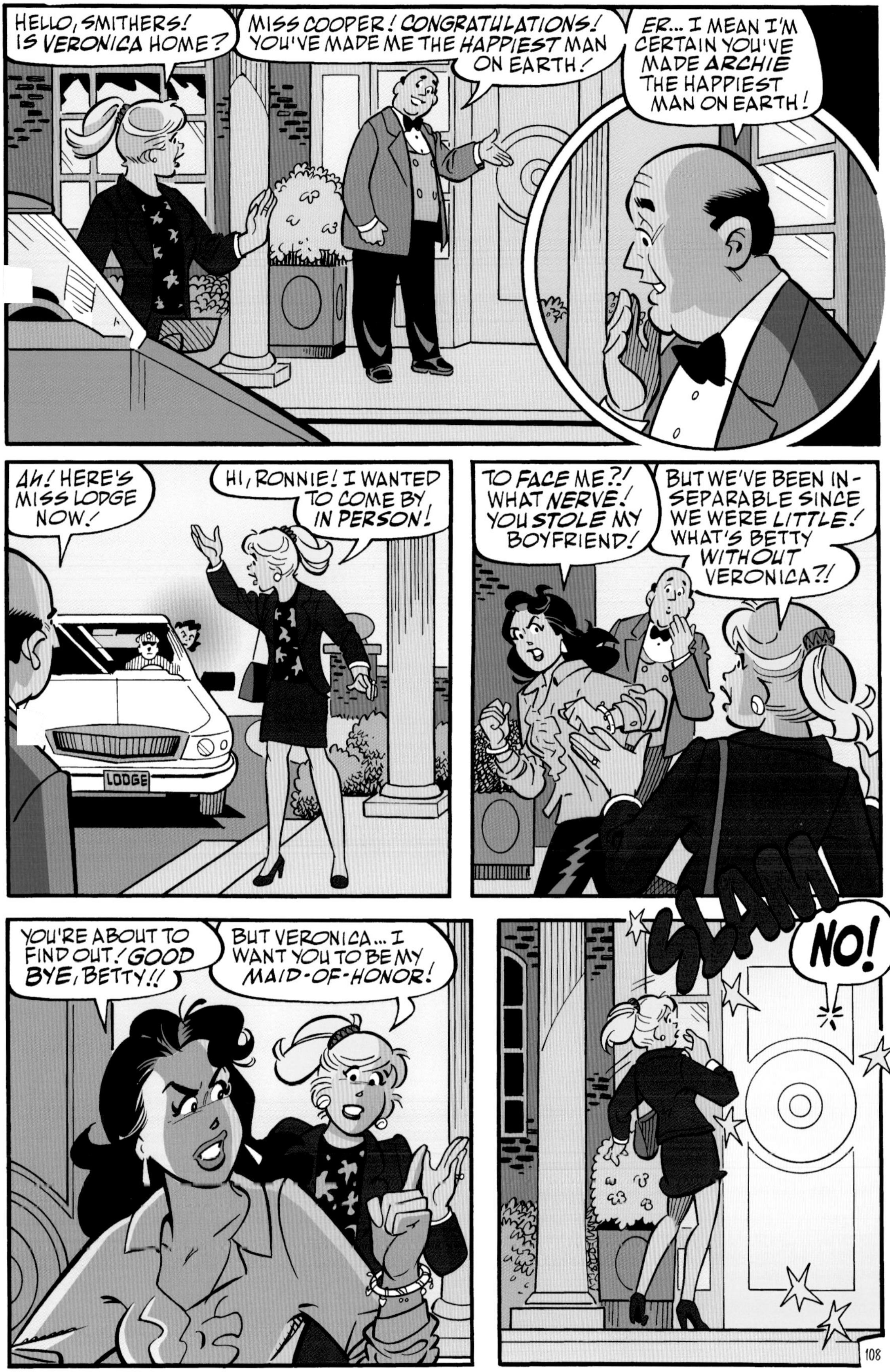
HELLO, SMITHERS! IS VERONICA HOME?
MISS COOPER! CONGRATULATIONS! YOU'VE MADE ME THE HAPPIEST MAN ON EARTH!
ER... I MEAN I'M CERTAIN YOU'VE MADE ARCHIE THE HAPPIEST MAN ON EARTH!
AH! HERE'S MISS LODGE NOW!
HI, RONNIE! I WANTED TO COME BY IN PERSON!
LODGE
TO FACE ME?! WHAT NERVE! YOU STOLE MY BOYFRIEND!
BUT WE'VE BEEN IN-SEPARABLE SINCE WE WERE LITTLE! WHAT'S BETTY WITHOUT VERONICA?!
YOU'RE ABOUT TO FIND OUT! GOOD BYE, BETTY!!
BUT VERONICA... I WANT YOU TO BE MY MAID-OF-HONOR!
SLAM
NO!

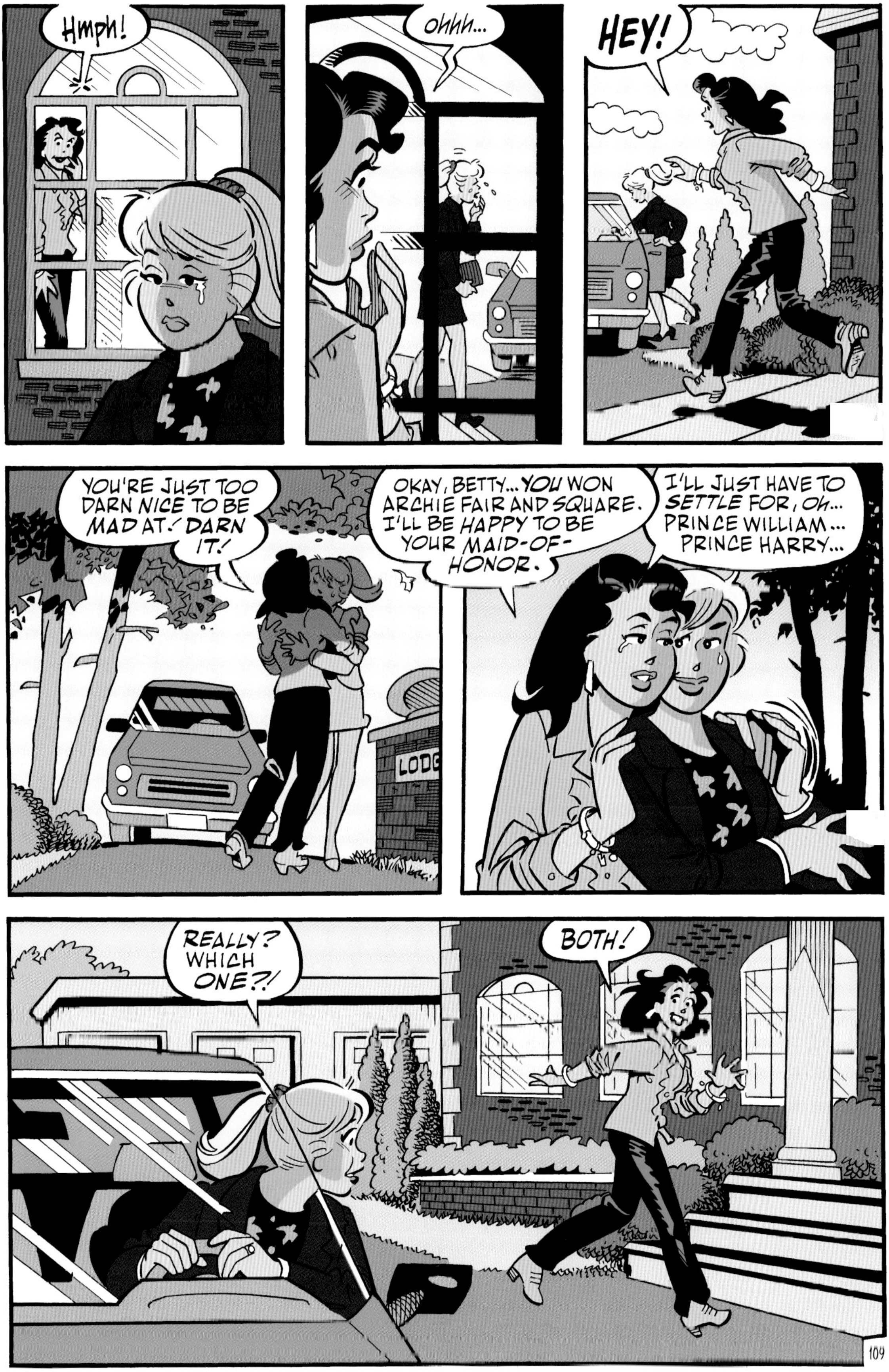
Hmph!
ohhh...
HEY!
YOU'RE JUST TOO DARN NICE TO BE MAD AT.' DARN IT!
OKAY, BETTY... YOU WON ARCHIE FAIR AND SQUARE. I'LL BE HAPPY TO BE YOUR MAID-OF-HONOR.
I'LL JUST HAVE TO SETTLE FOR, Oh... PRINCE WILLIAM... PRINCE HARRY...
LODG
REALLY? WHICH ONE?!
BOTH!

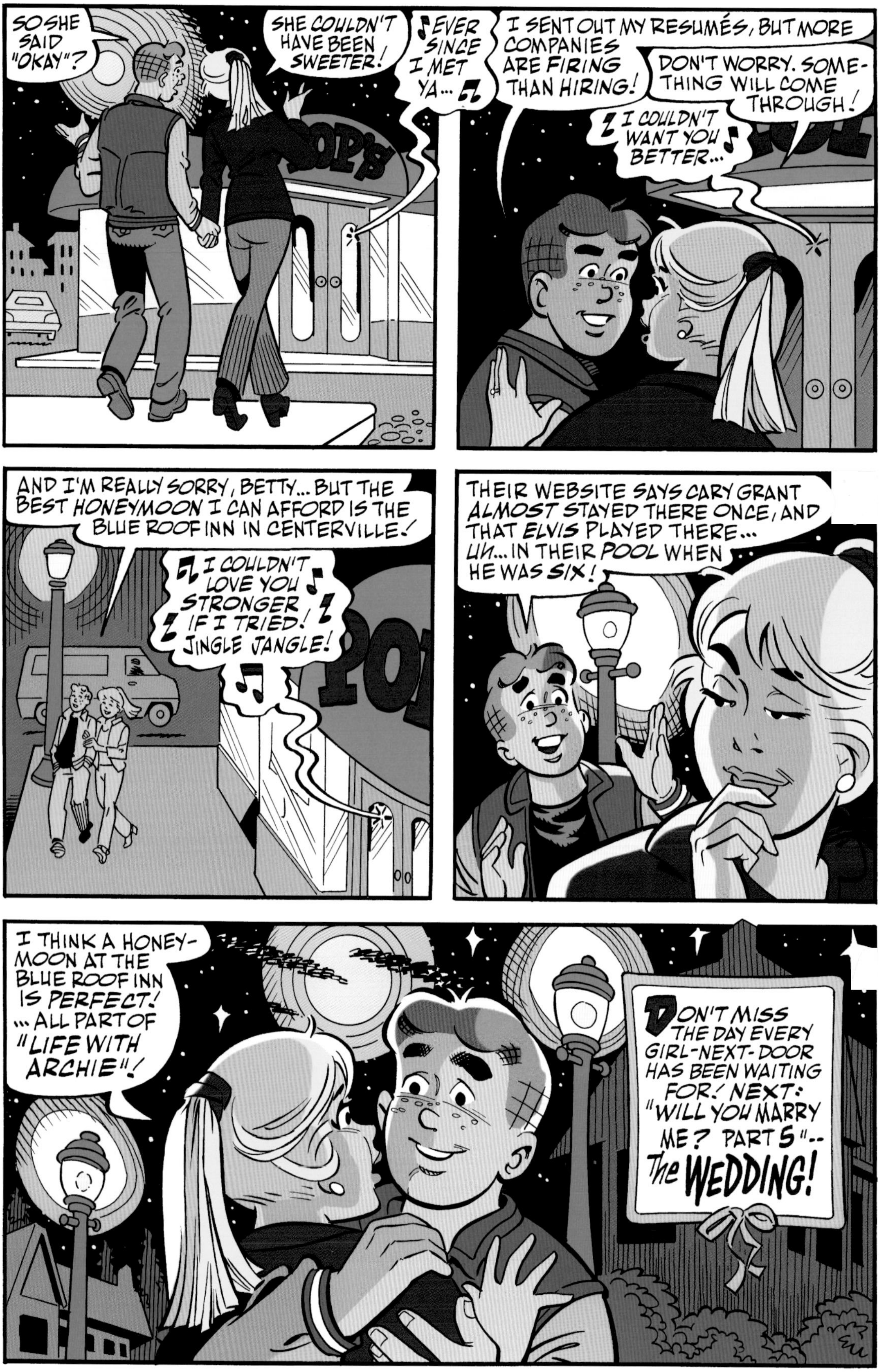
SO SHE SAID "OKAY"?
SHE COULDN'T HAVE BEEN SWEETER!
EVER SINCE I MET YA...
I SENT OUT MY RESUMÉS, BUT MORE COMPANIES ARE FIRING THAN HIRING!
DON'T WORRY. SOMETHING WILL COME THROUGH!
I COULDN'T WANT YOU BETTER...
AND I'M REALLY SORRY, BETTY... BUT THE BEST HONEYMOON I CAN AFFORD IS THE BLUE ROOF INN IN CENTERVILLE!
I COULDN'T LOVE YOU STRONGER IF I TRIED! JINGLE JANGLE!
THEIR WEBSITE SAYS CARY GRANT ALMOST STAYED THERE ONCE, AND THAT ELVIS PLAYED THERE... UH... IN THEIR POOL WHEN HE WAS SIX!
I THINK A HONEYMOON AT THE BLUE ROOF INN IS PERFECT! ...ALL PART OF "LIFE WITH ARCHIE"!
DON'T MISS THE DAY EVERY GIRL-NEXT-DOOR HAS BEEN WAITING FOR! NEXT: "WILL YOU MARRY ME? PART 5"-- The WEDDING!

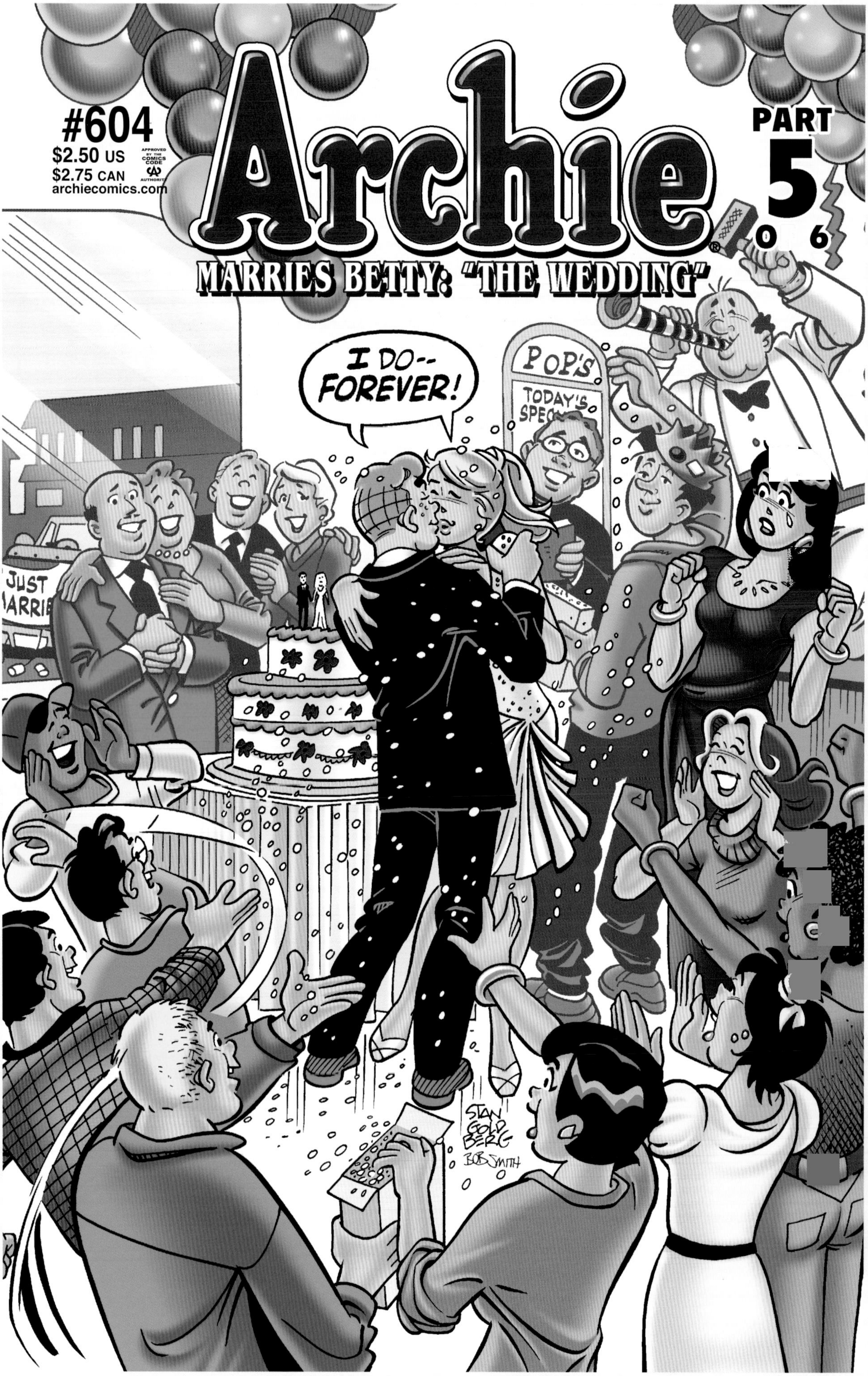

#604
$2.50 US
$2.75 CAN
archiecomics.com
APPROVED BY THE COMICS CODE AUTHORITY
Archie®
PART 5 of 6
MARRIES BETTY: "THE WEDDING"
I DO--
FOREVER!
POP'S
TODAY'S SPEC
JUST MARRIE
STAN GOLDBERG
BOB SMITH

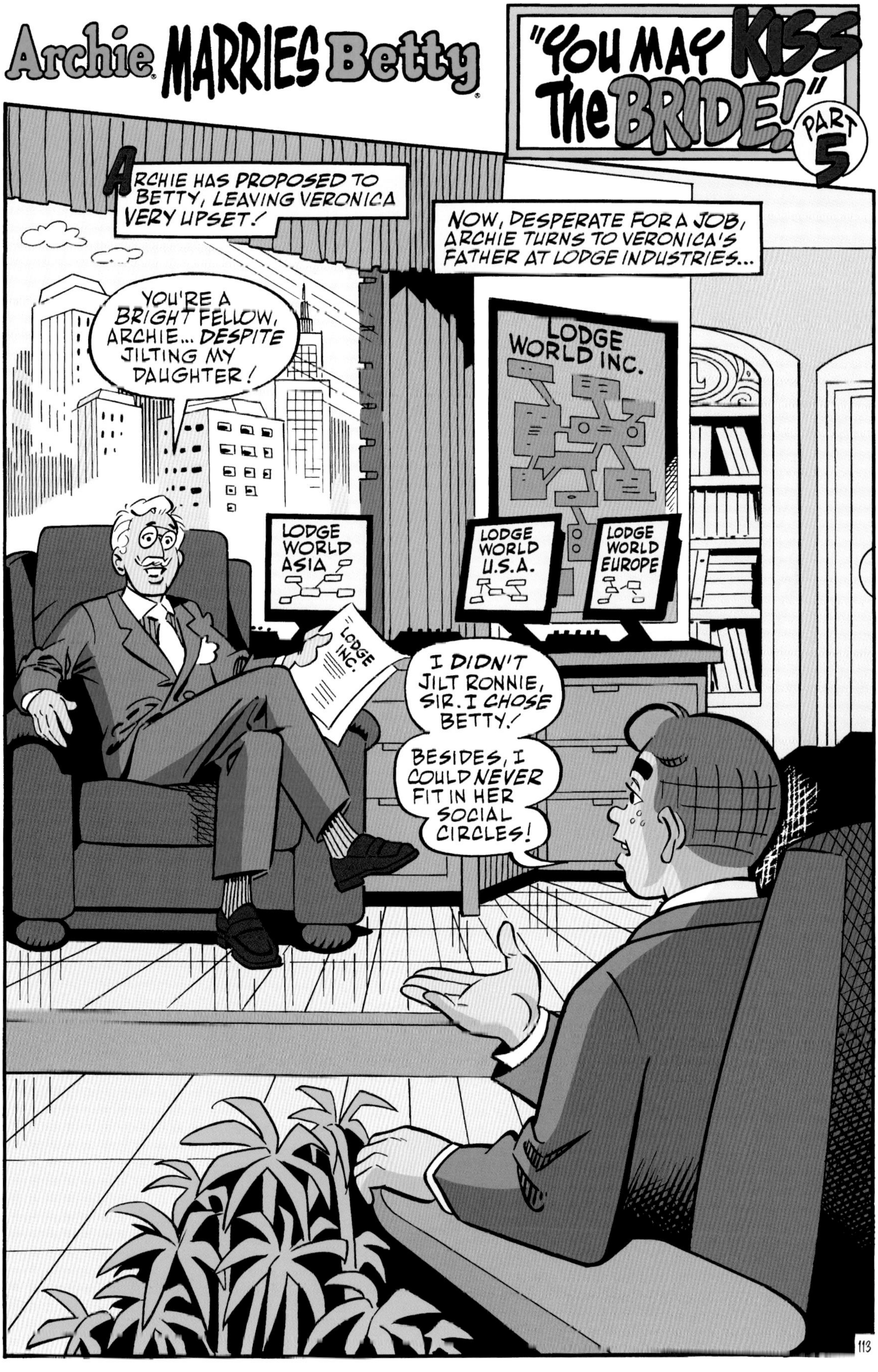

Archie MARRIES Betty
"YOU MAY KISS The BRIDE!" PART 5
ARCHIE HAS PROPOSED TO BETTY, LEAVING VERONICA VERY UPSET!
NOW, DESPERATE FOR A JOB, ARCHIE TURNS TO VERONICA'S FATHER AT LODGE INDUSTRIES...
YOU'RE A BRIGHT FELLOW, ARCHIE... DESPITE JILTING MY DAUGHTER!
LODGE WORLD INC.
LODGE WORLD ASIA
LODGE WORLD U.S.A.
LODGE WORLD EUROPE
LODGE INC.
I DIDN'T JILT RONNIE, SIR. I CHOSE BETTY!
BESIDES, I COULD NEVER FIT IN HER SOCIAL CIRCLES!

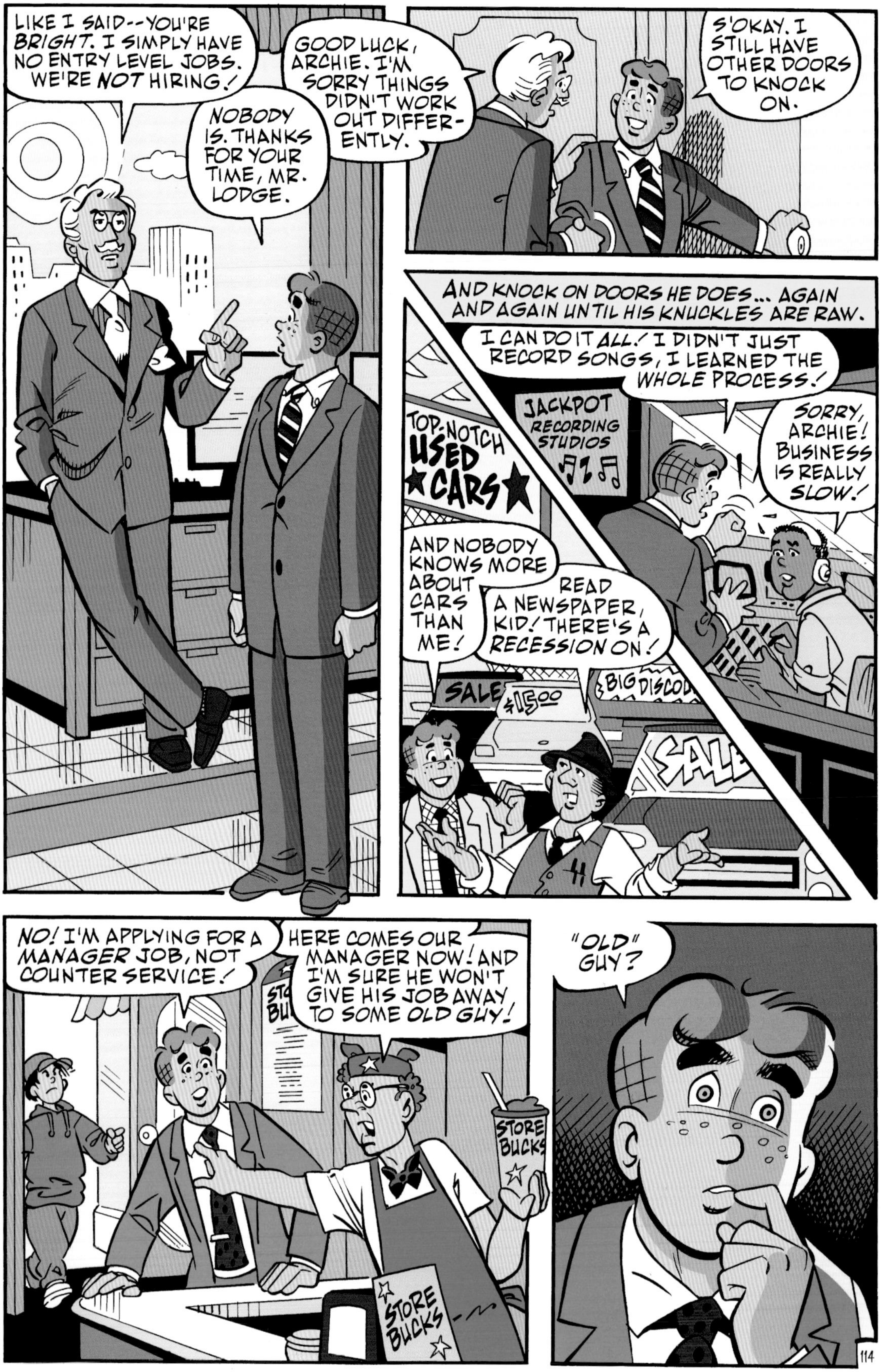
LIKE I SAID--YOU'RE BRIGHT. I SIMPLY HAVE NO ENTRY LEVEL JOBS. WE'RE NOT HIRING!
NOBODY IS. THANKS FOR YOUR TIME, MR. LODGE.
GOOD LUCK, ARCHIE. I'M SORRY THINGS DIDN'T WORK OUT DIFFER-ENTLY.
S'OKAY. I STILL HAVE OTHER DOORS TO KNOCK ON.
AND KNOCK ON DOORS HE DOES... AGAIN AND AGAIN UNTIL HIS KNUCKLES ARE RAW.
I CAN DO IT ALL! I DIDN'T JUST RECORD SONGS, I LEARNED THE WHOLE PROCESS!
JACKPOT RECORDING STUDIOS
SORRY, ARCHIE! BUSINESS IS REALLY SLOW!
TOP-NOTCH USED CARS
AND NOBODY KNOWS MORE ABOUT CARS THAN ME!
READ A NEWSPAPER, KID! THERE'S A RECESSION ON!
SALE
$15.00
BIG DISCO
SALE
NO! I'M APPLYING FOR A MANAGER JOB, NOT COUNTER SERVICE!
HERE COMES OUR MANAGER NOW! AND I'M SURE HE WON'T GIVE HIS JOB AWAY TO SOME OLD GUY!
STORE BUCKS
STORE BUCKS
"OLD" GUY?

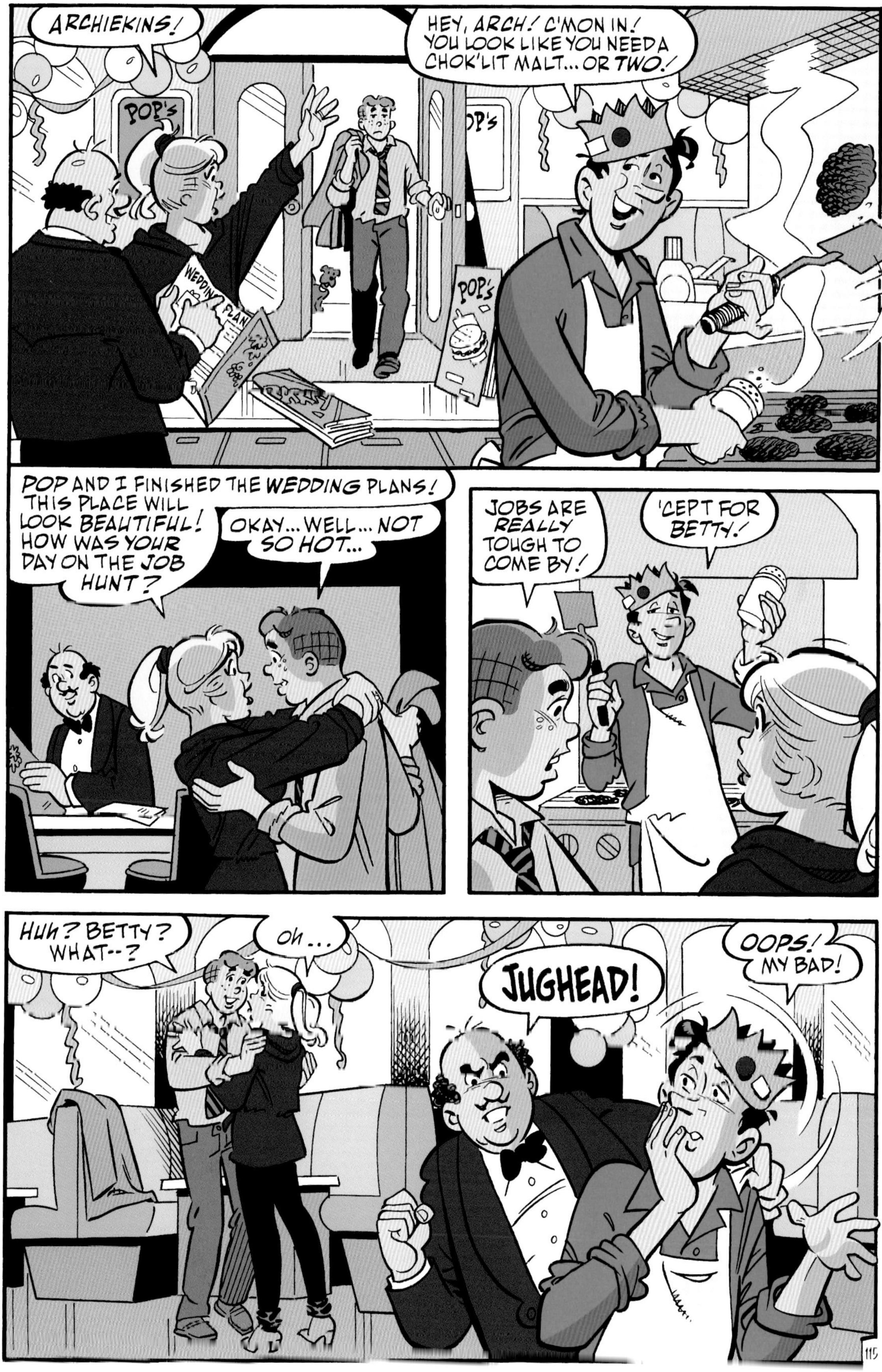
ARCHIEKINS!
HEY, ARCH! C'MON IN! YOU LOOK LIKE YOU NEED A CHOK'LIT MALT... OR TWO!
POP'S
WEDDING PLAN
POP AND I FINISHED THE WEDDING PLANS! THIS PLACE WILL LOOK BEAUTIFUL! HOW WAS YOUR DAY ON THE JOB HUNT?
OKAY... WELL... NOT SO HOT...
JOBS ARE REALLY TOUGH TO COME BY!
'CEPT FOR BETTY!
HUH? BETTY? WHAT--?
OH...
JUGHEAD!
OOPS! MY BAD!

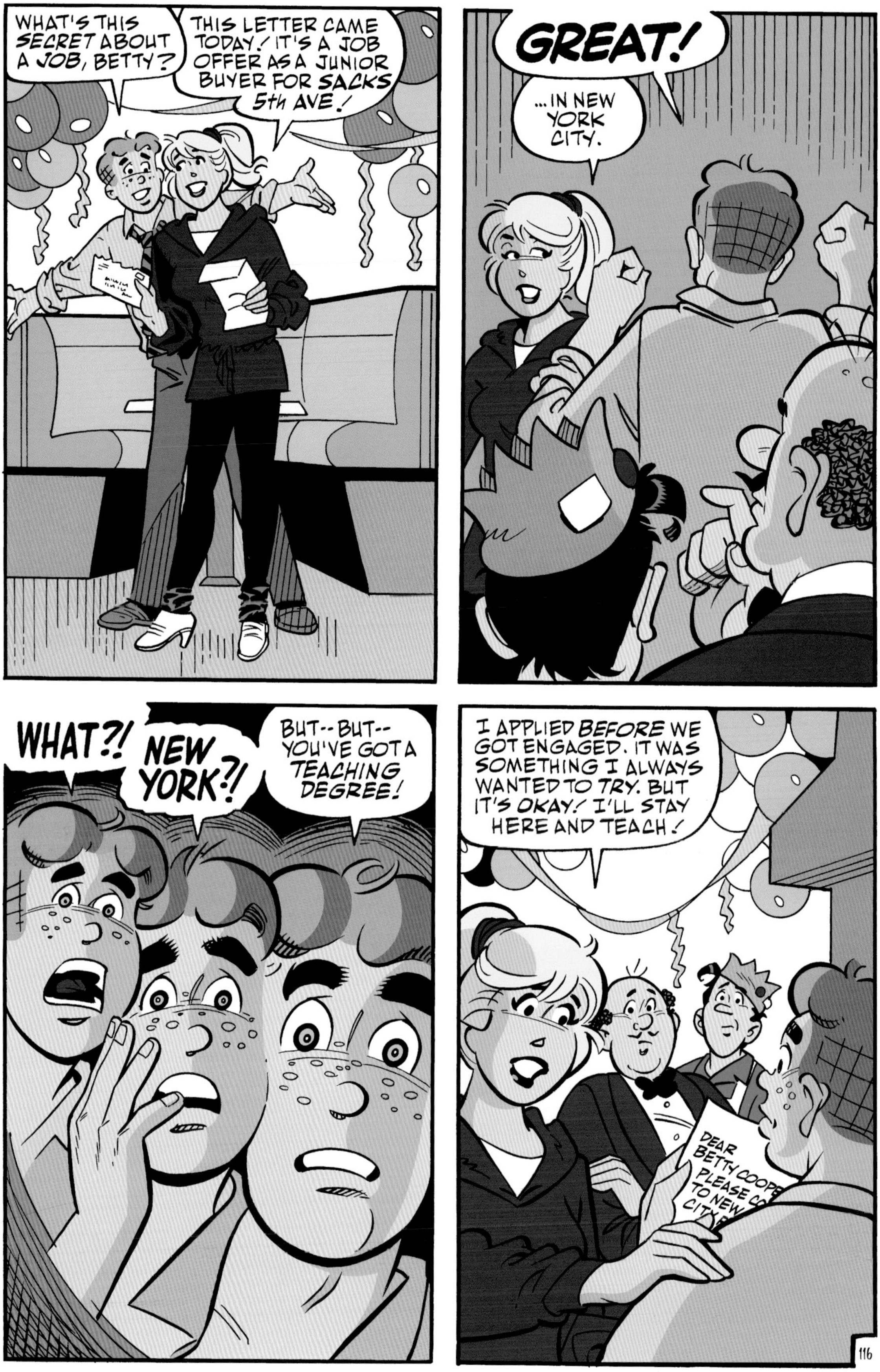
WHAT'S THIS SECRET ABOUT A JOB, BETTY?
THIS LETTER CAME TODAY! IT'S A JOB OFFER AS A JUNIOR BUYER FOR SACKS 5th AVE!
GREAT!
...IN NEW YORK CITY.
WHAT?!
NEW YORK?!
BUT--BUT-- YOU'VE GOT A TEACHING DEGREE!
I APPLIED BEFORE WE GOT ENGAGED. IT WAS SOMETHING I ALWAYS WANTED TO TRY. BUT IT'S OKAY! I'LL STAY HERE AND TEACH!
DEAR BETTY COOPE PLEASE CO TO NEW CITY

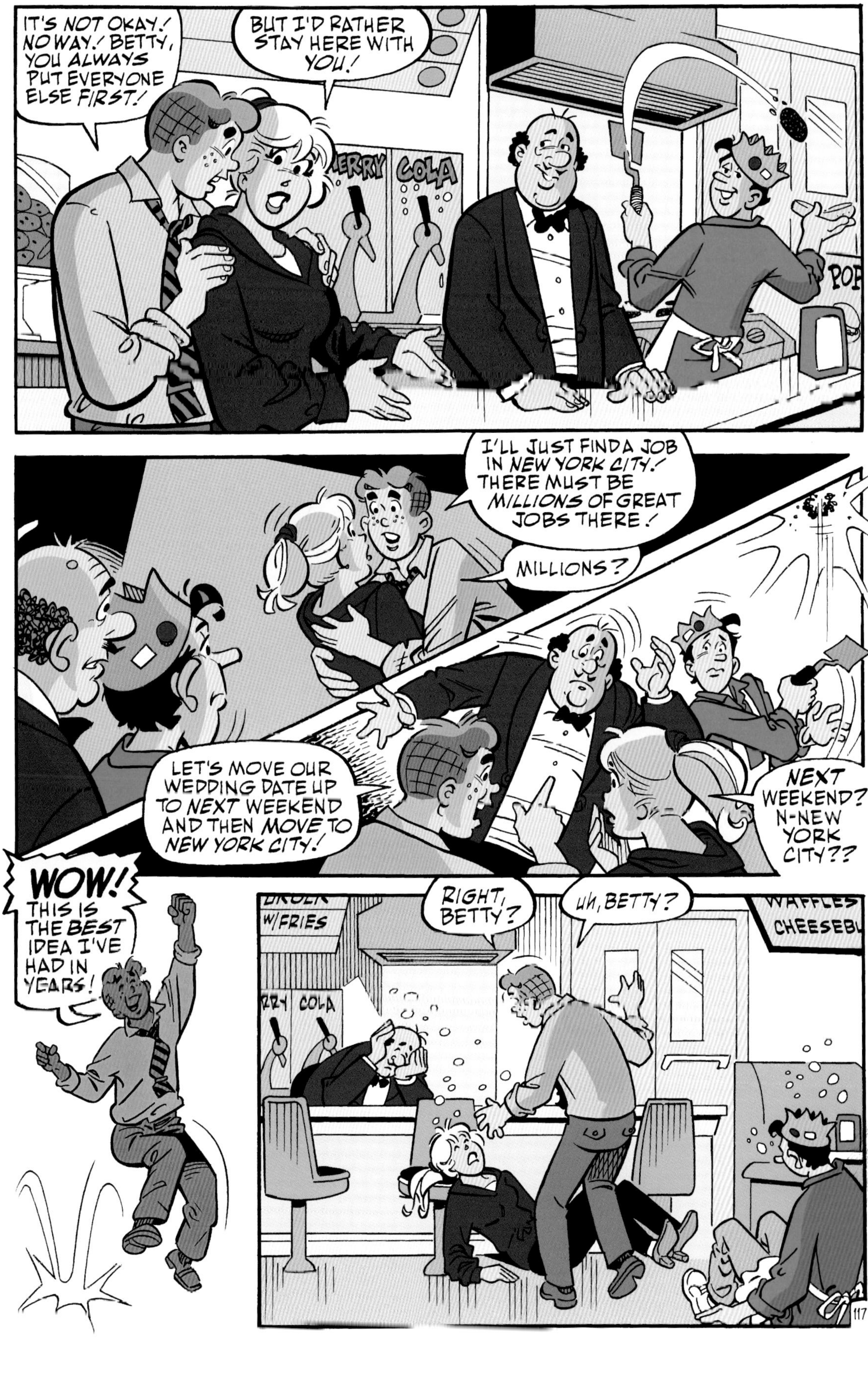
IT'S NOT OKAY! NO WAY! BETTY, YOU ALWAYS PUT EVERYONE ELSE FIRST!
BUT I'D RATHER STAY HERE WITH YOU!
ERRY
COLA
POP
I'LL JUST FIND A JOB IN NEW YORK CITY! THERE MUST BE MILLIONS OF GREAT JOBS THERE!
MILLIONS?
LET'S MOVE OUR WEDDING DATE UP TO NEXT WEEKEND AND THEN MOVE TO NEW YORK CITY!
NEXT WEEKEND? N-NEW YORK CITY??
WOW! THIS IS THE BEST IDEA I'VE HAD IN YEARS!
W/FRIES
WAFFLES
CHEESEBU
RIGHT, BETTY?
uh, BETTY?
RRY
COLA

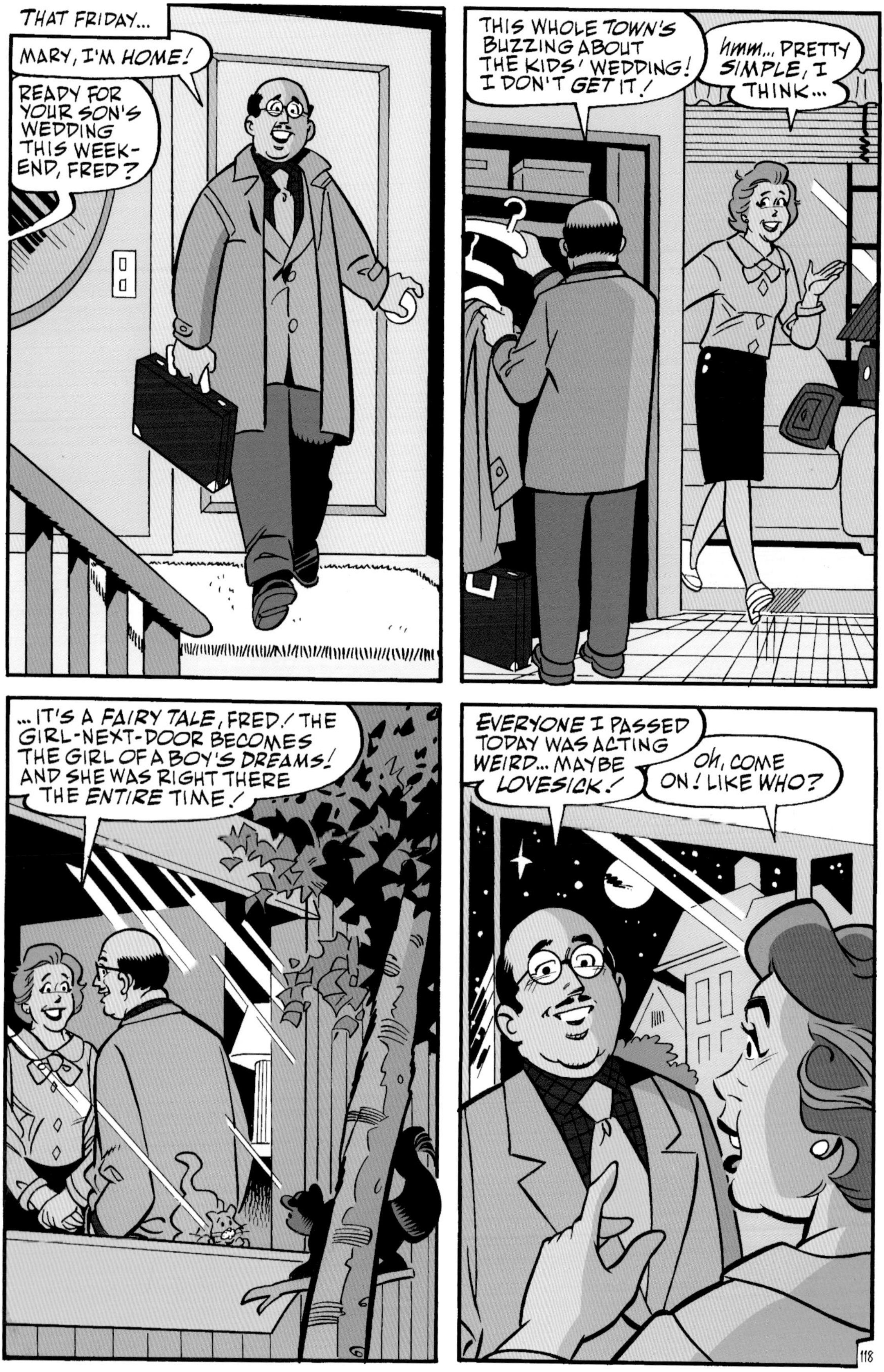
THAT FRIDAY...
MARY, I'M HOME!
READY FOR YOUR SON'S WEDDING THIS WEEK-END, FRED?
THIS WHOLE TOWN'S BUZZING ABOUT THE KIDS' WEDDING! I DON'T GET IT!
hmm... PRETTY SIMPLE, I THINK...
...IT'S A FAIRY TALE, FRED! THE GIRL-NEXT-DOOR BECOMES THE GIRL OF A BOY'S DREAMS! AND SHE WAS RIGHT THERE THE ENTIRE TIME!
EVERYONE I PASSED TODAY WAS ACTING WEIRD... MAYBE LOVESICK!
Oh, COME ON! LIKE WHO?

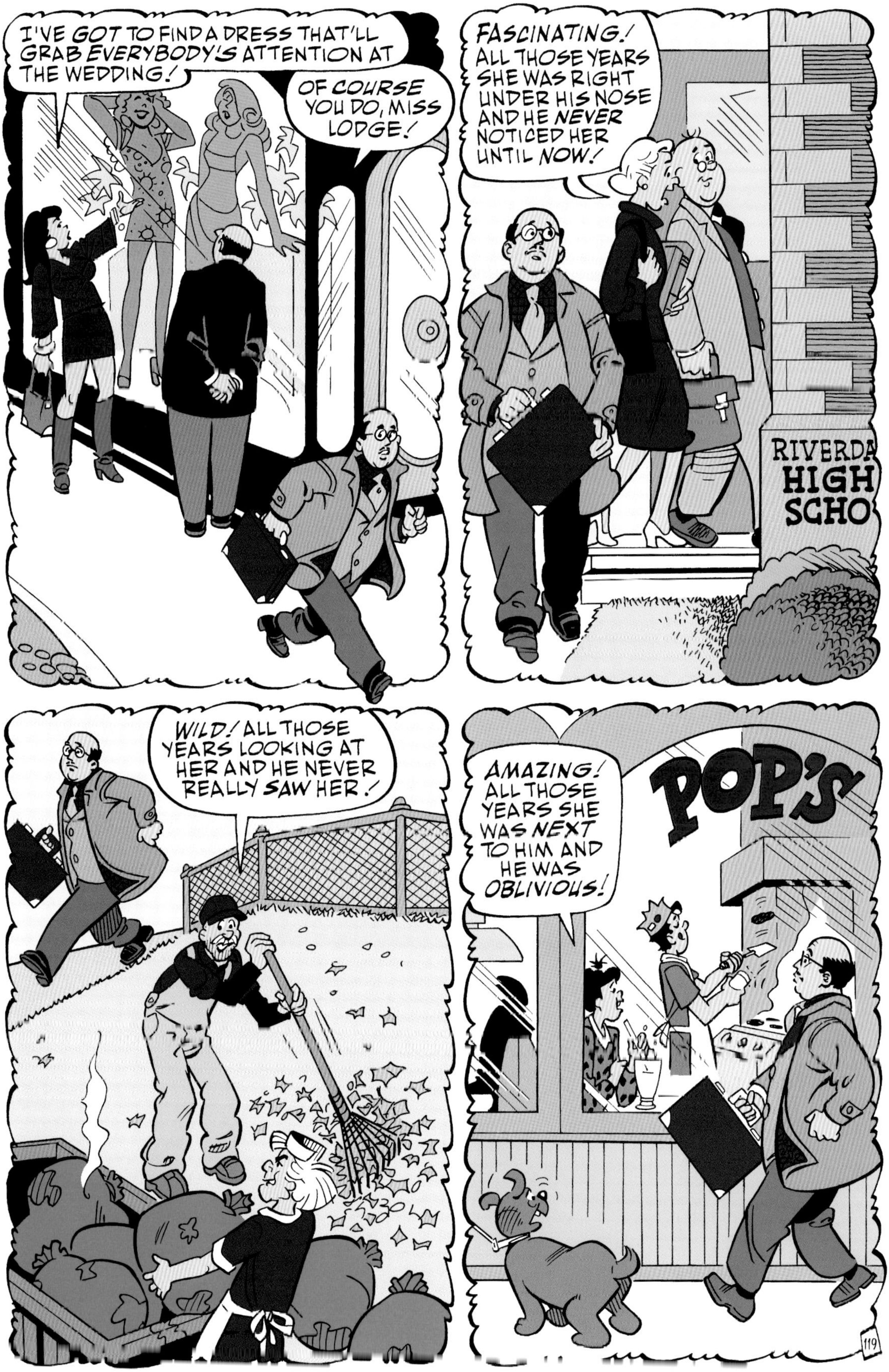
I'VE GOT TO FIND A DRESS THAT'LL GRAB EVERYBODY'S ATTENTION AT THE WEDDING!
OF COURSE YOU DO, MISS LODGE!
FASCINATING! ALL THOSE YEARS SHE WAS RIGHT UNDER HIS NOSE AND HE NEVER NOTICED HER UNTIL NOW!
RIVERDA
HIGH
SCHO
WILD! ALL THOSE YEARS LOOKING AT HER AND HE NEVER REALLY SAW HER!
POP'S
AMAZING! ALL THOSE YEARS SHE WAS NEXT TO HIM AND HE WAS OBLIVIOUS!

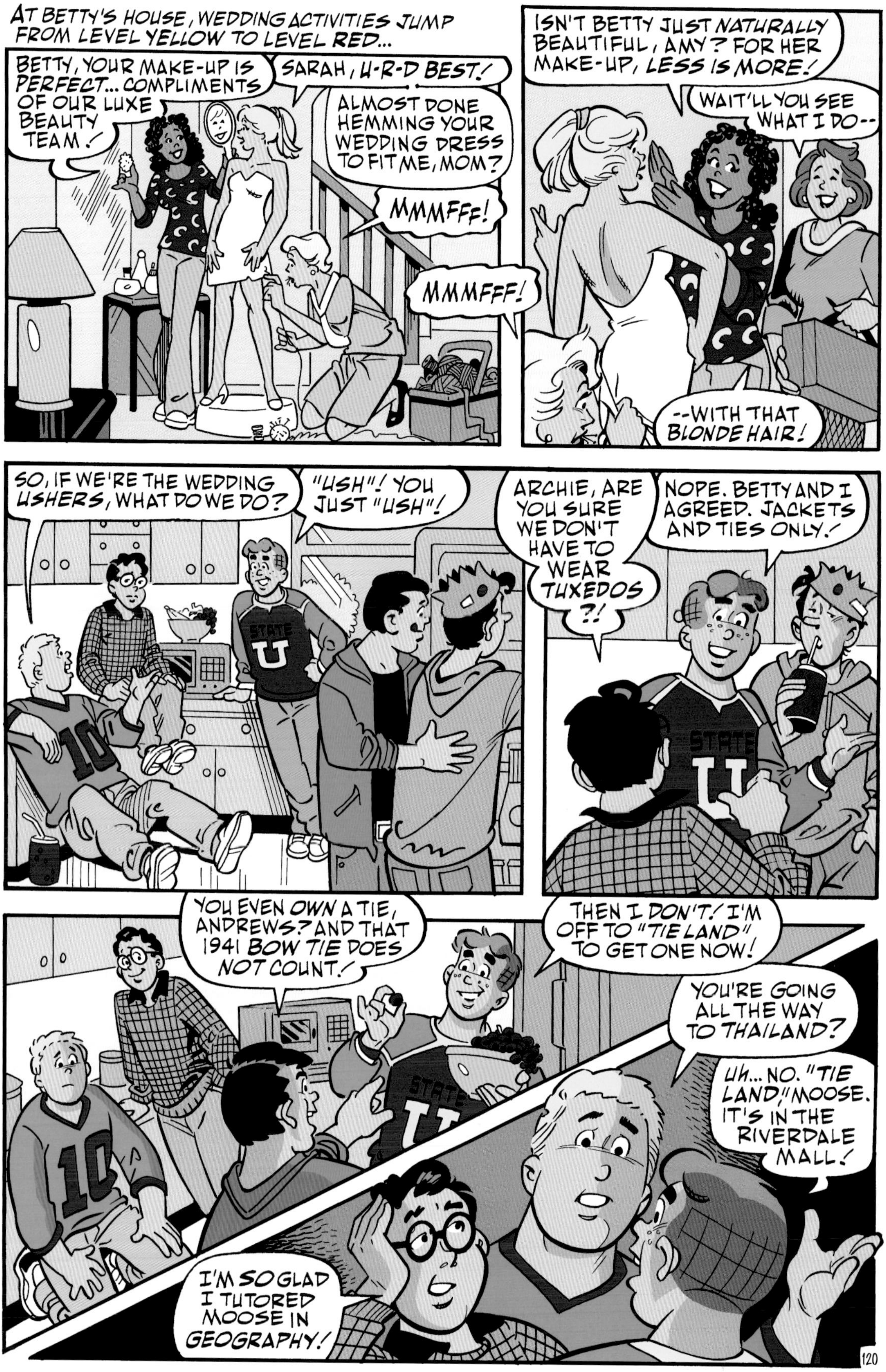
AT BETTY'S HOUSE, WEDDING ACTIVITIES JUMP FROM LEVEL YELLOW TO LEVEL RED...
BETTY, YOUR MAKE-UP IS PERFECT... COMPLIMENTS OF OUR LUXE BEAUTY TEAM!
SARAH, U-R-D BEST!
ALMOST DONE HEMMING YOUR WEDDING DRESS TO FIT ME, MOM?
MMMFFF!
MMMFFF!
ISN'T BETTY JUST NATURALLY BEAUTIFUL, AMY? FOR HER MAKE-UP, LESS IS MORE!
WAIT'LL YOU SEE WHAT I DO--
--WITH THAT BLONDE HAIR!
SO, IF WE'RE THE WEDDING USHERS, WHAT DO WE DO?
"USH"! YOU JUST "USH"!
ARCHIE, ARE YOU SURE WE DON'T HAVE TO WEAR TUXEDOS?!
NOPE. BETTY AND I AGREED. JACKETS AND TIES ONLY!
YOU EVEN OWN A TIE, ANDREWS? AND THAT 1941 BOW TIE DOES NOT COUNT!
THEN I DON'T! I'M OFF TO "TIE LAND" TO GET ONE NOW!
YOU'RE GOING ALL THE WAY TO THAILAND?
UH... NO. "TIE LAND," MOOSE. IT'S IN THE RIVERDALE MALL!
I'M SO GLAD I TUTORED MOOSE IN GEOGRAPHY!

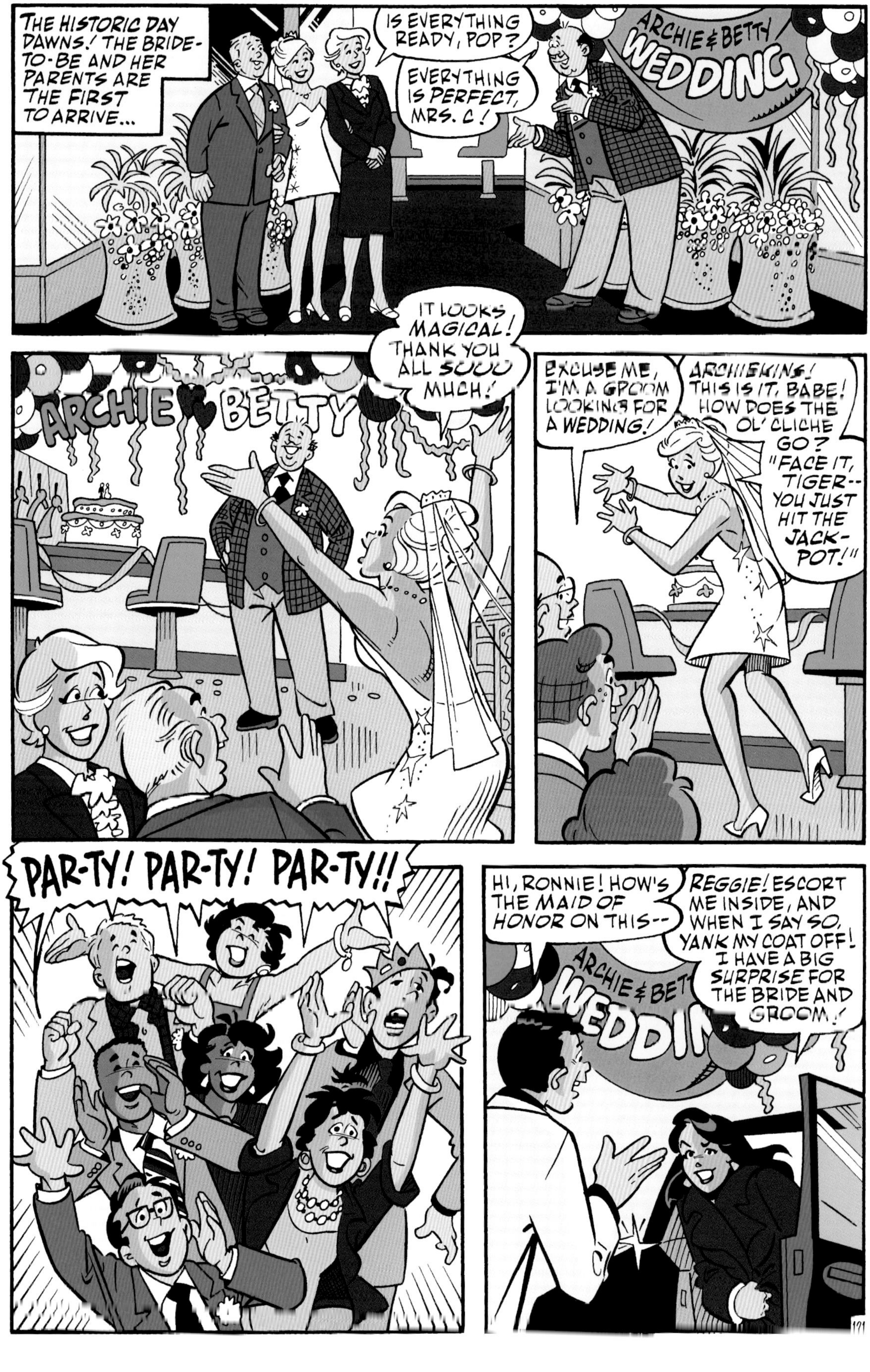
THE HISTORIC DAY DAWNS! THE BRIDE-TO-BE AND HER PARENTS ARE THE FIRST TO ARRIVE...
IS EVERYTHING READY, POP?
EVERYTHING IS PERFECT, MRS. C!
ARCHIE & BETTY WEDDING
IT LOOKS MAGICAL! THANK YOU ALL SOOO MUCH!
ARCHIE BETTY
EXCUSE ME, I'M A GROOM LOOKING FOR A WEDDING!
ARCHIEKINS! THIS IS IT, BABE! HOW DOES THE OL' CLICHE GO? "FACE IT, TIGER--YOU JUST HIT THE JACK-POT!"
PAR-TY! PAR-TY! PAR-TY!!
HI, RONNIE! HOW'S THE MAID OF HONOR ON THIS--
REGGIE! ESCORT ME INSIDE, AND WHEN I SAY SO, YANK MY COAT OFF! I HAVE A BIG SURPRISE FOR THE BRIDE AND GROOM!
ARCHIE & BET- WEDDIN
121

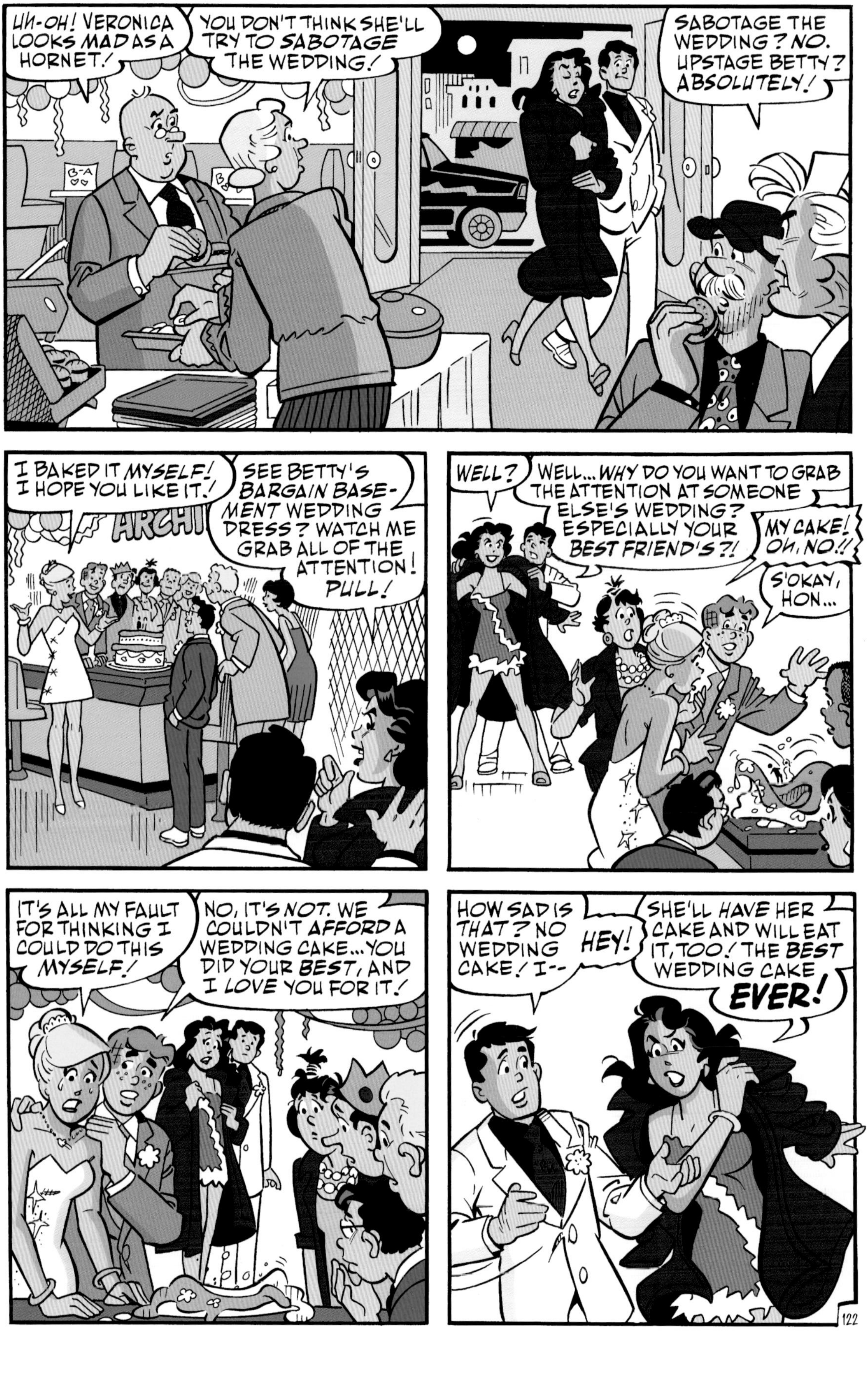
UH-OH! VERONICA LOOKS MAD AS A HORNET!
YOU DON'T THINK SHE'LL TRY TO SABOTAGE THE WEDDING!
SABOTAGE THE WEDDING? NO. UPSTAGE BETTY? ABSOLUTELY!
I BAKED IT MYSELF! I HOPE YOU LIKE IT!
SEE BETTY'S BARGAIN BASEMENT WEDDING DRESS? WATCH ME GRAB ALL OF THE ATTENTION! PULL!
ARCHI
WELL?
WELL... WHY DO YOU WANT TO GRAB THE ATTENTION AT SOMEONE ELSE'S WEDDING? ESPECIALLY YOUR BEST FRIEND'S?!
MY CAKE! OH, NO!!
S'OKAY, HON...
IT'S ALL MY FAULT FOR THINKING I COULD DO THIS MYSELF!
NO, IT'S NOT. WE COULDN'T AFFORD A WEDDING CAKE... YOU DID YOUR BEST, AND I LOVE YOU FOR IT!
HOW SAD IS THAT? NO WEDDING CAKE! I--
HEY!
SHE'LL HAVE HER CAKE AND WILL EAT IT, TOO! THE BEST WEDDING CAKE EVER!

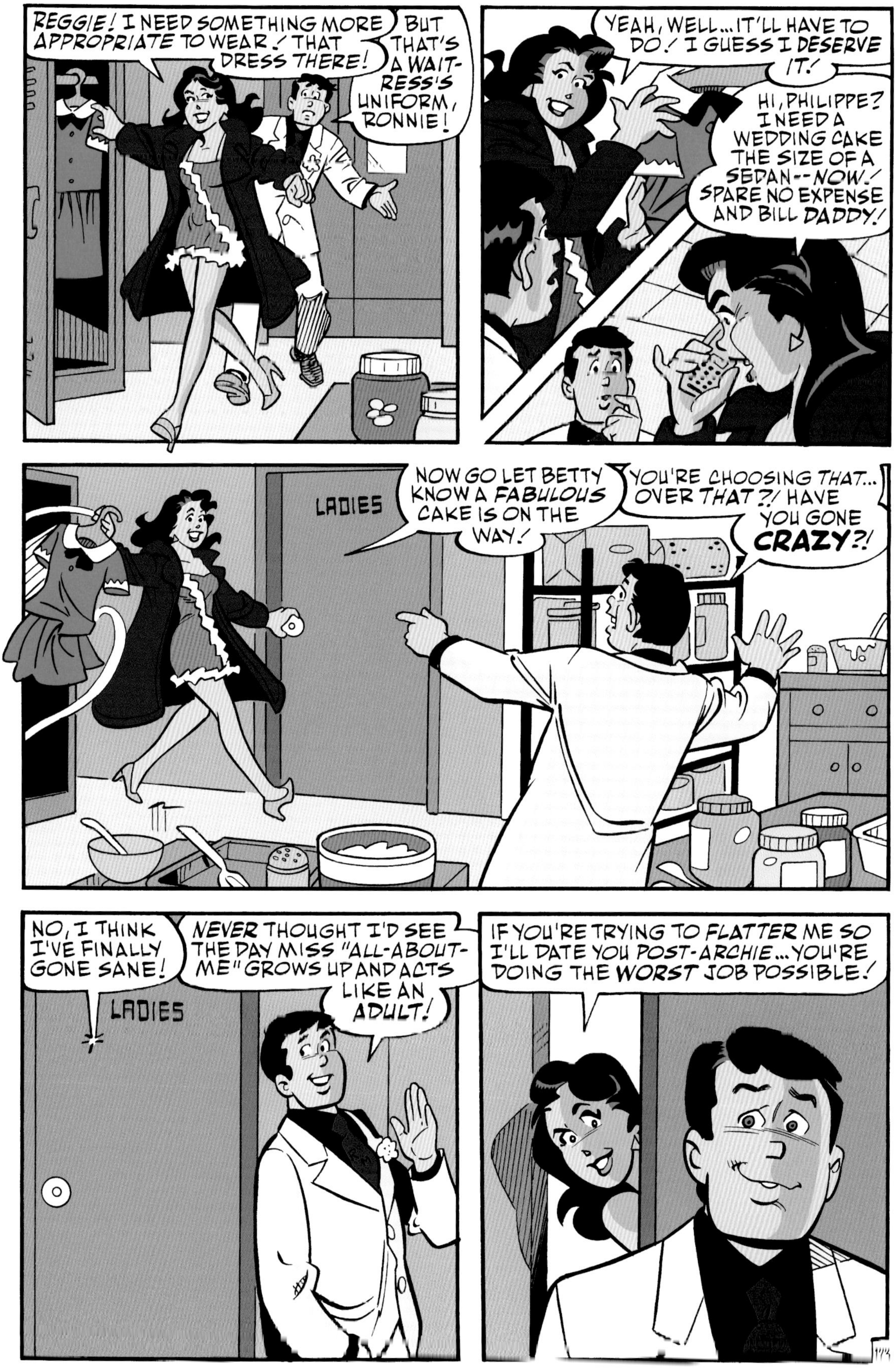
REGGIE! I NEED SOMETHING MORE APPROPRIATE TO WEAR! THAT DRESS THERE!
BUT THAT'S A WAITRESS'S UNIFORM, RONNIE!
YEAH, WELL...IT'LL HAVE TO DO! I GUESS I DESERVE IT!
HI, PHILIPPE? I NEED A WEDDING CAKE THE SIZE OF A SEDAN--NOW! SPARE NO EXPENSE AND BILL DADDY!
LADIES
NOW GO LET BETTY KNOW A FABULOUS CAKE IS ON THE WAY!
YOU'RE CHOOSING THAT... OVER THAT?! HAVE YOU GONE CRAZY?!
LADIES
NO, I THINK I'VE FINALLY GONE SANE!
NEVER THOUGHT I'D SEE THE DAY MISS "ALL-ABOUT-ME" GROWS UP AND ACTS LIKE AN ADULT!
IF YOU'RE TRYING TO FLATTER ME SO I'LL DATE YOU POST-ARCHIE...YOU'RE DOING THE WORST JOB POSSIBLE!

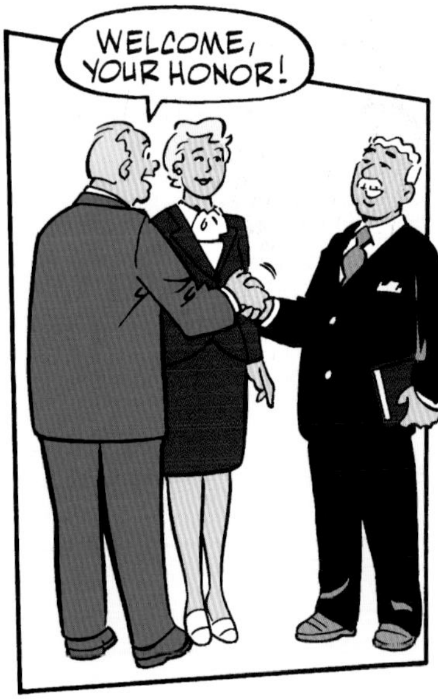
WELCOME, YOUR HONOR!

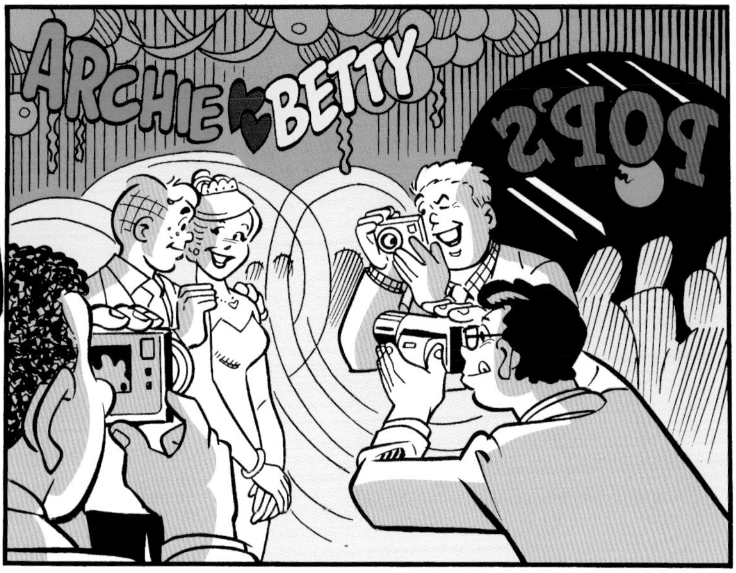
ARCHIE ♥ BETTY
POP'S

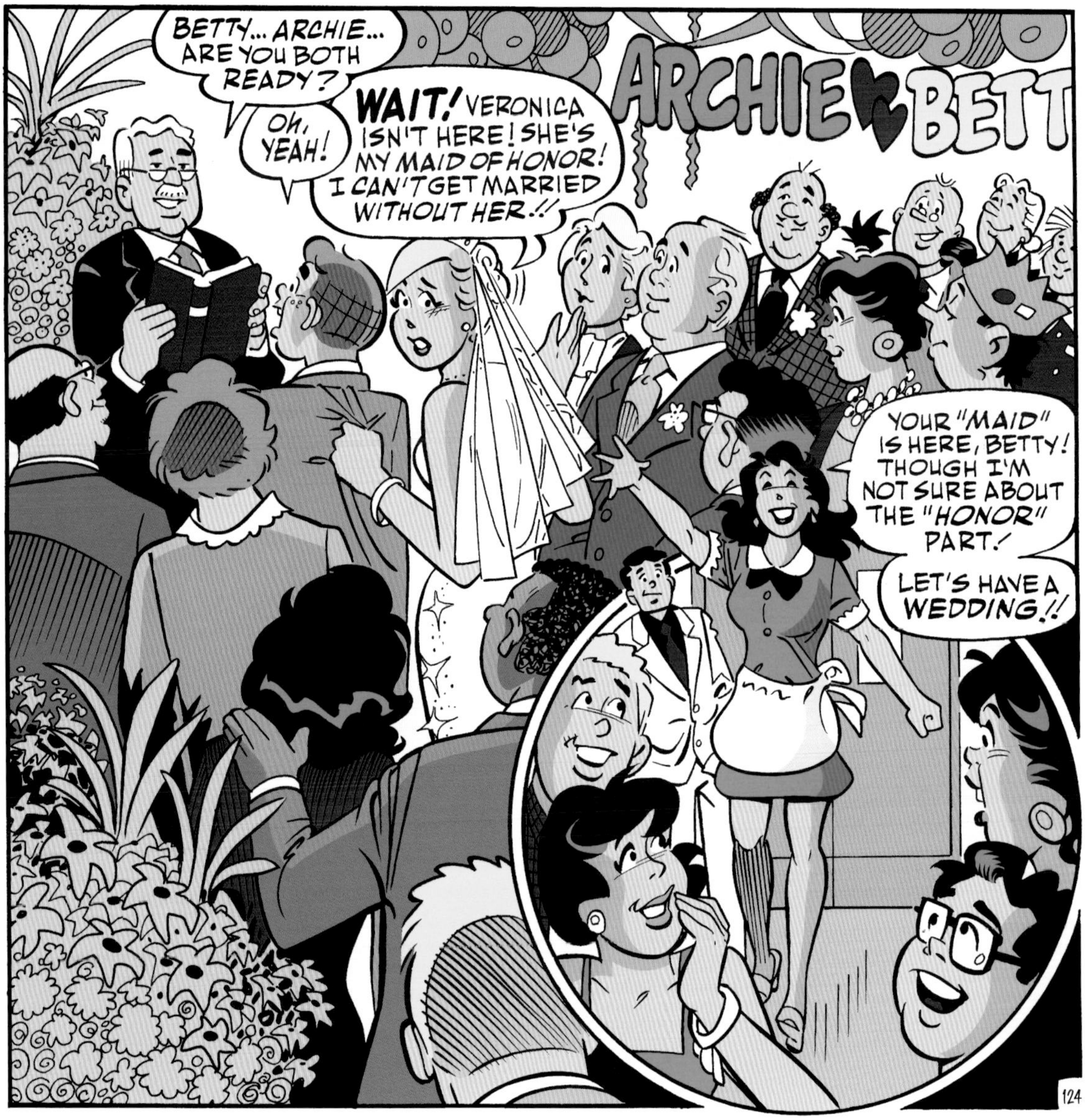
ARCHIE ♥ BETT
BETTY... ARCHIE... ARE YOU BOTH READY?
OH, YEAH!
WAIT! VERONICA ISN'T HERE! SHE'S MY MAID OF HONOR! I CAN'T GET MARRIED WITHOUT HER!!
YOUR "MAID" IS HERE, BETTY! THOUGH I'M NOT SURE ABOUT THE "HONOR" PART!
LET'S HAVE A WEDDING!!

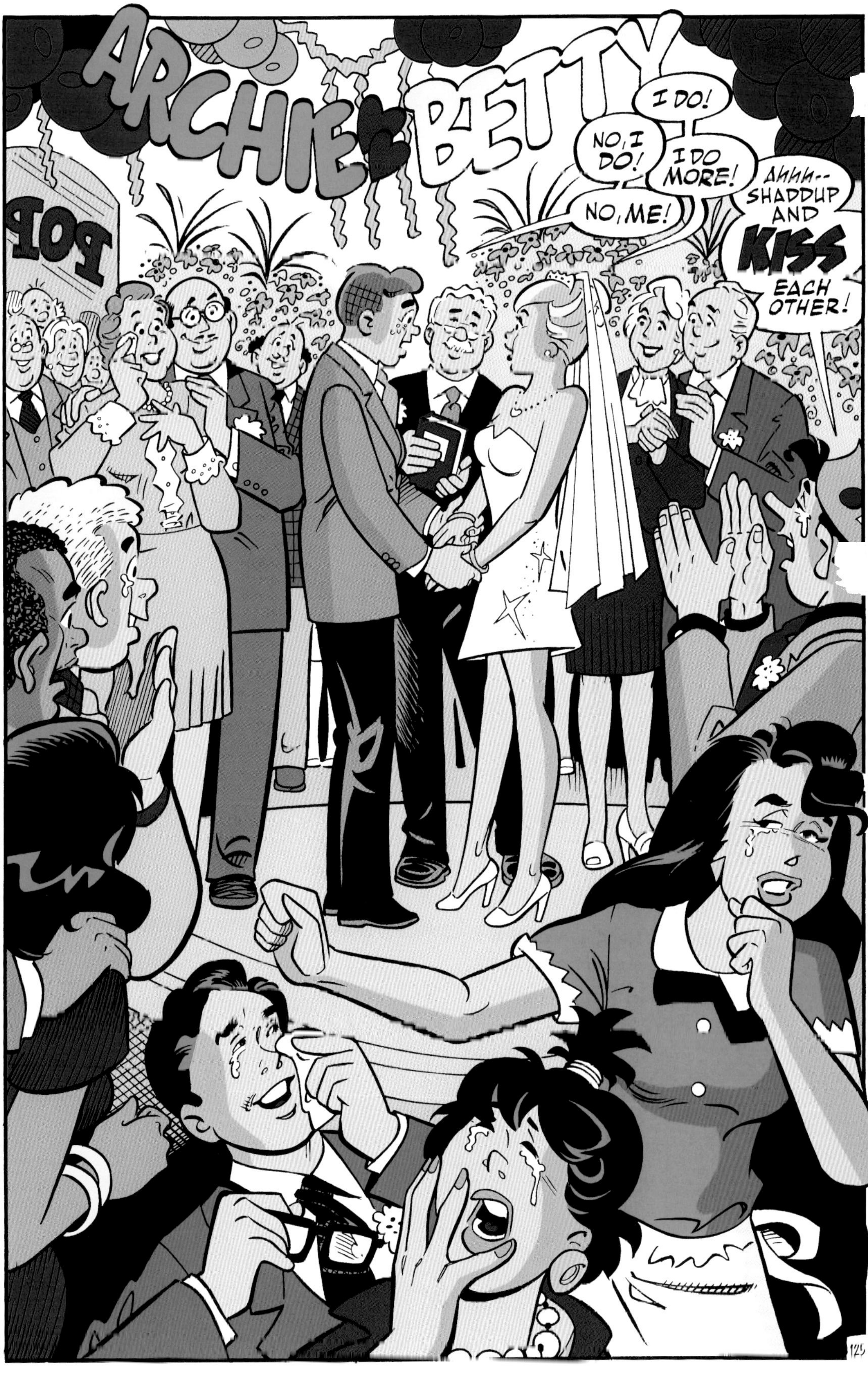
ARCHIE ♥ BETTY
POP
I DO!
NO, I DO!
I DO MORE!
NO, ME!
AHHH-- SHADDUP AND KISS EACH OTHER!

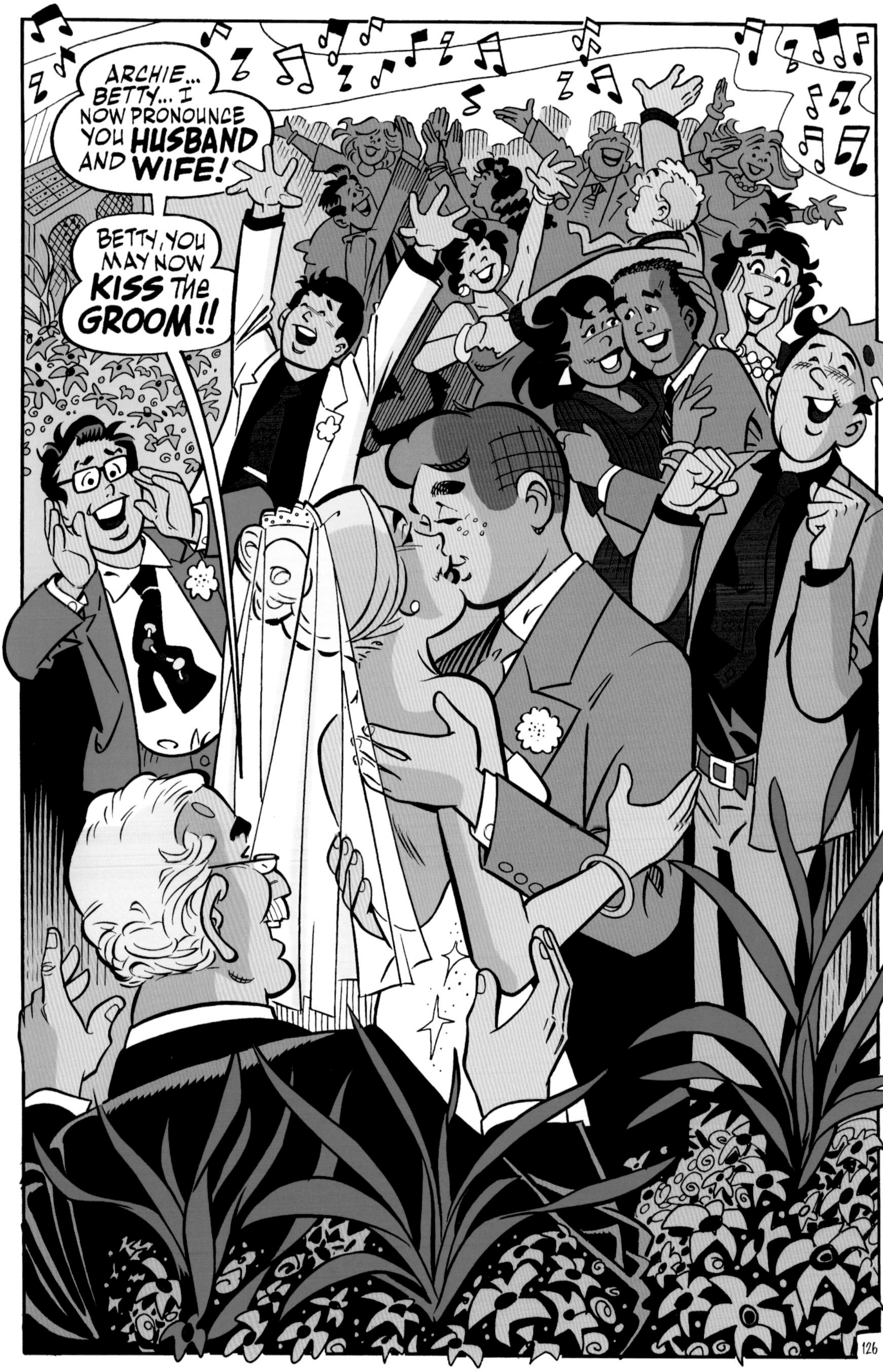
ARCHIE... BETTY... I NOW PRONOUNCE YOU HUSBAND AND WIFE!
BETTY, YOU MAY NOW KISS THE GROOM!!

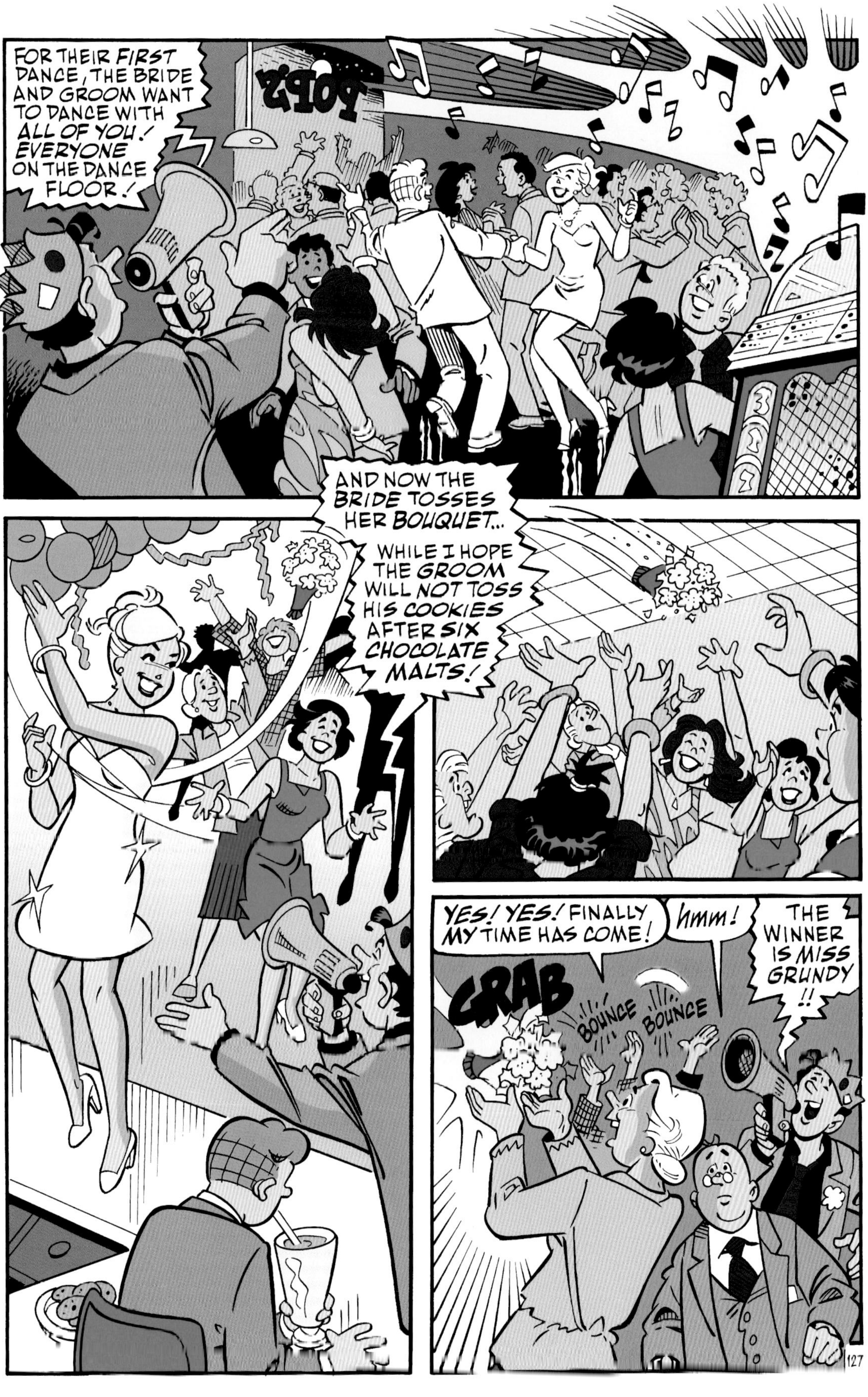
FOR THEIR FIRST DANCE, THE BRIDE AND GROOM WANT TO DANCE WITH ALL OF YOU! EVERYONE ON THE DANCE FLOOR!
POP'S
AND NOW THE BRIDE TOSSES HER BOUQUET...
WHILE I HOPE THE GROOM WILL NOT TOSS HIS COOKIES AFTER SIX CHOCOLATE MALTS!
YES! YES! FINALLY MY TIME HAS COME!
hmm!
THE WINNER IS MISS GRUNDY !!
GRAB
BOUNCE
BOUNCE

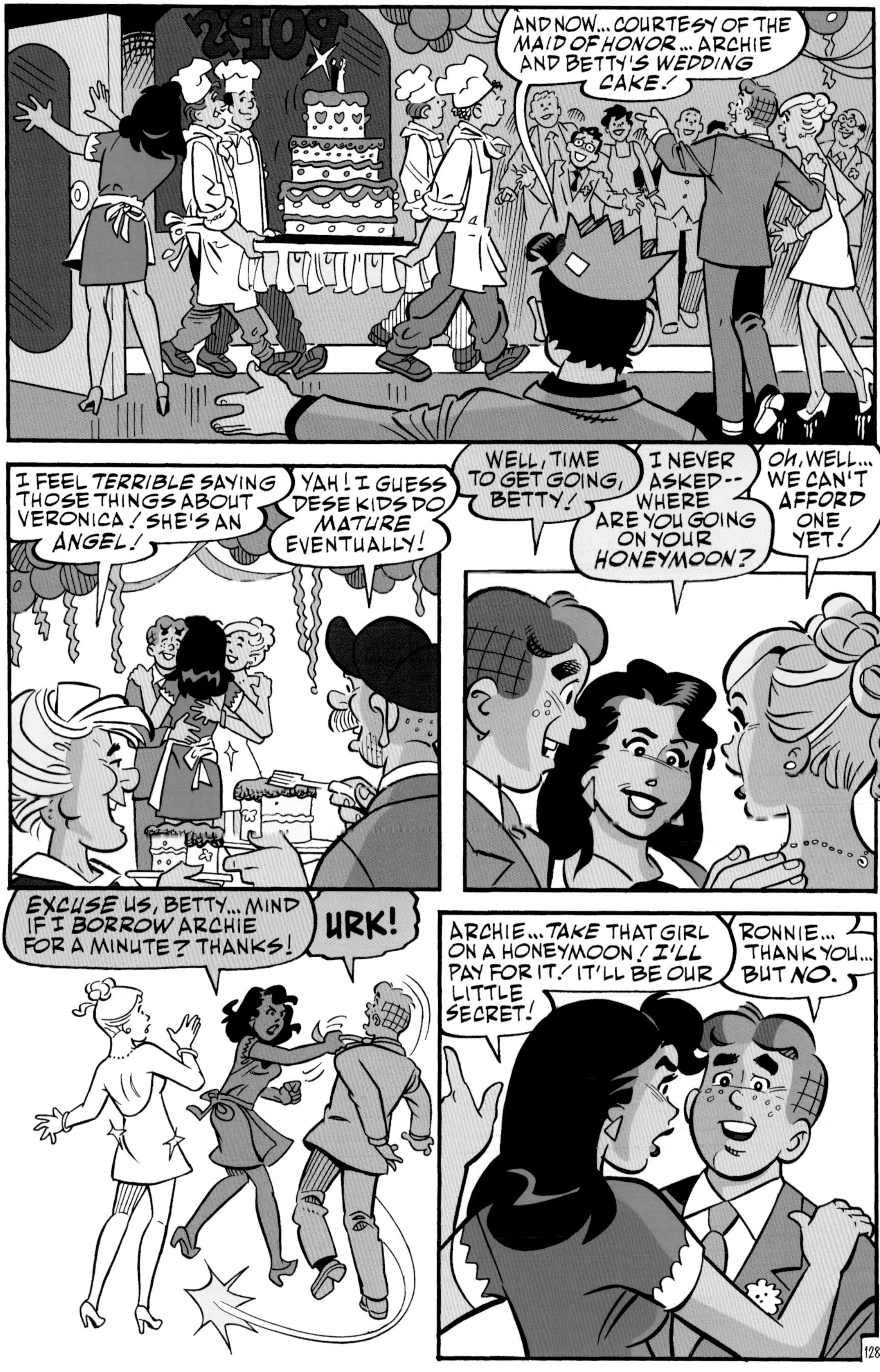
POP'S
AND NOW... COURTESY OF THE MAID OF HONOR... ARCHIE AND BETTY'S WEDDING CAKE!
I FEEL TERRIBLE SAYING THOSE THINGS ABOUT VERONICA! SHE'S AN ANGEL!
YAH! I GUESS DESE KIDS DO MATURE EVENTUALLY!
WELL, TIME TO GET GOING, BETTY!
I NEVER ASKED-- WHERE ARE YOU GOING ON YOUR HONEYMOON?
OH, WELL... WE CAN'T AFFORD ONE YET!
EXCUSE US, BETTY... MIND IF I BORROW ARCHIE FOR A MINUTE? THANKS!
URK!
ARCHIE... TAKE THAT GIRL ON A HONEYMOON! I'LL PAY FOR IT! IT'LL BE OUR LITTLE SECRET!
RONNIE... THANK YOU... BUT NO.

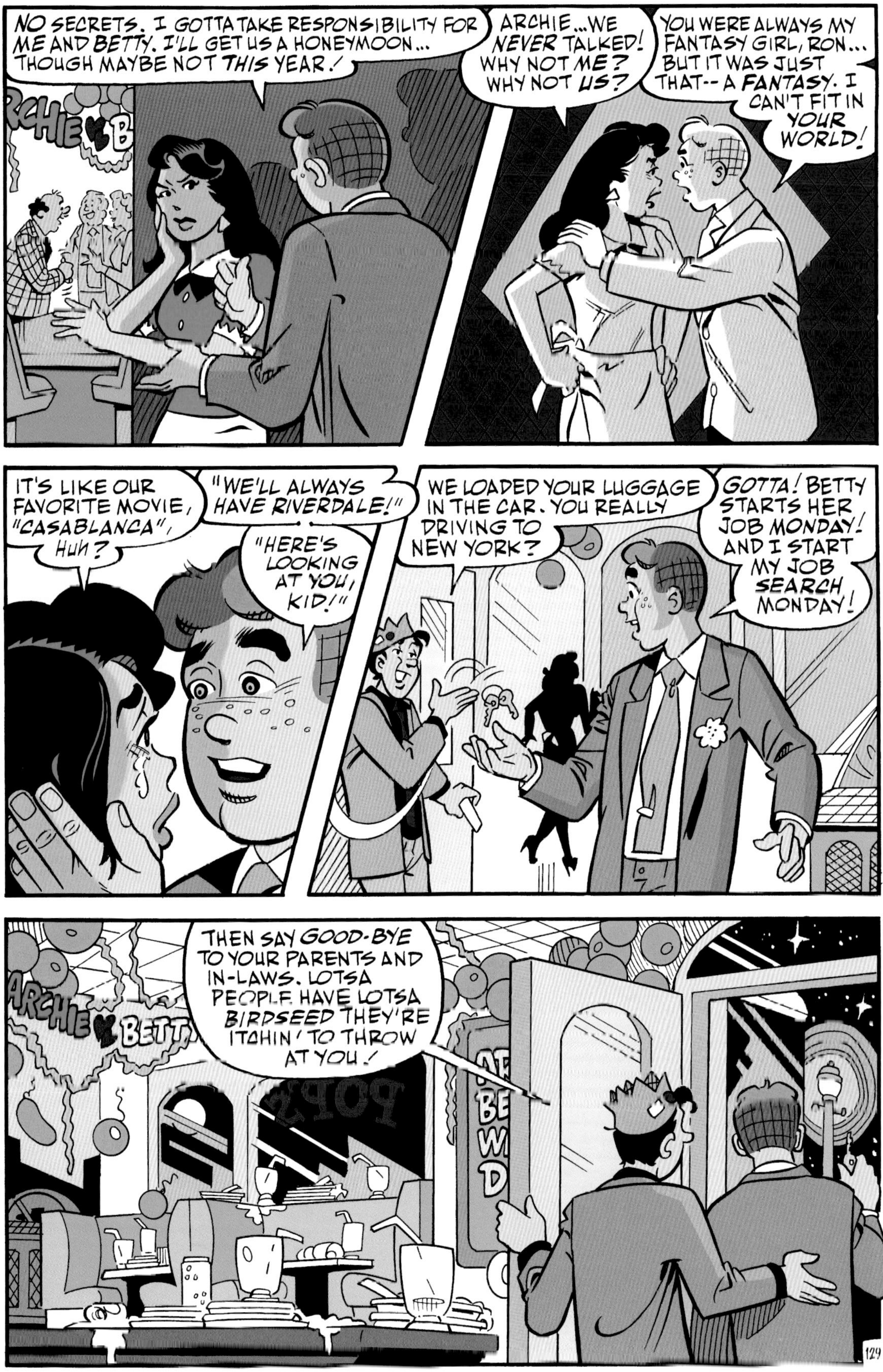
NO SECRETS. I GOTTA TAKE RESPONSIBILITY FOR ME AND BETTY. I'LL GET US A HONEYMOON... THOUGH MAYBE NOT THIS YEAR!
ARCHIE...WE NEVER TALKED! WHY NOT ME? WHY NOT US?
YOU WERE ALWAYS MY FANTASY GIRL, RON... BUT IT WAS JUST THAT-- A FANTASY. I CAN'T FIT IN YOUR WORLD!
IT'S LIKE OUR FAVORITE MOVIE, "CASABLANCA", HUH?
"WE'LL ALWAYS HAVE RIVERDALE!"
"HERE'S LOOKING AT YOU, KID!"
WE LOADED YOUR LUGGAGE IN THE CAR. YOU REALLY DRIVING TO NEW YORK?
GOTTA! BETTY STARTS HER JOB MONDAY! AND I START MY JOB SEARCH MONDAY!
THEN SAY GOOD-BYE TO YOUR PARENTS AND IN-LAWS. LOTSA PEOPLE HAVE LOTSA BIRDSEED THEY'RE ITCHIN' TO THROW AT YOU!

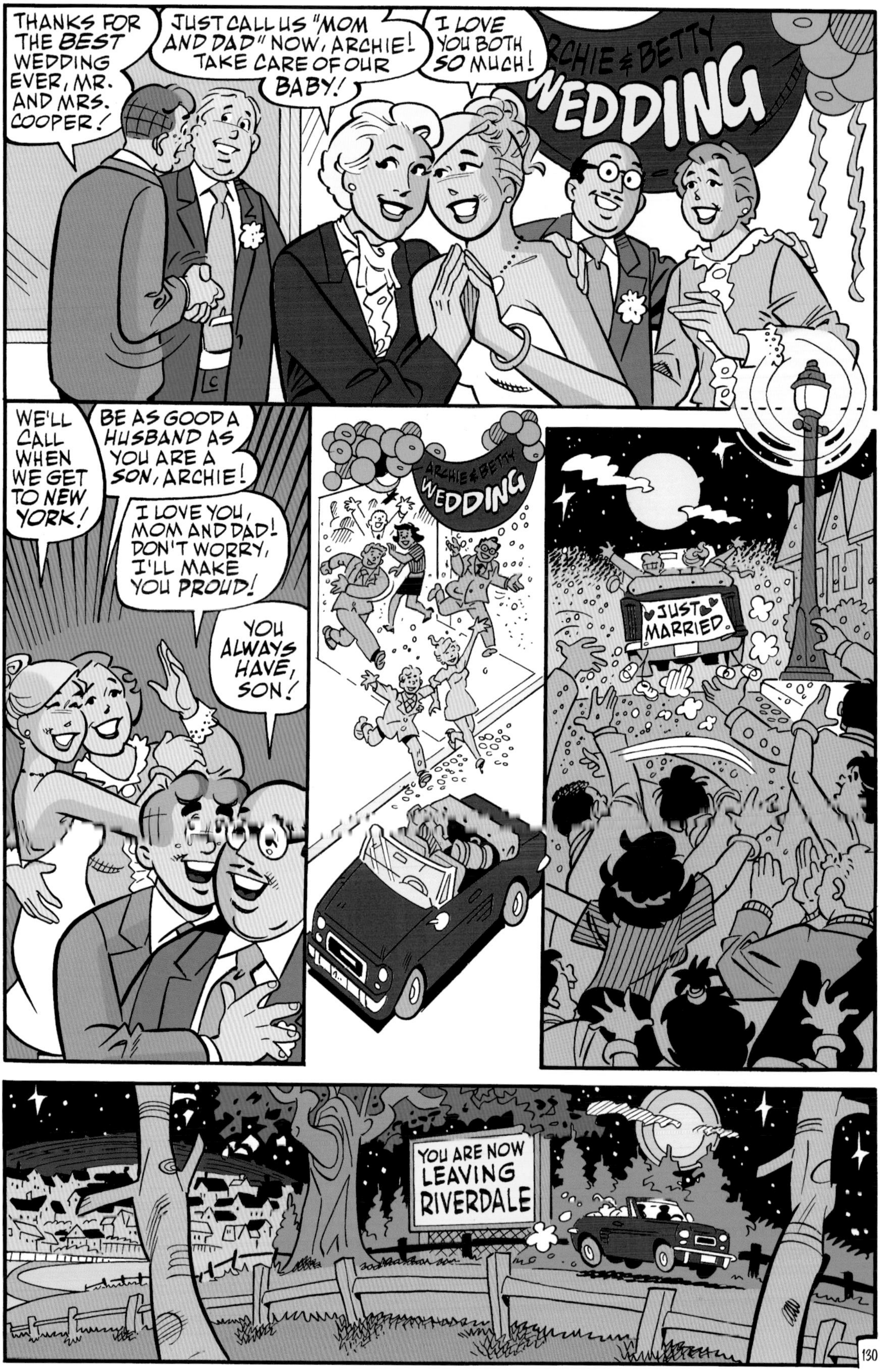

THANKS FOR THE BEST WEDDING EVER, MR. AND MRS. COOPER!
JUST CALL US "MOM AND DAD" NOW, ARCHIE! TAKE CARE OF OUR BABY!
I LOVE YOU BOTH SO MUCH!
ARCHIE & BETTY WEDDING
WE'LL CALL WHEN WE GET TO NEW YORK!
BE AS GOOD A HUSBAND AS YOU ARE A SON, ARCHIE!
I LOVE YOU, MOM AND DAD! DON'T WORRY, I'LL MAKE YOU PROUD!
YOU ALWAYS HAVE, SON!
ARCHIE & BETTY WEDDING
JUST MARRIED
YOU ARE NOW LEAVING RIVERDALE

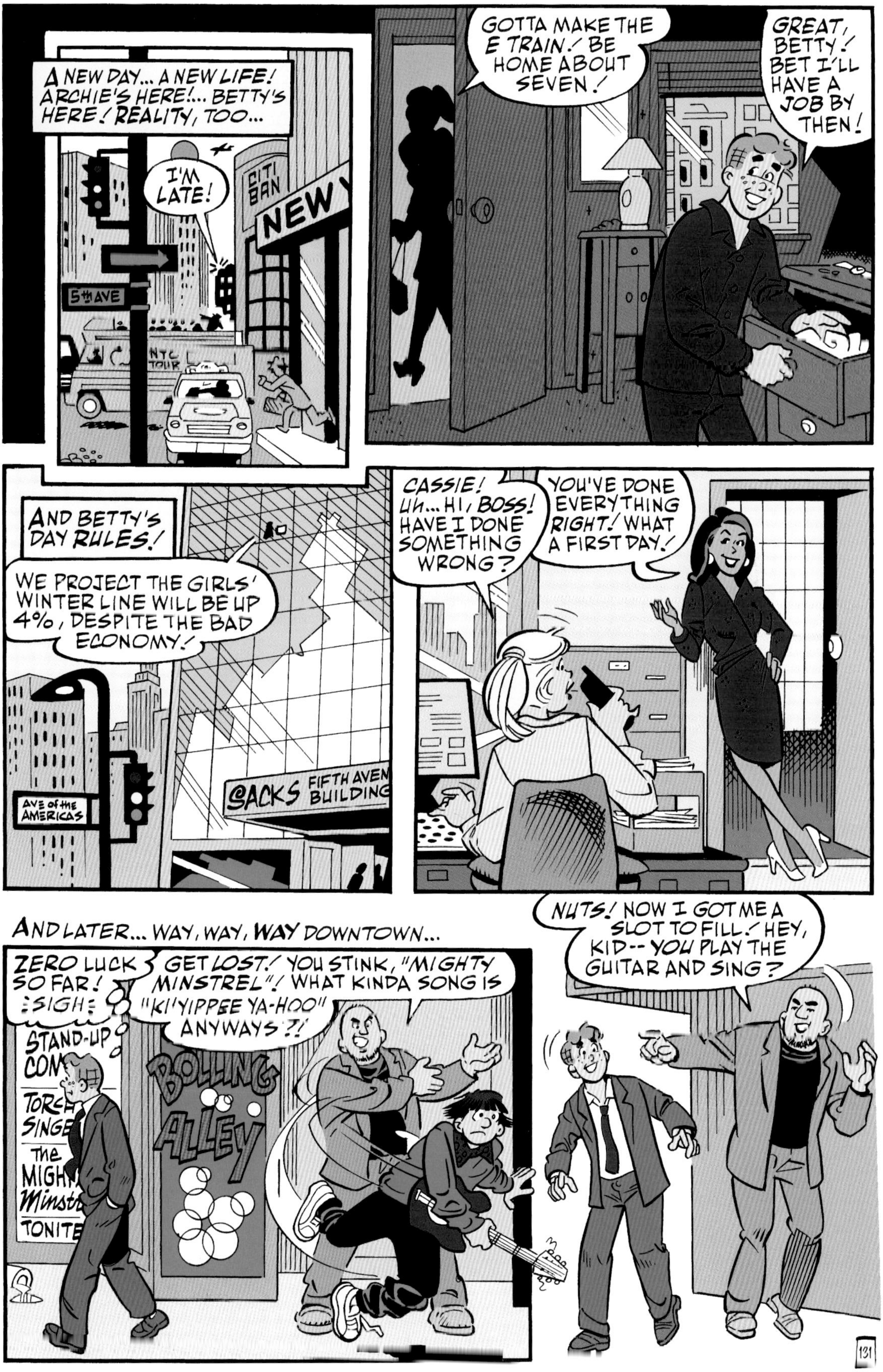

A NEW DAY... A NEW LIFE! ARCHIE'S HERE!... BETTY'S HERE! REALITY, TOO...
I'M LATE!
CITI BAN
NEW Y
5th AVE
NYC TOUR
GOTTA MAKE THE E TRAIN! BE HOME ABOUT SEVEN!
GREAT, BETTY! BET I'LL HAVE A JOB BY THEN!
AND BETTY'S DAY RULES!
WE PROJECT THE GIRLS' WINTER LINE WILL BE UP 4%, DESPITE THE BAD ECONOMY!
AVE of the AMERICAS
SACKS FIFTH AVEN BUILDING
CASSIE! UH...HI, BOSS! HAVE I DONE SOMETHING WRONG?
YOU'VE DONE EVERYTHING RIGHT! WHAT A FIRST DAY!
AND LATER... WAY, WAY, WAY DOWNTOWN...
ZERO LUCK SO FAR! SIGH
GET LOST! YOU STINK, "MIGHTY MINSTREL"! WHAT KINDA SONG IS "KI'YIPPEE YA-HOO" ANYWAYS?!
STAND-UP COM
TORCH SINGE
The MIGH Minstr
TONITE
BOWLING ALLEY
NUTS! NOW I GOT ME A SLOT TO FILL! HEY, KID-- YOU PLAY THE GUITAR AND SING?

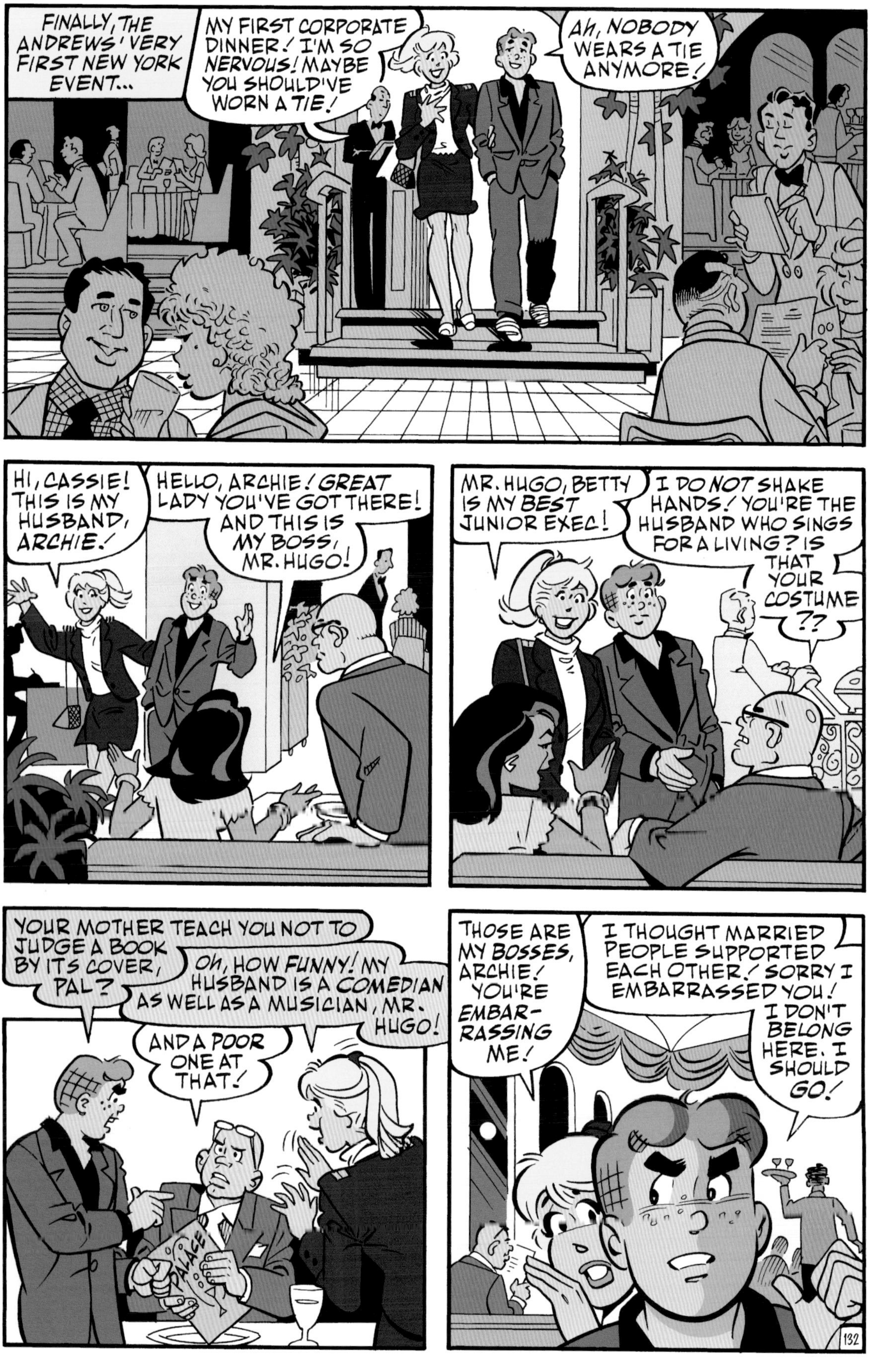
FINALLY, THE ANDREWS' VERY FIRST NEW YORK EVENT...
MY FIRST CORPORATE DINNER! I'M SO NERVOUS! MAYBE YOU SHOULD'VE WORN A TIE!
Ah, NOBODY WEARS A TIE ANYMORE!
HI, CASSIE! THIS IS MY HUSBAND, ARCHIE!
HELLO, ARCHIE! GREAT LADY YOU'VE GOT THERE! AND THIS IS MY BOSS, MR. HUGO!
MR. HUGO, BETTY IS MY BEST JUNIOR EXEC!
I DO NOT SHAKE HANDS! YOU'RE THE HUSBAND WHO SINGS FOR A LIVING? IS THAT YOUR COSTUME??
YOUR MOTHER TEACH YOU NOT TO JUDGE A BOOK BY ITS COVER, PAL?
Oh, HOW FUNNY! MY HUSBAND IS A COMEDIAN AS WELL AS A MUSICIAN, MR. HUGO!
AND A POOR ONE AT THAT!
PALACE
THOSE ARE MY BOSSES, ARCHIE! YOU'RE EMBARRASSING ME!
I THOUGHT MARRIED PEOPLE SUPPORTED EACH OTHER! SORRY I EMBARRASSED YOU! I DON'T BELONG HERE. I SHOULD GO!

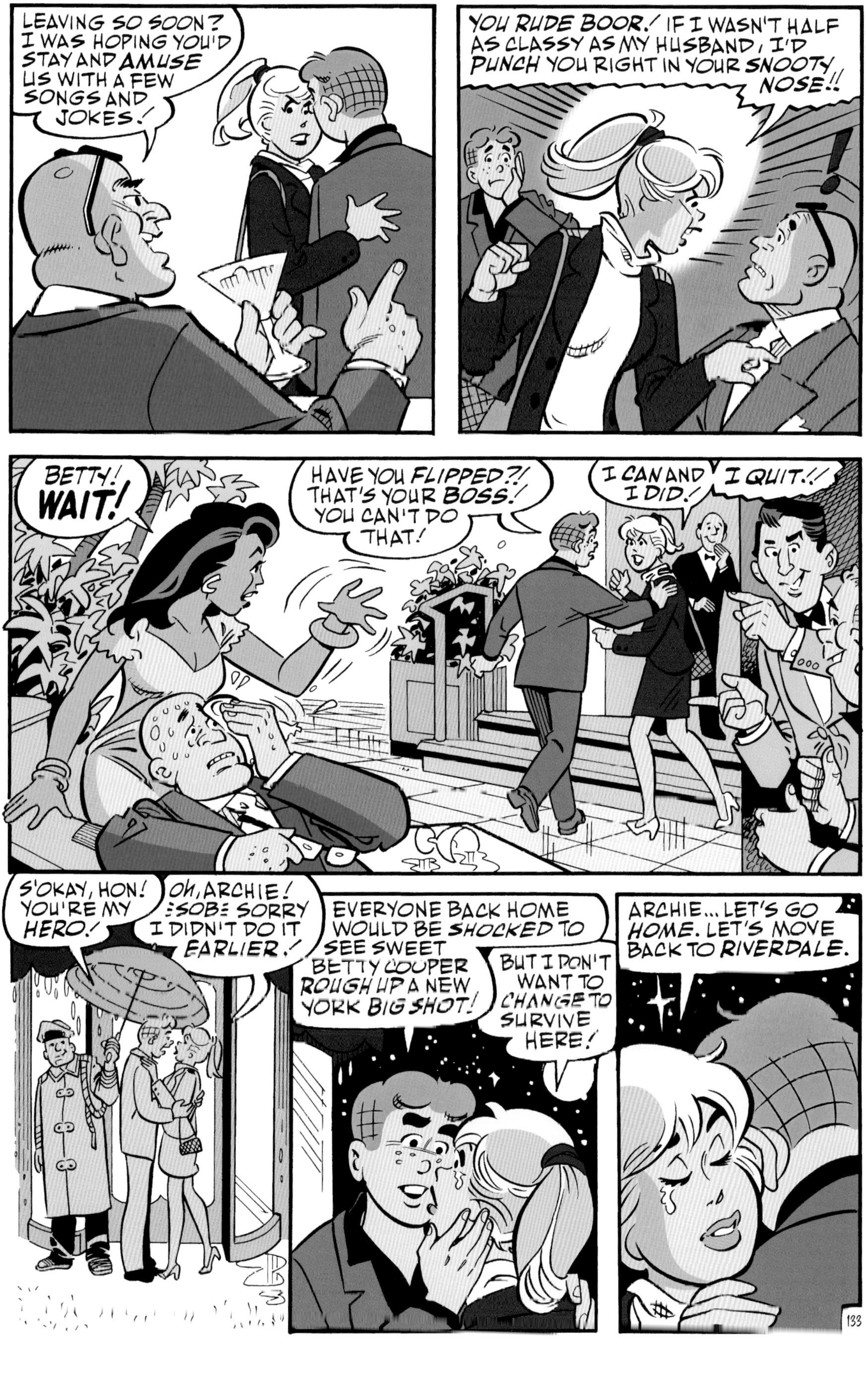
LEAVING SO SOON? I WAS HOPING YOU'D STAY AND AMUSE US WITH A FEW SONGS AND JOKES!
YOU RUDE BOOR! IF I WASN'T HALF AS CLASSY AS MY HUSBAND, I'D PUNCH YOU RIGHT IN YOUR SNOOTY NOSE!!
!
BETTY! WAIT!
HAVE YOU FLIPPED?! THAT'S YOUR BOSS! YOU CAN'T DO THAT!
I CAN AND I DID!
I QUIT!!
S'OKAY, HON! YOU'RE MY HERO!
OH, ARCHIE! SOB SORRY I DIDN'T DO IT EARLIER!
EVERYONE BACK HOME WOULD BE SHOCKED TO SEE SWEET BETTY COOPER ROUGH UP A NEW YORK BIG SHOT!
BUT I DON'T WANT TO CHANGE TO SURVIVE HERE!
ARCHIE... LET'S GO HOME. LET'S MOVE BACK TO RIVERDALE.

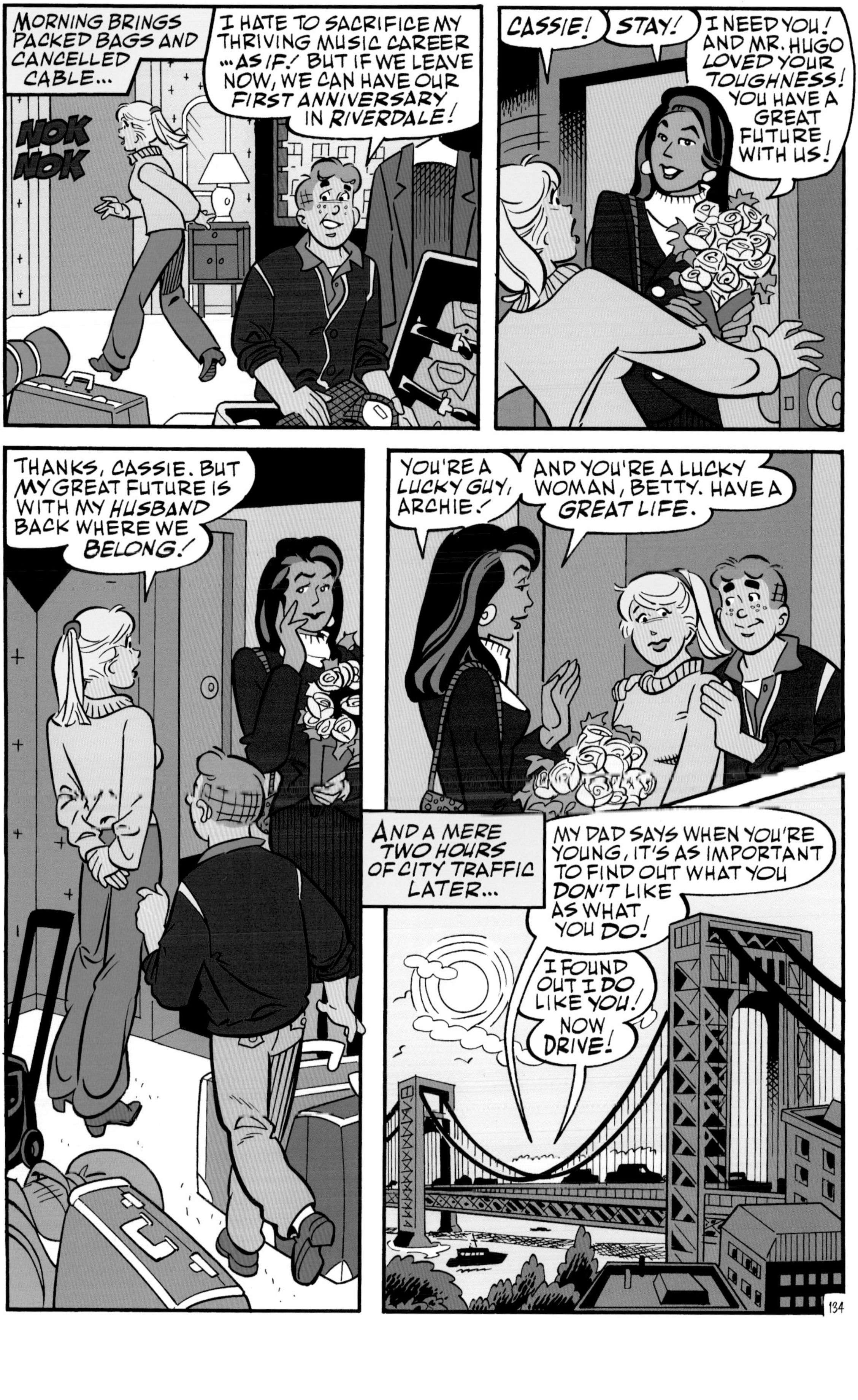
MORNING BRINGS PACKED BAGS AND CANCELLED CABLE...
NOK NOK
I HATE TO SACRIFICE MY THRIVING MUSIC CAREER ...AS IF! BUT IF WE LEAVE NOW, WE CAN HAVE OUR FIRST ANNIVERSARY IN RIVERDALE!
CASSIE!
STAY!
I NEED YOU! AND MR. HUGO LOVED YOUR TOUGHNESS! YOU HAVE A GREAT FUTURE WITH US!
THANKS, CASSIE. BUT MY GREAT FUTURE IS WITH MY HUSBAND BACK WHERE WE BELONG!
YOU'RE A LUCKY GUY, ARCHIE!
AND YOU'RE A LUCKY WOMAN, BETTY. HAVE A GREAT LIFE.
AND A MERE TWO HOURS OF CITY TRAFFIC LATER...
MY DAD SAYS WHEN YOU'RE YOUNG, IT'S AS IMPORTANT TO FIND OUT WHAT YOU DON'T LIKE AS WHAT YOU DO!
I FOUND OUT I DO LIKE YOU! NOW DRIVE!

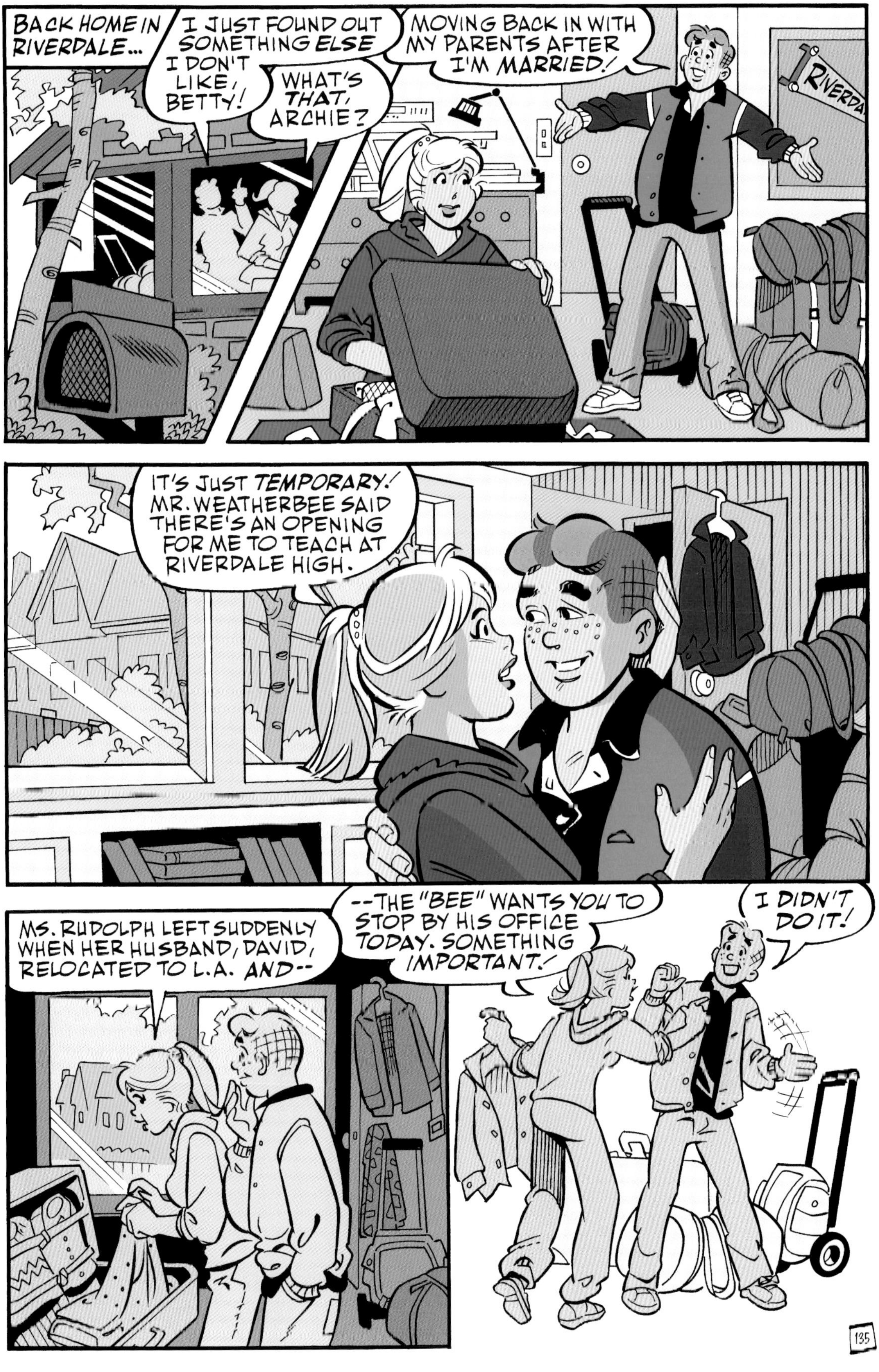
BACK HOME IN RIVERDALE...
I JUST FOUND OUT SOMETHING ELSE I DON'T LIKE, BETTY!
WHAT'S THAT, ARCHIE?
MOVING BACK IN WITH MY PARENTS AFTER I'M MARRIED!
RIVERDA
IT'S JUST TEMPORARY! MR. WEATHERBEE SAID THERE'S AN OPENING FOR ME TO TEACH AT RIVERDALE HIGH.
MS. RUDOLPH LEFT SUDDENLY WHEN HER HUSBAND, DAVID, RELOCATED TO L.A. AND--
--THE "BEE" WANTS YOU TO STOP BY HIS OFFICE TODAY. SOMETHING IMPORTANT!
I DIDN'T DO IT!

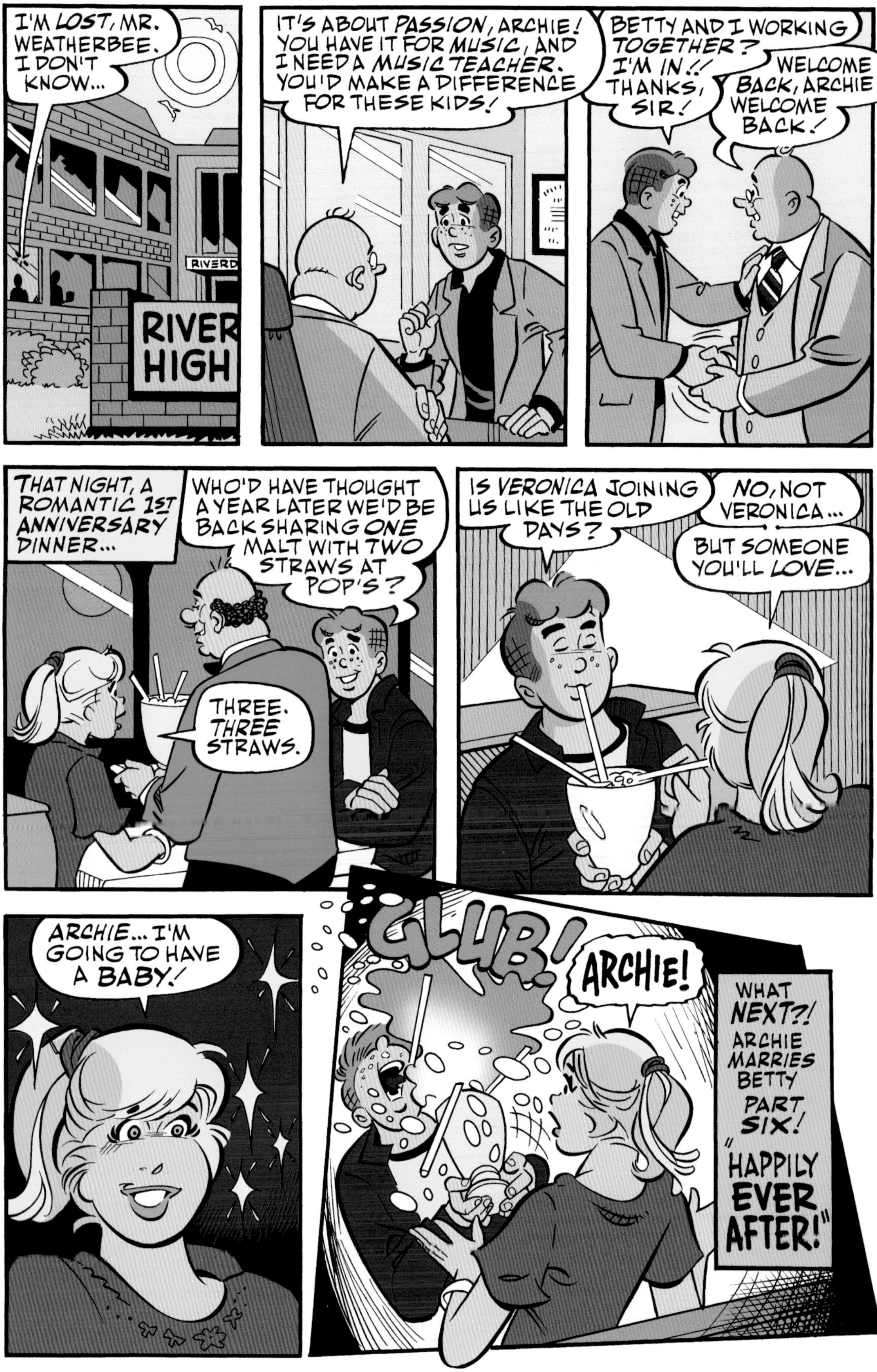
I'M LOST, MR. WEATHERBEE. I DON'T KNOW...
RIVERD
RIVER HIGH
IT'S ABOUT PASSION, ARCHIE! YOU HAVE IT FOR MUSIC, AND I NEED A MUSIC TEACHER. YOU'D MAKE A DIFFERENCE FOR THESE KIDS!
BETTY AND I WORKING TOGETHER? I'M IN!! THANKS, SIR!
WELCOME BACK, ARCHIE! WELCOME BACK!
THAT NIGHT, A ROMANTIC 1ST ANNIVERSARY DINNER...
WHO'D HAVE THOUGHT A YEAR LATER WE'D BE BACK SHARING ONE MALT WITH TWO STRAWS AT POP'S?
THREE. THREE STRAWS.
IS VERONICA JOINING US LIKE THE OLD DAYS?
NO, NOT VERONICA...
BUT SOMEONE YOU'LL LOVE...
ARCHIE... I'M GOING TO HAVE A BABY!
GLUB!
ARCHIE!
WHAT NEXT?! ARCHIE MARRIES BETTY PART SIX! "HAPPILY EVER AFTER!"

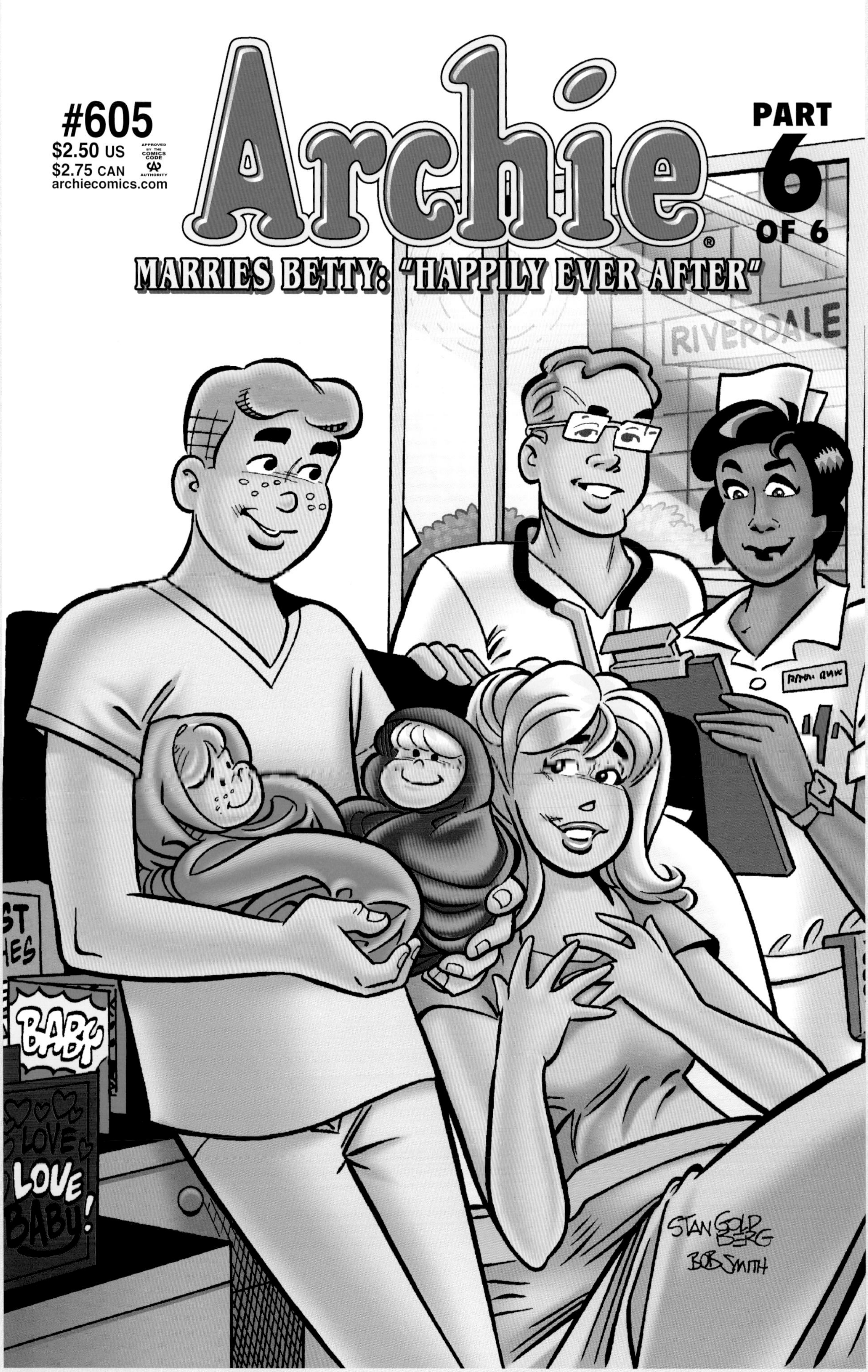
#605
$2.50 US
$2.75 CAN
archiecomics.com
APPROVED BY THE COMICS CODE AUTHORITY
Archie
PART 6 OF 6
MARRIES BETTY: "HAPPILY EVER AFTER"
RIVERDALE
BABY
LOVE
LOVE
BABY!
STAN GOLDBERG
BOB SMITH

Archie MARRIES Betty

"HAPPILY EVER AFTER" PART 6

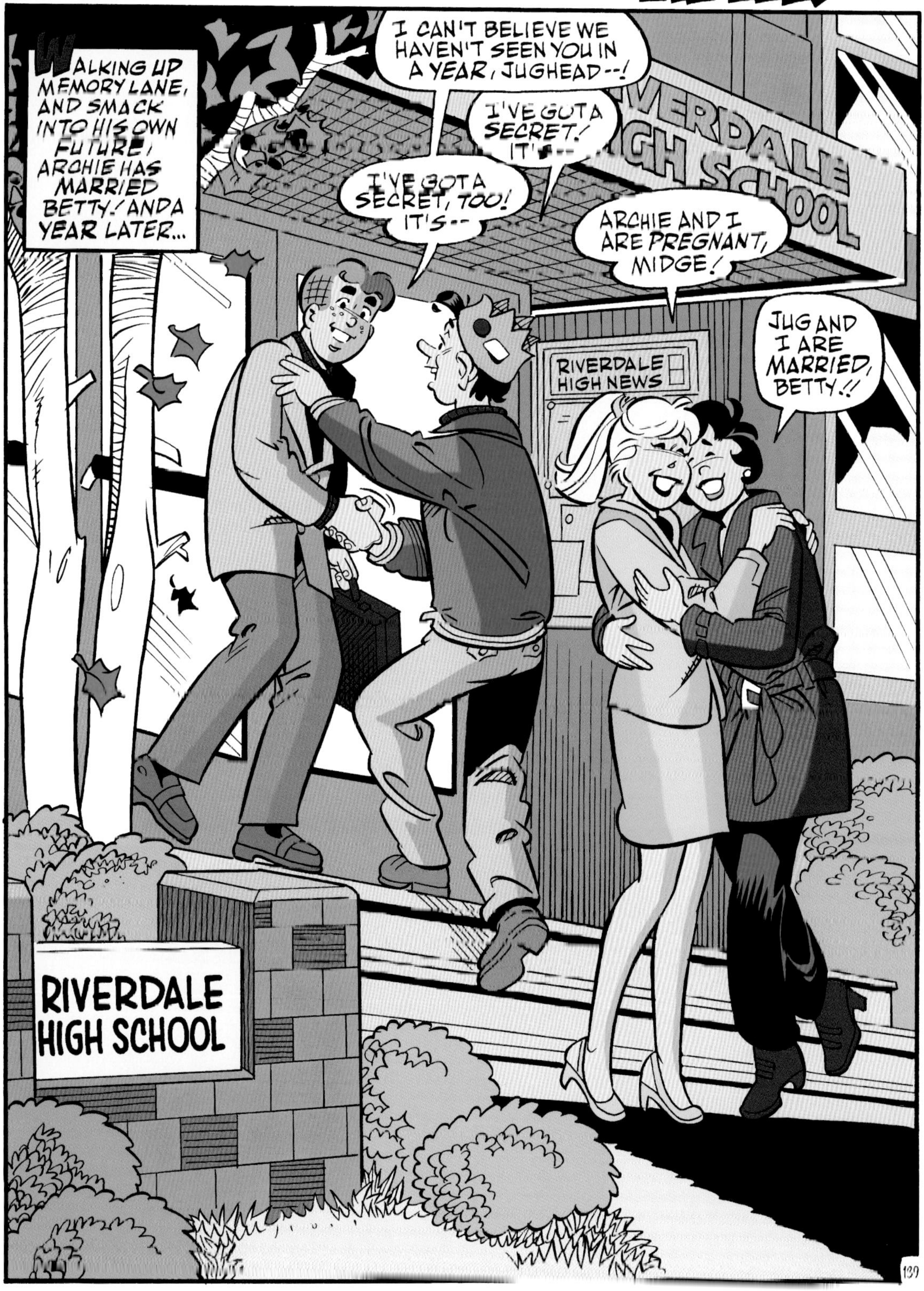
WALKING UP MEMORY LANE, AND SMACK INTO HIS OWN FUTURE, ARCHIE HAS MARRIED BETTY! AND A YEAR LATER...
I CAN'T BELIEVE WE HAVEN'T SEEN YOU IN A YEAR, JUGHEAD--!
I'VE GOT A SECRET, TOO! IT'S--
I'VE GOT A SECRET! IT'S--
ARCHIE AND I ARE PREGNANT, MIDGE!
JUG AND I ARE MARRIED, BETTY!!
RIVERDALE HIGH SCHOOL
RIVERDALE HIGH NEWS
RIVERDALE HIGH SCHOOL

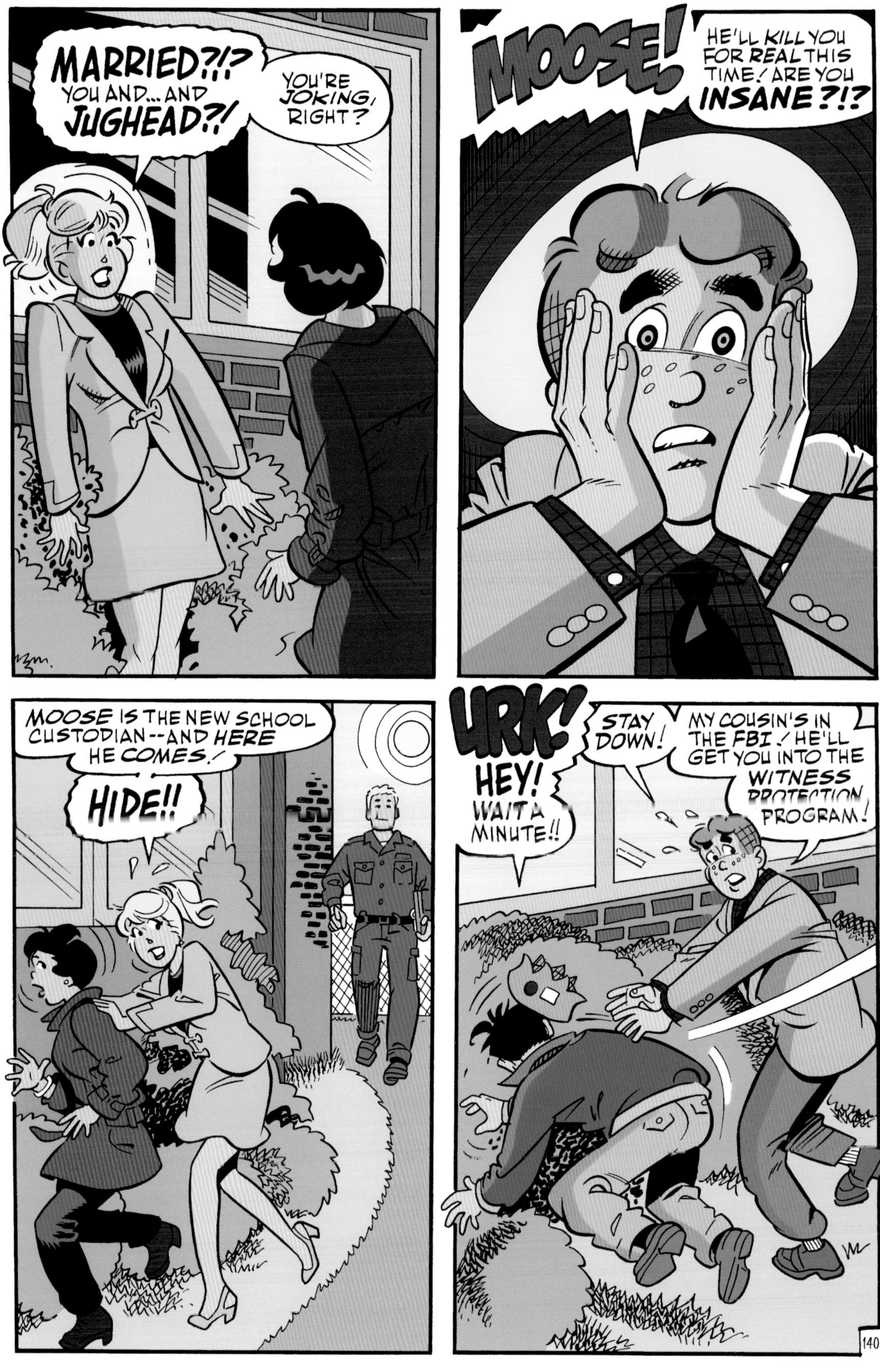

MARRIED?!? YOU AND... AND JUGHEAD?!
YOU'RE JOKING, RIGHT?
MOOSE!
HE'LL KILL YOU FOR REAL THIS TIME! ARE YOU INSANE?!?
MOOSE IS THE NEW SCHOOL CUSTODIAN--AND HERE HE COMES!
HIDE!!
URK!
HEY! WAIT A MINUTE!!
STAY DOWN!
MY COUSIN'S IN THE FBI! HE'LL GET YOU INTO THE WITNESS PROTECTION PROGRAM!

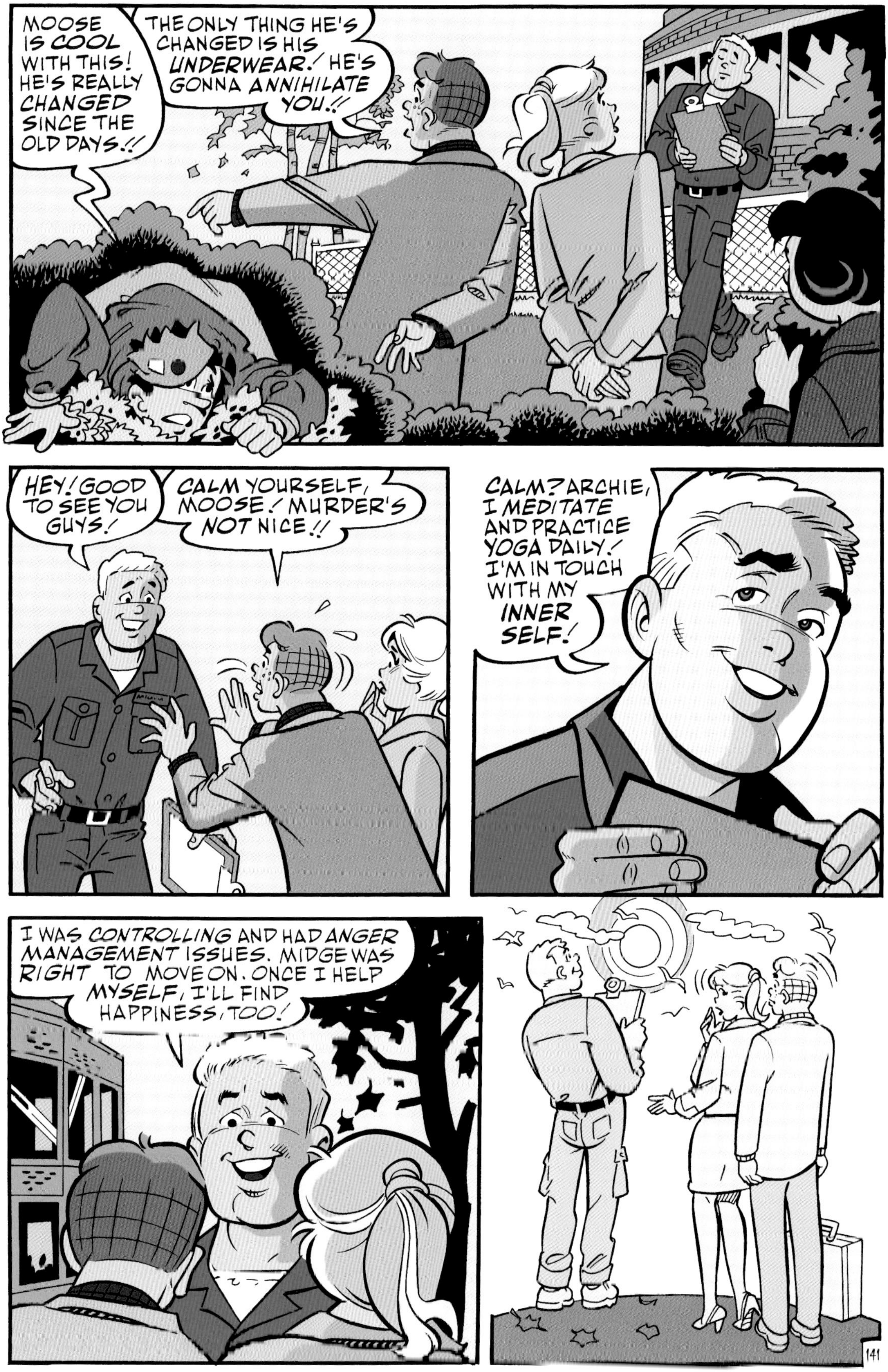
MOOSE IS COOL WITH THIS! HE'S REALLY CHANGED SINCE THE OLD DAYS!!
THE ONLY THING HE'S CHANGED IS HIS UNDERWEAR! HE'S GONNA ANNIHILATE YOU!!
HEY! GOOD TO SEE YOU GUYS!
CALM YOURSELF, MOOSE! MURDER'S NOT NICE!!
CALM? ARCHIE, I MEDITATE AND PRACTICE YOGA DAILY! I'M IN TOUCH WITH MY INNER SELF!
I WAS CONTROLLING AND HAD ANGER MANAGEMENT ISSUES. MIDGE WAS RIGHT TO MOVE ON. ONCE I HELP MYSELF, I'LL FIND HAPPINESS, TOO!

HOW ABOUT WE ALL GO TO DINNER AT *POP'S*?

I FORGOT...YOU JUST GOT BACK AFTER A YEAR AWAY!

THERE *IS* NO MORE POP'S!

RIVERDALE HIGH SCHOOL

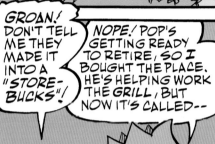

GROAN! DON'T TELL ME THEY MADE IT INTO A "STORE-BUCKS"!

NOPE! POP'S GETTING READY TO RETIRE, SO *I* BOUGHT THE PLACE. HE'S HELPING WORK THE GRILL, BUT NOW IT'S CALLED--

I GOT *STIMULUS* MONEY TO BUY IT! MIDGE AND I RUN IT!

WOW! HAS *EVERYTHING* CHANGED IN RIVERDALE IN JUST *ONE* YEAR?!

JUGGIE'S

MENU

JUGGIE'S

RONNIE! REGGIE!

I THOUGHT YOU WERE IN *EUROPE*, GIRL!

CAME HOME FOR A BREAK FROM RICH SUITORS WHO I COULDN'T *STAND*!

JUGGIE'S
BURGER-
FRIES-

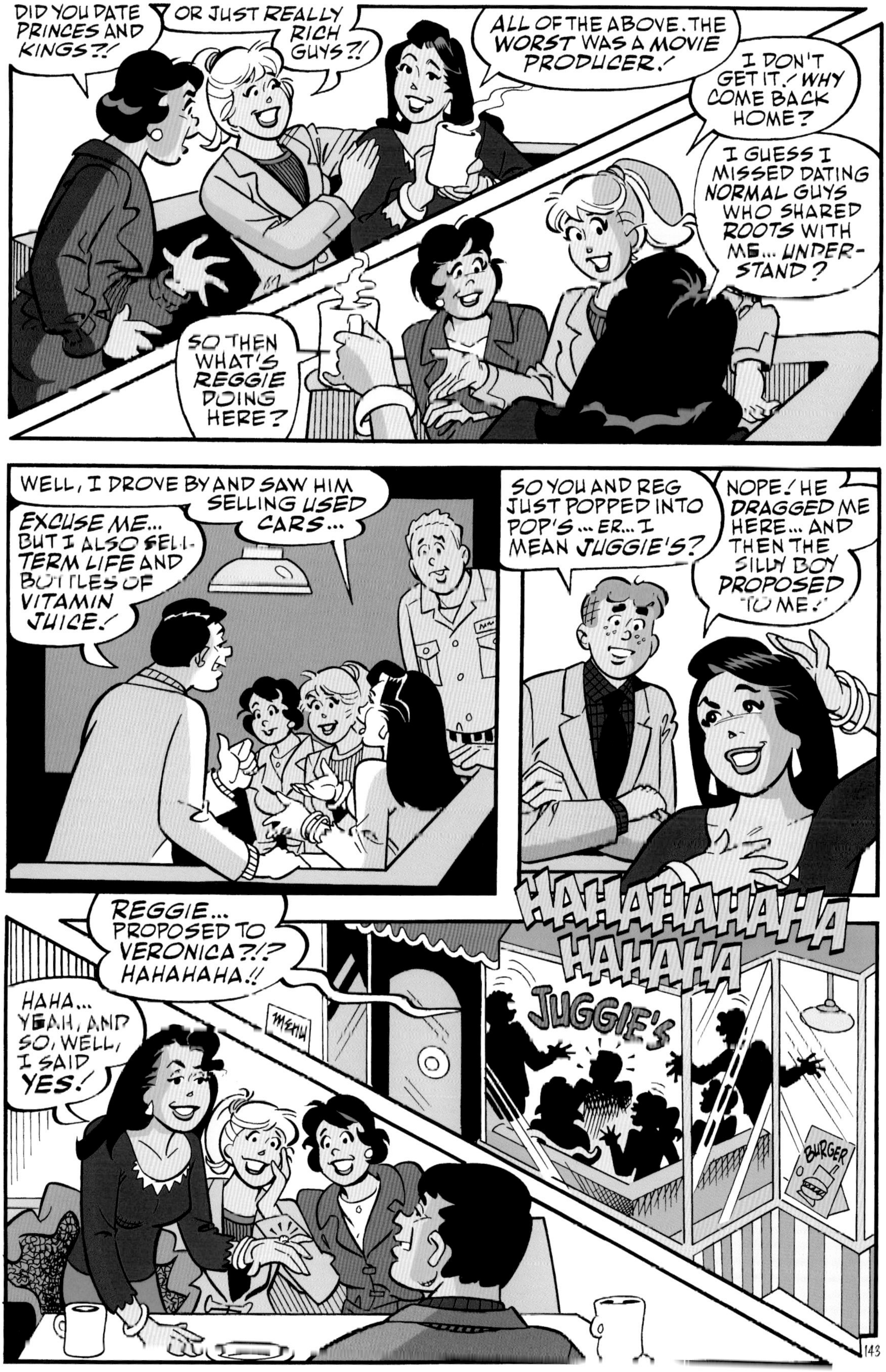
DID YOU DATE PRINCES AND KINGS?!
OR JUST REALLY RICH GUYS?!
ALL OF THE ABOVE. THE WORST WAS A MOVIE PRODUCER!
I DON'T GET IT! WHY COME BACK HOME?
I GUESS I MISSED DATING NORMAL GUYS WHO SHARED ROOTS WITH ME... UNDER-STAND?
SO THEN WHAT'S REGGIE DOING HERE?
WELL, I DROVE BY AND SAW HIM SELLING USED CARS...
EXCUSE ME... BUT I ALSO SELL TERM LIFE AND BOTTLES OF VITAMIN JUICE!
SO YOU AND REG JUST POPPED INTO POP'S... ER... I MEAN JUGGIE'S?
NOPE! HE DRAGGED ME HERE... AND THEN THE SILLY BOY PROPOSED TO ME!
HAHAHAHAHAHA HAHAHA
REGGIE... PROPOSED TO VERONICA?!? HAHAHAHA!!
HAHA... YEAH, AND SO, WELL, I SAID YES!
MENU
JUGGIE'S
BURGER

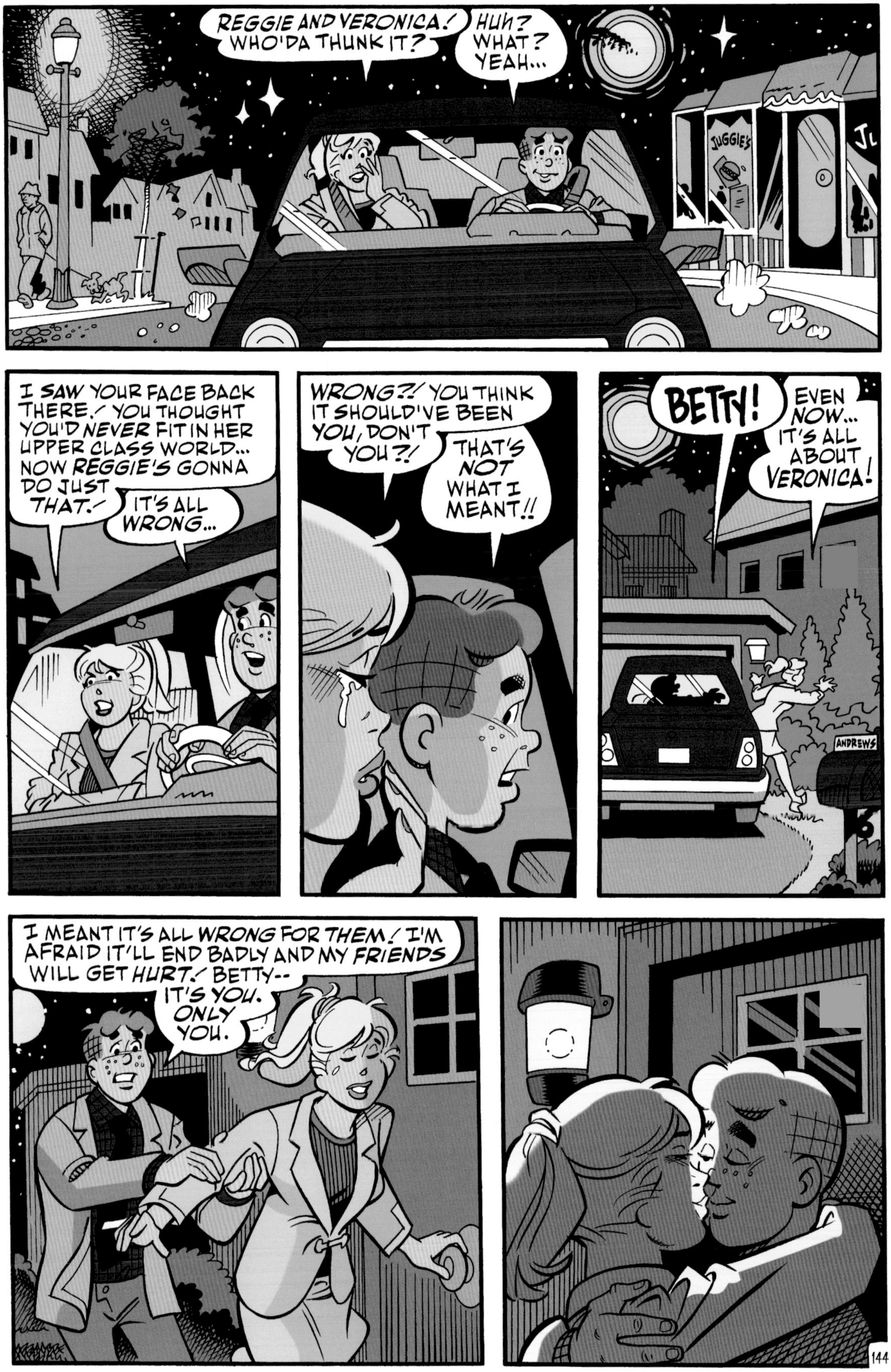
REGGIE AND VERONICA! WHO'DA THUNK IT?
HUH? WHAT? YEAH...
JUGGIE'S
I SAW YOUR FACE BACK THERE! YOU THOUGHT YOU'D NEVER FIT IN HER UPPER CLASS WORLD... NOW REGGIE'S GONNA DO JUST THAT!
IT'S ALL WRONG...
WRONG?! YOU THINK IT SHOULD'VE BEEN YOU, DON'T YOU?!
THAT'S NOT WHAT I MEANT!!
BETTY!
EVEN NOW... IT'S ALL ABOUT VERONICA!
ANDREWS
I MEANT IT'S ALL WRONG FOR THEM! I'M AFRAID IT'LL END BADLY AND MY FRIENDS WILL GET HURT! BETTY--
IT'S YOU. ONLY YOU.

A MARVELOUS BRAND NEW DAY AT RIVERDALE HIGH...

RI-I-ING!

FOR MONDAY-- RESEARCH "ANDY HARDY" AND HIS INFLUENCE ON POP CULTURE!

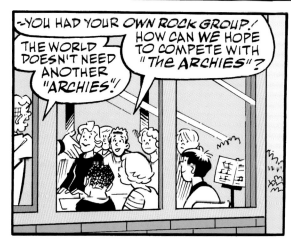

MUSIC DEFINES US! WHEN ALIENS INTERCEPT OUR VOYAGER 1 SATELLITE, THEY'LL HEAR BACH'S "BRANDENBURG CONCERTO #2"!

SURE YOU LOVE MUSIC, MR. ANDREWS--

--YOU HAD YOUR OWN ROCK GROUP! HOW CAN WE HOPE TO COMPETE WITH "THE ARCHIES"?

THE WORLD DOESN'T NEED ANOTHER "ARCHIES"!

IT NEEDS THE BEST JESSICAS, AND SAMANTHAS AND BOBBYS! EXPRESS YOURSELVES THROUGH MUSIC!

RI-I-ING!

MRS. ANDREWS IS SO COOL! SHE MAKES ME WANT TO LEARN!

MR. ANDREWS LOVES MUSIC, AND MAKES ME LOVE IT, TOO!

I KNEW BETTY WOULD MAKE A WONDERFUL TEACHER... BUT ARCHIE--?

MY HUNCH WAS RIGHT! HE FOUND HIS CALLING.

145

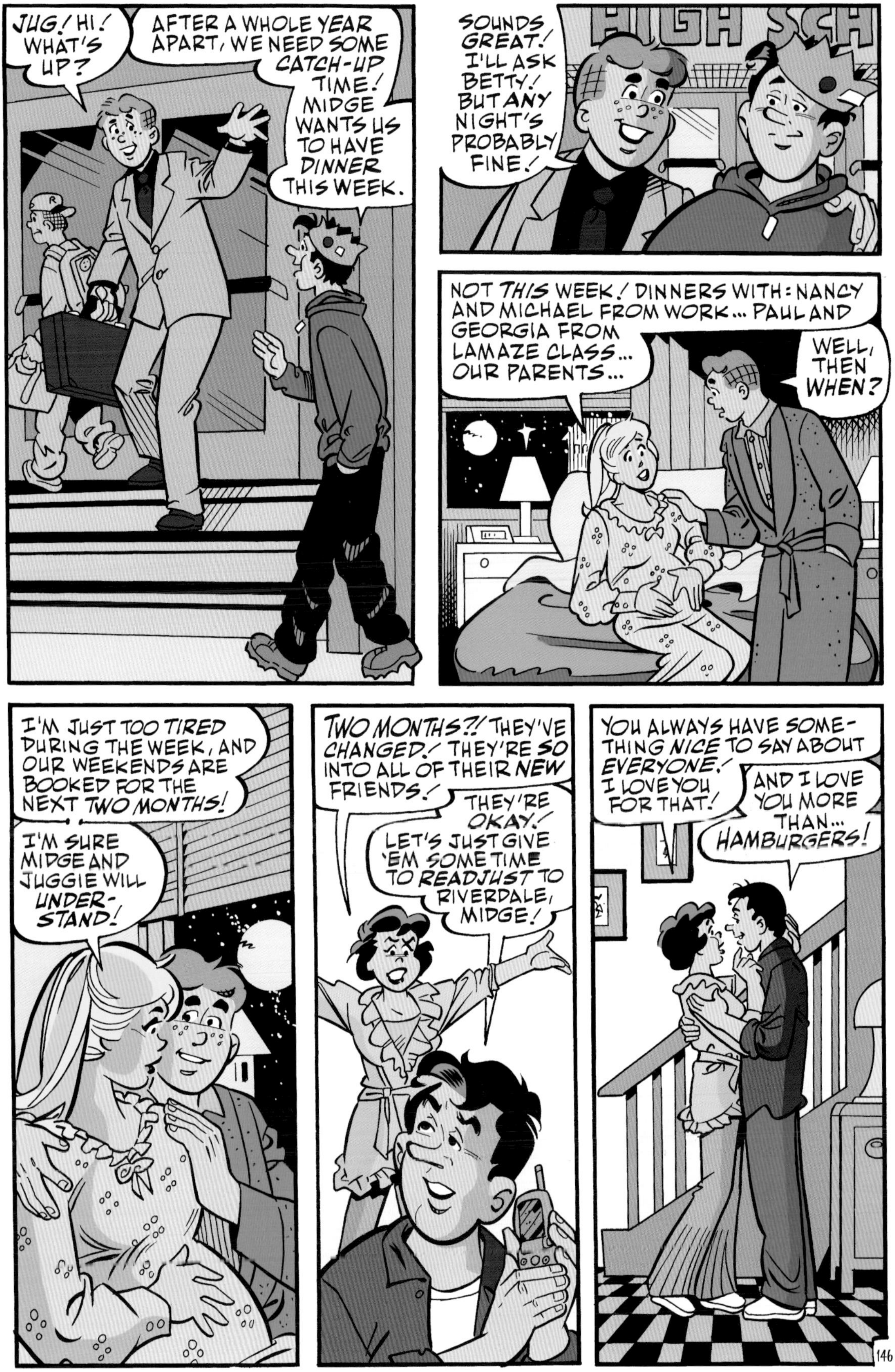
JUG! HI! WHAT'S UP?
AFTER A WHOLE YEAR APART, WE NEED SOME CATCH-UP TIME! MIDGE WANTS US TO HAVE DINNER THIS WEEK.
SOUNDS GREAT! I'LL ASK BETTY! BUT ANY NIGHT'S PROBABLY FINE!
NOT THIS WEEK! DINNERS WITH: NANCY AND MICHAEL FROM WORK... PAUL AND GEORGIA FROM LAMAZE CLASS... OUR PARENTS...
WELL, THEN WHEN?
I'M JUST TOO TIRED DURING THE WEEK, AND OUR WEEKENDS ARE BOOKED FOR THE NEXT TWO MONTHS!
I'M SURE MIDGE AND JUGGIE WILL UNDERSTAND!
TWO MONTHS?! THEY'VE CHANGED! THEY'RE SO INTO ALL OF THEIR NEW FRIENDS!
THEY'RE OKAY! LET'S JUST GIVE 'EM SOME TIME TO READJUST TO RIVERDALE, MIDGE!
YOU ALWAYS HAVE SOMETHING NICE TO SAY ABOUT EVERYONE! I LOVE YOU FOR THAT!
AND I LOVE YOU MORE THAN... HAMBURGERS!

THE BABY'S KICKING AND I'M *EXHAUSTED*. WHY DON'T YOU HANG OUT WITH THE GUYS TONIGHT?

NAH! I'LL STAY AND WORK ON MY NEW SONGS... MY *OPUS!*

BUT REGGIE AND MOOSE ARE HANGING OUT AT *JUGGIE'S!*

ARCHIE HASN'T CHILLED WITH US *ONCE* SINCE HE MOVED BACK!

HE'S *MARRIED,* REG! GIVE HIM A BREAK!

AT LEAST HE CAME *BACK!* UNLIKE *DILTON!*

JUGGIE'S

MENU

MY COUSIN SENT ME THIS CLIPPING FROM A *ROSWELL, NEW MEXICO* NEWSPAPER!

ROSWELL STAR-LEDGER

DOILEY DISCOVERS PARALLEL UNIVERSE, DISAPPEARS

DILTON DOILEY

MAN! HOW *WEIRD!*

ANY *MORE* WEIRD THAN ARCHIE MARRYING BETTY... MIDGE MARRYING JUGHEAD... OR *YOU* ENGAGED TO VERONICA?

LIFE'S FULL OF *SURPRISES!*

ROSWELL STAR LEDGER

LOCAL FIND!

LIKE YOU BEING MORE MATURE THAN ALL OF US?

LUCKILY, I DIDN'T *PEAK IN HIGH SCHOOL!*

ROSWELL DOILEY D PARALLEL UNIVERSE SAR

147

Ahhhh...THE WEEKEND COMETH...

I'LL DO MY BIKING AND BE BACK IN A COUPLE OF HOURS!

YOU OKAY?

UH-HUH! BUT...YOU *SURE* WE'RE REALLY PREPARED FOR WHEN I GO INTO *LABOR?!*

WELL, THE DOC SAYS THAT'S *DAYS* AWAY... BUT LET ME SHOW YOU HOW *PREPARED* WE ARE!

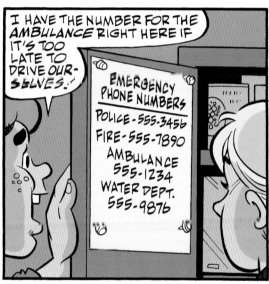

I HAVE THE NUMBER FOR THE *AMBULANCE* RIGHT HERE IF IT'S TOO LATE TO DRIVE OUR-SELVES!

EMERGENCY PHONE NUMBERS
POLICE - 555-3456
FIRE - 555-7890
AMBULANCE 555-1234
WATER DEPT. 555-9876

THERE'S YOUR PACKED SUITCASE... PERFECT! THERE'S OUR LAMAZE STUFF...PERFECT!

"NOTHING CAN GO WRONG!"

JUST ONE MORE THING, ARCHIE...

CALL THE *DOCTOR.* MY WATER BROKE. IT'S *TIME* TO GO TO THE HOSPITAL.

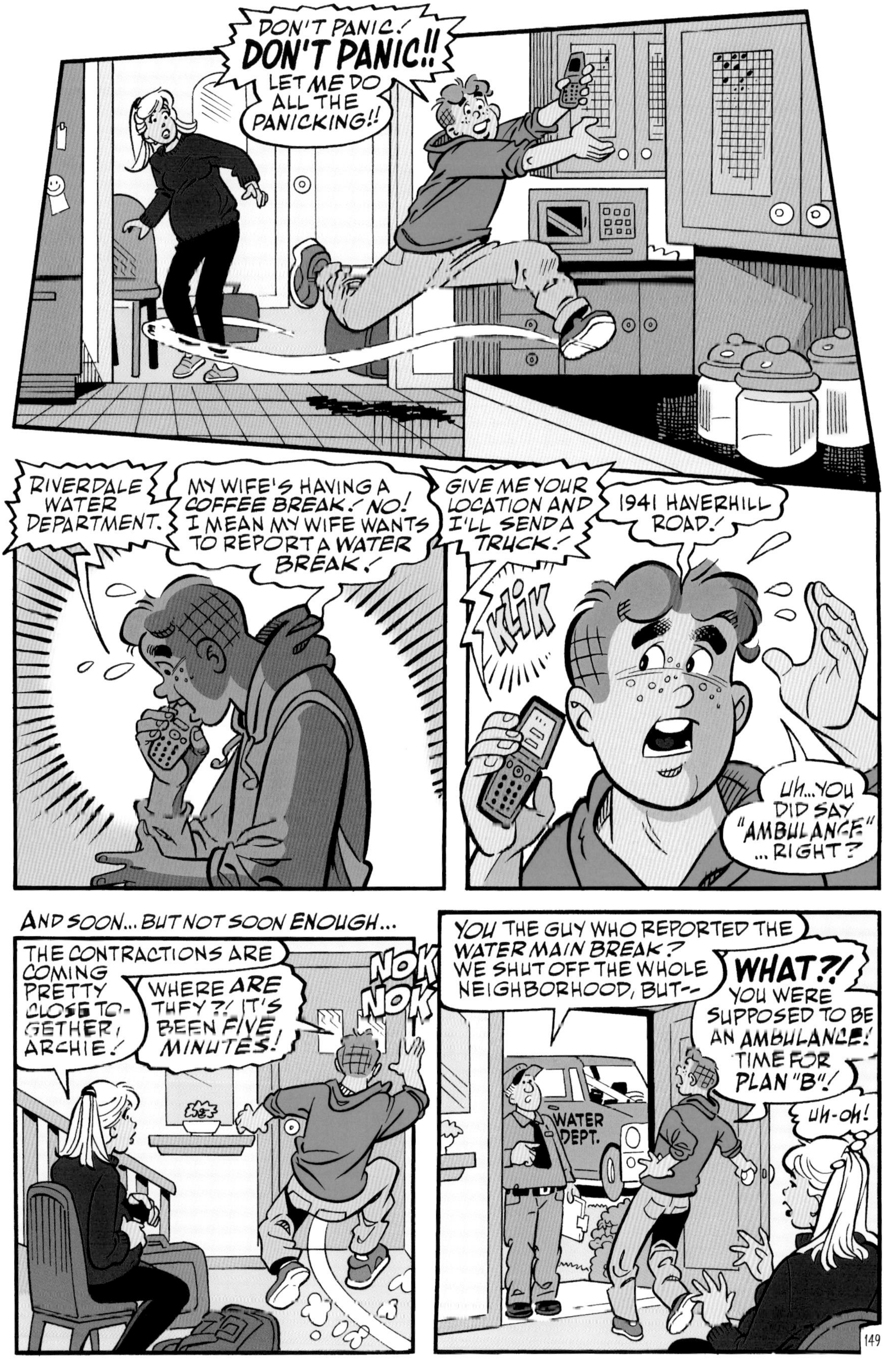
DON'T PANIC! DON'T PANIC!! LET ME DO ALL THE PANICKING!!
RIVERDALE WATER DEPARTMENT.
MY WIFE'S HAVING A COFFEE BREAK! NO! I MEAN MY WIFE WANTS TO REPORT A WATER BREAK!
GIVE ME YOUR LOCATION AND I'LL SEND A TRUCK!
KLIK
1941 HAVERHILL ROAD!
UH...YOU DID SAY "AMBULANCE" ...RIGHT?
AND SOON... BUT NOT SOON ENOUGH...
THE CONTRACTIONS ARE COMING PRETTY CLOSE TOGETHER, ARCHIE!
WHERE ARE THEY?! IT'S BEEN FIVE MINUTES!
NOK NOK
YOU THE GUY WHO REPORTED THE WATER MAIN BREAK? WE SHUT OFF THE WHOLE NEIGHBORHOOD, BUT--
WHAT?! YOU WERE SUPPOSED TO BE AN AMBULANCE! TIME FOR PLAN "B"!
UH-OH!
WATER DEPT.

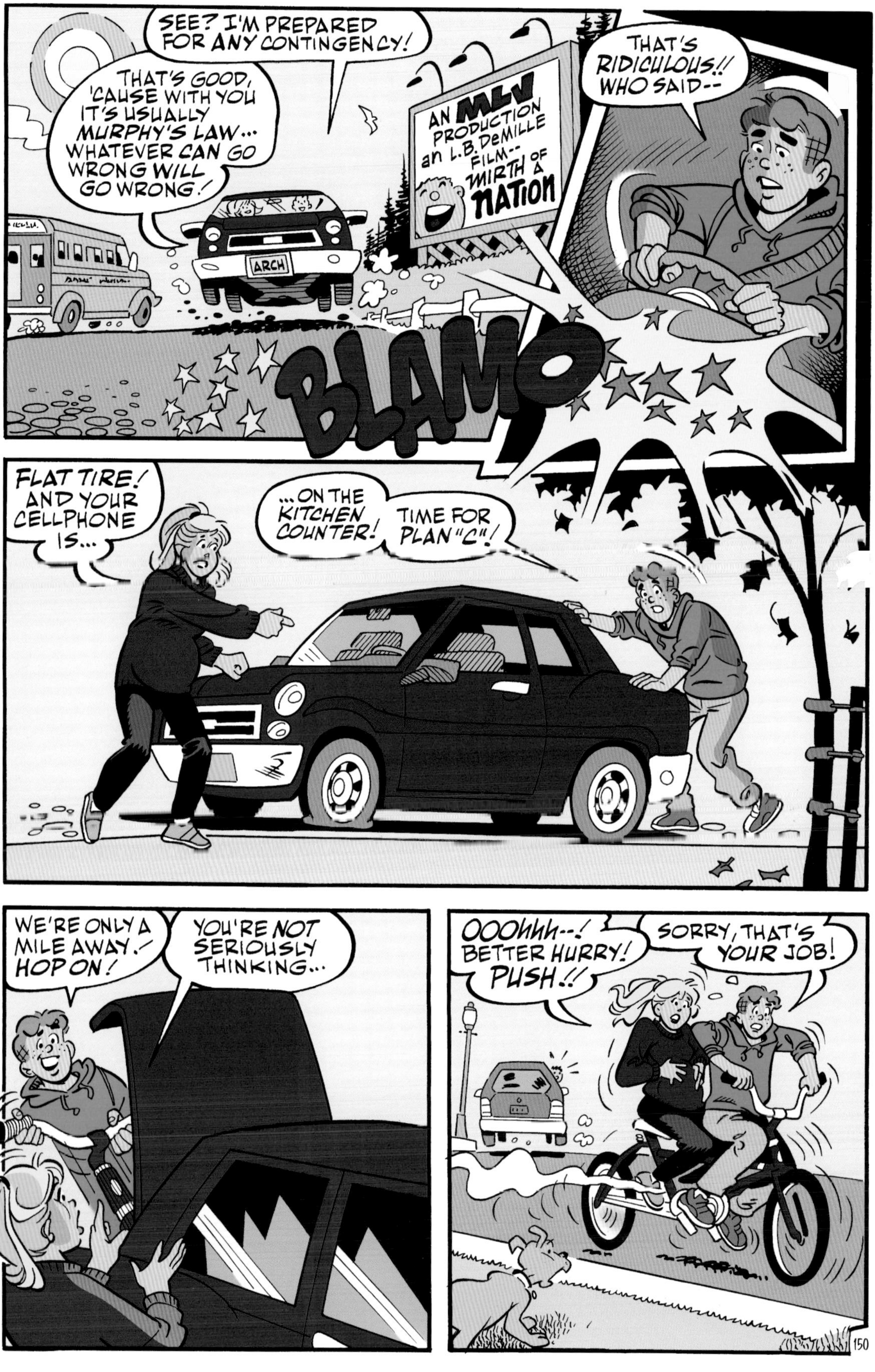
SEE? I'M PREPARED FOR ANY CONTINGENCY!
THAT'S GOOD, 'CAUSE WITH YOU IT'S USUALLY MURPHY'S LAW... WHATEVER CAN GO WRONG WILL GO WRONG!
AN MLV PRODUCTION an L.B. DeMILLE FILM-- MIRTH OF A NATION
ARCH
THAT'S RIDICULOUS!! WHO SAID--
BLAMO
FLAT TIRE! AND YOUR CELLPHONE IS...
...ON THE KITCHEN COUNTER!
TIME FOR PLAN "C"!
WE'RE ONLY A MILE AWAY! HOP ON!
YOU'RE NOT SERIOUSLY THINKING...
OOOhhh--! BETTER HURRY! PUSH!!
SORRY, THAT'S YOUR JOB!

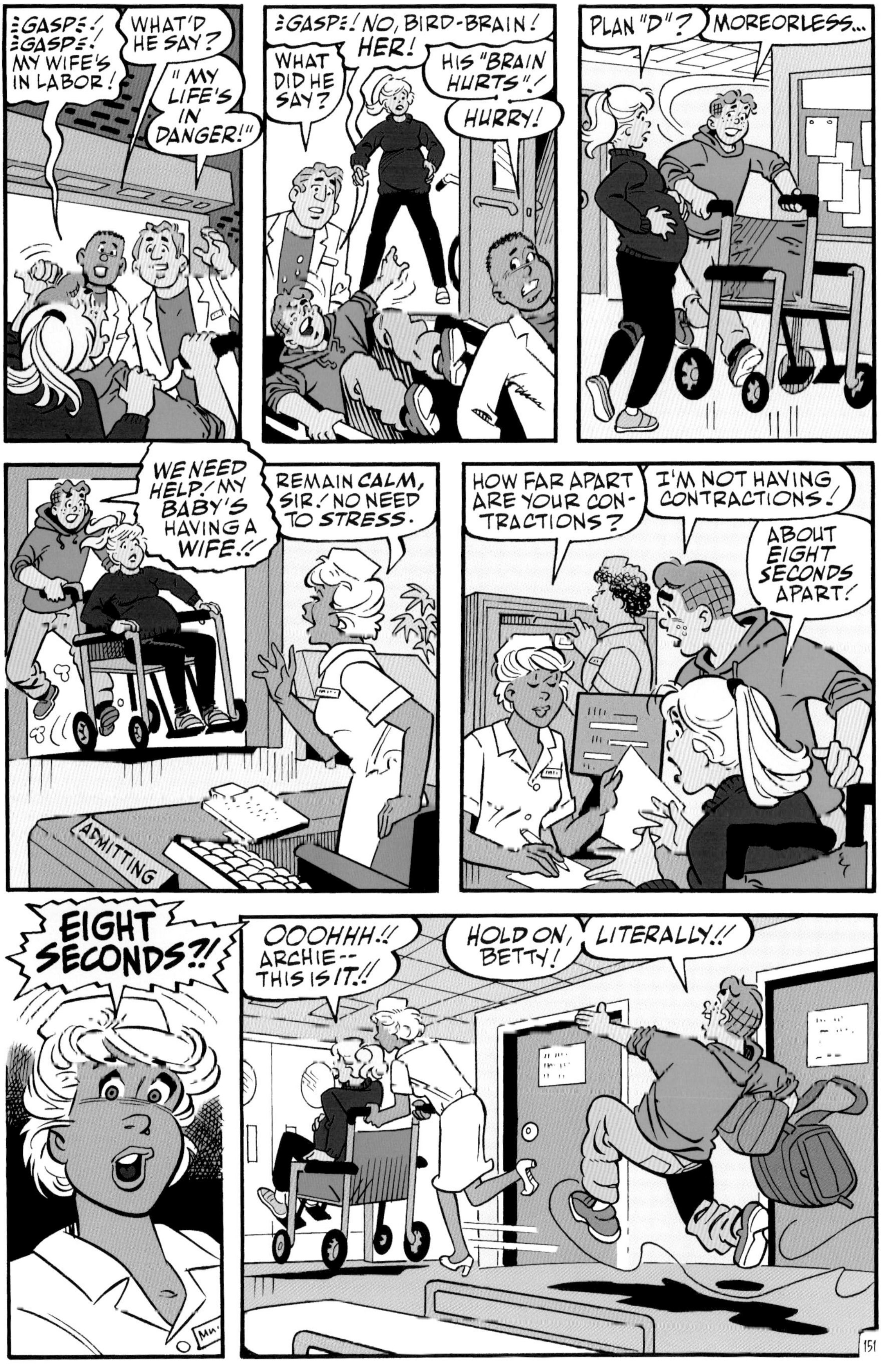

:GASP:! :GASP:! MY WIFE'S IN LABOR!
WHAT'D HE SAY?
"MY LIFE'S IN DANGER!"
:GASP:! NO, BIRD-BRAIN! HER!
WHAT DID HE SAY?
HIS "BRAIN HURTS"!
HURRY!
PLAN "D"?
MOREORLESS...
WE NEED HELP! MY BABY'S HAVING A WIFE!!
REMAIN CALM, SIR! NO NEED TO STRESS.
ADMITTING
HOW FAR APART ARE YOUR CONTRACTIONS?
I'M NOT HAVING CONTRACTIONS!
ABOUT EIGHT SECONDS APART!
EIGHT SECONDS?!
OOOHHH!! ARCHIE-- THIS IS IT!!
HOLD ON, BETTY!
LITERALLY!!

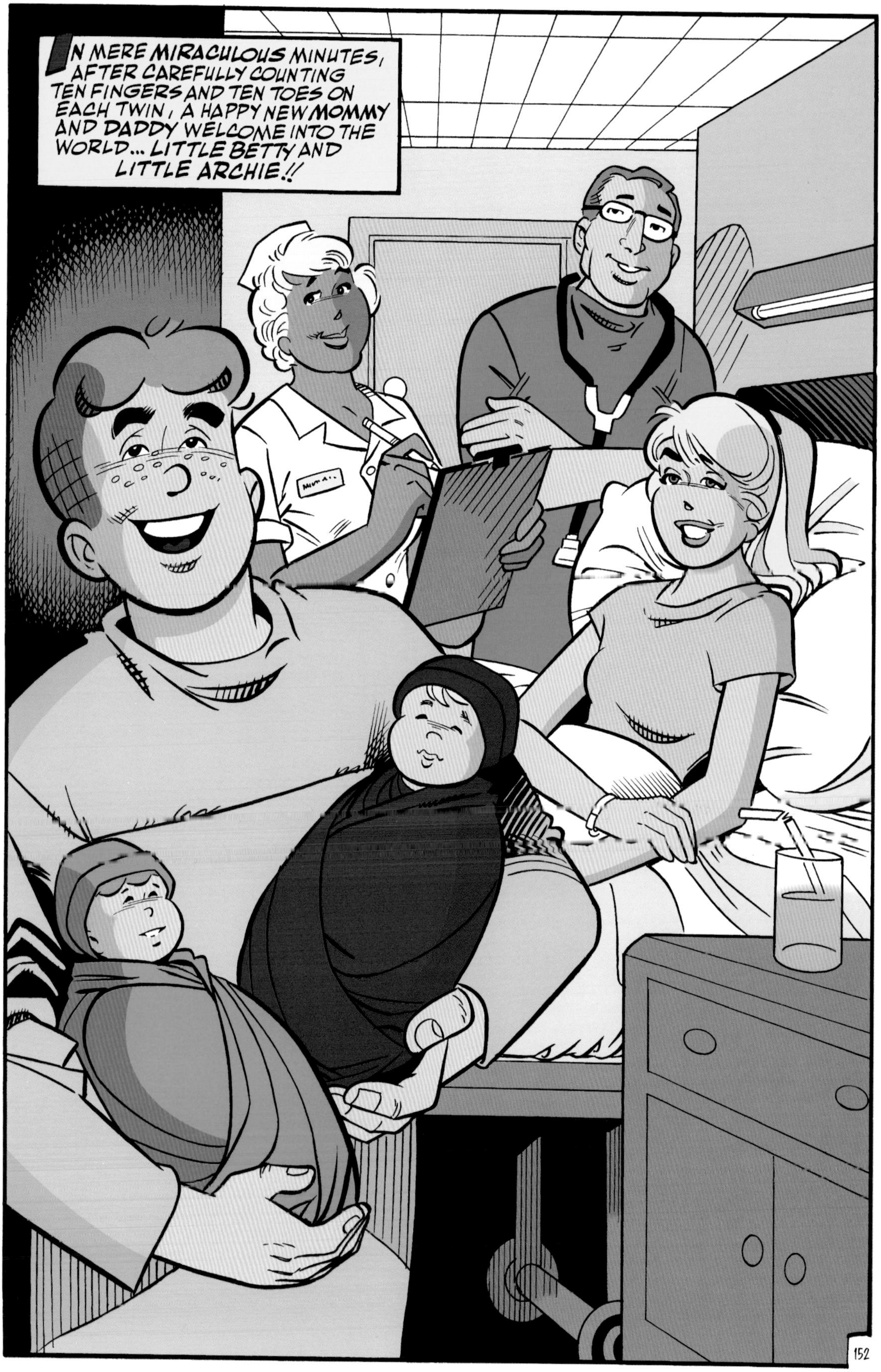
IN MERE MIRACULOUS MINUTES, AFTER CAREFULLY COUNTING TEN FINGERS AND TEN TOES ON EACH TWIN, A HAPPY NEW MOMMY AND DADDY WELCOME INTO THE WORLD... LITTLE BETTY AND LITTLE ARCHIE!!

MOM! DADDY!

Oh, BETTY! MY BABY HAS BABIES!! THEY'RE SO BEAUTIFUL! YOU'RE SO BEAUTIFUL!

NICE WORK, SON.

MOM! POP!

THE BABIES AND BETTY ARE ALL HEALTHY?

WE'RE GREAT, DAD!

THAT'S ALL THAT COUNTS!

EEEEEEEEEE!!

JUG, WILL YOU TWO BE THE GOD-PARENTS TO LITTLE ARCHIE?

ARCH... I... I... ≡CHOKE≡ IT WOULD BE THE GREATEST HONOR OF MY LIFE─!

EEEEEEEEEE!!

TWINS?! DIDN'T THINK YA HAD IT IN YA, ARCH! WAY TA GO!!

GEE, THANKS!

I DIDN'T APPRECIATE WHAT I HAD UNTIL I LOST IT! DON'T EVER MAKE MY MISTAKE!

I WON'T, RONNIE. THANKS.

155

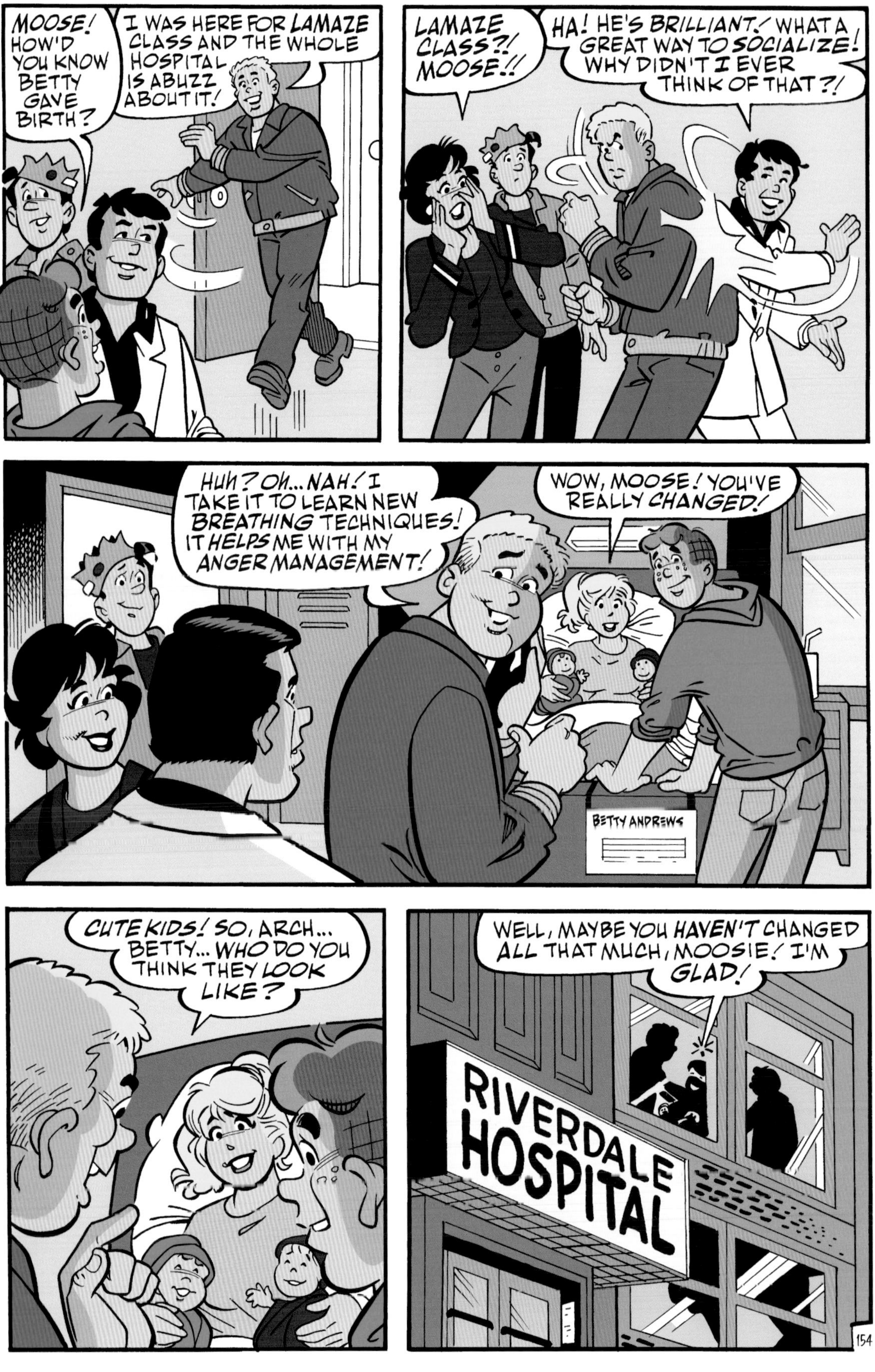
MOOSE! HOW'D YOU KNOW BETTY GAVE BIRTH?
I WAS HERE FOR LAMAZE CLASS AND THE WHOLE HOSPITAL IS ABUZZ ABOUT IT!
LAMAZE CLASS?! MOOSE!!
HA! HE'S BRILLIANT! WHAT A GREAT WAY TO SOCIALIZE! WHY DIDN'T I EVER THINK OF THAT?!
HUH? OH... NAH! I TAKE IT TO LEARN NEW BREATHING TECHNIQUES! IT HELPS ME WITH MY ANGER MANAGEMENT!
WOW, MOOSE! YOU'VE REALLY CHANGED!
BETTY ANDREWS
CUTE KIDS! SO, ARCH... BETTY... WHO DO YOU THINK THEY LOOK LIKE?
WELL, MAYBE YOU HAVEN'T CHANGED ALL THAT MUCH, MOOSIE! I'M GLAD!
RIVERDALE HOSPITAL

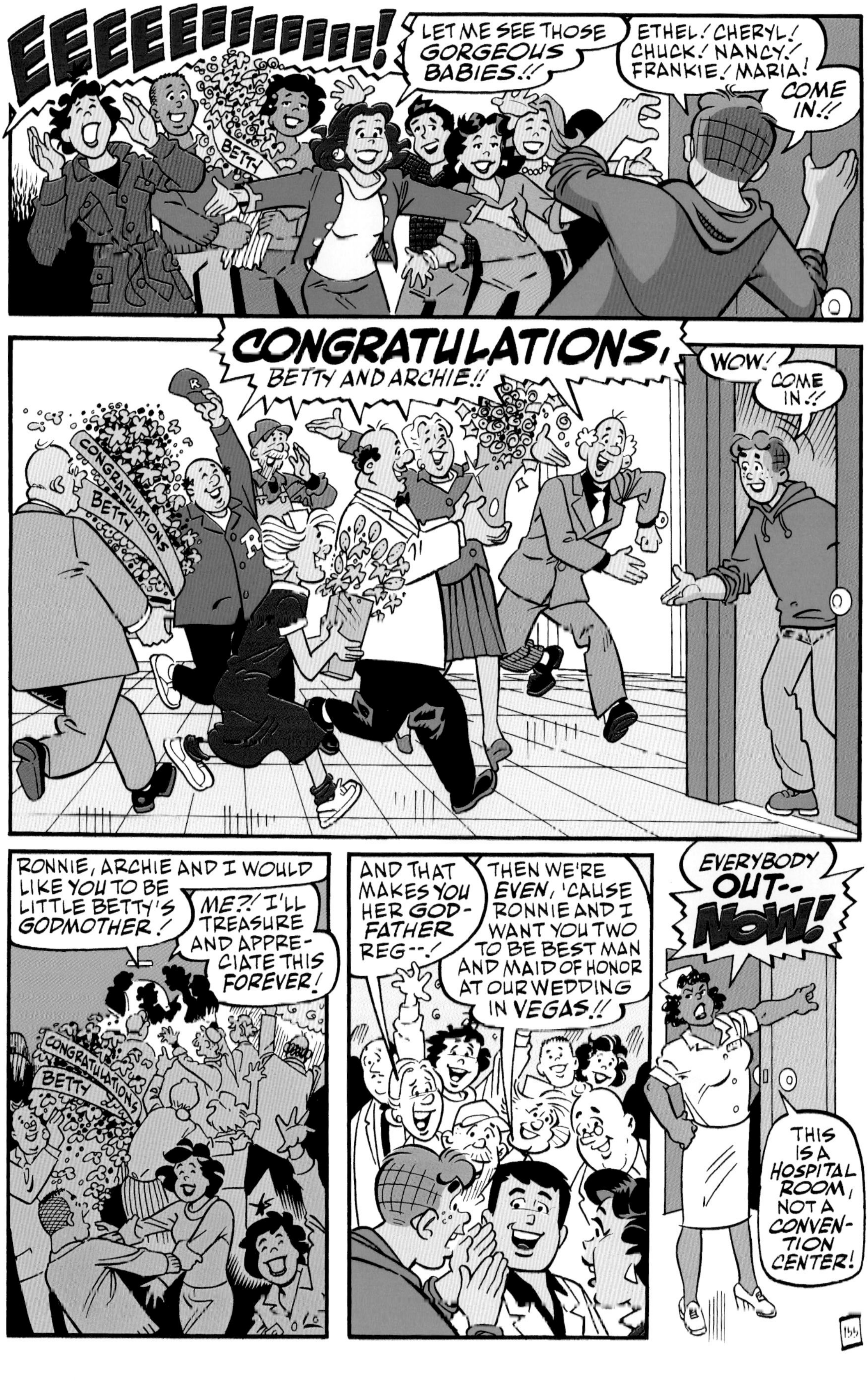
EEEEEEEEEEEEE!
LET ME SEE THOSE GORGEOUS BABIES!!
ETHEL! CHERYL! CHUCK! NANCY! FRANKIE! MARIA!
COME IN!!
BETTY
CONGRATULATIONS, BETTY AND ARCHIE!!
WOW!
COME IN!!
CONGRATULATIONS
BETTY
RONNIE, ARCHIE AND I WOULD LIKE YOU TO BE LITTLE BETTY'S GODMOTHER!
ME?! I'LL TREASURE AND APPRECIATE THIS FOREVER!
CONGRATULATIONS
BETTY
AND THAT MAKES YOU HER GODFATHER REG--!
THEN WE'RE EVEN, 'CAUSE RONNIE AND I WANT YOU TWO TO BE BEST MAN AND MAID OF HONOR AT OUR WEDDING IN VEGAS!!
EVERYBODY OUT--NOW!
THIS IS A HOSPITAL ROOM, NOT A CONVENTION CENTER!

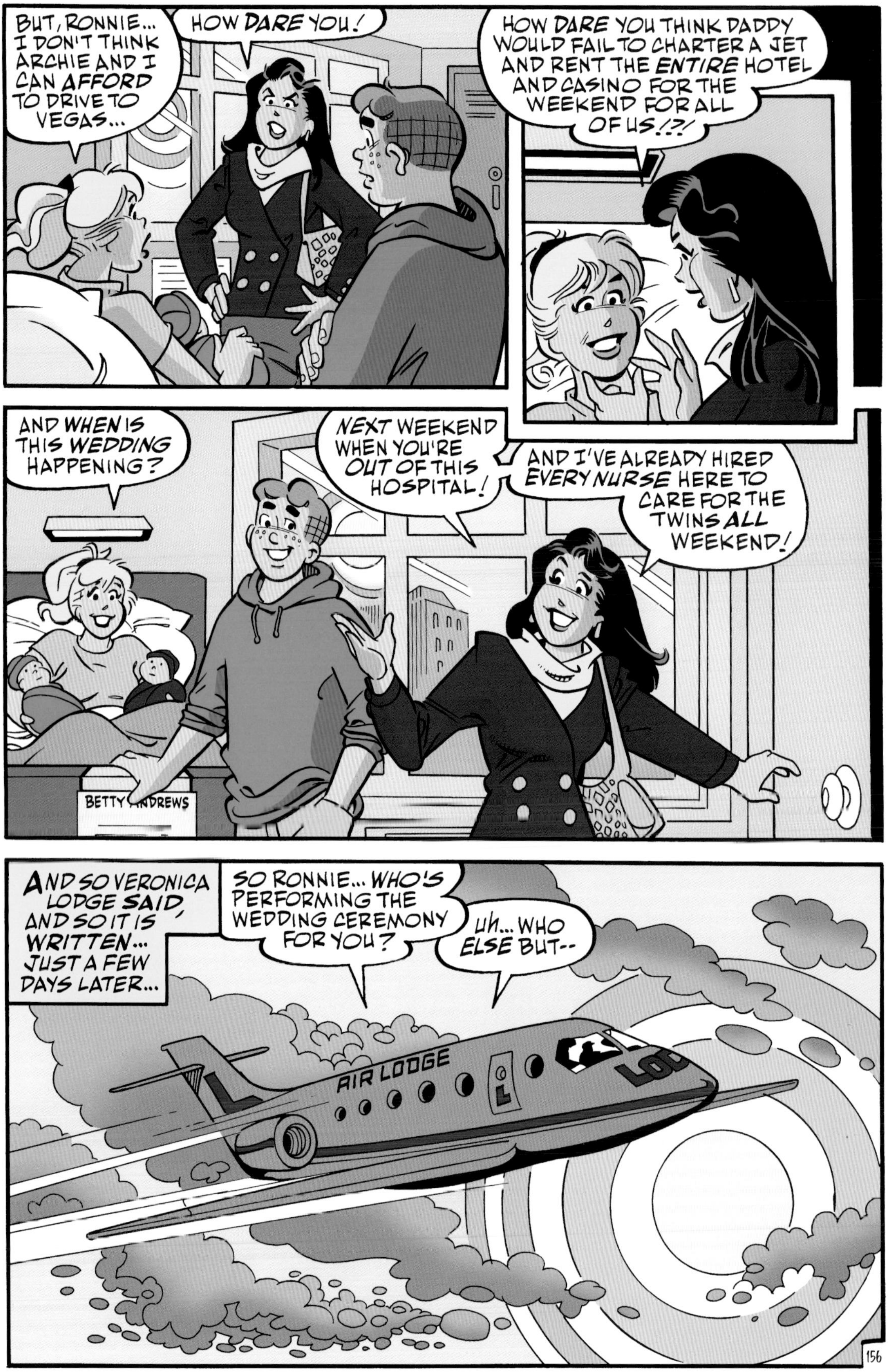

BUT, RONNIE... I DON'T THINK ARCHIE AND I CAN AFFORD TO DRIVE TO VEGAS...
HOW DARE YOU!
HOW DARE YOU THINK DADDY WOULD FAIL TO CHARTER A JET AND RENT THE ENTIRE HOTEL AND CASINO FOR THE WEEKEND FOR ALL OF US!?!
AND WHEN IS THIS WEDDING HAPPENING?
NEXT WEEKEND WHEN YOU'RE OUT OF THIS HOSPITAL!
AND I'VE ALREADY HIRED EVERY NURSE HERE TO CARE FOR THE TWINS ALL WEEKEND!
BETTY ANDREWS
AND SO VERONICA LODGE SAID, AND SO IT IS WRITTEN... JUST A FEW DAYS LATER...
SO RONNIE... WHO'S PERFORMING THE WEDDING CEREMONY FOR YOU?
UH... WHO ELSE BUT--
AIR LODGE

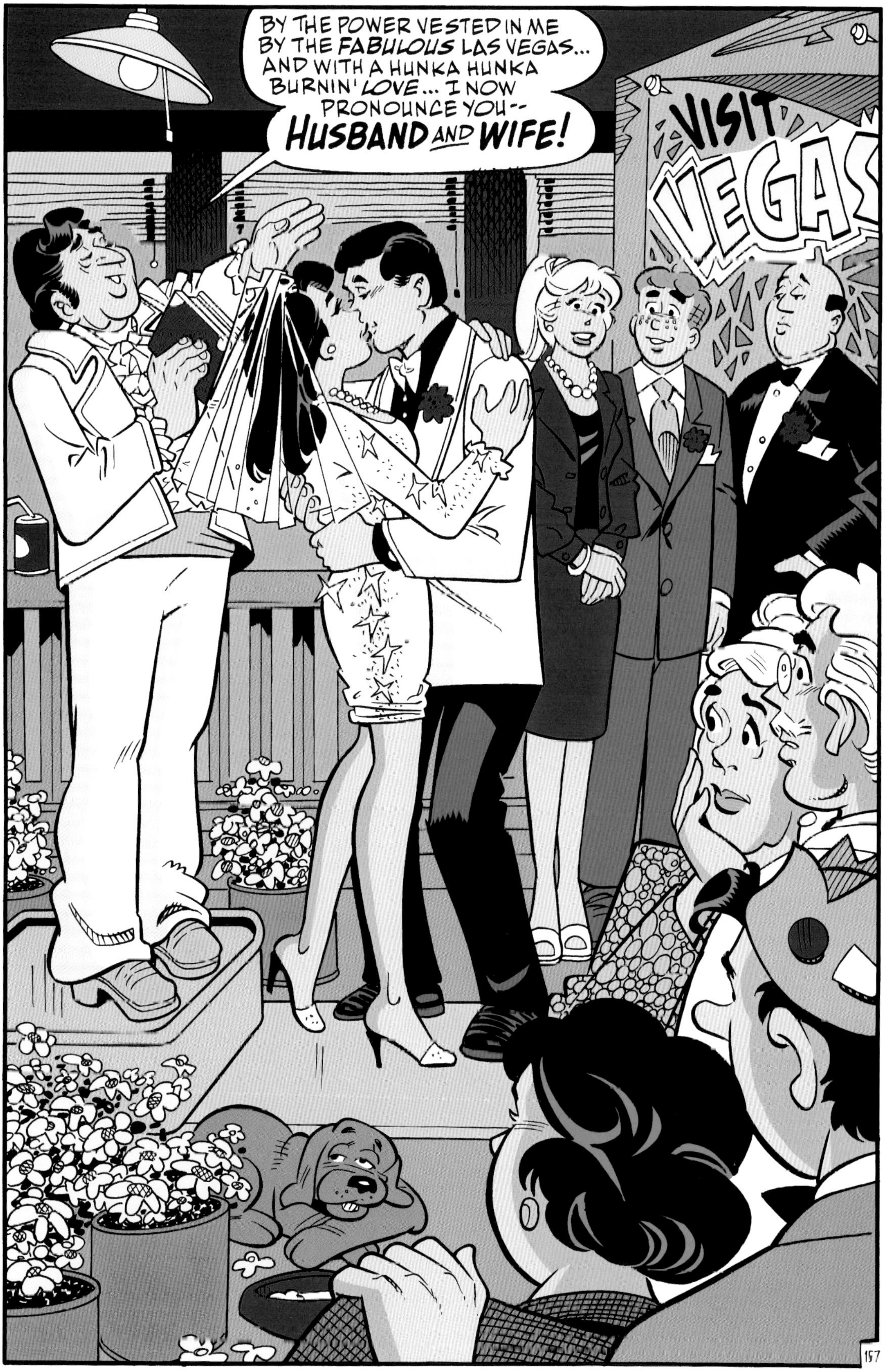
BY THE POWER VESTED IN ME BY THE FABULOUS LAS VEGAS... AND WITH A HUNKA HUNKA BURNIN' LOVE... I NOW PRONOUNCE YOU-- HUSBAND AND WIFE!
VISIT VEGAS

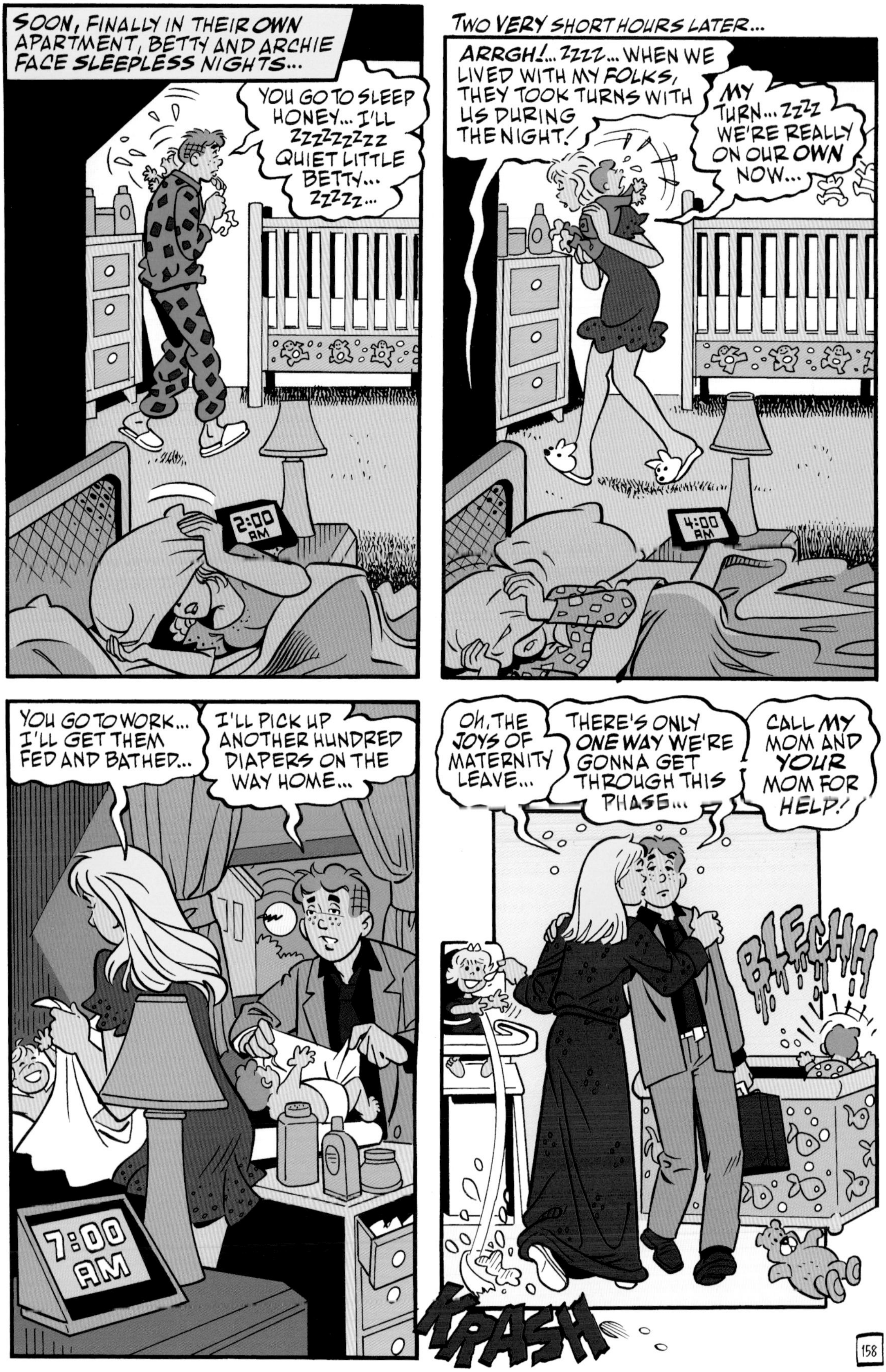
SOON, FINALLY IN THEIR OWN APARTMENT, BETTY AND ARCHIE FACE SLEEPLESS NIGHTS...
YOU GO TO SLEEP HONEY... I'LL ZZZZZZZZZ QUIET LITTLE BETTY... ZZZZZ...
2:00 AM
TWO VERY SHORT HOURS LATER...
ARRGH!... ZZZZ... WHEN WE LIVED WITH MY FOLKS, THEY TOOK TURNS WITH US DURING THE NIGHT!
MY TURN... ZZZZ WE'RE REALLY ON OUR OWN NOW...
4:00 AM
YOU GO TO WORK... I'LL GET THEM FED AND BATHED...
I'LL PICK UP ANOTHER HUNDRED DIAPERS ON THE WAY HOME...
7:00 AM
OH, THE JOYS OF MATERNITY LEAVE...
THERE'S ONLY ONE WAY WE'RE GONNA GET THROUGH THIS PHASE...
CALL MY MOM AND YOUR MOM FOR HELP!
BLECHH
KRASH

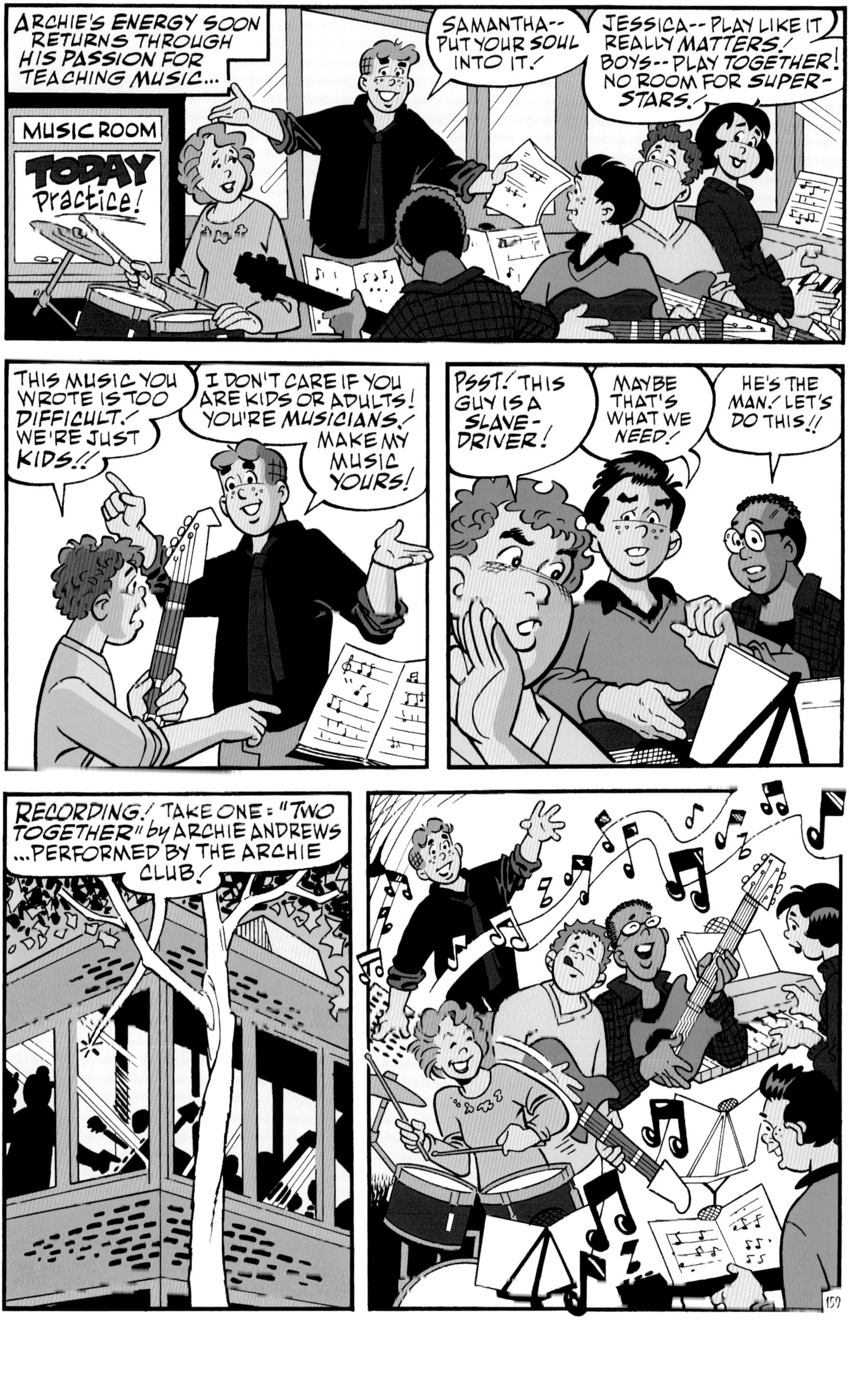
ARCHIE'S ENERGY SOON RETURNS THROUGH HIS PASSION FOR TEACHING MUSIC...
SAMANTHA-- PUT YOUR SOUL INTO IT!
JESSICA-- PLAY LIKE IT REALLY MATTERS! BOYS-- PLAY TOGETHER! NO ROOM FOR SUPER-STARS!
MUSIC ROOM
TODAY Practice!
THIS MUSIC YOU WROTE IS TOO DIFFICULT! WE'RE JUST KIDS!!
I DON'T CARE IF YOU ARE KIDS OR ADULTS! YOU'RE MUSICIANS! MAKE MY MUSIC YOURS!
PSST! THIS GUY IS A SLAVE-DRIVER!
MAYBE THAT'S WHAT WE NEED!
HE'S THE MAN! LET'S DO THIS!!
RECORDING! TAKE ONE: "TWO TOGETHER" by ARCHIE ANDREWS ...PERFORMED BY THE ARCHIE CLUB!

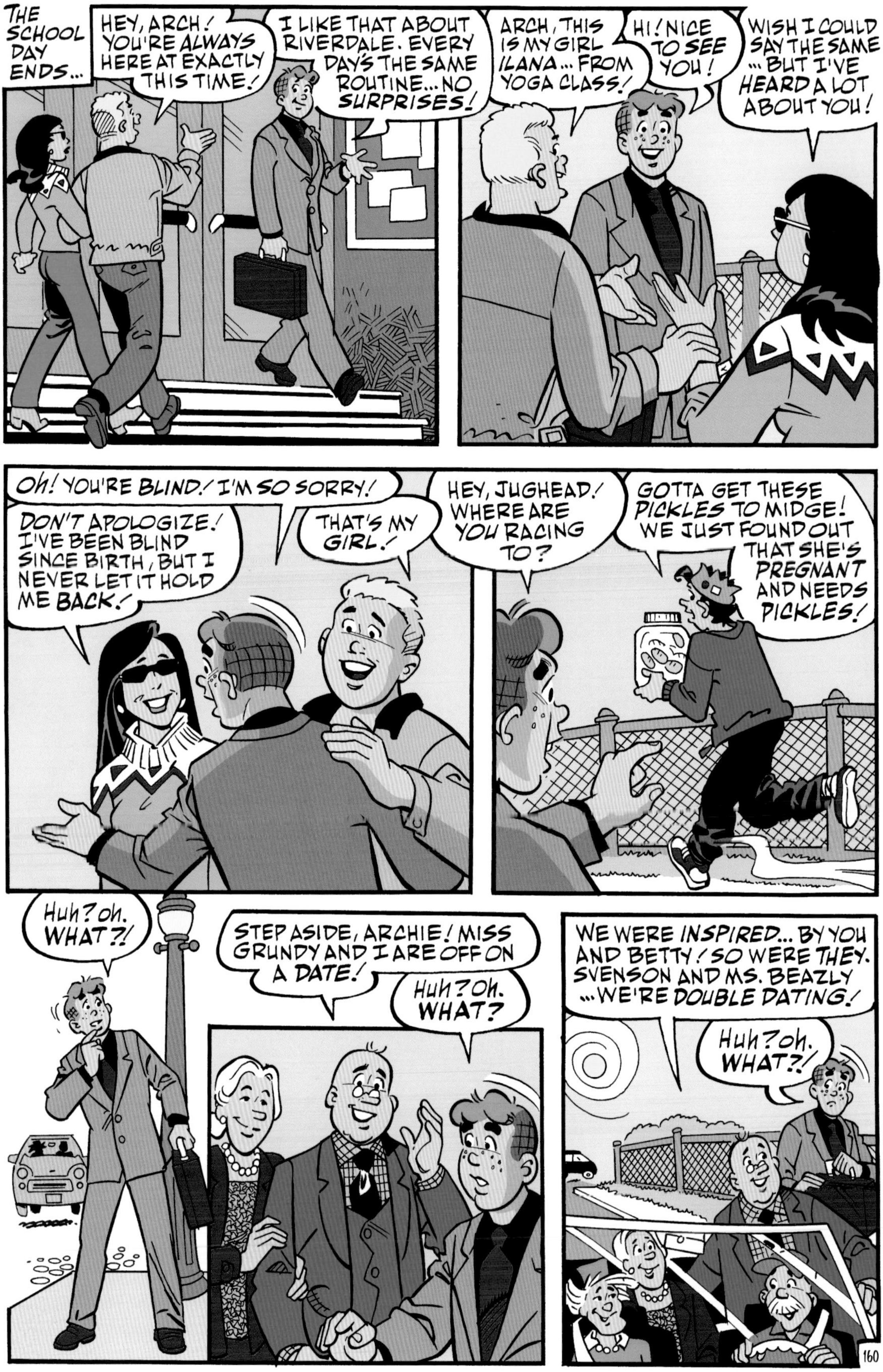
THE SCHOOL DAY ENDS...
HEY, ARCH! YOU'RE ALWAYS HERE AT EXACTLY THIS TIME!
I LIKE THAT ABOUT RIVERDALE. EVERY DAY'S THE SAME ROUTINE...NO SURPRISES!
ARCH, THIS IS MY GIRL ILANA... FROM YOGA CLASS!
HI! NICE TO SEE YOU!
WISH I COULD SAY THE SAME ...BUT I'VE HEARD A LOT ABOUT YOU!
Oh! YOU'RE BLIND! I'M SO SORRY!
DON'T APOLOGIZE! I'VE BEEN BLIND SINCE BIRTH, BUT I NEVER LET IT HOLD ME BACK!
THAT'S MY GIRL!
HEY, JUGHEAD! WHERE ARE YOU RACING TO?
GOTTA GET THESE PICKLES TO MIDGE! WE JUST FOUND OUT THAT SHE'S PREGNANT AND NEEDS PICKLES!
Huh? oh. WHAT?!
STEP ASIDE, ARCHIE! MISS GRUNDY AND I ARE OFF ON A DATE!
Huh? oh. WHAT?
WE WERE INSPIRED... BY YOU AND BETTY! SO WERE THEY. SVENSON AND MS. BEAZLY ...WE'RE DOUBLE DATING!
Huh? oh. WHAT?!

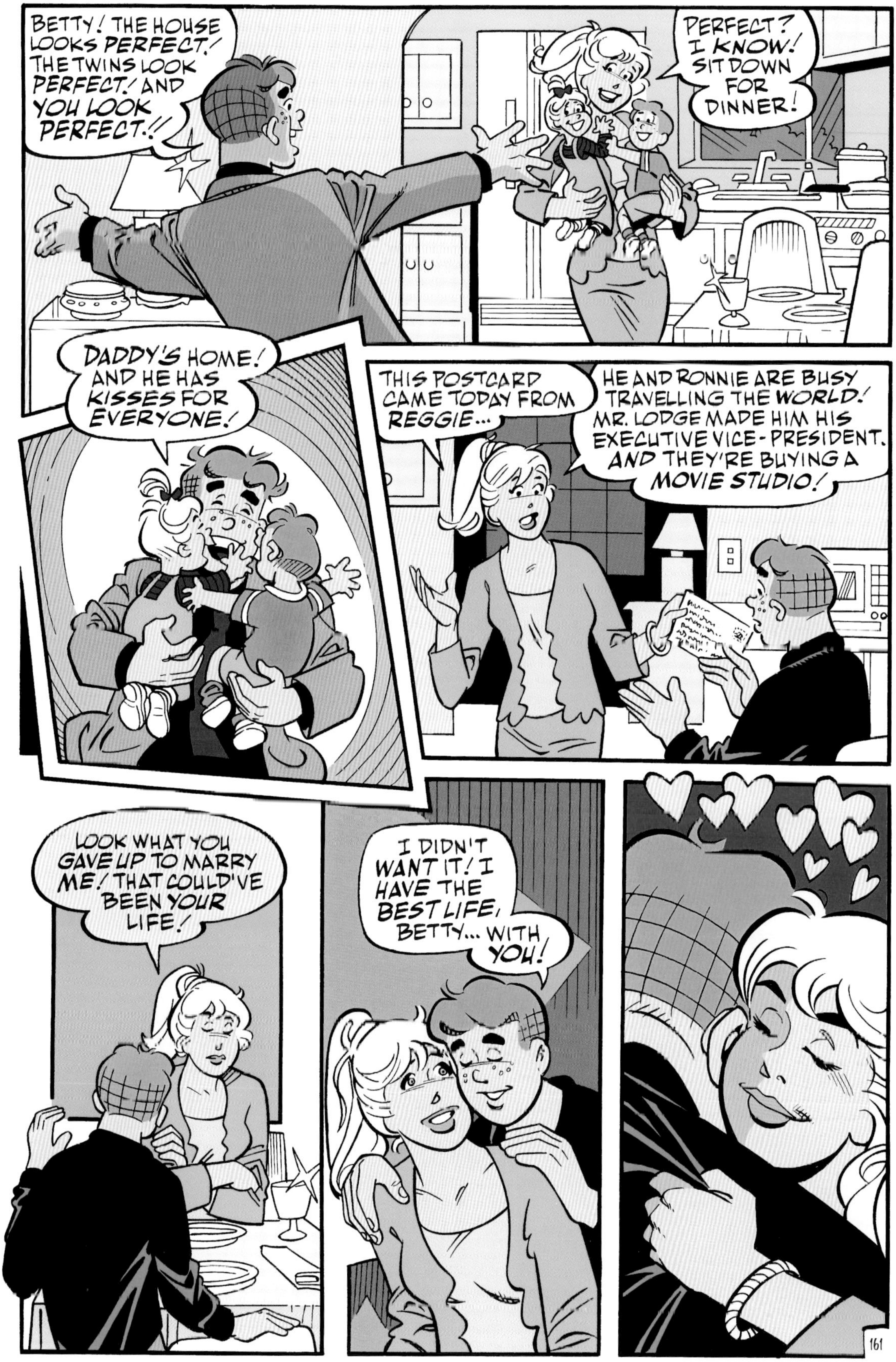

BETTY! THE HOUSE LOOKS PERFECT! THE TWINS LOOK PERFECT! AND YOU LOOK PERFECT!!
PERFECT? I KNOW! SIT DOWN FOR DINNER!
DADDY'S HOME! AND HE HAS KISSES FOR EVERYONE!
THIS POSTCARD CAME TODAY FROM REGGIE...
HE AND RONNIE ARE BUSY TRAVELLING THE WORLD! MR. LODGE MADE HIM HIS EXECUTIVE VICE-PRESIDENT. AND THEY'RE BUYING A MOVIE STUDIO!
LOOK WHAT YOU GAVE UP TO MARRY ME! THAT COULD'VE BEEN YOUR LIFE!
I DIDN'T WANT IT! I HAVE THE BEST LIFE, BETTY... WITH YOU!

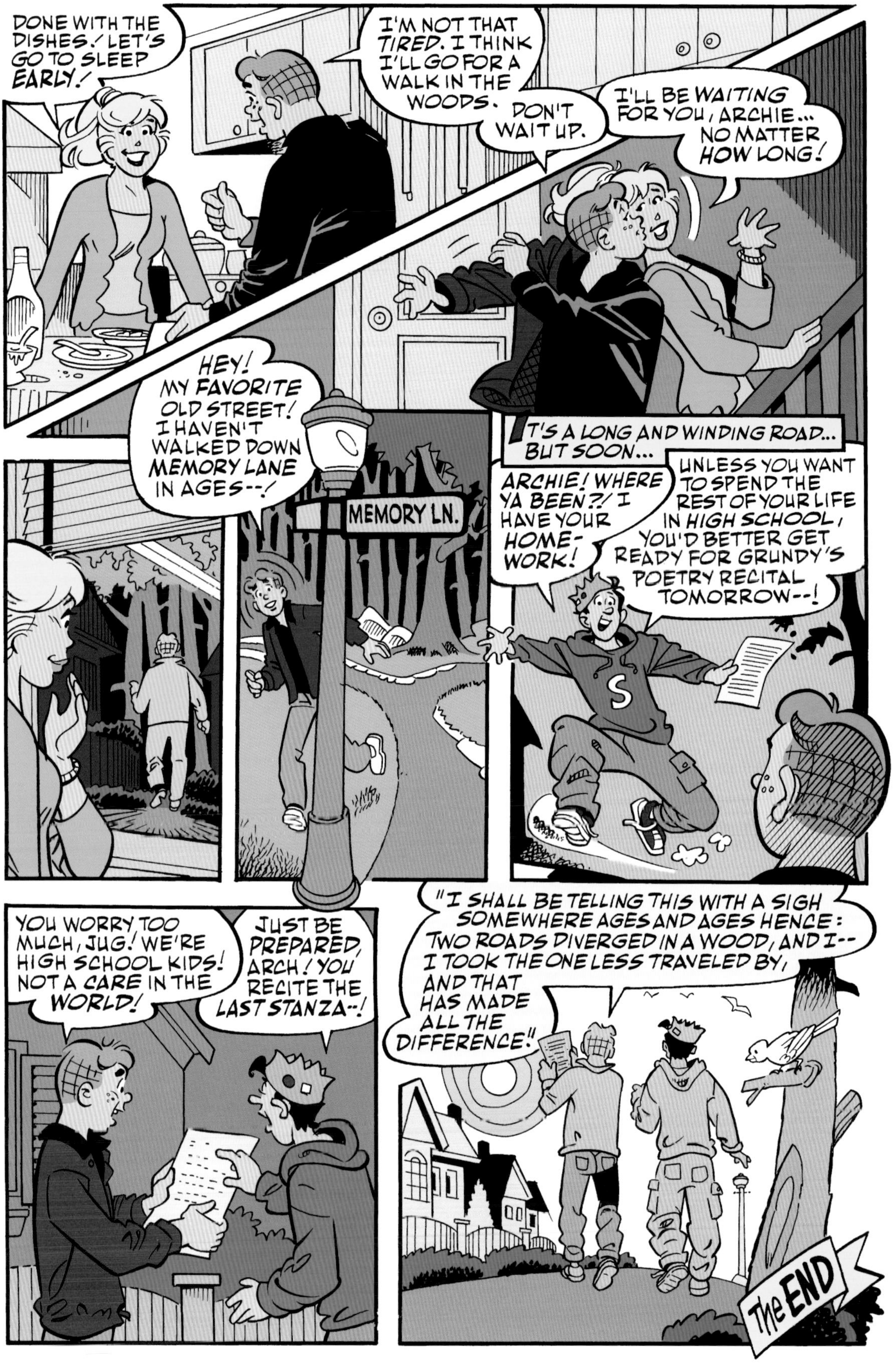
DONE WITH THE DISHES! LET'S GO TO SLEEP EARLY!
I'M NOT THAT TIRED. I THINK I'LL GO FOR A WALK IN THE WOODS.
DON'T WAIT UP.
I'LL BE WAITING FOR YOU, ARCHIE... NO MATTER HOW LONG!
HEY! MY FAVORITE OLD STREET! I HAVEN'T WALKED DOWN MEMORY LANE IN AGES--!
MEMORY LN.
IT'S A LONG AND WINDING ROAD... BUT SOON...
ARCHIE! WHERE YA BEEN?! I HAVE YOUR HOME-WORK!
UNLESS YOU WANT TO SPEND THE REST OF YOUR LIFE IN HIGH SCHOOL, YOU'D BETTER GET READY FOR GRUNDY'S POETRY RECITAL TOMORROW--!
YOU WORRY TOO MUCH, JUG! WE'RE HIGH SCHOOL KIDS! NOT A CARE IN THE WORLD!
JUST BE PREPARED, ARCH! YOU RECITE THE LAST STANZA--!
"I SHALL BE TELLING THIS WITH A SIGH SOMEWHERE AGES AND AGES HENCE: TWO ROADS DIVERGED IN A WOOD, AND I-- I TOOK THE ONE LESS TRAVELED BY, AND THAT HAS MADE ALL THE DIFFERENCE."
The END

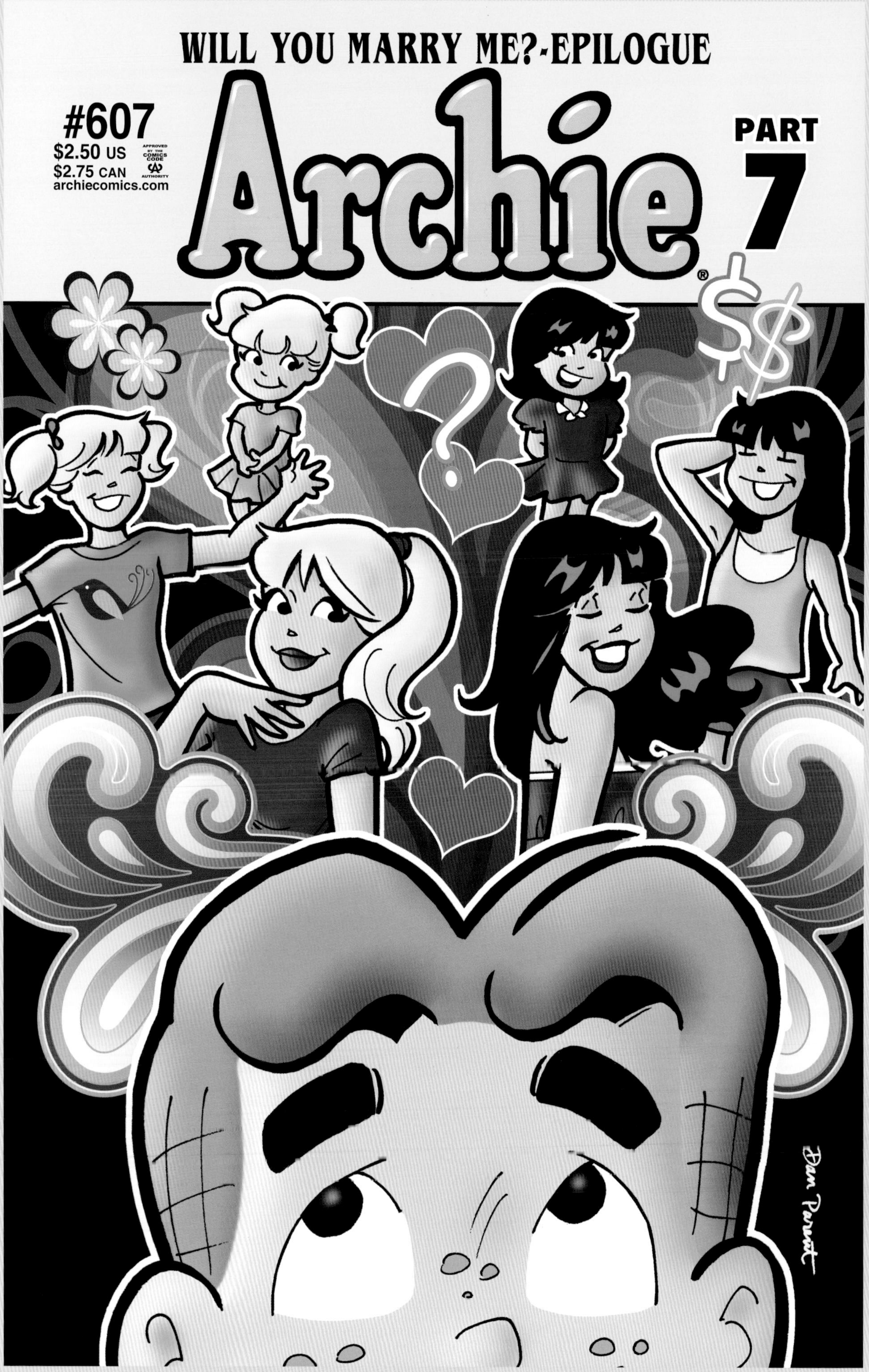
WILL YOU MARRY ME?-EPILOGUE
#607
$2.50 US
$2.75 CAN
archiecomics.com
APPROVED BY THE COMICS CODE AUTHORITY
Archie
PART 7
Dan Parent

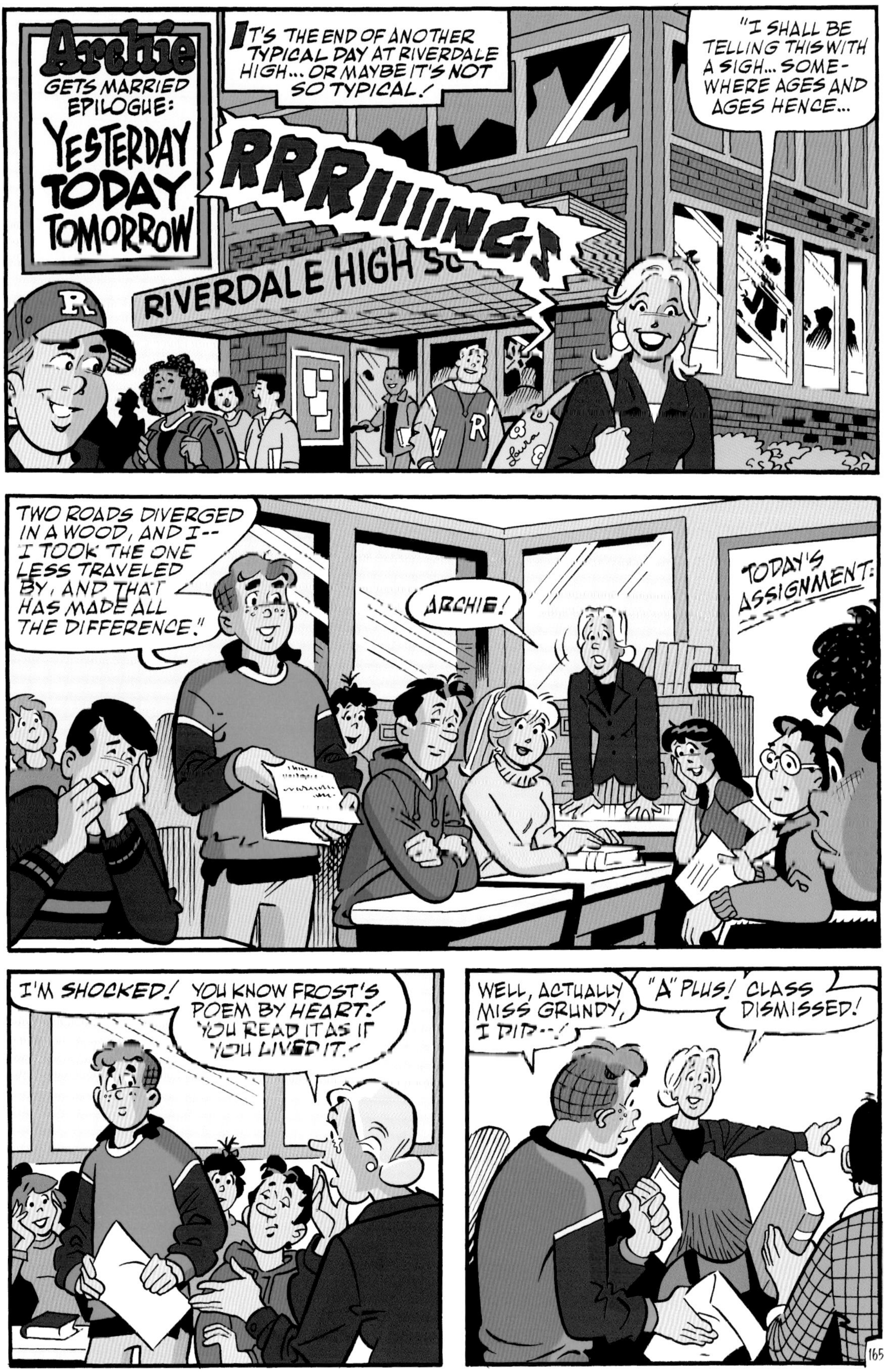
Archie
GETS MARRIED
EPILOGUE:
YESTERDAY TODAY TOMORROW
IT'S THE END OF ANOTHER TYPICAL DAY AT RIVERDALE HIGH... OR MAYBE IT'S NOT SO TYPICAL!
"I SHALL BE TELLING THIS WITH A SIGH... SOMEWHERE AGES AND AGES HENCE...
RRRIIIIING!
RIVERDALE HIGH SC
R
R
Laura
TWO ROADS DIVERGED IN A WOOD, AND I-- I TOOK THE ONE LESS TRAVELED BY, AND THAT HAS MADE ALL THE DIFFERENCE."
ARCHIE!
TODAY'S ASSIGNMENT:
I'M SHOCKED!
YOU KNOW FROST'S POEM BY HEART! YOU READ IT AS IF YOU LIVED IT!
WELL, ACTUALLY MISS GRUNDY, I DID--!
"A" PLUS! CLASS DISMISSED!

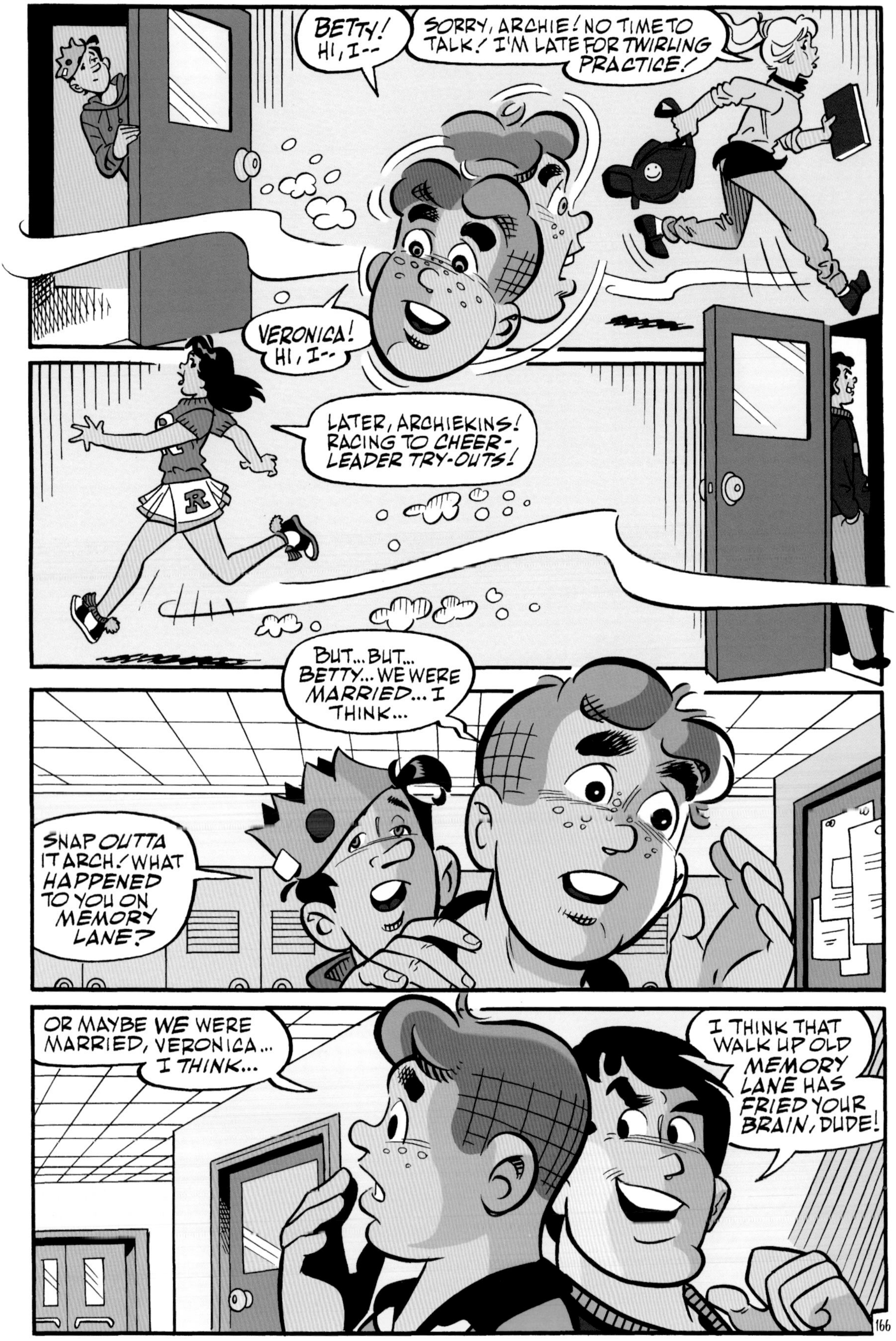
BETTY! HI, I--
SORRY, ARCHIE! NO TIME TO TALK! I'M LATE FOR TWIRLING PRACTICE!
VERONICA! HI, I--
LATER, ARCHIEKINS! RACING TO CHEER-LEADER TRY-OUTS!
BUT... BUT... BETTY... WE WERE MARRIED... I THINK...
SNAP OUTTA IT ARCH! WHAT HAPPENED TO YOU ON MEMORY LANE?
OR MAYBE WE WERE MARRIED, VERONICA... I THINK...
I THINK THAT WALK UP OLD MEMORY LANE HAS FRIED YOUR BRAIN, DUDE!

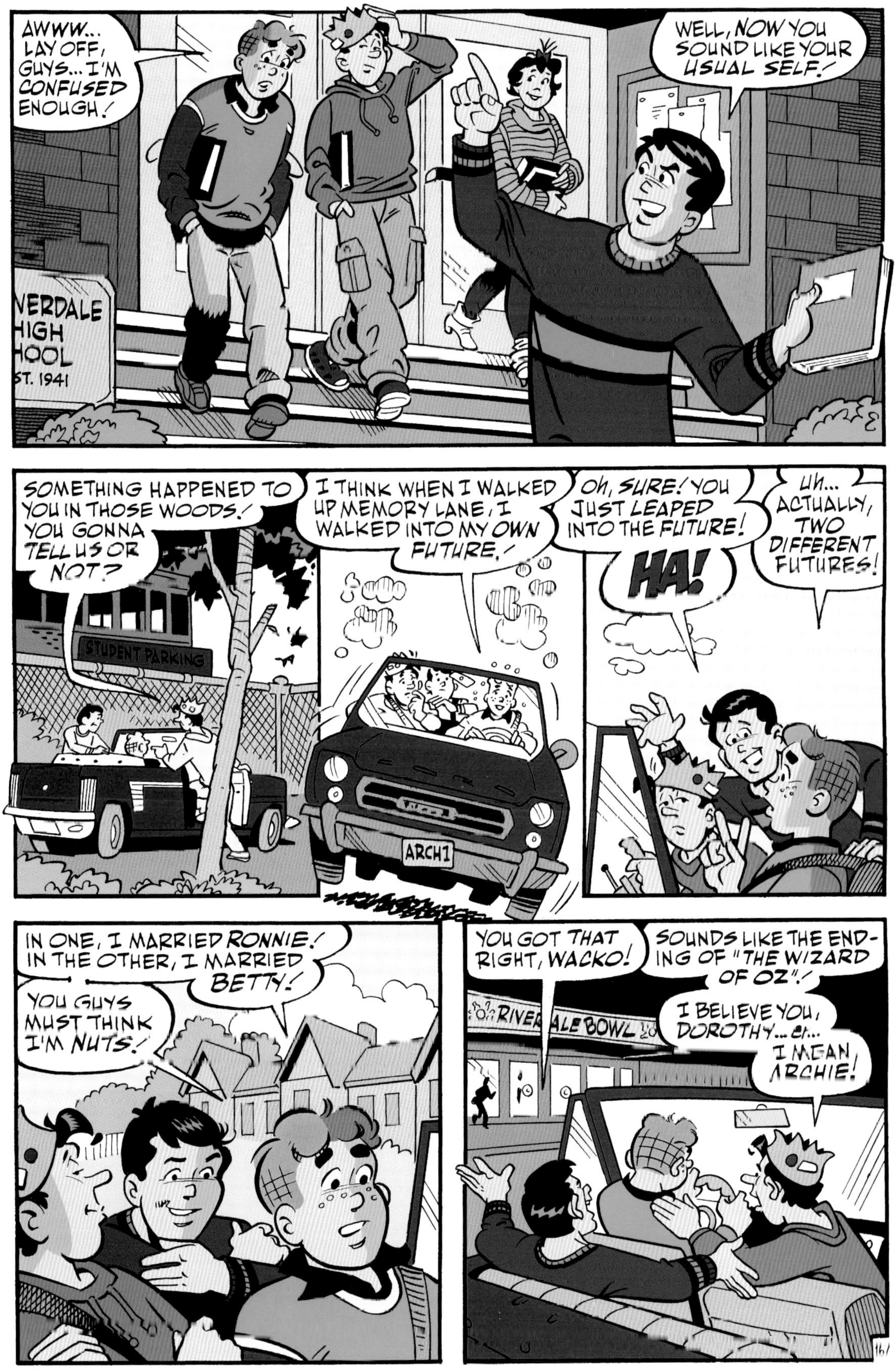
AWWW... LAY OFF, GUYS... I'M CONFUSED ENOUGH!
WELL, NOW YOU SOUND LIKE YOUR USUAL SELF!
VERDALE HIGH HOOL ST. 1941
SOMETHING HAPPENED TO YOU IN THOSE WOODS! YOU GONNA TELL US OR NOT?
STUDENT PARKING
I THINK WHEN I WALKED UP MEMORY LANE, I WALKED INTO MY OWN FUTURE!
ARCH1
OH, SURE! YOU JUST LEAPED INTO THE FUTURE!
HA!
UH... ACTUALLY, TWO DIFFERENT FUTURES!
IN ONE, I MARRIED RONNIE! IN THE OTHER, I MARRIED BETTY!
YOU GUYS MUST THINK I'M NUTS!
YOU GOT THAT RIGHT, WACKO!
SOUNDS LIKE THE ENDING OF "THE WIZARD OF OZ"!
RIVERDALE BOWL
I BELIEVE YOU, DOROTHY... ER... I MEAN ARCHIE!
161

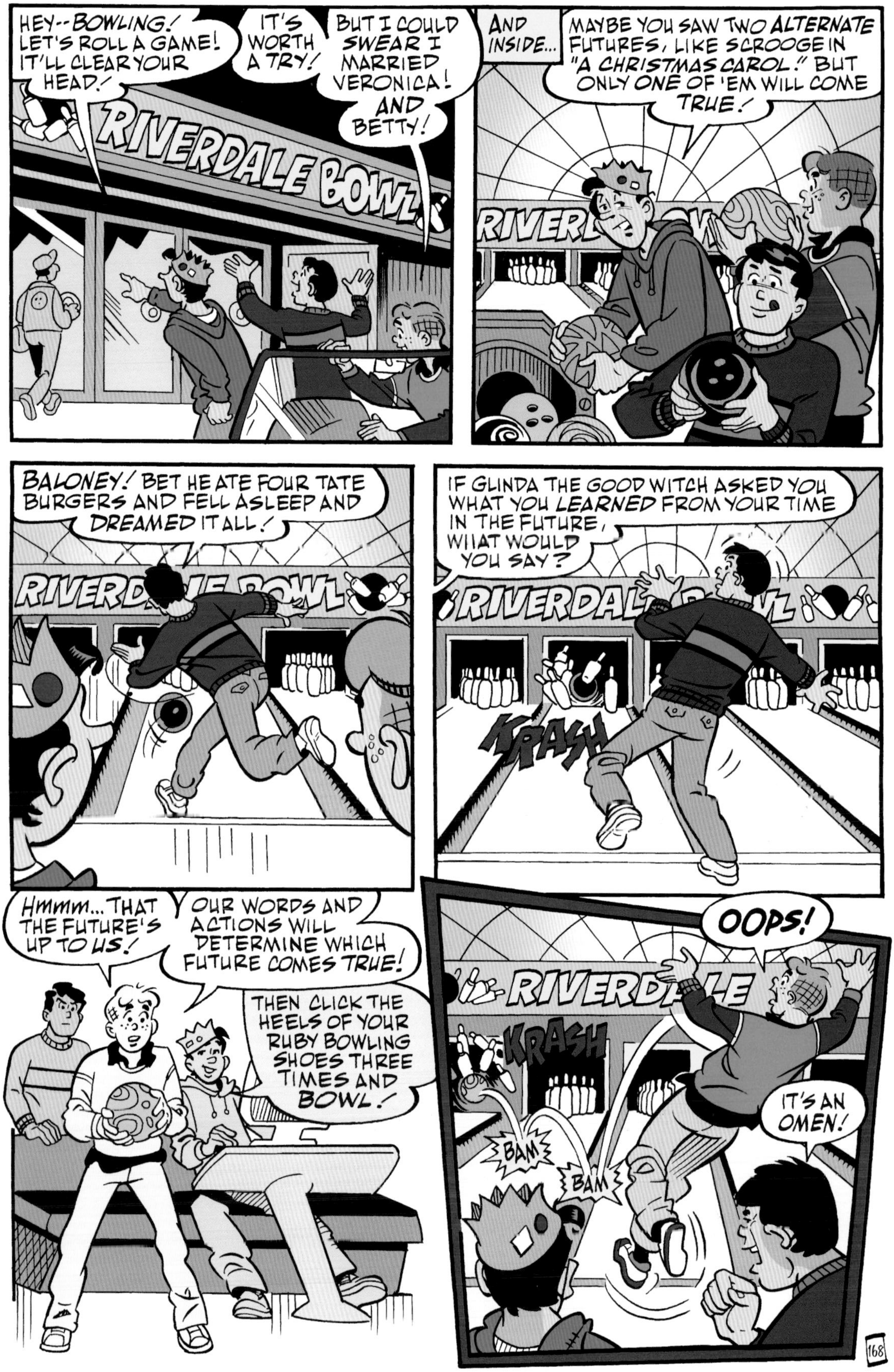
HEY--BOWLING! LET'S ROLL A GAME! IT'LL CLEAR YOUR HEAD!
IT'S WORTH A TRY!
BUT I COULD SWEAR I MARRIED VERONICA! AND BETTY!
RIVERDALE BOWL
AND INSIDE...
MAYBE YOU SAW TWO ALTERNATE FUTURES, LIKE SCROOGE IN "A CHRISTMAS CAROL!" BUT ONLY ONE OF 'EM WILL COME TRUE!
BALONEY! BET HE ATE FOUR TATE BURGERS AND FELL ASLEEP AND DREAMED IT ALL!
IF GLINDA THE GOOD WITCH ASKED YOU WHAT YOU LEARNED FROM YOUR TIME IN THE FUTURE, WHAT WOULD YOU SAY?
KRASH
HMMM... THAT THE FUTURE'S UP TO US!
OUR WORDS AND ACTIONS WILL DETERMINE WHICH FUTURE COMES TRUE!
THEN CLICK THE HEELS OF YOUR RUBY BOWLING SHOES THREE TIMES AND BOWL!
OOPS!
RIVERDALE
KRASH
BAM
BAM
IT'S AN OMEN!

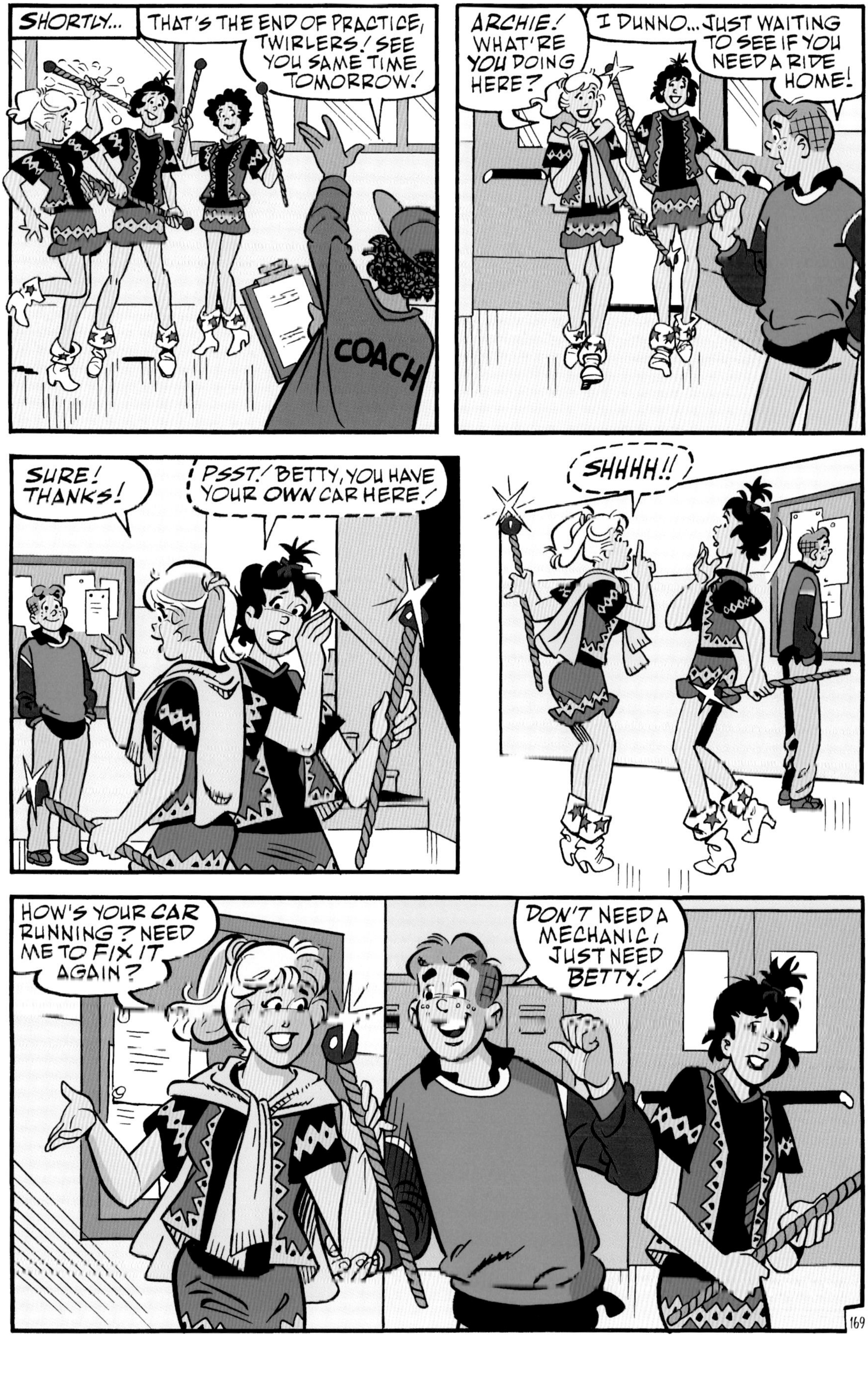
SHORTLY...
THAT'S THE END OF PRACTICE, TWIRLERS! SEE YOU SAME TIME TOMORROW!
COACH
ARCHIE! WHAT'RE YOU DOING HERE?
I DUNNO... JUST WAITING TO SEE IF YOU NEED A RIDE HOME!
SURE! THANKS!
PSST! BETTY, YOU HAVE YOUR OWN CAR HERE!
SHHHH!!
HOW'S YOUR CAR RUNNING? NEED ME TO FIX IT AGAIN?
DON'T NEED A MECHANIC, JUST NEED BETTY!

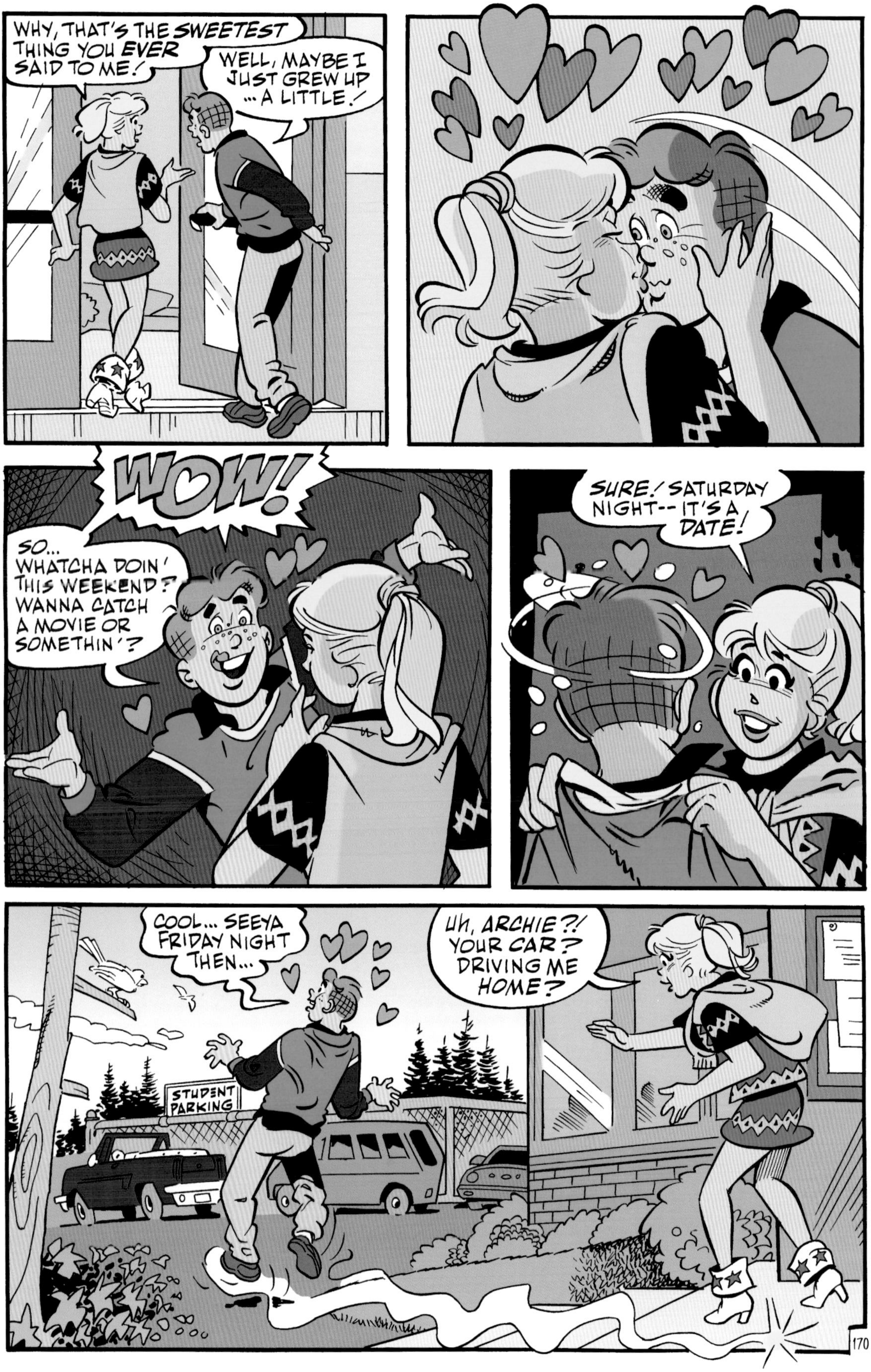
WHY, THAT'S THE SWEETEST THING YOU EVER SAID TO ME!
WELL, MAYBE I JUST GREW UP ...A LITTLE!
WOW!
SO... WHATCHA DOIN' THIS WEEKEND? WANNA CATCH A MOVIE OR SOMETHIN'?
SURE! SATURDAY NIGHT-- IT'S A DATE!
COOL... SEEYA FRIDAY NIGHT THEN...
UH, ARCHIE?! YOUR CAR? DRIVING ME HOME?
STUDENT PARKING

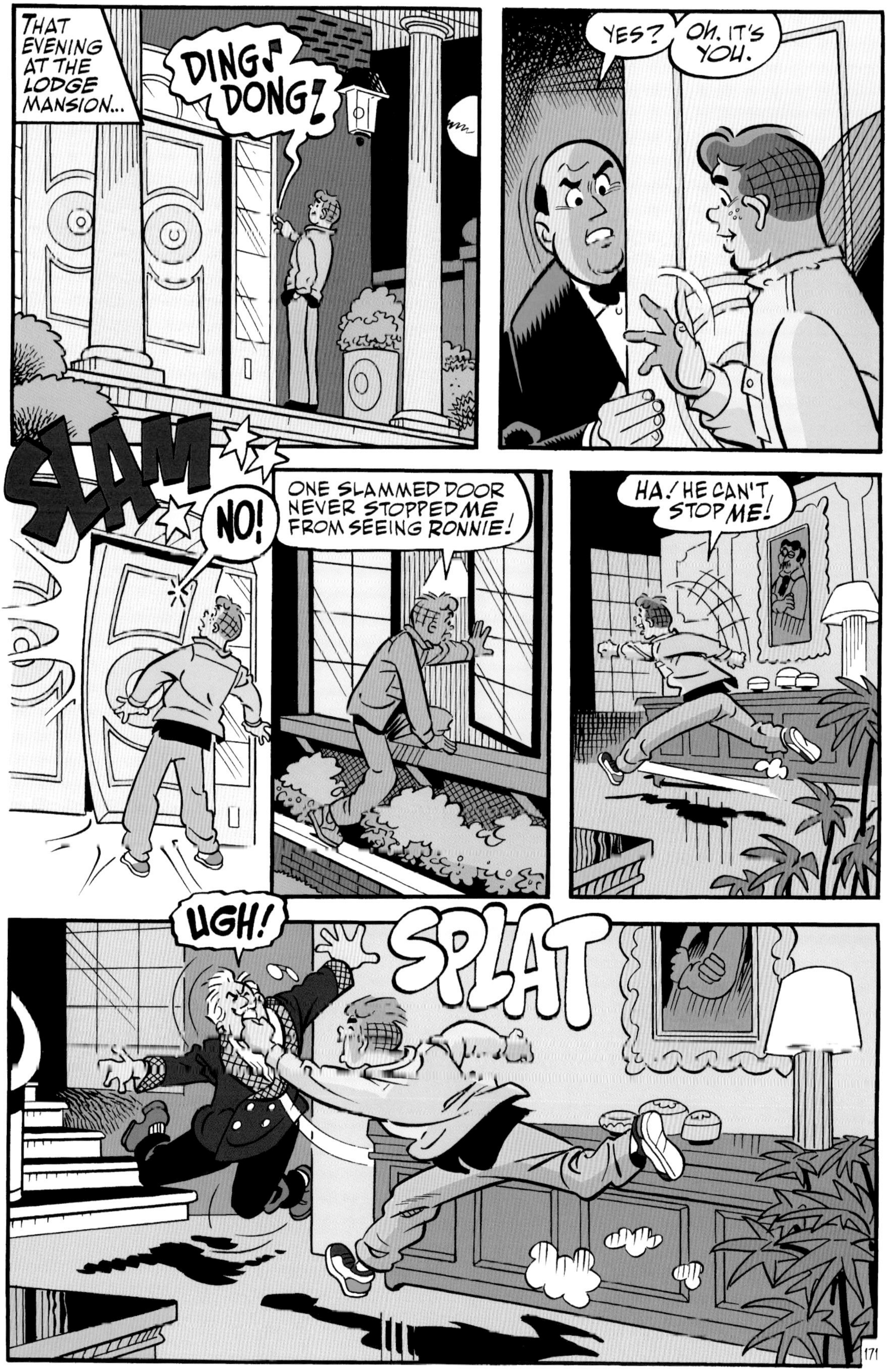
THAT EVENING AT THE LODGE MANSION...
DING DONG
YES?
OH. IT'S YOU.
SLAM
NO!
ONE SLAMMED DOOR NEVER STOPPED ME FROM SEEING RONNIE!
HA! HE CAN'T STOP ME!
UGH!
SPLAT

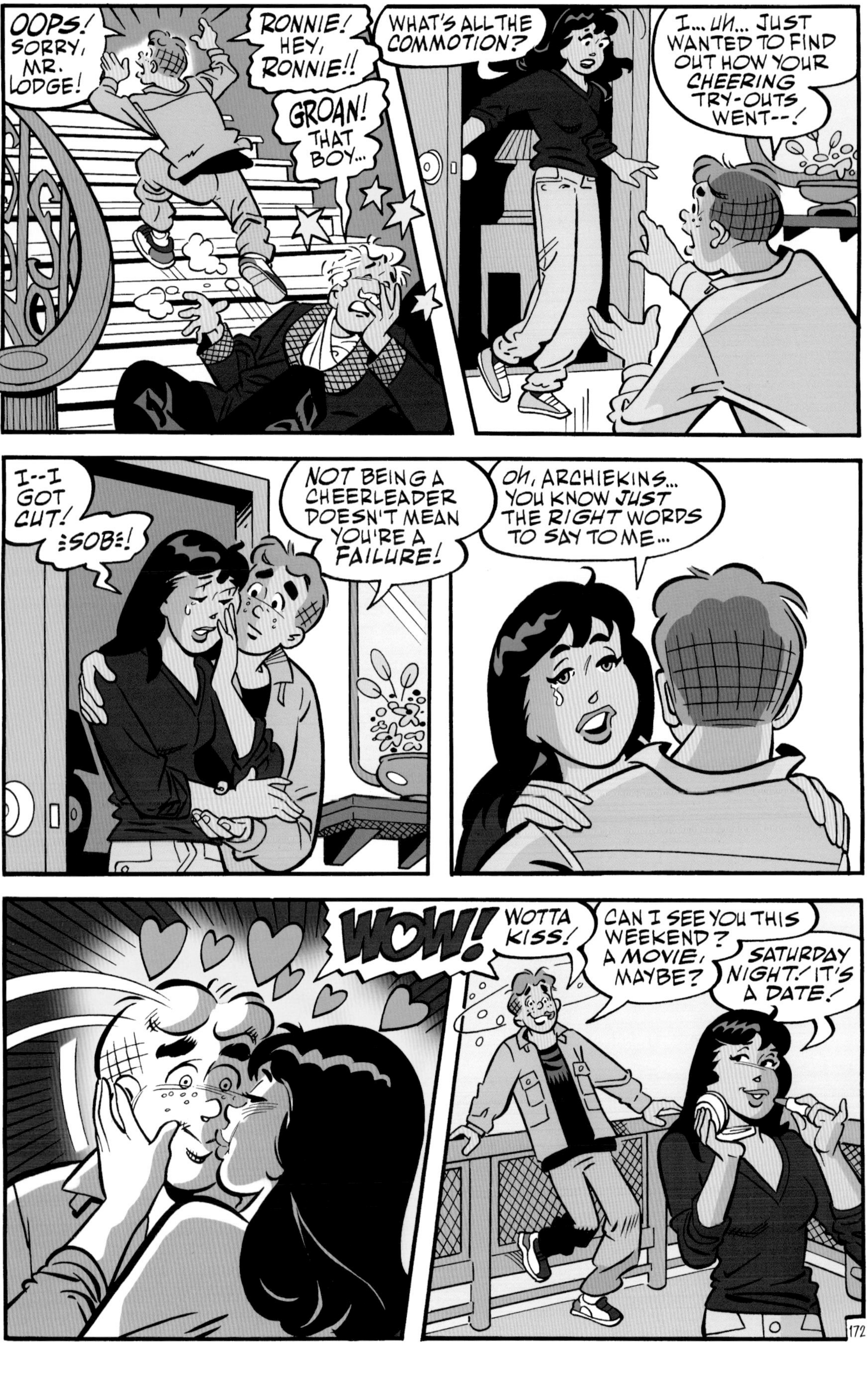

OOPS! SORRY, MR. LODGE!
RONNIE! HEY, RONNIE!!
GROAN! THAT BOY...
WHAT'S ALL THE COMMOTION?
I... UH... JUST WANTED TO FIND OUT HOW YOUR CHEERING TRY-OUTS WENT--!
I--I GOT CUT!
SOB!
NOT BEING A CHEERLEADER DOESN'T MEAN YOU'RE A FAILURE!
OH, ARCHIEKINS... YOU KNOW JUST THE RIGHT WORDS TO SAY TO ME...
WOW!
WOTTA KISS!
CAN I SEE YOU THIS WEEKEND? A MOVIE, MAYBE?
SATURDAY NIGHT! IT'S A DATE!

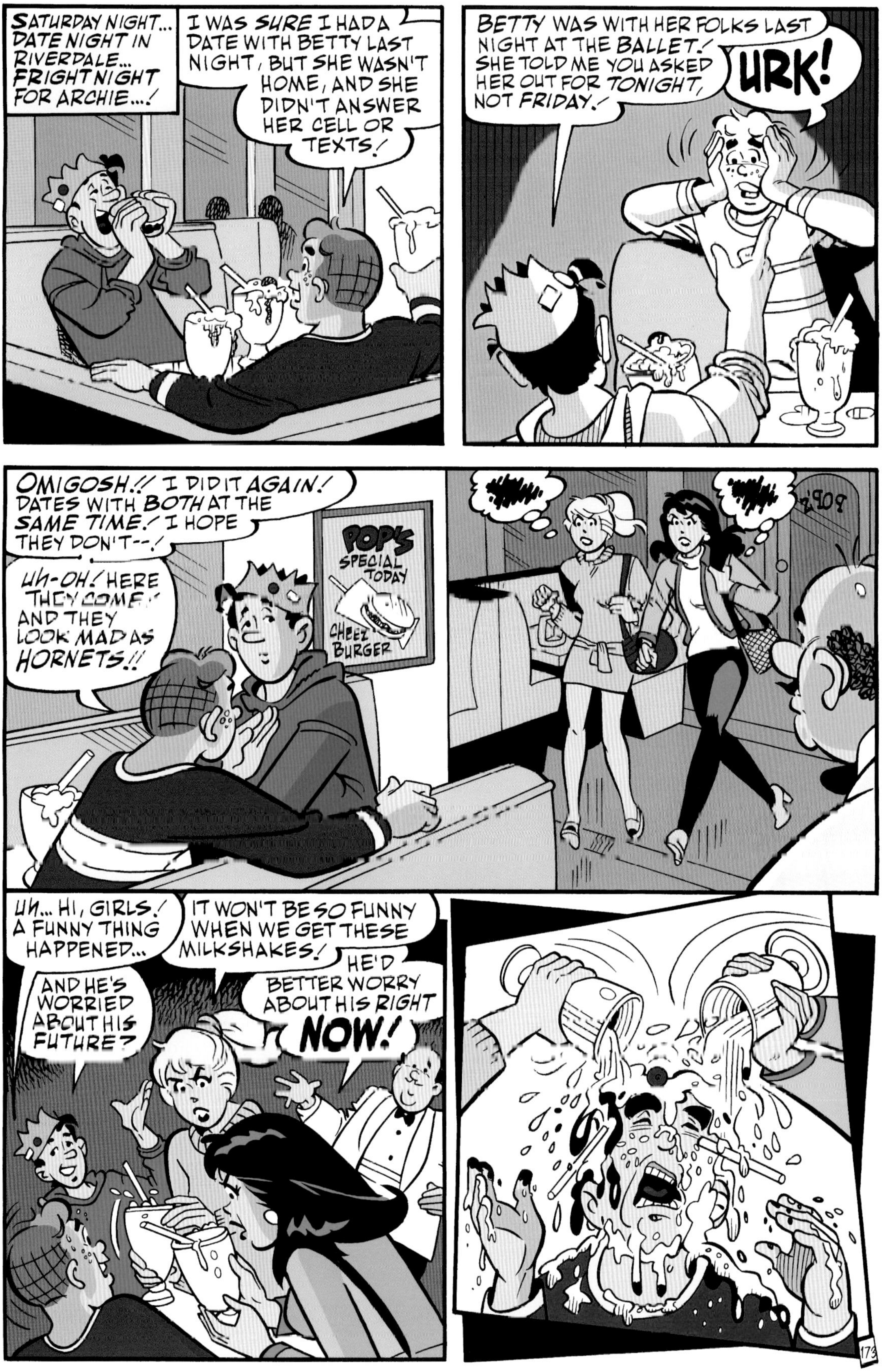
SATURDAY NIGHT... DATE NIGHT IN RIVERDALE... FRIGHT NIGHT FOR ARCHIE...!
I WAS SURE I HAD A DATE WITH BETTY LAST NIGHT, BUT SHE WASN'T HOME, AND SHE DIDN'T ANSWER HER CELL OR TEXTS!
BETTY WAS WITH HER FOLKS LAST NIGHT AT THE BALLET! SHE TOLD ME YOU ASKED HER OUT FOR TONIGHT, NOT FRIDAY!
URK!
OMIGOSH!! I DID IT AGAIN! DATES WITH BOTH AT THE SAME TIME! I HOPE THEY DON'T--!
UH-OH! HERE THEY COME! AND THEY LOOK MAD AS HORNETS!!
POP'S SPECIAL TODAY
CHEEZ BURGER
POP'S
UH... HI, GIRLS! A FUNNY THING HAPPENED...
IT WON'T BE SO FUNNY WHEN WE GET THESE MILKSHAKES!
AND HE'S WORRIED ABOUT HIS FUTURE?
HE'D BETTER WORRY ABOUT HIS RIGHT NOW!

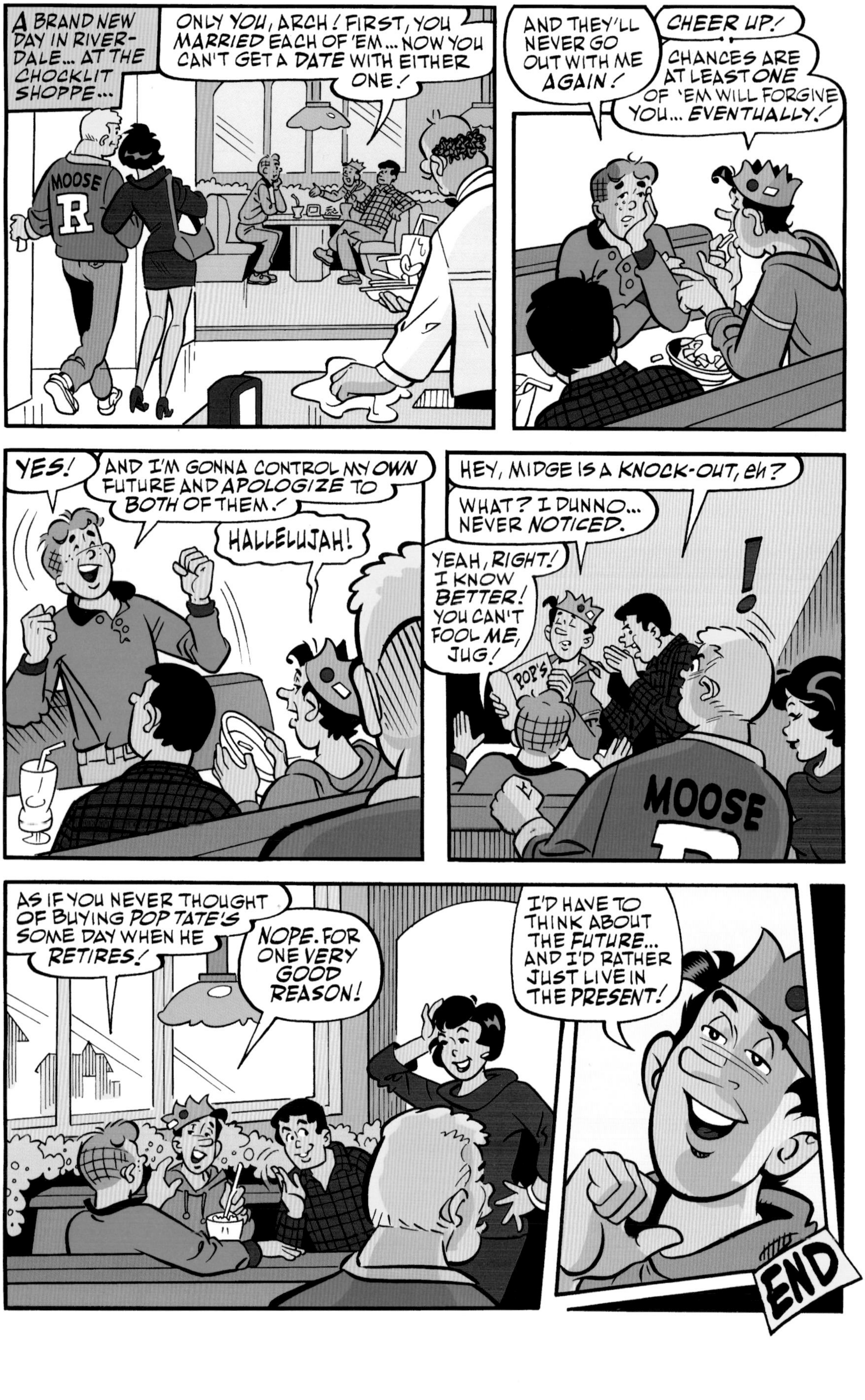
A BRAND NEW DAY IN RIVER-DALE... AT THE CHOCKLIT SHOPPE...
ONLY YOU, ARCH! FIRST, YOU MARRIED EACH OF 'EM... NOW YOU CAN'T GET A DATE WITH EITHER ONE!
MOOSE
R
AND THEY'LL NEVER GO OUT WITH ME AGAIN!
CHEER UP!
CHANCES ARE AT LEAST ONE OF 'EM WILL FORGIVE YOU... EVENTUALLY!
YES!
AND I'M GONNA CONTROL MY OWN FUTURE AND APOLOGIZE TO BOTH OF THEM!
HALLELUJAH!
HEY, MIDGE IS A KNOCK-OUT, eh?
WHAT? I DUNNO... NEVER NOTICED.
YEAH, RIGHT! I KNOW BETTER! YOU CAN'T FOOL ME, JUG!
!
POP'S
MOOSE
AS IF YOU NEVER THOUGHT OF BUYING POP TATE'S SOME DAY WHEN HE RETIRES!
NOPE. FOR ONE VERY GOOD REASON!
I'D HAVE TO THINK ABOUT THE FUTURE... AND I'D RATHER JUST LIVE IN THE PRESENT!
END

Interviews & Supplementary Material

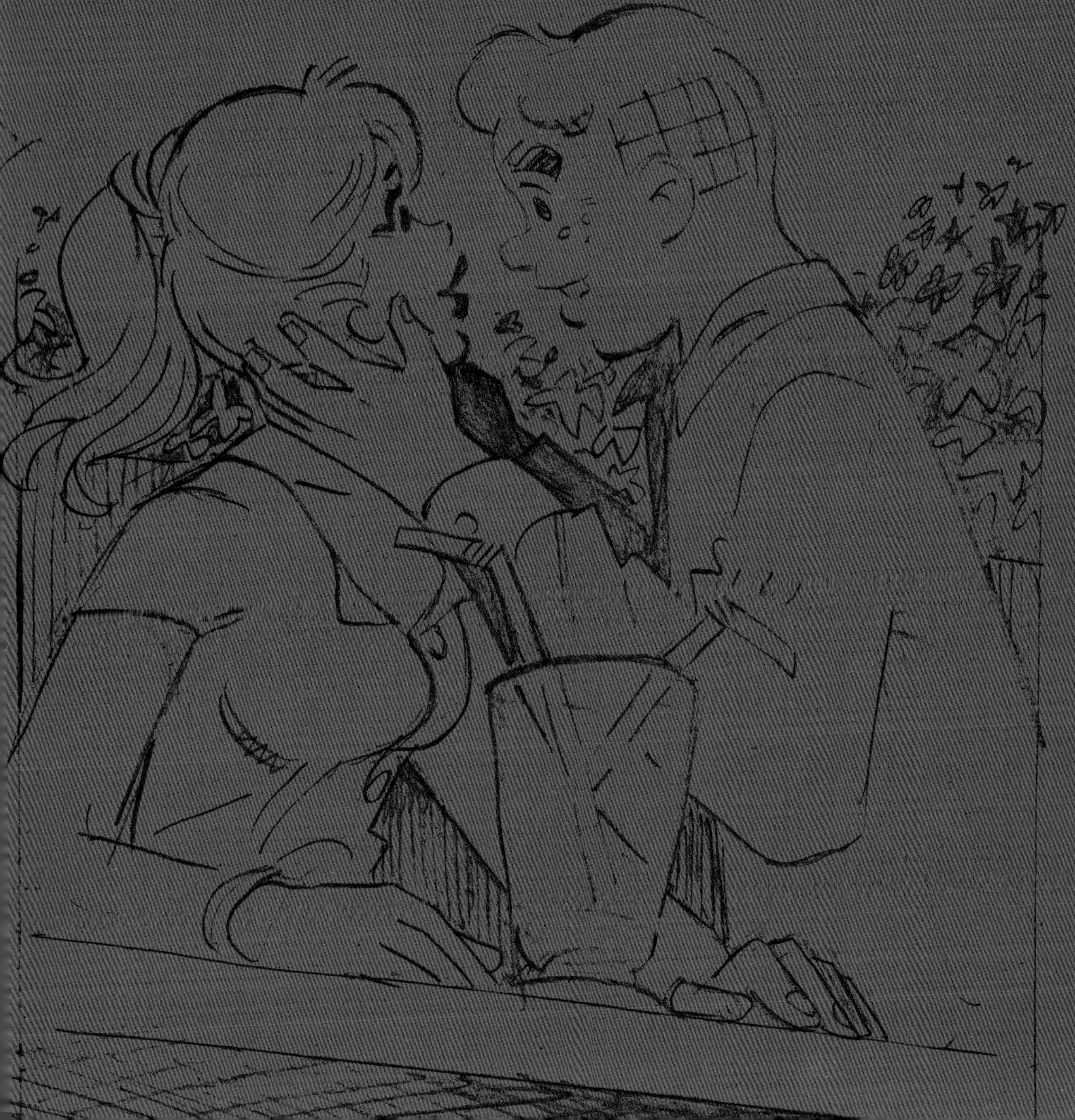

Abrams ComicArts Executive Editor **Charles Kochman** spoke with the seven creators of *Archie Marries . . .* about their roles in the creation of the story line, the reaction to the wedding of Archie and Veronica and the wedding of Archie and Betty, the endurance of the Archie characters, and their fellow collaborators. The interview with writer **Michael Uslan** took place on February 25 and 26, 2010. Archie President/Editor in Chief **Victor Gorelick** was interviewed on April 1, 2010. Penciler **Stan Goldberg** was interviewed on April 2, 2010. Letterer **Jack Morelli** was interviewed on April 2, 2010. Inker **Bob Smith** was interviewed on March 18, 2010. Colorist **Glenn Whitmore** was interviewed on March 30, 2010. And Archie Co-CEO **Jon Goldwater** was interviewed on March 30, 2010. These interviews were transcribed by **Helen Chin** and edited for publication in April 2010 by Kochman and Assistant Editor **Sofia Gutiérrez**.

MICHAEL USLAN

Charles Kochman: I remember reading on CNN back in May 2009 that Archie was going to marry Veronica, and like everyone else who heard the news, I was taken aback. This was such a radical approach to an Archie story. How did you conceive of the idea? And even more to the point, how on earth did you get Archie folks to approve the story line?

Michael Uslan: I'm told by my mother that I learned to read before I was four years old from comic books like *Casper, Richie Rich,* and *Archie.* When I was growing up, I was an *Archie* comics reader, and like most people in my baby-boomer generation, the preconceived notions I had as to what high school was going to be like and what dating was going to be like largely came from reading *Archie* comics. Maybe a little bit came from *Ozzie and Harriet,* maybe a little from *Leave It to Beaver,* but primarily my frame of reference for being a teenager came from *Archie* comics. I guess you could say that Archie played an important role in my life, as it has in the lives of many people since 1941.

After *The Dark Knight* came out in 2008—that was a film I was executive producer of—my wife, Nancy, sat me down and said, "Okay, what do you want to do when you grow up?" I sat and thought real hard about what I wanted to do, and I realized I wanted to write a few things. I've been lucky enough to have written Batman comics, and Batman was one of my biggest comic book heroes. I wrote a Batman graphic novel. I've written other characters I love, like the Shadow, Steve Ditko's the Question, and Will Eisner's the Spirit, but I always wanted to write an Archie comic. I wanted to do something important, something historical, something significant. So I thought about it and went to see Victor Gorelick, who has been at Archie for over fifty years, I believe. Victor and I know each other going back thirty years. A friend of mine, Jeff Mendel, and I wrote a book, the first hardcover Archie collection ever. It was a history of Archie called *The Best of Archie,* and it was published in 1980 by G.P. Putnam's Sons. In order to do that book we interviewed the people who were around

then, including John L. Goldwater, the founder of Archie Comics, and we also met Victor. Victor opened up the Archie vaults for us, and Jeff and I read every single issue of *Archie* comics ever made up until then. That way we could pick out the best stories, and write the history, too. So my background with Victor goes all the way back, and I said, "Victor, I would love to write an important Archie comic." And he said, "That's great. What would you like to do?" I said, "I'd like to do a story where Archie gets married." And he looked at me like I was crazy and said, "You can't do that." And I said, "Why not?" And that sparked a discussion, a very creative discussion, and a number of e-mails, that led us onto the path of Archie getting married.

The reason I wanted to do the marriage story was because in the world of comic books today, attention is drawn to the world's greatest super heroes—from Spider-Man to Superman to Batman—by major events in their lives. Pivotal stories that appeal not only to the hardcore fans and collectors, but that reach out to the mainstream audience, who in many cases don't even know comic books are still being published today. These are not people who show up at their local comic book shops every Wednesday in order to get the latest issues. A lot of them read comic books for years, especially when they were younger; a lot of them have moved on, or live in areas where there are no comic book shops. Well, I felt it was time for the media spotlight to turn on Archie. His comic books are still very successful. Amazingly, seventy years later, Archie and the gang are still doing the same kinds of things in school, and the same kinds of things at Pop Tate's malt shop and on the beach, and they're still magically relevant to readers today. I wanted to be able to appeal not only to the current generation of young fans but to the parents and grandparents who had moved on from reading *Archie* since they were kids. I wanted to let the world know that these comic books are still being published, that Archie is still relevant. But what we did not anticipate was the firestorm that erupted in the worldwide media. And when I say worldwide, I'm not just talking the United States and Canada. I'm talking Kenya, India, Australia, England. The story just seemed to register with fans everywhere; that was something we never did anticipate.

Kochman: Let's talk about that. What happens when you're writing a story like this, a monumental story, the equivalent of the death of Superman, or the wedding of Lois and Clark or of Peter Parker and Mary Jane Watson, or the death of Gwen Stacy, or even the death of Jason Todd's Robin? I know from my time at DC Comics that sometimes these stories hit big when you're not expecting them to, and sometimes they're published and for whatever reason they don't get the media attention you were hoping for. Obviously, that wasn't the case with Archie. So when you're writing that first issue, you have no idea how it's going to be received. And then by the time you're writing the last issue, a lot of people are now paying attention, readers all over the world. Is that pressure intimidating or helpful? All of a sudden you, as the writer, now have to live up to the hype you've created. Especially because people weren't happy with the fact that Archie was going to marry Veronica.

Uslan: [laughs] That's putting it mildly. Which is why we started with his marriage to Veronica first, to draw the attention we wanted to the story line. You know, all the great super heroes have had events like those you just mentioned: Superman married Lois Lane; Spider-Man married Mary Jane, then he *unmarried* Mary Jane; Batman had his back broken; Superman died, then it turned out he wasn't dead; Captain America died. But miraculously, in the world of comic books, somehow they all came back. So the idea of these major events in the world of comics that draw attention to the characters doesn't mean that they permanently change the status of those characters. The only major event I could imagine that would have a similar impact would be if Archie got married. After all, he's dated these two girls now for over sixty-eight years, and I thought, Isn't it about time he made a choice? By the time the first issue was published, we already had the whole story line mapped out and most of the issues written, so fortunately I didn't feel too much of the pressure. We knew where we were going and were confident in our story.

Kochman: Did you initially consider just one scenario, or did you always conceive the wedding story line as showing both sides?

Uslan: I always wanted to show both sides. I think that's the magic of it. Showing Archie marrying just one of the two would have cheated at least half of every generation of Archie readers. We needed to show the consequences, the butterfly effect, not only on Archie, Betty, and Veronica, but the butterfly effect his marriage would have on everybody in Riverdale, family and friends, because in real life a marriage does just that: It impacts everybody's lives, not just the lives of the two spouses. So it was important to me to show what Archie's life would be like if he married Veronica, and then show what it would be like if he married Betty, and then let the readers compare. Let the readers express their own feelings about it, their own thoughts, after seeing how these different decisions affected everyone's lives. And it brings up some interesting points, too. Thematically, the question becomes: Does a person marry for love or marry for money and security? I'm reminded of my freshman year in college. It was Parents' Weekend, and my dad was down, and my college roommate Marc Caplan's dad was down, and the four of us were having lunch somewhere, and we got onto this discussion of marriage. And my father said, "Oh, absolutely, you should marry for love," and Marc's father said, "Absolutely, you should marry for love . . . but if she happens to come from money, that's not a bad thing, either." Definitely find somebody you love, but gee, wouldn't it be great if you happen to find somebody you love who also has money? That was always interesting to me, especially because Veronica was filthy rich and Betty was so not. The impact of money on a marriage—

what that would do for Archie in terms of his career, his lifestyle, and how that would allow him to fit in with the likes of Jughead, Moose, and people who he's been friends with since he was little—it was an interesting thing to explore, especially in this day and age and with the current recession. And I couldn't help but feel that in real life, if you can possibly call it real life, the news that Brad Pitt picked Angelina Jolie over Jennifer Aniston—to me that was the real-world equivalent of Archie picking Veronica over Betty. So does the exotic, rich woman win out all the time over the loyal girl next door? These were questions I wanted to address, and I needed to show both sides.

Kochman: Anything influence you as you were writing the story?

Uslan: I mainly had three inspirations: The first was my all-time favorite poem, a poem that has actually shaped my philosophy on life, which is Robert Frost's "The Road Not Taken": *Two roads diverged in a wood, and I— / I took the one less traveled by.* I used that as a primary source for this particular work. I wanted to show what would happen if you go down one path and then maybe you come back at a later day and try the other path.

Another inspiration was a movie starring Gwyneth Paltrow called *Sliding Doors.* In that movie, a young lady rushes to get onto the subway and different things happen to her. She's delayed slightly here and there crossing the streets, and she just misses the train. Then the film backs up and we're shown the same scenes all over again, only with the slightest bit of a twist and turn as she just barely makes that subway. We get to follow her life both ways—what happens to her if she made it and what happens to her if she did not make that train. And it was stunning, the differences in her life based on that one little incident. So to me, to show the differences in the lives of Archie and his family and friends based on whom he chooses to marry was something I absolutely wanted to explore.

The third inspiration was the Joni Mitchell song "Both Sides Now." I always knew the version sung by Judy Collins—*I've looked at love from both sides now / I've looked at life from both sides now*—that, too, made me absolutely want to set up this series where we would see what happened if Archie married Veronica and then the events if he married Betty.

Kochman: Did you ever consider opening the story line with Archie marrying Betty?

Uslan: If we had come out first with Betty, I think the world would have smiled a great big smile and given out a collective *Ah, isn't that sweet? Isn't that wonderful?* We would not have had the world event that we created by revealing that Archie was going to marry Veronica. That stirred the pot. That got a lot of people heated up from every generation. There was a poll taken by the *Today Show*, and after a few days twenty to thirty thousand people had responded. It ran about 80 percent to 20 percent Betty over Veronica, and we kind of suspected it might. But I would add that Jughead did place a strong third; the times they certainly are a-changin'.

ARCHIE #602, Page 24

PANEL 1. Archie puts on his coat and hat and scarf. He's taking something out of a pocket. Veronica takes some wrapping paper out of the same hall closet.

VERONICA

Come back SOON. It's snowing hard.

ARCHIE

Okay.

PANEL 2. Archie, in his coat and hat and gloves and scarf, goes to kiss Veronica at the open doorway as he holds up a mistletoe sprig over their heads. We can see how hard it's snowing and the cold wind blows in.

ARCHIE

It's MISTLETOE. I LOVE you, Veronica.

VERONICA

I LOVE you, too, Archie. Merry Christmas, darling.

PANEL 3. The kiss.

PANEL 4. Archie heads out into the snow as the door closes dramatically and symbolically.

PANEL 5. Archie finds himself back in the Yellow Woods in the driving snow. And there, just ahead, is that first signpost that reads "Memory Lane." In the distance ahead, it must be clear that the road diverges there and forks in two directions.

ARCHIE

The Yellow Woods! I haven't been here in AGES! And up ahead—"Memory Lane"! Hmmm . . . The road FORKS there!

PANEL 6. In the blinding snow, like the last shot in *Casablanca*, we see Archie take the right fork in the road and head out into the distance. Very dramatic.

BOTTOM CAPTION

Archie's about to walk right into an ALTERNATIVE FUTURE! Think you've seen it ALL? NO way!

Next: **"ARCHIE MARRIES BETTY!"**

Michael Uslan's script (**above**) and Stan Goldberg's pencils (**right**) for page 84 (*Archie* no. 602, December 2009).

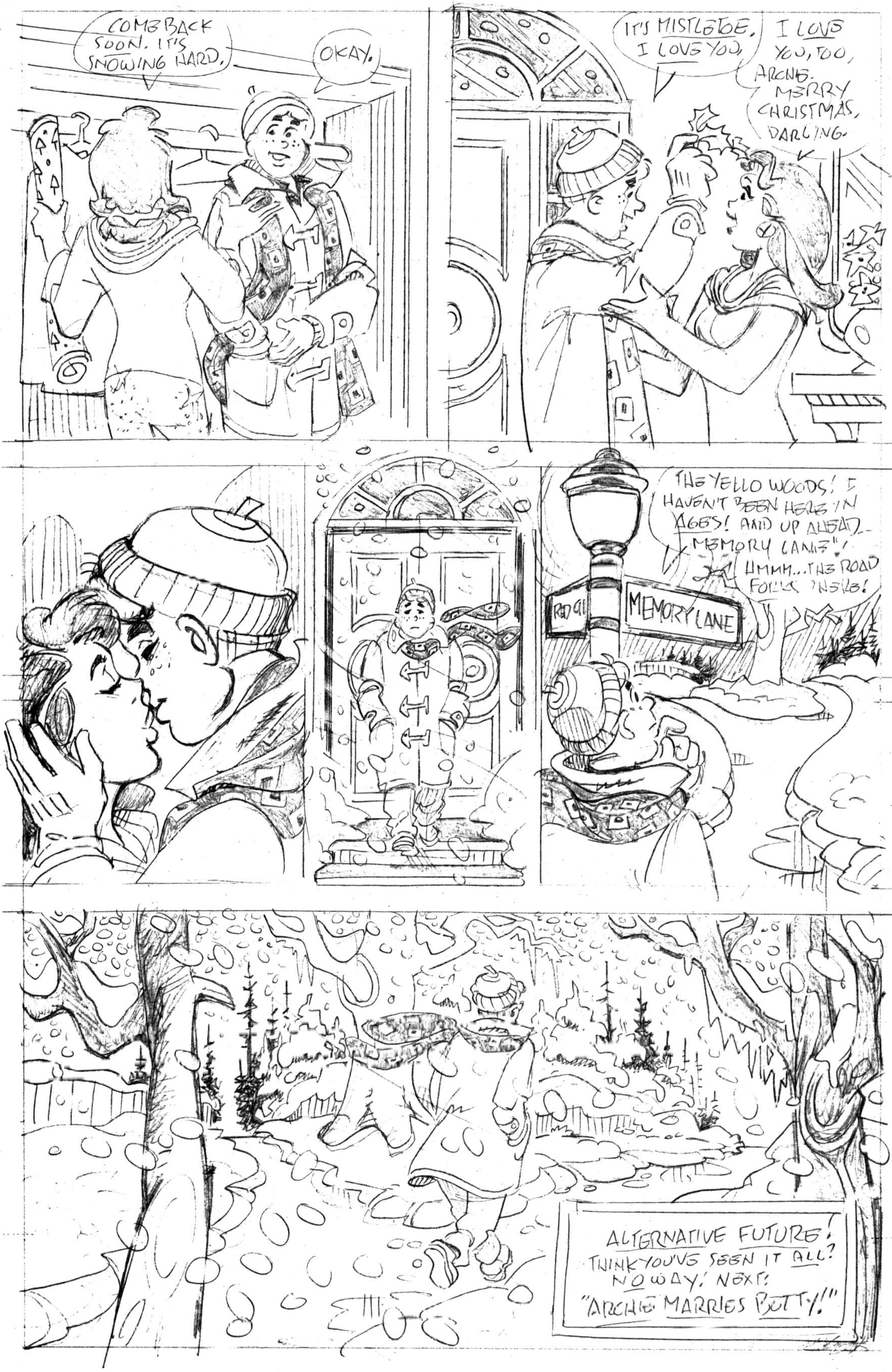
COME BACK SOON. IT'S SNOWING HARD.
OKAY.
IT'S MISTLETOE. I LOVE YOU.
I LOVE YOU, TOO, ARCHIE. MERRY CHRISTMAS, DARLING.
RED GI
MEMORY LANE
THE YELLO WOODS! I HAVEN'T BEEN HERE IN AGES! AND UP AHEAD-- "MEMORY LANE"!
HMMM...THE ROAD FORKS INSIDE!
ALTERNATIVE FUTURE! THINK YOU'VE SEEN IT ALL? NO WAY! NEXT: "ARCHIE MARRIES BETTY!"

There are probably at this point as many as fifty thousand postings on the Web dealing with this subject, with Archie getting married, or Archie marrying Veronica, or Archie marrying Betty, and I've been able to troll around and read about fifteen thousand of them. There are certain elements that I love to read. The same things are said over and over again. Archie readers are split into different camps, and they debate hot and heavy about Betty and Veronica. Do good girls ever win, or do they always lose to the sexy rich girls? The generations that have grown up with Archie over the decades—they responded with such emotion. Their e-mails would go on and on and on, and they'd comment in their blogs, *How can Archie grow up?* You know, *He was such an important part of our lives when we were young.* Somehow they needed that constant, even if they hadn't checked in on him over the years, you know? They've all grown up, but how can he grow up, too? They would go on and on about it, opening themselves up. Some were absolutely furious; some were concerned. And the same thing would crop up at the end of each of these postings: *I don't know why I'm going on and on and on about this, or why I'm so fired up about it, or even why it means so much to me—but it just does.* It's important. It's a part of so many of our childhoods, for generations now. It's like going to your high school reunion, when all of a sudden you get to see your high school friends who you grew up with. There's often an extended-family feeling. An awful lot of people have this vis-à-vis Archie, Betty, Veronica, and Jughead.

Kochman: And to be a part of that mythology, to create such a meaningful story that has touched so many readers, must be really satisfying.

Uslan: Thank you, it is. It requires . . . you must be true to the characters and to the integrity of the characters. We're dealing with characters who are now four years older. This story line takes place . . . it starts on graduation day from college, and in my life's experience, most of the people that I knew from high school did evolve to some degree or another—I'm not saying negatively or positively, but they did change by the time they graduated college. So I didn't want everyone to just read "Archie marries Veronica" and say, *Oh, she's so snooty. She's going to wreck his life. She's going to do this, she's going to do that. She's just going to drive him crazy. She's going to be spoiled*—because Veronica four years from now would inevitably be more mature. When people were asking, *What about poor Betty?* my answer was to point out that for all these years Betty has hung around doing everything she could to get Archie to look at her, to pay attention to her, to date her. . . . This girl has her *own* self-esteem, self-confidence issues, and maybe she deserves someone *better* than Archie. Maybe this is a great maturing wake-up call for her. Archie was making a choice as he was graduating college, which would put him around age twenty-two. He was making a choice, but I never said it was the best choice or the right choice. At age twenty-two, he, like I think many young people today, is a man-boy. He's not all that mature, and not necessarily

capable of making the wisest choices based on his experiences in life and his emotional maturity. So inevitably it is the sexier, hotter, richer girl that gets his attention over the wholesome girl next door, and that needed to be explored. So I was very happy with the reception that we got to our story. Even the people who were so violently appalled that he was going to marry Veronica initially, I think, were surprised that it wasn't turning out to be the complete disaster they thought it would turn out to be.

Kochman: When you're working on a story like this, obviously you have your initial idea, you run it by the Archie editorial team, you get the go-ahead. . . . I want to segue now to something that most readers don't know about Archie, but that is incredibly important to the ongoing success of these characters and comics. What was it like working with Archie Comics President and Editor in Chief Victor Gorelick on this?

Uslan: Working with Victor was one of the best, most creative experiences I ever had writing comic books and graphic novels. This is a man who literally grew up working for Archie Comics. Victor is, I believe, the only person in the history of the comic book industry who for over fifty years has been with one company, publishing primarily one set of characters. He knows Archie personally; he knows what Archie thinks, he knows how he acts and reacts, and he knows all of the people in Riverdale with the same degree of insight and understanding and integrity. Now you would think that this background would be a trap for someone who has been doing it for so long, who is so close to these characters; that he would play it conservatively and say, *Oh no, you can't do that.* But Victor is a very creative and innovative and daring editor. And he's willing to look around the next corner and look ahead instead of looking back over his shoulder with Archie.

Once we started to talk about the story creatively, well, it was Victor who came up with the idea of Memory Lane. I thought that was a great idea. People are always going down Memory Lane, but nobody ever goes *up* Memory Lane. If Archie walks up Memory Lane, he can theoretically step into his own future. And being comic book fans, Victor and I were both very familiar with the concept of parallel universes, which are an important part of the DC Comics mythos. Marvel has used this device, too. So Victor and I liked the concept of walking up Memory Lane and having two alternative futures that may or may not come to pass. As we indicate in the epilogue, now that Archie is back in high school again, it's going to be the function of all of the actions or the inactions of Archie and Betty and Veronica that determines their future. Of everything that's said between Archie and Betty or between Archie and Veronica or, maybe even more important, of everything unsaid between them that will ultimately determine which of these two futures is the one that will come true.

Kochman: You got to work with the dream team on this story. I mean, besides Victor, you got to work with Stan Goldberg and Bob Smith. What was it like to work with Stan Goldberg, and how did that collaboration work?

Uslan: I'm a comic book fan *and* a comic book historian. Stan Goldberg is a legend in the comic book industry. He is probably the longest—Victor could tell you this for sure—but Stan is probably the longest-running Archie artist in history, and the last connection to the early days. The great artists and writers who started in the early days of comic books never received the accolades, the respect, or the admiration that comic book and graphic novel artists get today. Theirs was a generation where comic books were not considered the legitimate art form they are today, but instead were often looked down upon as simply cheap entertainment for children. There was no concept of these comics as our modern mythology, as contemporary American folklore, which has now been acknowledged by everyone from the Smithsonian to the New York Metropolitan Museum of Art to the Louvre. But because of the work of, in particular, Dr. Fredric Wertham and his book *Seduction of the Innocent* in the 1950s, comic book artists, writers, and editors were denigrated in society.

Stan tells these great stories about how he used to hate going to cocktail parties because he was afraid somebody was going to corner him and ask what he did for a living. And whenever he was asked, he would say, "Well, I illustrate children's literature." Or he might say, "I work for magazines." And they would try to get specifics, and were interested in talking to him, until he revealed that he wrote comic books, and then nobody wanted to talk to him at any of these parties. So for Stan Goldberg, who has worked at all the major comic book companies—in particular, he colored all of the covers for Marvel in the sixties, including the first appearance of Spider-Man, and he did *Millie the Model*, which had a wonderfully popular long run—for Stan Goldberg to get this kind of international attention and to be responsible for what has turned out to be the single most important, historic story line in the history of Archie, I think it was great that he was the artist who got to illustrate it, because it brought a lot of attention and recognition to him, and he deserves all the acclaim. For me personally, the greatest thing was the opportunity to work with Stan and to have this talented artist be the one to bring my words and my stories to life. It was an experience I will always treasure. I treasured it as it was happening because I knew how special it was. I may be getting old and gray, but there is still a twelve-year old comic book fan alive and kicking inside me.

Kochman: The funny thing about Stan is that he's this legend, but he's also such a mensch, so sweet and humble. You're right, he's one of the great comic book artists of all time, and he's been in the trenches for decades doing such amazing art. And the work that he's done on this story, even at this point in his career, is as good, if not better, than the stuff he's been doing for Archie for over five decades. When I first heard about the story, I was really excited it was being illustrated by Stan and not some new flavor-of-the-month artist who never drew an Archie comic before. Having Stan be the illustrator made it a true Archie story. He made it matter. And that made me pay attention.

Uslan: When I got confirmation that Stan would be doing the art, I sat down and took a different approach to my scripting. Writing an Archie comic is not like writing the DC or Marvel super heroes. The approach *had* to be different: no more than six panels to a page. Plus we were adding background gags, and we were adding a lot of soap opera, a lot of drama, a lot of emotion. But artistically, I wanted to break Archie out of the traditional Archie page and panel. Knowing Stan was going to be doing the artwork, we incorporated the use of splash pages. And even centerfold splashes, which were dramatic and impactful. We gave readers full-page illustrations of Archie at these key, historic moments in his life, and they just popped off the page. And all of them, seriously, could be printed as posters—that's how beautiful they are.

Kochman: Anything we didn't cover? Any other influences that contributed to the story?

Uslan: There were a handful of other things, two more movies in particular, that influenced what I wrote. Certainly *The Wizard of Oz*. For example, when Archie comes back to Riverdale in the epilogue, it's meant to evoke Dorothy's return to Kansas from Oz. At different moments throughout the story line, you'll see references to *The Wizard of Oz* pop up. Another influence, certainly, was the Frank Capra film *It's a Wonderful Life*. Archie has these two completely different experiences, one with Veronica and one with Betty, and we're able to see what his life might be like depending on the choices he makes. Another influence on the story was *A Christmas Carol*—the novella by Charles Dickens more than any particular movie version. I always liked the idea of the visitations by the ghosts and Scrooge getting to see what his fate might be, and being given an opportunity to go back and do something about it, to take some control of his own future. Those were all certainly among my influences as I wrote the story.

Overall, I think it's important to Archie readers today, to the kids who are reading this stuff, that the idea of choices and consequences gets explored. And in the context of these characters being four years older, it gives us a chance for some surprising twists and turns that, taken in the context of those four years, do not violate the characters but instead enhance our understanding of them. It's been a lot of fun and an incredible experience and an honor. ◆

VICTOR GORELICK

Charles Kochman: You must be feeling pretty good these days.

Victor Gorelick: Well, yes, I am. This was a very successful project, to say the least. I've been with Archie Comics for a long time, and I can't remember getting this kind of publicity on a comic book before.

Kochman: As I talk to people in the industry about this book, everyone says the same thing, without any prompting: that you are a first-rate editor. Across the board, there is universal respect for you and for the work you've done over the decades. Stan Lee, Julie Schwartz, Mort Weisinger, Dick Giordano, Denny O'Neil, Archie Goodwin—these are the great comic book editors, and you're in that pantheon.

Gorelick: Now you're making me blush. [laughs]

Kochman: It's true. I don't think there's another editor, even Julie, who worked with the same group of characters for as long as you have, who knows them as well as you do the Archie characters. When did you get into the business?

Gorelick: Well, I started at Archie Comics right out of high school, in October 1958. I attended the School of Art and Design in New York City, which was called the School of Industrial Art at the time. I majored in cartooning. My senior year, just before graduation, there was a person working in the art department at Archie Comics, Sheldon Brodsky, who handled the production. He graduated from SIA the year before I did. He needed to hire someone to replace Dexter Taylor. Dexter was working on *Little Archie* with Bob Bolling and was going freelance, so they needed someone to fill in his spot in production. Sheldon called up the school—they had a job placement service—and said, "Anybody from cartooning interested in a job?" So I went up for an interview, and the rest is history.

Kochman: Wait, you can't condense fifty-two years just like that. [laughs] Let's talk a little about the rest of that history.

Gorelick: Well, I came up for the interview and met with Richard Goldwater, the managing editor, and Sheldon Brodsky. At the time the company was located on Church Street, in Lower Manhattan. I received a phone call a few days later and was told that I had the job. I started working in the art department, doing corrections, working on production, learning the business. Production was very involved, and we were putting out a lot of books. It required a lot of know-how, but I was learning everything little by little, working with the engraver and the printer. [laughs] At the time, they were called engravers. The comics were actually engraved on zinc plates. It was interesting. There have been a lot of changes in the industry since then.

Kochman: So how did you make the transition to editorial?

Gorelick: Well, I'd been working closely with Richard Goldwater, who was managing editor at that time. There was only one editor, and that was Richard. I worked with the artists in particular. Every so often Richard would have me go through some scripts and give him my opinion of them. Eventually, around the mid-eighties, Richard Goldwater and Michael Silberkleit took over the company; their fathers went into semiretirement. Richard promoted me to managing editor, so then I was responsible for all the scripts and all the artwork that was going into the books. It was a little different at Archie Comics. At DC or Marvel, they had editors and assistant editors and assistants to the assistants and so forth. At Archie, I was my own assistant. [laughs]

Kochman: Okay, let's fast-forward a little. I'm sure over the years people have pitched you all sorts of Archie stories that you've turned down for one reason or another. Maybe even a story along the lines of the wedding: "Why not have Archie get married?" Or, "Let's kill off Jughead." That kind of thing. I guess my question is, what made you go for Michael Uslan's pitch?

Gorelick: Well, let me go back a little bit. Michael was writing a book called *The Best of Archie*. He worked on it with another fellow by the name of Jeff Mendel. I worked closely with Mike and Jeff, helping them find material for the book at the time. I believe it was around 1980. Michael and I had a very good relationship. However, he went his way, becoming a successful producer and writer. I kept bumping into him at conventions over the years, and we'd bring each other up to date. I knew he was interested in producing an Archie movie. And with a lot of the changes going on at Archie, when I saw Mike at the New York Comic Con [in April 2008], I said, "You know, maybe you want to think about doing this now." We started talking and he said, "Well, you know, what I really want to do is write for you. Write an Archie story." And I said, "That would be great. Let's get together and talk about it." So we met and he pitched this idea to me, the idea of Archie getting married. And my first reaction was . . . I hesitated. I hesitated for about ten seconds, and then I thought, "You know, this might be a really good idea." So I said let's develop it and see how it goes.

Kochman: Was his idea fully fleshed out, or was it something you collaborated with him on?

Gorelick: I had already established this Memory Lane in a couple of issues. You know, where Archie went back in time and Archie from the year 2000 met Archie from the forties. I don't know if you've seen that. Betty and Veronica met the Betty and Veronica of the fifties, and Jughead met the Jughead of the forties. So we had this Memory Lane device already established, and I'm thinking, what if they walked *up* Memory Lane instead of down. And Michael came up with this story line where Archie goes up Memory Lane. So he sent me a proposal and I really liked it. I'm just glad I didn't hesitate too much, because obviously it has been very successful.

Kochman: But you get a million proposals all the time, and most of them you turn down. You have to. People always think they know what's best for your characters, or they want to do something with them that you just wouldn't want to do. Or couldn't do. It would be too radical.

Gorelick: Well, you're right. It's really difficult to do stuff with Archie. I mean, it's not like you can kill off a character easily and bring him back. They can't fall out of a spaceship and onto Genesis. [laughs]

Kochman: [laughs] But still, you took a chance on this story. It doesn't follow the same formula that you've established for seventy years. It was risky.

Gorelick: Well, to be honest, at the beginning I didn't know where Michael was going to go with the story exactly. And when he laid it out, I knew that we were going to get some reaction, especially with Archie choosing Veronica first. That was the big thing. But you know, Archie's sort of . . . what are you going to do with Archie that's really going to create some sort of attention? Years ago we had an Archie crossover with the Punisher. We've had Archie as a super hero, Pureheart the Powerful. We had him as the Man from R.I.V.E.R.D.A.L.E., a takeoff on the *Man from U.N.C.L.E.* television show. But you need something dynamic to grab the reader's attention, and what's bigger than Betty and Veronica? Who's Archie going to pick? One time we had a love showdown where Archie decided . . . everybody thought he decided who he was going to go steady with and who was going to be his best girl. And that created some media attention. But nothing like this. Who's he going to marry? Not only did we grab the attention of our current readers, but people who'd read Archie from the past fifty, sixty years were calling us up, trying to get copies of the comics.

Kochman: It was crazy, I know. But you couldn't expect . . . there's no way to anticipate that kind of reaction.

Gorelick: I don't know how I'm going to follow this up—you try, you keep banging your head against the wall trying to figure out some other great idea that's going to compete with this one. But I don't know what it's going to be.

Kochman: I don't think you have to top yourself. You told a great story, and it brought attention to the characters and renewed interest in the comics. I think you just have to continue to tell good, solid stories and remind people that these characters haven't gone away and that they're still relevant.

Gorelick: That was the whole purpose of doing something like this in the first place, to bring Archie back. You get tired of going to functions and hearing people say, "Oh, you work for Archie Comics? Do they still publish those? Are they still around?" You hear things like that. Well . . . people know we're around now.

Kochman: Absolutely, absolutely. I like how Jon Goldwater recently put it. He said, "Archie is open for business." It's a very exciting time. And it's clear to fans and to readers that there is a sense of renewal at Archie, that you're looking to the future.

Gorelick: We are. We're starting to try some other things, too. We're going to be doing some longer stories, some with continuing story lines, some crossovers to other titles and other companies. We're going to try and generate interest for our readers. Give them a little more than just a bunch of short stories . . . even though

we're still going to be publishing the digest books you see in supermarkets and on newsstands. Our digests are very popular.

Kochman: And I understand that you're going to build on the wedding story line.

Gorelick: That's right. We're continuing the story line. Actually . . . we decided to publish them in a magazine format. Instead of two separate comics, there will be one magazine called *Life with Archie*. And it will follow his married life, with "Archie Loves Veronica" and "Archie Loves Betty" stories. Anyway, that's where we are.

Kochman: Very exciting. Now let's talk a little about the teams you have in place. But first I want to ask you something. I get asked this question all the time, so now I get to ask you. What does an editor do? How do you describe the job of an editor? I always say an editor is like being a director. You have this vision, and you then pull all the various elements together.

Gorelick: That's certainly part of it. But . . . well, a couple of things. You have to listen to your readers for one, and see what they like and what they're interested in. You have to know what your readership likes as far as movies, TV, and music, and keep up with what's happening in the news. I try and integrate all of those things in our story lines. That's important. Making sure that the writers, especially new writers, maintain the integrity of the characters. It's important to listen to your writers, too. I mean, look, Michael Uslan came up with a great idea. Another editor might not have recognized it. Or another writer, I don't know, he might have had the idea of marrying Archie, but he didn't come up with the two scenarios, and he might not have been as open as Michael was when he was developing the story.

I'm fortunate . . . I've always had good writers to work with. When I started working here at Archie, a lot of the writers and artists had young families, and were able to tap into the natural resources that were in their homes when they wrote their stories. I think it's important to give writers and artists a little bit of line, so to speak, and to not restrict them too much. You can do that, but don't try to beat them over the head and say they have to do it this way or they have to do it that way. An editor has to work with the writers, the artists, and with the readers.

Kochman: Exactly. It's more than just checking spelling and grammar and putting in periods and commas. That's a small part of our job, the actual physical line editing. Being an editor is really about managing your team and getting the best out of them.

Gorelick: Putting together the right team is key. And you want to develop new artists, and you want to develop new writers as well. You have to do that. With Archie, there's hardly any story line that you can think of that hasn't already been approached or done in some shape or form over the last seventy years. I mean, Archie making a date with Betty and Veronica for the same night—there are thousands of stories like that; we've had stories like that in every decade for the past seventy years. But with each decade their environment changes, technology changes, and these changes all have to be integrated into the story. And you have to remind the writers to be aware of that.

Kochman: Well, the team you have on this book couldn't have been better. Michael Uslan obviously brought a unique idea to the table. But then you have art by Stan Goldberg, who is a legend, and one of my heroes. Now you've worked with Stan for a long time. But you had a choice of any number of artists, obviously, to illustrate this story. Why did you choose Stan?

Gorelick: Well, basically the same reason you just said. I mean, certainly he's one of the best artists in the industry. He's been drawing Archie for I don't even know how many years now. Not that I don't change that every once in a while, depending on the story line we have planned. But Stan was my first choice for the book. He's also the fastest. [laughs] I just thought it was a good thing. You want to put your best team on something like this. Even if he was on something else, I would have taken him off to do this.

Kochman: I would imagine when you have someone in the trenches for a long time . . . that when the big, plum assignments come up, they've sort of earned the right to have first crack at them.

Gorelick: No question about it. Although, you know, Mike Uslan isn't one of my regular writers. But I thought to have him write something for us was certainly . . . well, it was such a great story. And having his name on it was a big plus.

Kochman: Definitely. And one of your regular writers didn't pitch you the story. It took someone from the outside. There's a benefit to having a different set of eyes look at the characters. They bring another perspective.

Gorelick: Right, exactly. Michael has a very good understanding of the characters. I did very little editing on his stories. Very little . . . a little spelling error here or there. Sometimes he was a little wordy in places, so I cut back on some of the copy. But other than that, I didn't restrict him at all.

Kochman: There's a difference between rewriting to make the text sound like you would want it to if you were the writer; it's another thing to edit with respect for the writer, instead helping him to write what he is trying to express as well as he can, removing your own voice from the process. It may not be his characters, but he is the writer, after all.

Gorelick: Exactly.

Kochman: Let's talk about Bob Smith, the inker on this story.

Gorelick: Oh, yeah. Bob's great.

Kochman: From an editor's point of view, I think it would be interesting to know why you put Bob on the book.

Gorelick: Well, Bob has been Stan's inker for many years. Bob came up one time looking for a little work and I told him, "I don't have that much, but I'll give you something. Let's see how you do with it." And he did this great job, and I thought, *What, am I out of my mind? I've*

got to give this guy more work to do. [laughs] Bob's great. Plus, he's dependable.

Kochman: Describe what makes an inker great, as opposed to . . . obviously, he's not just tracing. What does he bring to a project?

Gorelick: An inker has to be able to draw. A lot of artists come by and they say they want to work for Archie, and I say, "What do you want to do?" And they say, "Oh, I want to ink. I'd like to ink this, I'd like to ink that." And I say, "Well, can you draw?" "Well, I'm a really good inker." "Well, can you fix up this arm? Can you fix this figure if you had to?" "Well, I guess I could do something if I had to, but I really like to ink." [laughs] So, of course, a lot of these young kids that come out of school, you know, they think all they have to do is take out a pen or markers. Many don't even use brushes, which drives me crazy altogether. They're just tracing over the pencils, but that's not it. First of all, Archie is a very, very difficult character not only to draw but to ink as well, because if you're inking an Archie face and you ink it on the outside of the line, you're going to wind up with a big, round, puffy face; you have to ink it on the inside of the line. And depending on whether he's in the foreground, or if he's in the middle of the panel, or toward the back, everything has to be kept on different planes—heavier lines in the front, thinner lines for the backgrounds, et cetera.

Kochman: I like the combination of Bob and Stan. I've seen other inkers on Stan's pencils, and they're not as strong.

Gorelick: Yes, Bob's pretty clean, but it's very difficult to ink some of Stan's stuff, too. His lines don't always come together all of the time. You have to know what side of the pencil line to ink on and where it breaks, where it's connected. It's not easy. I've seen some of the best inkers in the business just not do well inking Stan's work. Archie is a cartoon character, to some degree a realistic character; it's not as if you can throw in a lot of lines and a lot of shading and wrinkles and creases and muscles and things like that. [laughs] You're not going to hide anything. If you make a mistake, it's out there.

Kochman: And the rest of the team—you had Jack Morelli as letterer.

Gorelick: Well, Jack Morelli has got to be one of the best, if not *the* best letterer in the industry right now. You know, some of the other companies no longer use hand lettering; they do all this electronic lettering. But I always felt that lettering is part of the artwork, and it's a very integral part of what the page looks like. If I collected artwork, and I went to one of the conventions like so many people do, and I bought an original page of art from a Batman comic or a Superman comic or one of those books, and it's just a page with no lettering on it, no words on it, I'd be upset. What's a piece of comic book art without the lettering on it?

Kochman: I agree, it's integral. And Jack has such a distinct style.

Gorelick: Oh, he can do anything.

Kochman: What about Glenn Whitmore?

Gorelick: Well, actually, Mike Pellerito found him.

When Mike recommended we use Glenn on the book, I looked at some of his work. He's been coloring for us a little while now, and I thought . . . I know my regular colorist is a little upset about it, but you know, I wanted to . . . I had a new writer on the book, and I wanted to give this story a different look. I wanted to try a different approach and get someone else to do the coloring.

Kochman: It does look a little different than the regular Archie comics.

Gorelick: It should look a little different. In fact, even Stan drew it a little differently. The characters are four years older. He had to make them look a little bit older. It needed some different types of embellishment, from the writing to the coloring, which I think we accomplished.

Kochman: You absolutely did. Any closing thoughts? You've had an amazing career working with these characters, and it's certainly far from over. You have so many new projects in the works. And with Jon Goldwater on board, it's clear there's a new direction and spirit in the company.

Gorelick: Well, that's exactly right. I mean, there are just so many new things going on. There's so much happening. It's like a breath of new life in the company. I'm glad Jon's here. I encouraged him to come on board as much as I could. He's really hands-on, and I'm very happy about it. I love working with Jon. All these new things that we're doing, I'm really excited. I can't wait to come to work every day. I was starting to get a little tired after fifty years, but now I have new energy. ♠

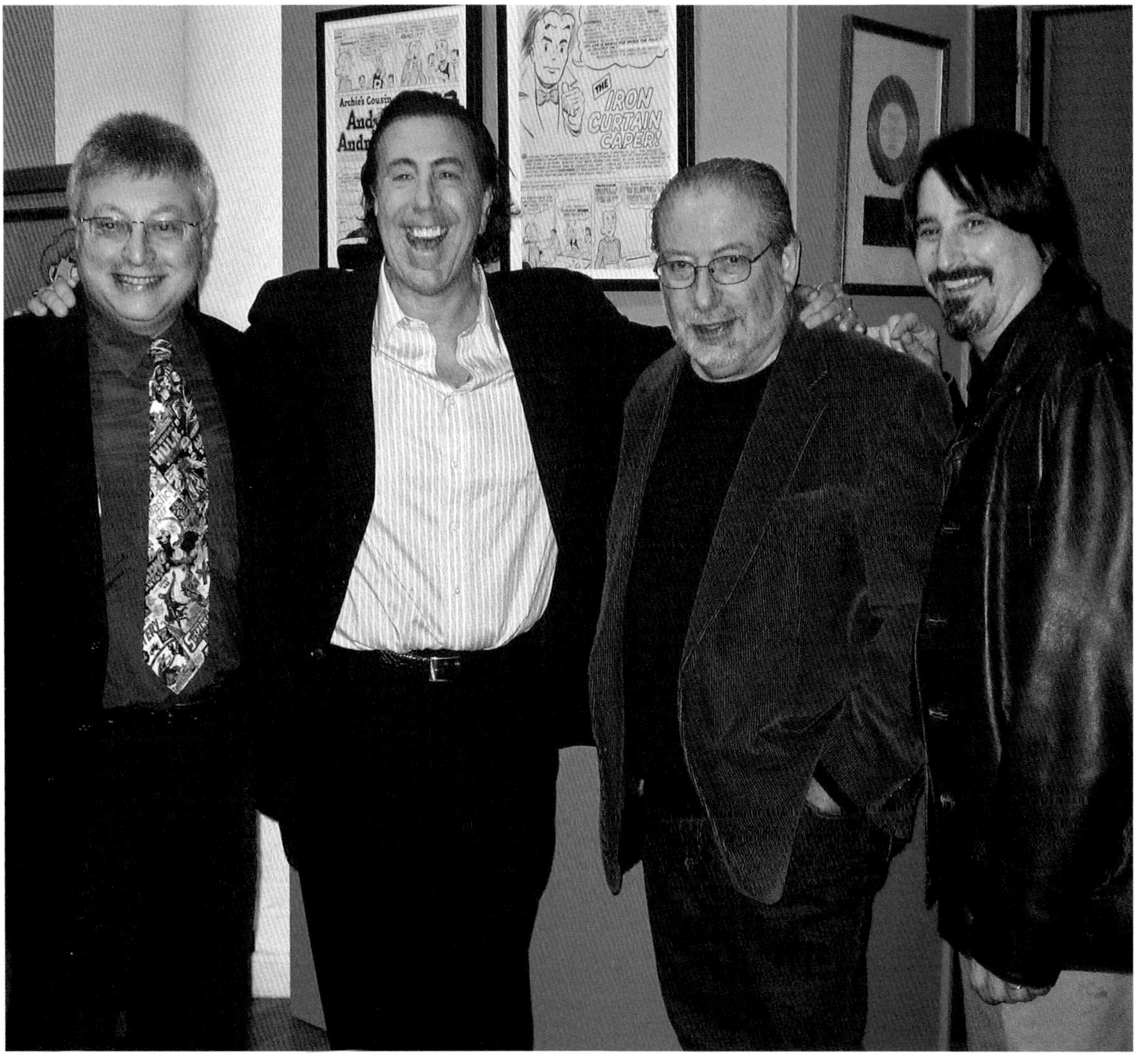
Archie's Cousin
Andy
Andr
THE IRON CURTAIN CAPER!

Left to right: Michael Uslan (writer), Jon Goldwater (Archie co-CEO), Victor Gorelick (Archie President/Editor in Chief), and Charles Kochman (Executive Editor, Abrams ComicArts) at the opening reception of "The Art of Archie" exhibit at the Museum of Comic and Cartoon Art (MoCCA) in New York City (November 19, 2009).

STAN GOLDBERG

Stan Goldberg: Do me a favor, try to correct my Bronx accent.

Charles Kochman: [laughs] No, we want the Bronx accent. I'm just sorry we don't have an audio chip in the book. So let's talk a little about your background, the kind of things you've done, and what led you to Archie.

Goldberg: My background? It's simple, really. It was kind of written in stone from when I was five or six years old. Just drawing pictures and telling stories. I always loved to tell stories with my pictures. I didn't realize it then, but I was always putting a little story to my drawings. Whenever I speak to boys and girls today and they show me their drawings, I try to encourage them as much as possible. And I always try to prompt the discussion a little if they show me something. If they draw this great-looking jet plane, I ask them to tell me who flies the plane. If the kids are really young, we have some fun with it. I say, "Well, usually you have to put the plane somewhere so it doesn't get wet in the rain or snowed on. Where does it sleep?" And then I help them draw a hangar. Growing up, I was just constantly drawing pictures. I remember my dad and . . . we would put pieces of notebook paper together and put holes in the sides of them so I could run a string through and make my own little books.

Kochman: Do you still have any of those?

Goldberg: [laughs] No, but I remember it so clearly—making a hole with a pencil and running some string through it, telling my little picture stories. They could be two pages, three pages if it was something I was enjoying. I was a little bit older when I was doing this. Always drawing. Another little fast story: Coming from an extended family in those days, not having any brothers or sisters but a lot of cousins, a lot of aunts and uncles, I was always picked on because I just sat and drew pictures. I didn't run around the house and break things. I had an uncle who would say, "Look at Stanley. Why can't all of you be more like him? Look, he's always sitting and drawing pictures." Then I'd get teased afterward by my cousins. But I didn't mind. It just worked out that way. Drawing was always just something I did, as far back as I can remember. And you can ask any artist, they'll probably have similar stories. I always drew pictures, even in school. It carried me through. In fact, I got out of high school early. They actually skipped me two grades because I did a lot of drawings for different departments in school, like the physical education department. I would copy pictures and draw them on oak tag and spread them around the room. I was a good kid, caused no problems, so I got out of school around sixteen, sixteen and a half, and went right to work for a company named Timely Comics. You know Timely, right?

Kochman: Sure. Timely became Marvel Comics in 1961, I believe it was. So were you working for Stan Lee?

Goldberg: Exactly. I was working for Stan at Timely. This was in 1949, before they became known as Marvel. In those days comic books were sixty-four pages, sometimes forty-eight. They were big books. You remember that book that came out about the comics industry? It was called, *All in Color for a Dime*. Well, that's what I was doing. Ten-cent comics. I was in the coloring department, and about a year or two in, the guy who was in charge left, and there was an opening in the department. There were only three or four of us, so I started running the coloring department and answering directly to Stan Lee. And I got to know exactly what he wanted and what he was looking for. We had a lot of books to put out, and I'd get the schedule each month and would handle the coloring. I was in charge of all our titles, doing the coloring for every cover that came out of Timely. This was from 1950 up until . . . I guess we all got laid off in 1959.

During this period, I did some drawings for Stan Lee, because he knew I wanted to draw comics, and he asked me to draw a new teenage title, *Kathy (The Teen-age Tornado!)*. I'd never done humor before, and this was a challenge for me. Needless to say, the rest is history. I was still young, and was nowhere near thinking of this as a career, or that I would be doing humor, romance, and funny animal comic books.

Kochman: I have to be careful not to get us sidetracked, because this is really fascinating, and we can spend all of our time talking about the work you did for Timely and Marvel. But one quick thing—you're talking about coloring, and I wanted to bring up something you once told me that I was surprised to learn. It makes sense that the covers of comic books are done first, before the stories on the inside are completed. I was unaware, however, that for books like *Amazing Fantasy* with Spider-Man, *The Incredible Hulk*, and all the great super heroes and villains who came out of Marvel in the sixties, you were the one who came up with the color schemes for the costumes, which you and the colorists on your team then followed for the interiors. That's something we take for granted—the blue and red of Spider-Man's costume—but I had no idea that you were involved in that aspect of the character creation.

Goldberg: I never really gave it much thought over the years. We were never credited for color; it was just part of the job. In fact, when Stan did start to add credits in the books, they still didn't add the names of the colorists. Later on, our names were added in the reprints. It's funny. I remember the first time somebody said they saw my name listed as colorist, and I said, "You're mistaken." But they brought the book with them, and sure enough, there was my name.

You know, I have to say, Stan Lee taught me a lot while we worked together all through the fifties and sixties. This helped me to lay the foundation for my career, which I'm still enjoying today. And he's still around, and I'm still around, so maybe what we do keeps us young.

Kochman: Amen to that. Now you've been with Archie Comics since the late sixties. For over *forty years* you've been illustrating Archie, Betty, Veronica, and the gang in Riverdale. That's incredible. How did you first come to work for the company?

Goldberg: In the early sixties, I was working for Stan Lee at Marvel, freelancing and drawing *Millie the Model*, *Life with Millie*, *Patsy Walker*, and *Kathy*, the first book I created. These were straight humor books. And that lasted for quite a while, but like everything else it came and went. And then after that I worked for DC Comics. I did *Date with Debbie*, *Swing with Scooter*, *Leave It to Binky*—books like that. Then I called Archie, and they more or less said, "When do you want to start?" They were producing a lot of books at that time and could use me right away, so I started. I worked for all three comic book companies at the same time—Archie, DC, and Marvel.

I was working for Stan for about three years doing Millie and Chili stories. Those books did well. We did two or three each month. And since Stan had a whole list of super-hero titles, some of which were in a "king-size" format, for Millie we put out "queen-size" annuals. They were fifty-two pages, and we did about twelve of those. I was turning out a lot of material, and basically that's why I never developed as an inker. I did some of my own inking, but mainly on the fashion pages, and on the covers of the Millie books, but not the insides. And at that time these were large-size comic book pages. You look at them now and say, "Wow, that's a lot of work!" And it was a lot of work, but that's what comic books were back then. They eventually came down to the ten-by-fifteen size they are now. And then these *Archie*-type humor books kind of drifted away and slowly died as super heroes took over. Eventually, DC canceled their books. Marvel didn't have any more humor or teenage books at that time, so Archie was the only game in town. And it was a good game, too, because the characters were great. I loved working on them, and I still do.

Kochman: Talk a little about how you, as a penciler, approach a story; how you take what's written on a manuscript page and translate it visually.

Goldberg: Well, first of all, let me just say something about Bob Smith. Bob is . . . I've had lots of inkers, some good, some not so good, some better than good. It's funny how you get locked into certain inkers working on your stuff. I remember working with Henry Scarpelli. We worked together very well. He was a terrific inker. And then Bob Smith—I didn't know Bob was at DC for so many years. He was just one of the guys whose work I noticed. He always did the most professional stuff around. And then he came to Archie. Now, I always said that the best inker on my stuff is Stan Goldberg. [laughs] But as the years go by, Bob gets better and better, to the point where I say there's nobody as good, nobody who has ever inked my stuff better—better than even I would attempt to do—than Bob Smith. I think the work he did on the wedding book is tremendous. I worked very hard on that book. I tried different shots and different angles, but Bob just took my stuff, and he knew exactly what I wanted to be done. I tried to create little moods, and he captured them with his marvelous brushstrokes and pen. I can't say enough about him.

Now to answer your question, every writer has a different way of scripting their story. Some will give you little stick figures. That's what I used to get from Stan Lee. Or he would loosely plot the stories, tell me an idea off the top of his head. Then I would do the drawings, bring them to him without any dialogue, and he would then first write the dialogue for the word balloons. That turned out to be the "Marvel method" of telling stories. He would give you a plot, and you would draw the whole thing. But with Archie, some writers give me stick figures, some do whole storyboard layouts for me, and sometimes, most times, I just get a full script.

Being the artist, I see things a little differently than the writer. I know what works on the page. Some writers put too much in. There's just no way to fit in everything they describe. But I'll figure out ways to squeeze and move and get in a big panel and reduce some of the panels down to a smaller size. I go over the script first before I even start any drawings, and I make little notes in my head, or I jot little notes I might have on the side of the manuscript pages. I don't want to lose those thoughts. After I go through the whole story, I then start doing my breakdowns right on the page. I don't do any little thumbnail sketches. To me that's a waste of time, because my breakdowns are on the paper that I'm drawing on. I'm working, moving and changing while I'm drawing. Changing things around.

I keep about three different erasers on my desk. One for erasing details, one for erasing larger areas, and one for erasing a whole page. And I don't think twice about using any of them. If there's something that's disturbing me, I don't start correcting an eye, a nose, or even one figure if there's ten on the page. I'll just knock out the whole set of figures and start over. It sounds like extra work, but it's not. To me, it's about getting something that feels right. It's about getting the story down on paper in the amount of time I have for the assignment and trying to feel good about the work. Sometimes I please myself 75 percent, sometimes 50 percent, because I have to meet my deadline. Most of the time I think it really works. When I used to smoke, I'd light up my pipe, sit back in my chair, and say, "Hey, Goldberg, that's not a bad drawing."

Kochman: You make it look so effortless, Stan. But it's not effortless, obviously. There's great craft to your work. It's clean and perfect. After all these decades you've internalized your process. Every line that's on the page is necessary. There's no excess. I have to say, across the board, that everybody I speak to about Archie has the highest regard for you and your work. These are not just Archie stories. These are Stan Goldberg Archie stories.

Goldberg: Believe me, I hear those things and it means a lot to me. It really does. I just try not to think

---

(**overleaf**) Stan Goldberg's pencils for the wedding of Archie and Veronica, pages 44–45 (*Archie* no. 601, November 2009).

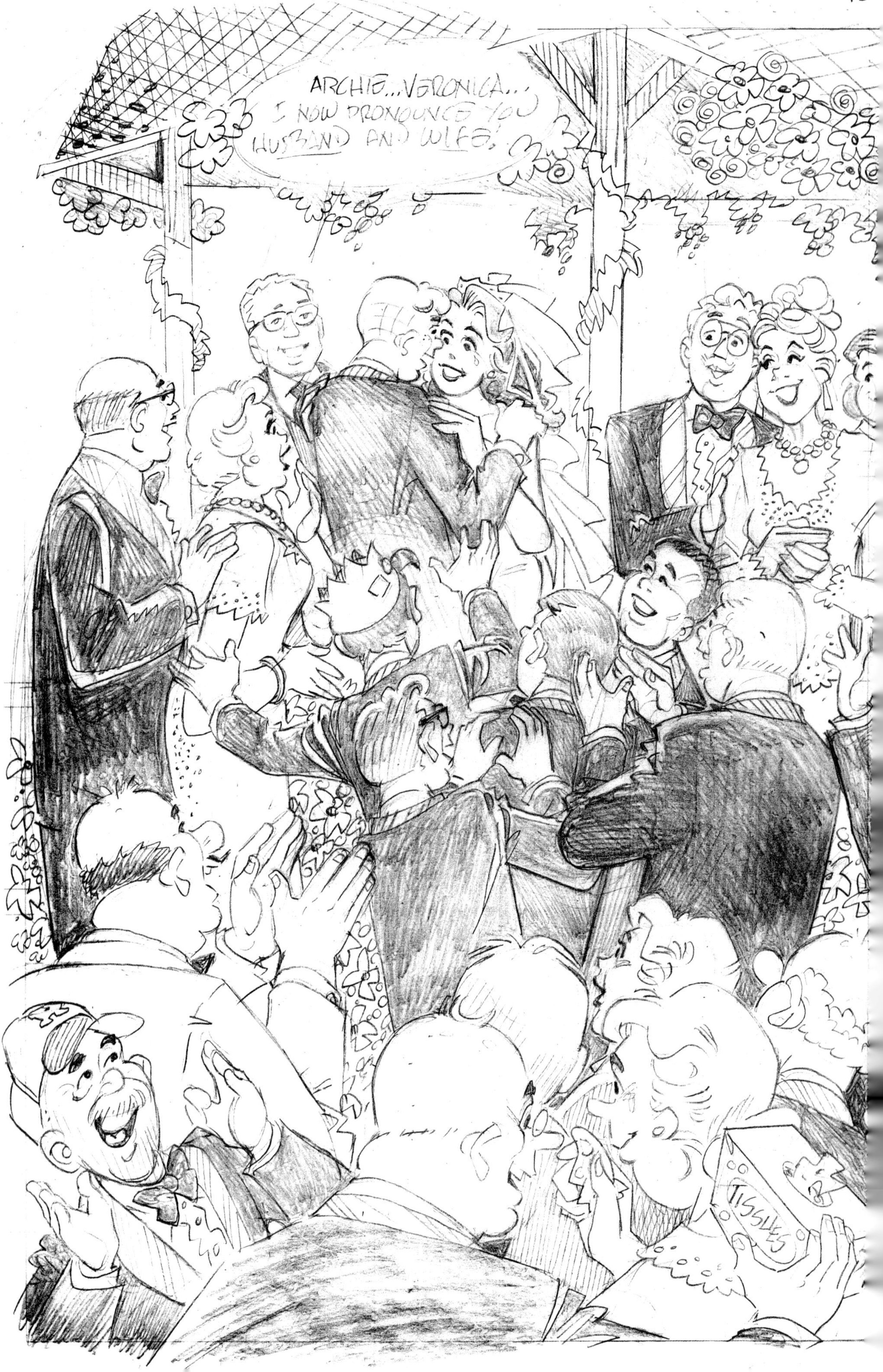
ARCHIE...VERONICA...
I NOW PRONOUNCE YOU
HUSBAND AND WIFE!
TISSUES

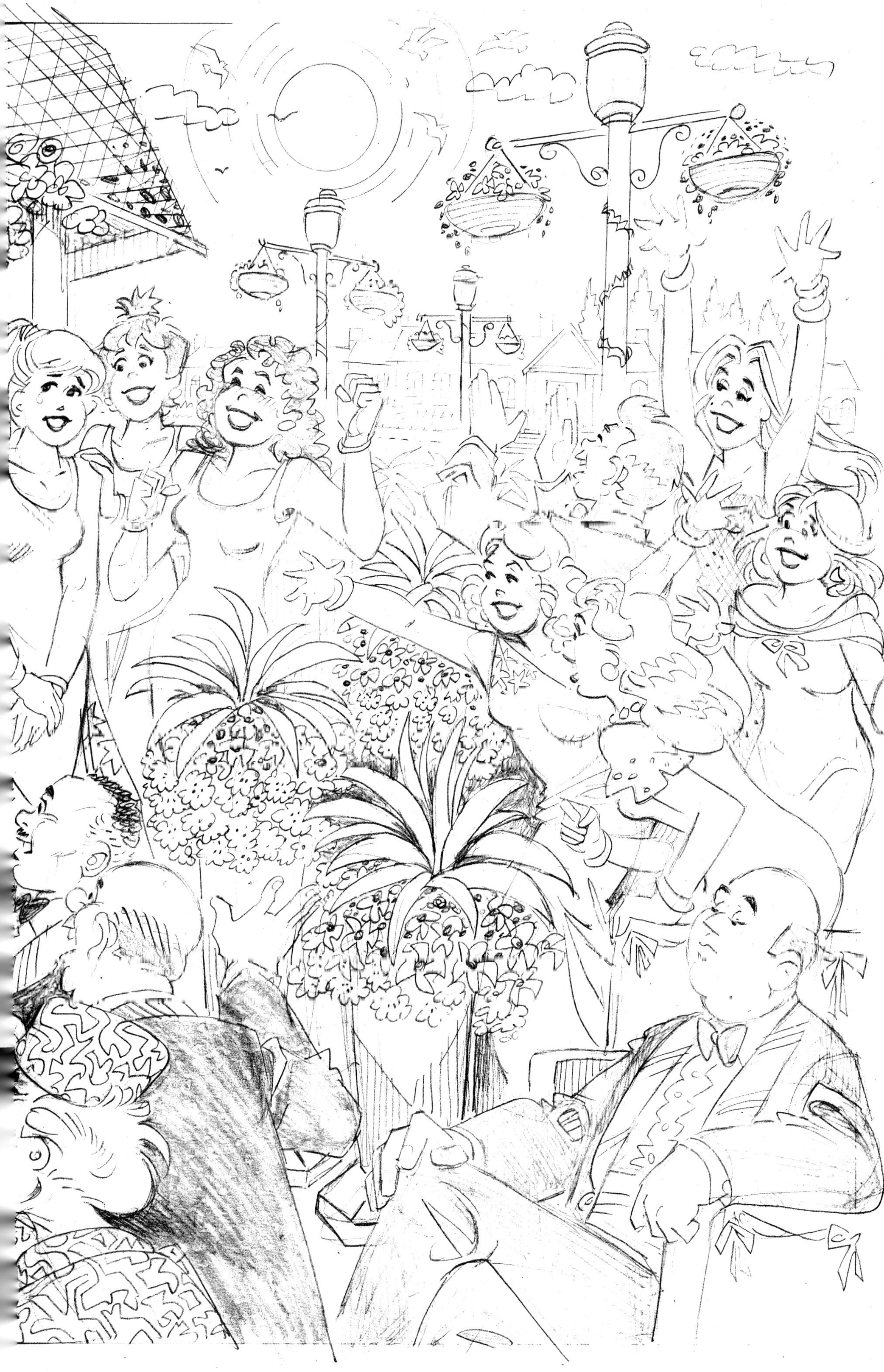

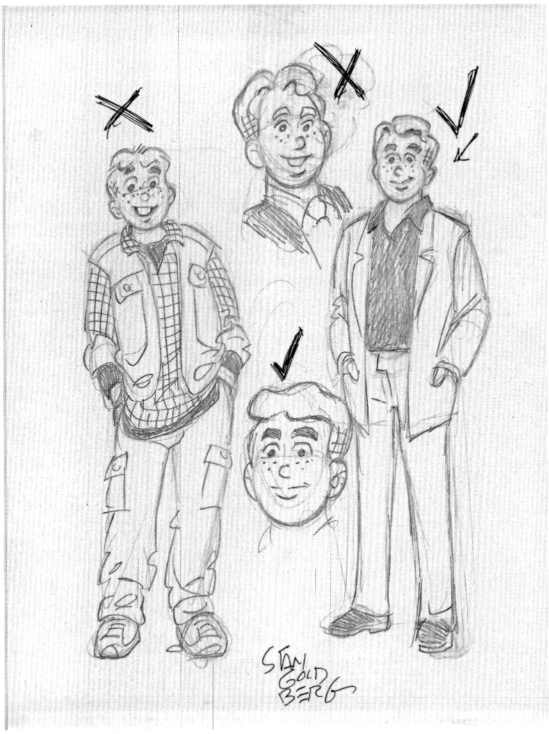
STAN GOLDBERG

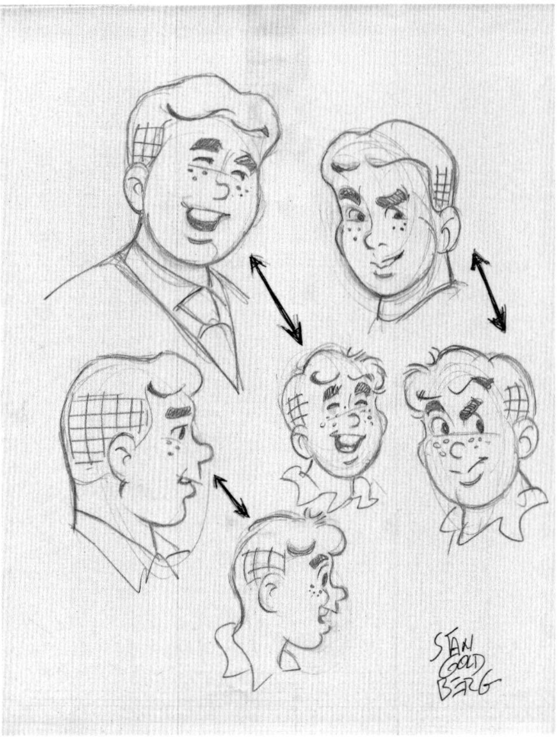
STAN GOLDBERG

about it too much. I don't want any medals or little pats on the back. You know, when you do something in life, and you do it for any period of time, you have to enjoy yourself. I'm very fortunate.

Kochman: Let's talk a little more about the wedding story line. How did you hear about it? I'm assuming Victor called you up one day and told you. What was your reaction?

Goldberg: Well, let's start from the beginning. Before the wedding was ever thought of, when we did issue number 400 [June 1992], and when we did issue 500 [October 2000], we prepared for those particular numbers. For any book that has a number and two zeroes after it, you want to come up with something special. I remember we had a nice concept for issue 500. It started in 490, I believe, and led up to issue 500. We had Betty and Veronica each realize that they were about to go on their five hundredth date with Archie. And of course, he makes a date with both of them for the same night. So I was talking to Victor, probably a little more than two years ago now, and I said, "We better start thinking about issue 600." I said, more or less, "I'll do the drawing; you come up with the idea. Or we can work on it together. I'll give you some concepts. But let's do something special for this one." Now I had no idea what the approach would be. Then Victor started to tell me what he was thinking of. And he told me about Michael Uslan's idea for the wedding. We started talking about it, and I thought it sounded like a good idea. But I still didn't know what the story line was going to be. I didn't know how they were going to do it, or how it was all going to come together. And then it did. They pulled it off. I think some of the dialogue and some of the concepts were fantastic, but there were also some concepts I didn't think would work that well in a comic book.

Kochman: Did you get to offer your feedback?

Goldberg: Oh, sure. When something was being suggested and I didn't think it was going to work, I had a meeting with Victor. We discussed it, and I gave him some suggestions, and Michael came up with his own ideas, and it all came together. But these are the things you do. You change things around; you make them work. You know, one of my favorite scenes in the series was in issue number 2, where the wedding takes place; I was able to do some nice big panels, which Michael suggested. A lot of his suggestions worked out really well. And I love the ending. There is so much in this story that people are enjoying. And all over the world; I can't begin to tell how many people are reading this and talking about it—people that haven't read an *Archie* comic in fifty years, sixty years. For our readers out there, I just want them to have the best time with our books. And they are. We were just in Mexico, and would you believe I was signing the wedding comics down in Mexico? This whole story, it put Archie right back on the map again. I mean, he's always been there, let me put it that way.

Kochman: But you're reminding readers about why they care about these characters.

Goldberg: Exactly. Here's one fast story. There are so many stories that come to mind, but this one in particular: I do some charity work for the East Hampton Library. A lot of famous authors live in the East End—about 120 of them—and they always invite me down. It's interesting, Archie always draws the biggest crowd.

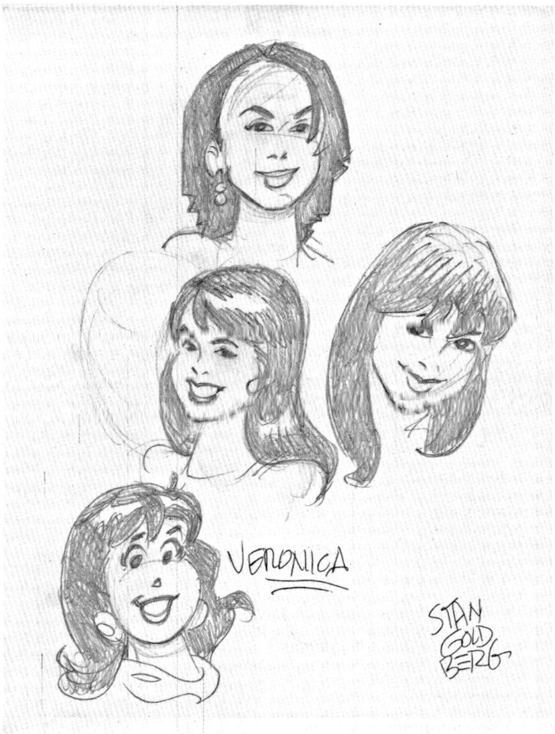
VERONICA
STAN GOLDBERG

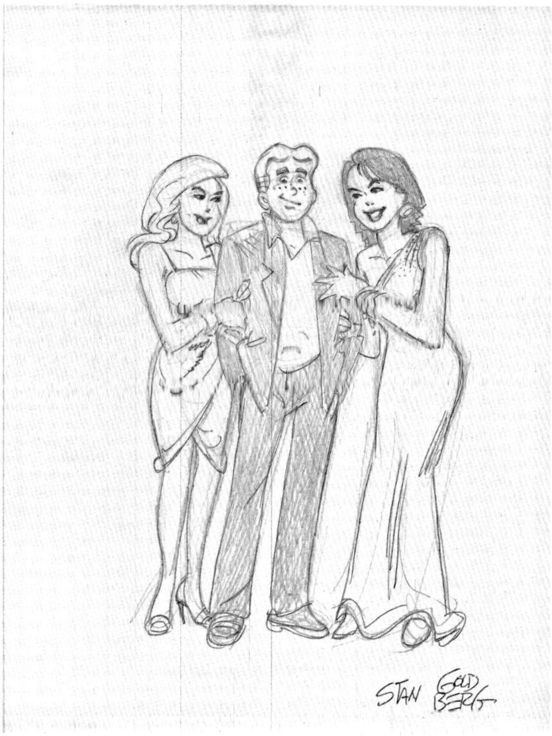
STAN GOLDBERG

[laughs] Well, at the last event, word was starting to get out about the wedding and Archie marrying Veronica. And there was one elderly couple, a very, very rich elderly couple that came over to my table. And the woman was very agitated. She had to be in her eighties, and she told me she used to read *Archie*, and now she's passed her comics on to her grandchildren. But she was so upset. "You're sending the wrong message to all the boys and girls in the world today. Archie picked the wrong girl. It was the wrong thing to do. Betty is so lovable and caring and devoted to him, and he's going for Veronica!" I couldn't tell her about the other part of the story, since it hadn't been revealed yet. So I just told her as much as I possibly could without giving anything away. But she still said, "It's not right. You shouldn't be doing that." So there you have it. It's just a comic book, but people are very involved.

Kochman: Well, keep doing what you've been doing, because clearly you're the best at it. And you enjoy doing it. And your fans and your readers love the work you do. Even the rich old ladies. They just don't know any better.

Goldberg: [laughs] You know, Charlie, this story is quite something. It's funny. Seven books is a lot of work. But for me this story wasn't work. Usually I look back on some jobs, the ones that entail a lot of reference or a lot of thinking, and I remember that they took up a lot of time, or there were a lot of pictures I didn't really like to draw. There are always some pictures I prefer drawing more than others. But I get through the slow periods of the story and try to make them as interesting as possible. But with this one, this wedding story, I don't remember having a hard time on any of the books.

Sometimes it feels like the pages draw themselves. I sit down at my desk, and I'm working away, and [my wife] Pauline will come into my studio. I don't hear anything—I figure she's doing something—but she's looking at me, watching me draw. And she says, "I don't know how you do it."

And I'll pick my head up slowly, and I'll look at her and say, "You know what? Neither do I!"

After all these years, I still don't know. ♦

(above) Concept sketches by Stan Goldberg. "I was playing around with Archie, Betty, and Veronica for the wedding story," Stan recalled, "getting a feel for how I would approach making them look four years older."

JACK MORELLI

Charles Kochman: I was talking with Victor Gorelick yesterday about lettering—he had very nice things to say about you, by the way—and he was explaining why he feels lettering is such an integral part of comic book art; that it's an important part of the story and the storytelling. So for those people who don't know what a letterer does, let's walk them through the process. You're working on the pencils. The art hasn't been inked yet. First the pages come from the penciler, Stan Goldberg, to you. Then you letter the writer's script onto the boards, and then you continue the assembly-line process by sending the lettered pages on to the inker when you're done.

Jack Morelli: Right, right. You know, before you called, I was wondering what I could say about this that would be pertinent or interesting. I'm just a letterer, and lettering is so old school. Very few people do hand lettering anymore. It's a lost art, and it's underappreciated. It's really nice to hear that Victor spoke well of me, because I know he appreciates good lettering. Victor started out as a letterer, forty-something years ago. And he's still lettering, just to keep his hand in it . . . he letters some of the covers. And I think he may letter the newspaper strip as well.

Kochman: I'm glad we're doing these interviews for the book, because I think it's important that everyone involved with the wedding story have an opportunity to discuss their roles. Most people don't know what a letterer does.

Morelli: Well, you try to capture the emotion and the feel of the artwork. You're not only lettering each panel, you're capturing the flavor of what's going on in the panel, whether it's something silly, scary, funny . . . whatever it may be. You try to think of the page the way the artist thought of it when he was drawing. I think that's especially true when you letter by hand—I don't believe you can fully capture that feeling with computer lettering. Lettering is organic. It's an organic art form. You want the reader to see the human being behind the work. Looking at the work, it should appear as if one person did it all; that the whole page was done by the same artist. So even though I have my style, and Stan has his style, and Bob has his style, it's all supposed to come together in this stew that you hope ends up delicious when you're done cooking it. [laughs]

Kochman: Haven't most letterers created fonts of their handwriting? Or does that feel impersonal to you?

Morelli: I have a font that I've created. I've worked on the computer before. But I just tend to think it looks too obvious; that these two things were done on different dimensions, on different planes, and then put together mechanically. I do things with my lettering where I wrap the words around objects on the page. I vary my balloon shapes. I don't know that you can actually re-create what I do on the computer. I guess you probably could, but it would take you so long that it would be . . . you wouldn't make any money at it.

Computer lettering, even at its best, looks like Colorforms; like something created by a machine is stuck over something that was created by a human. And when you hand letter—and to the people who know what they're looking at, to those who can see it and appreciate it—it's the melding of these two organic things. They need to exist together. To work together. Like a dance. Whereas computer lettering, to me, is never a dance. It's always Colorforms. And I'm not just knocking computer lettering because I'm a hand letterer—I've done both, and I appreciate both. But having done both for over a decade now . . . well, there's no contest between the two.

Kochman: As readers, we may not consciously notice it, but when the work is pleasing to the eye, as it is with Archie comics, hand lettering is one of the reasons. You know, there are lots of things we're able to do differently now because we have the machines to do it. But that doesn't mean we should. Here's a ten-cent analogy for you: You can easily make potato pancakes by putting them in a food processor. But the way my grandmother made them, she grated the potatoes and the onions by hand, and there was no comparison. So yeah, we have the tools to make things quicker or faster, but that doesn't necessarily make them better.

Morelli: Right! That's the thing. Somebody who doesn't know how to make latkes could easily buy them frozen and stick them in the microwave, and sure enough they're eating latkes. But your grandmother made a *latke*. [laughs]

Kochman: She did. But let's be honest: She was a lousy letterer.

Morelli: [laughs] Not to get too sappy about this, but Stan Goldberg was really good friends with Danny Crespi, who was the production manager up at Marvel. He was also a fantastic letterer, and he did all the classic cover copy for Marvel back in the sixties and seventies. All those great covers we grew up with. Well, Danny was the guy who taught me to letter. Stan was very, very close with Danny. They were like best friends. And Danny was my mentor at Marvel. So to work on Stan's stuff now . . . I try to bring Danny's sensibility to it. As someone from my generation working with Stan, I try to bring what I hope is the same passion and sensibility to it that our predecessors did. I try and marry it all together when I work on a book. You know, I think about that every time I sit down to do a page. I have a picture of Danny on the shelf above my desk, and every now and then I look up and think, *I'm trying Danny. I'm trying to live up to the history.* I really try to work hard and keep it all alive. And I try to do it in a world where Colorform lettering and microwave latkes are the norm. [laughs]

Kochman: I know exactly what you mean. For me, it's Joe Orlando. He was my mentor at DC. I think of him all the time. Every book I edit, every project, I hear his voice in my head pushing me to make it better.

Well, this is great, Jack. This is exactly what I wanted to get into. Now another aspect of lettering is leading the reader's eye through the story. Obviously, the penciler establishes that. He indicates where the captions and the word balloons will go. Stan will take a script like Michael Uslan's, and he will interpret it and leave room for the dialogue. But then the letterer has to go in there and make some choices. You help make sure the reader always knows how to go from panel to panel. You lead the eye in combination with the art.

Morelli: Well, actually, Stan is very good about this. He always indicates the balloon placement. But every now and then I see a better way, because it's what I do. I have thirty years of experience in this one particular area. Sometimes I can figure out a slightly better way to stack the balloons that leads the eye around into the next panel. Or sometimes I tweak the stacking of the balloons to create a different pacing, which, in a humor book, might make things a little funnier.

Sometimes, the way you letter things can—let me find the right way to put this—it can help with the joke telling. Some comedians get on stage and tell a joke with a flat delivery, and you hear crickets. Other comedians could deliver the same material, only their pacing and inflections are spot on. They've got comic timing. The words may be exactly the same, but some deliveries are just funnier than others. Now, the writers, artists, and editors by far do the lion's share of this. But as a member of the team, you can sometimes help convey that a little bit with the lettering. You know what I mean? I try to think about that when I'm working on a job.

The thing about Archie is that it's the same characters, the same setting. It's Riverdale, and the core dynamics don't change, as in any sitcom. You know all the characters so well. So even if the situation is familiar, there's always something new or funny, a unique take on the way they interact. And it makes me laugh. Michael Uslan did such a great job with this story; not only was it humorous, but it was compelling and interesting. And when I lettered it I thought, *Okay, can my part do anything to help capture this?* I read it, and I heard it in my head. And then I tried to get it down on paper. I can only do just so much, because an artist like Stan does indicate where he'd like the balloons to go, and he's drawn the panel to accommodate that. He's also thought about the timing himself. But sometimes I can capture the pacing with the placement.

Kochman: Have you really been doing this for thirty years?

Morelli: Thirty this year. The first story I lettered was an issue of *Star Trek* by Marty Pasko, and it was drawn by Gil Kane. That was the first full book I lettered. I had been doing lettering corrections and working at Marvel since 1978, but the first full comic I lettered start to finish was in 1980.

Kochman: So you worked for both DC and Marvel?

Morelli: I worked for Marvel for twenty years, and then they went computer. And then I worked at DC for five or six years. I worked on a lot of different things. Whatever came my way. I worked on Green Lantern, Superman, Batman, Azrael. I did a lot of stuff there. And then they too followed suit and switched over to computer lettering.

But to tell you the truth—and I'm not just saying this—in thirty years this is the most fun I've had

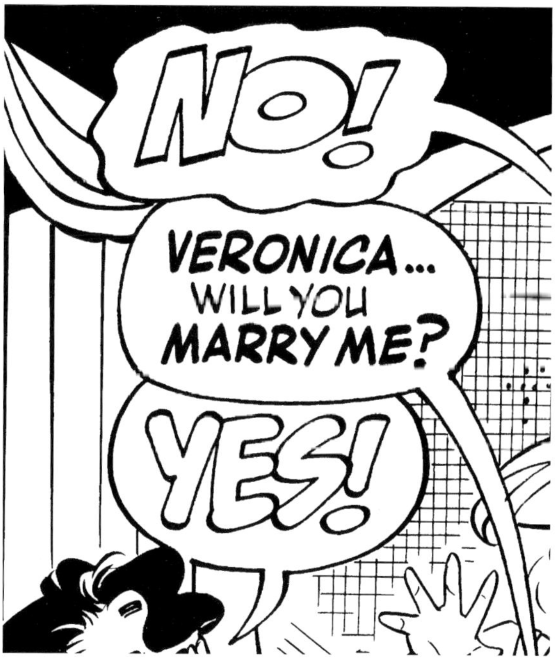
NO!
VERONICA... WILL YOU MARRY ME?
YES!

lettering comics. Don't get me wrong. I loved my time growing up at Marvel. I was a kid. I was fifteen, just turned sixteen, when I started there as an intern. And I loved the people. There's nothing like the people in this business. I had a wonderful time at the office, and I had a lot of fun with everybody. It was great. And when you come to Archie, it's the same thing. It's a great group of guys. And the actual work—sitting down every day and putting that first page on the board. You know, you've got your cup of coffee and you have your music on in the background . . . and then you're working on a Stan Goldberg story. Honestly, it's never drudge work. I'm having the most fun. I was actually out of the business for a little while, for two years, when computers had taken over and I wasn't working at Archie yet. And I thought, maybe I'm done. But luckily this came around, and now I'm having the time of my life.

Kochman: Not many people can say that. I'm going on twenty-five years, and I feel the same way you do.

Morelli: We're lucky. But I want to say one thing about the team at Archie, and I'm not trying to sound like an apple polisher, but you know what impresses me about them—about Victor and Mike Pellerito and Stephen Oswald? When I do something a little extra, when I add something special to a story—like I'll put in some scary lettering, or make a choice about something—those guys always notice and let me know. Not that long ago, Stan called me up to tell me that he thought I was doing a great job, and he enjoyed working with me. [laughs] I don't think I could work for the rest of the day; I was floating around the house.

Kochman: When we began this conversation, you said, "I'm just a letterer." But clearly you're not "just" a letterer, Jack, and that's why I wanted to include you in this interview section, and include Glenn Whitmore and Bob Smith, too. You guys are not just lettering or coloring or inking; you're all part of a team. The creators of a comic book intrinsically work together. There's a harmony in what you do, in the team Victor has put in place at Archie. And your contributions can each be seen on the pages, as part of the artwork of the finished product, issue after issue, month after month, year after year. Some of the players may be unsung, but all are equally important.

Morelli: Well, thank you. We were at the Smithsonian last year, and my son was looking at this display they had on literature through the ages. It's when you first walk in. There's this illuminated manuscript, this entire book that was lettered with a quill. And I'm just staring and it, and my son said, "You're probably the only guy who still does that." [laughs] And I thought, *Yeah. I'm the last scribe.* Basically, I'm taking a story that someone else has written, I'm making my own pen, and I'm literally dipping the quill in ink, bringing it over one letter at a time, and telling a tale. So in a way he's right.

Kochman: Wait, you make your own pen? There's not one out of the box you can use?

Morelli: No, not at all. But what I do is take a B6 pen. All Speedball pens—they have different shapes and sizes, but I find the B6 is about the right size for comic book lettering—they have a little tab at the end of the pen that creates the stroke. And I just cut that tab off at an angle with a fingernail clipper, believe it or not. I cut it off to the right thickness to turn it into a crow quill, like a calligraphy-style pen. But if you cut off too much, the line will be too thick; if you cut too little, it won't be thick enough. I like to have both thick and thin lines to my lettering because I think it looks more alive. So I use the fingernail clipper and clip the tab off, and I then take either wet or dry sandpaper, or I have a little jeweler's stone, and I'll start by making little ovals and figure eights until I smooth out the pen. I'll smooth out the rough sides, because it has nasty edges that snag when you clip the tab off like that. And I do that until I get the tip as smooth as I can, then test it on a piece of paper.

Very slowly I'll start lettering a word like "Kuramoto." I've taken to lettering "Kuramoto" because Morrie Kuramoto was an old production guy at Marvel, and he helped teach me how to letter. You want any word that has lots of ovals in it, as well as descenders and horizontals, that kind of stuff. Now, Archie uses nice paper, smooth paper, but depending on the tooth of the paper, the pen will snag more or less, so I work the pen around and around on either the sandpaper or the jeweler's stone. I angle the edges a little bit, round the edges, and get the tip to where it's as smooth as I can possibly get it, where it grabs up less of the tooth of the paper and it flows easily. Then the very last thing I do is take a shot glass—John Romita Sr. showed me this trick—I take a shot glass and pour a little bit of ink in and then run the pen in circles around the bottom. And the glass is so smooth, unlike sandpaper, but believe it or not, it takes any last little microscopic burrs off the point, and then you're ready to start to letter. And boy, when you get a pen that you've made, when you're just gliding, you treat that thing like gold.

Kochman: And how long do they last?

Morelli: Well, if you treat them right, they usually . . . well, some pens I've had for years. But I find I can sometimes get six months out of a pen. I'm talking normal-copy lettering. The pen I use 90 percent of the time. I can get six, eight months out of a pen, and then they start . . . they either start to come apart, from metal fatigue, and break down, or they begin to spread, so you start to use that as your bold pen, and you then need to create a new normal-body copy pen. They graduate up.

Kochman: Wow, that was fascinating. I learned more about pens in the past two minutes than I ever thought there was to know. [laughs]

Morelli: And that's why we're the last remaining buggy-whip company in North America! There are still a few other guys like me hand lettering comics. I always like to say, I'm not the last guy, but most of the time I just feel like I am. There are a few of us out there doing it like this, but not a whole lot of us.

Kochman: But that's just it. Most people don't notice the lettering. The average sort of reader—they read the story, and if they're entertained, they don't notice the lettering. They take for granted that it's good. Why would it not be? They expect it to be good.

Morelli: But bad lettering is like . . . when someone's playing Beethoven and the C key isn't working. Don't think that doesn't change the whole performance. And that's what it's like for us. In our humble sort of way, we're an ensemble. But I have to say, Charlie, I appreciate that you included me and Glenn and Bob in these interviews. I appreciate that you took the time. It's nice when other professionals recognize you. It's nice when Stan calls—it's *fantastic* when Stan calls—but colorists and inkers and letterers, we sort of toil in anonymity. [laughs] I sound like Eeyore: "Thanks for noticing me." ◆

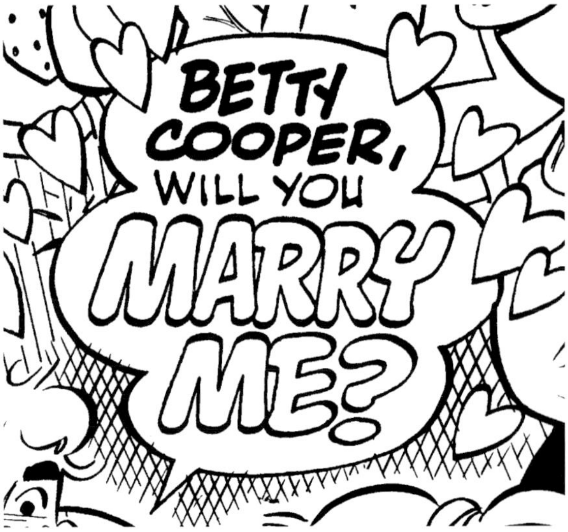
BETTY COOPER, WILL YOU MARRY ME?

BOB SMITH

Charles Kochman: How did you find out about the wedding story line, and what was your reaction to it?

Bob Smith: I'm one of the regular inkers on the Archie books, so it just kind of fell in with my monthly work assignment inking Stan Goldberg's pencils. I think Mike Pellerito first told me about it, probably several months ahead of time, about a year ago, and I found it very interesting, the whole . . . you know, Archie getting married to both of them, and his going up Memory Lane and back. I didn't know what the reader reaction was going to be. But there was a strong reaction when Archie married Veronica first. A lot of people are very partisan about the whole Betty and Veronica thing.

Kochman: And when it was announced, everyone was all up in arms. They didn't expect anything like that. I know from working at DC Comics that when we published the "Death of Superman" story line in 1992 and '93, which started out as just a regular story and then made headlines on a slow news day, we were all surprised it became so big and that people all over the world took notice. You realize how important these iconic comic book characters are to people—especially to adults who haven't read a comic in decades.

Smith: Certainly, after experiencing the Superman story, I figured there would probably be some sort of a reaction to this. But I didn't expect it to be *as* big because I didn't realize just how popular the Archie characters are, so I wasn't expecting such an extreme reaction, especially with the press. I didn't expect any press reaction.

Kochman: What's it like when you get the penciled pages from Stan Goldberg? I assume, like all of us, you're a fan of Stan's. What's it like to ink his stories, and to read Michael Uslan's story as you're doing it?

Smith: Well, with Stan it's always a lot of fun because his books have a lot of energy to them. There's always a lot of . . . people aren't just standing around talking. There's a lot of movement. So I always enjoy working with Stan. Reading the stories, I would get the book in chunks, six to eight pages a shot, and it was fun, seeing how things would turn out, and then from issue to issue not knowing where things were going to go. Michael was always adding a lot of little sight gags and references to Archie's history in the stories, and those were always fun to ink. And there are even little outside references; I think there was a Spider-Man reference in one of them, so that makes it interesting. If you're a real fan you might catch all these little things going on in the panels, and they all add to the enjoyment of the story.

Kochman: Can you explain what an inker does? I think most people think like the character in the Kevin Smith film *Chasing Amy*, that an inker just traces.

Smith: People often ask me if I do the coloring and the lettering—they always assume I do the coloring for some reason—but the way it works is that the penciler draws it in pencil, and then I go over it later with pen and brush and ink, and make the lines more solid and darker for reproduction purposes.

Kochman: But it's not as simple as just tracing the lines. There's a lot more nuance to it. Can you explain that a little?

Smith: Well, there's a certain amount of interpretation—working with line weights, rendering, adding details like textures, and making minor corrections to anatomy or to the backgrounds. An inker makes the art more readable and more interesting and brings it to life, because if the pages were shot using just the pencil, it would be sort of gray and flat. Some pencilers are a little sketchier than others; it really wouldn't work to use just the pencils. Even if you were to just trace the pencils, you'd have to . . . the inker has to know how to draw as well as ink, and how to catch things in order to bring the page together as a whole.

Kochman: I think everyone always misinterprets the role of an inker. I mean, a penciler obviously lays out the page, but you're going in there and you create depth of field by adding the black areas, accentuating different parts of a page or a panel to focus the reader's eye.

Smith: Exactly. A lot of pencilers use sort of a dead line, so what I try to do with thick and thin line weights is create a sense of perspective, making things up front a little heavier and things in the background a little lighter.

Kochman: And you've been working with Stan for a long time now, so you guys have a good rapport when you collaborate. I'm sure there are certain things he leaves for you to add that he probably wouldn't leave for another inker to fill in. But with you, he knows you're going to add your style to it and accentuate what he pencils. So you two make a good team. I've seen Stan inked by some other inkers, and the art never reads the same as when he's inked by you.

Smith: Well, he also knows that no matter what he pencils, I'll ink it. No matter how much detail he throws in, I'm going to put it all in there on the final page.

Kochman: So some inkers will actually leave some stuff out?

Smith: Due to deadline situations or something like that. Or they feel like maybe there's too much detail, so they'll throw a black wash over some of the art. But I'll just put everything in there. [laughs]

Kochman: You recently wrapped up the series. And as you're working on it—I asked this of Michael and I'm curious about your take—the first book is not released yet, and then it comes out and you haven't even finished working on the series yet when it starts to get all this media attention. And you yourself don't even know how it's going to all play out. What's that like as an artist? Was it intimidating? Did you feel any pressure now that so many people were paying attention? When you were working on the first issue, it was just another monthly assignment. You didn't have millions of eyes watching what you were doing, caring as much as they did all of a sudden.

Smith: Once the story broke, people started asking me what was going to happen—how it was going to turn out. They wanted to know how it was going to end. And I couldn't tell them, you know, because even *I* didn't know.

And when I did finally know, I wouldn't tell, because I wanted them to find out for themselves. I had to keep the story secret so it could be enjoyed.

Kochman: When you finished the epilogue, did you look at the first issue and wish you had the chance to go back and do anything differently?

Smith: Oh yeah. Every time I ink a job, I always feel like I could've done better. And I'm sure Michael probably felt the same way; when he finally finished writing the epilogue, he probably wished he could go through and rewrite the first couple of issues. Because there are always things you wish you could have done better or differently, you realize, given the perspective you gain later. Looking it over you notice certain inconsistencies.

Kochman: These days almost all individual issues are collected into trade paperback or hardcover. But when you read the work of, say, Jack Kirby in the seventies, which was written in monthly installments, you can see that the comics weren't meant to be read in one sitting, as a complete work. When you read these collected editions, you definitely notice a lot of inconsistencies.

Smith: And there's certainly a lot of repetition, stuff like that.

Kochman: You mentioned adding details and things in the background. Is there anything you wish to share? Any Easter eggs you planted in the stories?

Smith: There's nothing I added. It's mostly stuff Michael and Stan added, and I enjoyed seeing them. I don't usually put things in myself; I used to when I was much younger—slipping in the names of friends and things like that—but I don't do much of that anymore.

Kochman: Overall, are you happy with the work? Do you feel like this is one of those career milestones?

Smith: Yeah, I haven't had too many of them, so I really enjoyed this one.

Kochman: What does it feel like to work on something that becomes . . . that so many people are paying attention to?

Smith: I like the fact that it's being collected and remembered and enjoyed by a lot of people; that it's being discussed and criticized. To be involved in something like that at this stage of my career, when a lot of times people . . . when creators reach a certain point in their careers, they don't get this opportunity anymore. It's usually reserved for younger creators.

Kochman: Let's talk a little bit about your career. How did you get into comics?

Smith: I started in 1975, working with DC Comics on Plastic Man.

Kochman: You started as an inker?

Smith: As an inker, yeah. I didn't work as an assistant to anyone. I just came in and got right to work. I showed my portfolio at DC and was able to get work almost immediately.

Kochman: How did you decide to start as an inker? Why not as a penciler?

Smith: I just fell into it. I came in with my own pencil samples. Back then I didn't have access to photocopies of other artists' pencils or anything to work with, so I had to pencil my own samples, and then I inked them. They seemed to like my inking, so they started me out as an inker, and I just kind of stuck with it. I never got back into the penciling.

Kochman: Which characters have you worked on since, besides Plastic Man and Archie?

Smith: Oh boy. [laughs] The Flash, Black Canary— there were so many at DC. I was working on so many books there. Batman and *Detective Comics*.

Kochman: Superman?

Smith: I really didn't do any Superman. I did just one issue of Superman. I worked on the Justice League, Robin, Catwoman, Captain Atom, Green Lantern, Blue Beetle, Teen Titans . . . a lot of early stuff like *House of Mystery*. Some of the war titles . . . so many of them, especially early on. *Adventure Comics. World's Finest.* I didn't really have a regular book.

Kochman: Any characters that you haven't worked on that you'd like to?

Smith: I wish I had done more work at Marvel. I think I inked only one book for Marvel. I kind of got locked in with DC and stayed there for a long time. I wish I could have inked Spider-Man or Fantastic Four, or something like that.

Kochman: How did you transition to Archie?

Smith: Well, in the late nineties the work at DC started to thin down quite a bit, and I wasn't getting as many assignments, so I figured I'd better start looking around at other companies for work. I called up Victor Gorelick at Archie and asked him if he had anything, and he sent me some photocopies and asked me to send in some samples. He told me he liked my work and he would hire me to do some stuff, but he couldn't promise he'd be able to keep me busy. But within a month I had so much work there, I didn't have time to work for anyone else. And I've been with Archie ever since. I have done some work for other companies, like Bongo Comics on *Radioactive Man*, and I did a few pages of a *Star Trek* story for IDW, but mostly I've been working for Archie for the last decade or so.

Kochman: How long does it take to do what you do? I mean, how long does it take to ink a page or an issue?

Smith: I try to do at least two pages a day if I can. I'm getting slower as I get older; my eyes get tired earlier in the day. Like now. [laughs] ◆

(**right**) Bob Smith's final inks for page 81 (*Archie* no. 602, December 2009).

Archie #602 Dec. '09

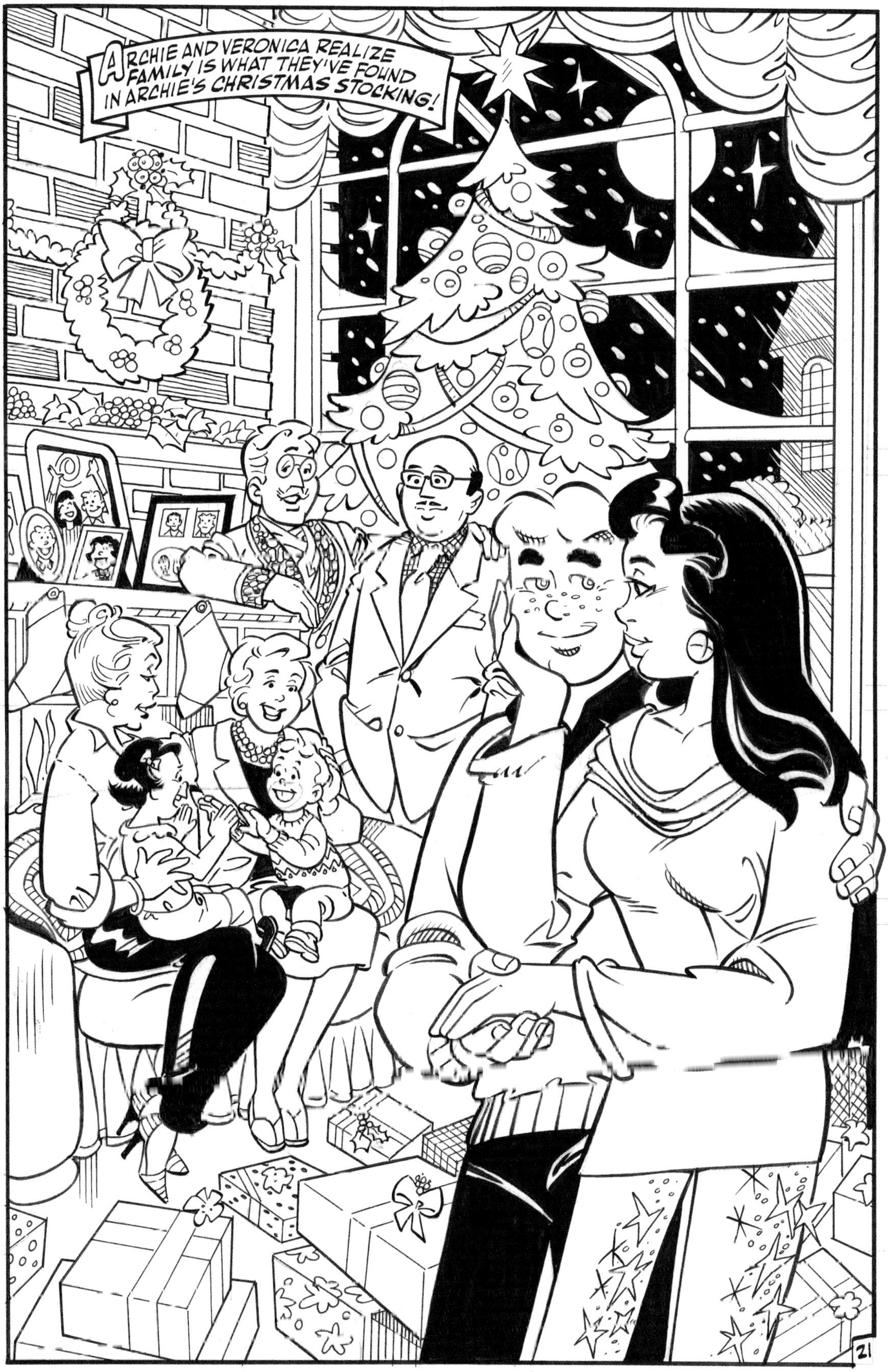
ARCHIE AND VERONICA REALIZE FAMILY IS WHAT THEY'VE FOUND IN ARCHIE'S CHRISTMAS STOCKING!
21

GLENN WHITMORE

Charles Kochman: How long have you been coloring for Archie?

Glenn Whitmore: I've been doing it since the beginning of 2008. Fernando Ruiz, who pencils for Archie, recommended me. We're fellow alumni from the Joe Kubert School of Cartoon and Graphic Art in New Jersey. Fernando recommended me to Mike Pellerito. Mike and I talked, and he sent me some stuff to color, and the next thing I know I'm working for Archie. I find it easy working for Mike and everybody up there. Right now, that's the majority of the stuff I'm doing, pretty much all of the stuff I'm doing at the moment, coloring-wise. But it's working out real well. I really enjoy coloring for them.

Kochman: What is your background? Where did you train?

Whitmore: Right out of high school, I went to the Joe Kubert School. I took their Cartoon and Graphics curriculum, and at the time I was still a little weak on my drawing, but coloring and design were my strong suits. They taught the way coloring worked, which was something I really gravitated to because it was this definite system that I could really comprehend. I liked coding and I liked figuring out how to make different things pop out, different elements in the panel, and emphasize the artist's design of a page.

I graduated from the Kubert School in 1987, and about a year later I was able to pick up some freelance from DC Comics. In the meantime, I worked in the production department at Marvel a couple of days a week. And then DC started giving me some work, beginning with the *Hawk & Dove* series, which was penciled by Rob Liefeld. I worked with DC editor Mike Carlin on that series, and he liked me well enough to give me Superman later on when a colorist assignment opened up.

Kochman: That's when you and I first met, when you were working on the "Death of Superman" story line for DC Comics in 1992 and '93.

Whitmore: Right. I was fortunate enough to be around for that. I'd begun working for Mike in 1988, 1989, right around there. I was young at the time and eager to learn, and he knew what he wanted, so he was able to instill in me what he was looking for in a colorist. I stayed on the Superman books for the next eleven years, which was a great thrill. Especially to be around for the big multipart story lines, like Clark Kent's engagement to Lois Lane, their marriage, and the death of Superman—all the big events from the nineties. That was a lot of fun.

Kochman: Let's talk more about what a colorist does. I think most people don't realize the artistry and skill involved—that a good colorist can really make a book, or that a bad colorist can hinder the reader's enjoyment.

Whitmore: When I was growing up as a comics fan, I never really paid attention to the color in the comics

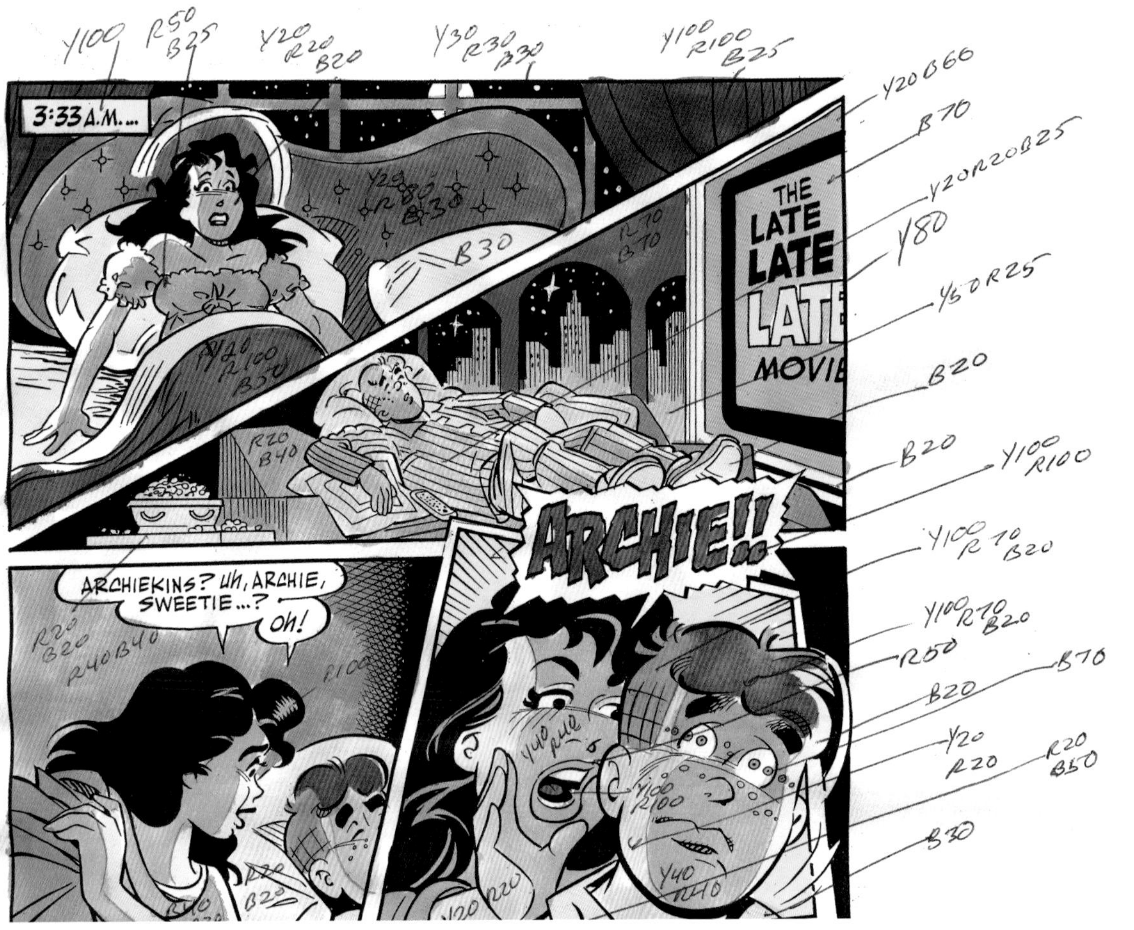
3:33 A.M....
THE
LATE
LATE
ARCHIE!!
ARCHIEKINS? UH, ARCHIE, SWEETIE...?
OH!

Glenn Whitmore's color guides for page 73 (*Archie* no. 602, December 2009).

I read. I mean, I knew it was there, but it was just something that if it wasn't bad, you didn't really notice it; it was just part of the artwork, at least for me. But after I went to the Kubert School and broke into comics, I realized how important the colorist is. Back then it wasn't computer coloring at all, it was all watercolor dyes. We would spec up a black-and-white Xerox of the inks with watercolor dyes, and then put the codes on them for the separator to add the color at the printer.

Kochman: Those codes appear on the color guides the Archie guys sent us to include in this book. So it's still being done that way? I thought it was all computer coloring now.

Whitmore: Well, Archie still does it that way. Archie is very traditional as far as that's concerned. They still use color guides and give them to a separator. It's what they've traditionally done for years. I'm able to do both. I can do computer coloring *and* spec color guides.

Kochman: When you're doing color, when you're looking at an inked page, how do you approach your work? One thing I learned from your coloring style is that it's not so black and white, so to speak. For instance, there are, surprisingly, a number of different ways to color Superman. Obviously, his cape is red and his uniform is blue; however, you use different values of those colors as you take into consideration lighting or given time of day or location, and you alter the intensity of those primary colors depending on what else is on the page. If you can, talk a little about how it's not just that each character has a specific color, but that you have to take into consideration other factors when you approach coloring a page.

Whitmore: With super-hero comics there's a little more leeway in using coloring effects, because there are all kinds of crazy things going on when they use their powers, that kind of stuff. Or if you have a nighttime character like Batman, obviously you try to use as many cool colors (blues, greens) in the scene as possible. With Metropolis, a lot of the sets, like the *Daily Planet* building or Clark Kent's apartment—or with Riverdale, for Pop's Malt Shop or Archie's house or Betty's house—I try to be consistent issue to issue in the colors I use. I also treat the sets as characters, unless there's some kind of special effect going on, or there's some kind of cue in the story or dialogue, like, "It's a late afternoon, after school," or if it's nighttime. With the Archie characters, there's freedom in that they don't wear the same clothes all the time. They don't wear uniforms. But I still have a set color palette for each. I try to keep Archie in primaries mostly, sort of like Superman was in his series. And then I have a certain set of colors for each character; like Jughead would be in either burgundy or dark blue. For Veronica and Betty, I usually pick one and assign her a pink or purple or green or one of the secondary colors, then use complimentary colors for the other.

Kochman: So you approach it by starting with the characters first on each page, and then building around them. Or do you look at each part of the story and determine that this scene, say, takes place in Pop's Malt

Shop, so it needs to have a kind of overhead fluorescent lighting effect because it takes place inside in the middle of the day, and that determines the values of your palette?

Whitmore: The latter. But it doesn't affect the characters as much as everything else in the scene. Archie Comics has very specific color codes for each character's flesh tones and hair color, so there's not much leeway there. When I physically color a page, I decide what my light colors are, and that usually ends up being the background. For daytime scenes, I always put down the light blue first, and then I work my strongest colors, because, with watercolor dyes, if you put your strong colors down first and then try to add the light colors, the strong colors will bleed into them. So you have to be careful like that. But I always make sure that when there's a scene change I don't always use the same color as before, so I can cue the reader in and indicate that the scene has changed. They might not be reading the story, but they can take a glance at it and know that the scene has changed. It might be going from somebody's house to another person's house—you need to be able to differentiate; maybe the artist draws the room or the houses similar, but the color can be a very effective tool in giving the reader a clue that we've just changed scenes.

Kochman: A lot of it, I'm sure, is very intuitive. You just know after doing this for over twenty years how to approach your craft. You look at a particular scene and you know how to make it look right. Now, in terms of the Archie wedding story line, what was your take? How did you first hear about it? Did you read about it like everyone else, or did they give you a heads up that you were going to be working on this story and it was going to be really huge?

Whitmore: Actually, I assumed somebody else was going to be coloring the story because it had been announced and was already out in the media, so I just assumed one of the other colorists was assigned to it. Then one day I got an e-mail or a phone call from Stephen Oswald at Archie saying, "We're sending you these pages, and there's going to be a tight deadline on them." And I was really, really happy to get the assignment.

Kochman: That's cool. So you got the inks for the first issue. You knew the basic story line, but you hadn't read it until then, obviously. What was your impression?

Whitmore: After twenty-some odd years it's still hard to gauge. By the time the comic comes out on the stands, I forget that there's a whole public audience that has not read it yet. But I had to be careful about what I said with friends who were not involved in the story, because I felt like I had a responsibility to keep it as secret as possible until it came out. But there's always the temptation to talk about it because there was such excitement surrounding it.

Kochman: Sure. And you had to do that once before with the death of Superman, where you're part of a small creative team that knows what's going to happen with Doomsday and how Superman's going to come back. Not many creators have worked on more than one of these major comic book events. I think that's pretty cool. Anything else you want to cover?

Whitmore: We haven't mentioned Stan. He's the dean of all the Archie guys. I really felt that I was given the keys to the Cadillac when I was sent these pages. As a colorist, you can always tell when you are given a job whether you're going to have to work hard to make it work. But with Stan, it's easy. He's really great at designing panels and pages, and his were easier than those of most artists I've colored. I guess that's about all I have to say. I hope I've given you enough. ◆

JON GOLDWATER

Charles Kochman: So you're relatively new to Archie. When did you join as CEO?

Jon Goldwater: Actually, I'll have been at Archie one year come April 1. This coming Thursday is my one-year anniversary. Being at Archie has been, for me, a dream come true. Obviously, my father is the founder of the company, and I grew up with it every day, so Archie was not just . . . it's in my blood, quite honestly. From the second I could read, I read *Archie* comics. My dad would bring home the new books as soon as they came out, so I'm intimately familiar with not just the characters themselves but with the backstory, and everything that went on with the genesis of the company. When my half-brother Richard Goldwater passed away—I guess it's going on just over two years now—and then his partner Michael Silberkleit passed away nine months later, there was a big void in the day-to-day operations of Archie Comics. Through a series of remarkable events, I was offered the opportunity to come in and buy some stock in the company and run Archie. So now it's been a year, and it's been probably the greatest year of my life. Just about every day I pinch myself and say it's a dream come true. It's really fantastic.

Kochman: So, was it always in the back of your mind that you would one day take over the company, or was it just the circumstances?

Goldwater: I always wanted to work at Archie. I always wanted to run the company. But you know, there's family dynamics involved. And sometimes you don't always get to the front of the line, if you know what I mean. So when the opportunity presented itself, I embraced it. But yes, I always thought about it. I dreamed about it. Like I said, it's part of my heritage. It's part of my blood. From day one, it just felt really natural.

Kochman: Well, from an outsider's perspective, it's been an amazing year for Archie Comics. You've totally rejuvenated the brand. We now hear about the company in mainstream news and also within the industry. Suddenly it feels like Archie's back. For a long time Archie was taken for granted. You were still putting out great comics that sold week in and week out, year after year, but nobody was talking about Archie. Now you've put the characters back on the map and reestablished Archie as a major comic book company once again.

Goldwater: I really appreciate your saying that, Charlie. You know, it's funny. Comic-Con in San Diego this past July was the first Comic-Con I ever attended, and I found it remarkable. Not just the passion that people feel for comic books in general, but I left there with the feeling that we don't give the world enough Archie. We don't give readers enough opportunities to embrace our characters, whether it be, like you say, in mainstream news, or in new initiatives we weren't undertaking. There just wasn't enough Archie out there. It really resonated with me that we have to do something to (a) satisfy our fan base and (b) grow the company. I mean, we have to move forward. With the print medium right now, and the emergence of digital platforms, you know this better than anybody, there's so much information available from so many places—how do you distinguish yourself? Well, the way you separate yourself from everyone else is to be creative, to be vibrant, to be current, and by doing things sometimes that people don't expect. Well, I've been looking at opportunities outside the framework of our company and our characters, while still maintaining the integrity of who our characters are. That's what we've been doing here at Archie these past twelve months. We need to invigorate this brand within the integrity of the characters. And so we've been moving forward, and we are doing tons of new initiatives. We have many media opportunities in the works. We have digital books out there on multiple platforms. In fact, we're the number one most downloaded comic book on iTunes. There are so many things we're proud of. It's been a remarkable year.

Kochman: Congratulations. Talking to your team, I hear how respected they all feel and how you treat everyone like they're family. Even though it was always an Archie family, guys like Stan and Victor—both of whom have basically worked their whole lives for Archie Comics—really feel the positive changes you've made. No disrespect to the people who were there before you.

Goldwater: Well, that's great to hear, Charlie, because honestly, without the writers, without the artists, without all the people who put their time, their energy, their talent, and their creativity in the books day after day, we would have nothing. So we embrace them, like you were saying, as part of the family. I want everyone to feel that they can come to me with new ideas, with new initiatives, and they will be looked at with respect and with seriousness. And you know what? Dealing with the artists and dealing with the writers has probably been the most fun part of my job. I feel like I've unleashed them. I've freed them up to be able to come to me with all sorts of new ideas. We now have a whole new outlook on how to do things, and I love it. I love working with them because they also love our characters so much. It's been such a pleasure. I want everyone involved, everyone who puts our books together and who writes our stories and does all that stuff, to feel not just respected, because I would hope they would always feel respected, but I want them to feel like family. They're part of what we do here. These books are our lifeblood, and the creators are the blood that goes into the comics. We really embrace our contributors.

Kochman: Well, I know it's appreciated. Most of your creators have given so much of their lives and their creativity to the company and to the characters over the years, so it's great to hear that attitude and see it reflected in the new projects you are getting involved in. Now, you came to Archie a year ago. Was the idea of the wedding comic in the works? Did it predate you, or was it a result of your mandate to change the status quo?

Goldwater: The idea for the wedding predated me. It was actually . . . Michael Uslan had gone to Victor a few months before I came on board. And Victor, being incredibly intuitive and brilliant, immediately recognized it as something that could make an impact. It was Victor who green-lit the idea, so I give him all the credit in the world for that. And he did a brilliant job with it, too. And then there's Michael Uslan, of course. When I first got here, one of my great honors was to meet Mike. I mean, if there's anyone who embodies what a comic book is, it's Michael Uslan, for goodness' sake. To sit with him and to hear him discuss his vision for the wedding story . . . to me, he just made it crystal-clear that this was something special. Something this company had never done before.

Kochman: Were you surprised by the reaction?

Goldwater: Shocked. And thrilled, simultaneously. Once again, it just goes back to the fact that people really, really love our characters. They feel invested in what happens to them. Michael and Victor's stroke of brilliance was to have Archie marry Veronica in the first book out. Marrying Betty—that would have been expected. That would have been the easy thing to do. But Michael picked up on the fact that if Archie married Veronica, people would be shocked by that. So yeah, the reaction to the story was really incredible. You know, we didn't have a publicist on board; we really did nothing to promote it. I think we posted something on our website. And from there it spread like wildfire.

Kochman: Were you planning a regular print run, or once you announced it and the news exploded, did you adjust your print run accordingly?

Goldwater: We had to adjust the print run. We absolutely had to. I mean, I would like to say we anticipated the reaction . . . of course, you always hope for the best, but you can't really plan for it. You can't expect this kind of fervor for a story, so, I mean, as soon as we saw things taking off the way they were, we had to adjust our print runs. It's now our best-selling book in over twenty-five years. It's just monumental, the impact that book has had on our company. And I mean the whole story line—six books in a row and the epilogue. Without getting into specific numbers, a lot of Archie comics were sold.

Kochman: Did it help the backlist, and your other titles, too?

Goldwater: This story has impacted everything we do here at Archie. It's been amazing, because it's brought so many new eyeballs to the company. So yes, the wedding stories sold great, but our subscriptions have been through the roof since then. And it's impacted the way we do business here at Archie Comics. Everything is way, way up for us now.

Kochman: After seventy years, to continue to surprise your readers, and to reinvent the characters and yet to remain true to who they are . . . I think that says a lot about the brand.

Goldwater: It's amazing the amount of passion that people feel for our characters. I gotta tell you, I'm really, really proud that people have such strong feelings about them. And it's multigenerational. You have people, men and women, who are in their fifties and sixties, who have grown up reading *Archie* comics their whole lives. And you have younger readers who are, you know, eight to ten years old. So it really runs the whole gamut. It's inspirational.

Kochman: So all of a sudden the story line is announced, and a whole media firestorm erupts. And it's not just in the comics community, but on regular, mainstream news as well. And internationally, too. Can you speak a little about the international appeal of the characters?

Goldwater: It's crazy. Victor has done a bunch of interviews with the BBC. This story really helped us establish a foothold in the UK market. And in India, where Archie has always been strong, we had articles on the front pages of their papers! You're talking about millions and millions and millions of readers. Our sales in that territory have gone through the roof. It's been absolutely remarkable. In the Middle East, too. It's really been an international phenomenon. Australia—huge. Various parts of Europe—huge. I mean, this story really has translated internationally. So it really has been this international phenomenon. And, of course, Canada, which is probably the strongest territory outside of the United States for Archie. This whole thing just went crazy in Canada.

Kochman: And here at home you had the dream team on these books. Michael Uslan brought his whole Hollywood background to the story, and has a deep knowledge and reverence for the characters. And then there's Stan and Bob and Jack and Glenn. Can you talk a little about your creative team on the books?

Goldwater: Well, you just said it perfectly, Charlie. It's the dream team. I mean, you're talking legends. You're talking the best of the best. So when you have that sort of team, it all comes together. Michael is just brilliant at what he does. And Stan and Bob—these guys are the best. All the reviews say it, our sales say it, and so do our fans. It's black and white. Working with them was phenomenal. But once again I have to give credit to Victor. Victor shepherded this thing through on a day-to-day basis. He recognized the potential of the story from the outset. And most important, he set up an environment where a story like this could be pitched and not just dismissed out of hand. We couldn't have done this without Victor. He's phenomenal.

Kochman: I'm so glad to hear you say that. It's rare

for a boss to speak so candidly about an employee, especially with such reverence and praise. And it's all well deserved. Victor holds a very special place in the history of comics. He's well respected in the community. And I gather that these days he's doing even more in addition to editing. He's part of your management team. He's the brand manager.

Goldwater: Victor is brilliant. He looks at a story and, in a no-nonsense way, but in a very professional way, gets right to the heart of it: "This is what I like." "This is what works." "This is what needs to be changed." And every time, he makes it better. And I don't mean that just in terms of the story itself—but from an artistic point of view, he will have suggestions that almost always make the book better aesthetically. So Victor Gorelick *is* Archie Comics. He embodies Archie Comics. Victor is irreplaceable. He is a legend, but you know what? He's been here fifty years, Charlie, but he's still as current, and as contemporary, as any editor in the business. Victor knows more about contemporary comics and what's going to work for Archie in today's world than anybody. That's how good Victor is.

Kochman: [laughs] No argument from me. I think you're absolutely right.

Goldwater: He knows our characters better than anyone. He's lived with them, he's breathed them, every day for the last fifty years. They are truly his family— Archie, Betty, Veronica, and the gang. And Victor is part of Riverdale, without a doubt.

Kochman: So, where does Archie and the gang go from here? What's next?

Goldwater: Well, what's next is we're continuing the wedding story lines. We're actually launching a brand-new magazine called *Life with Archie*. It contains both "Archie Loves Veronica" and "Archie Loves Betty"—two new titles. And it follows them as married couples and deals with all the things that young married couples deal with, like husband-wife relationship issues, friendship issues, domestic issues, money issues. One story from the Betty point of view, and one from the Veronica point of view. And there's a little bit more meat on the bone than in your typical Archie story. They're geared for an older audience, thirteen and up. Michael Uslan has written the first issue, and he's done an absolutely brilliant job setting them up. So we are actually increasing the number of our titles here at Archie Comics. We're expanding.

I've gotta tell you something. This is not the end of it, either. This is a very exciting time at Archie Comics. The wedding was just the beginning. I promise you, we're moving things forward. We never left, but we're back, big-time. ◆

THE PITCH

From: Michael Uslan
Date: Sat, 6 Sept 2008 10:01:36 -0400
To: Victor Gorelick
Subject: Archie Gets Married

Hi Victor . . .

In the afterglow of my success with *The Dark Knight*, I've been thinking about all the things I always wanted to do but never got around to doing. Believe it or not, one is to write either an Archie comic book or graphic novel. I have a wild idea for a story that I think would generate great publicity. Is this something feasible you and I could discuss?

Let me know. If nothing else, it'll be a good excuse for us to meet for lunch.

Best,
Michael Uslan

From: Victor Gorelick
Sent: Thu, 16 Oct 2008 10:22:31 -0400
To: Michael Uslan
CC: 'Mike Pellerito'; 'Fred Mausser'
Subject: RE: RE: Archie Gets Married

Hi Michael,

Looks like this storyline will work best over six issues, starting with *Archie* no. 600. I'm already working on issue no. 592 and would like to start promoting this story arc in issue no. 593, even no. 592, if I can start putting together cover art. I like the idea of using Memory Lane and the fork in the road idea. Let's discuss this as soon as possible, so we can get the ball rolling. Since you'll be on the road for a couple of weeks, please do not hesitate to call me at home if you can't reach me during the day.

Victor

From: Michael Uslan
Date: Fri, 17 Oct 2008 7:17:21 -0400
To: Victor Gorelick
Subject: Archie no. 600

Hi Vic . . .

It was great to see you last week! And it will be a lot of fun to work with you!

A few questions about this project before I get to the outline of content:

If I got it straight, the plan will be to first publish this as a five-part story arc beginning in ARCHIE COMICS no. 600 and then collect them into the format of the first ARCHIE graphic novel. Here's my question about length: Half of this is to be a tale of Archie's marrying Veronica and the other half is to be a tale of Archie marrying Betty. If we were doing six issues, then clearly each would have three issues devoted to the story. Is this possible or need we stick to five issues? If we do stick to five, how do you see the two stories breaking up?

Next question: I know a lot of people in the movie/TV industry and was wondering if it would be okay if I invited a number of well-known women to send me their wedding gown designs for Veronica or for Betty, the way they might have if they were still 8–12 years old and reading BETTY & VERONICA comics? Do I need them to sign some sort of release or can we just print what they send in? Spacewise, how many might I have room for in the books?

Pin-up pages have always been an important part of the comic book history of Betty and Veronica. Any interest in my approaching famous comic book artists of the past and present to do wedding pin-up pages of the two girls?

Titles: To me, there are two ways to go: The first is a proclamation designed to grab immediate media and reader attention. "ARCHIE MARRIES VERONICA!" and then "ARCHIE MARRIES BETTY!" The more reserved titles would be: "THE WEDDING OF ARCHIE & VERONICA" and "THE WEDDING OF ARCHIE AND BETTY." I like the first, in-your-face title better. What works for you?

As I mention this project to some people, I get such an immediate sheer excitement in response that I sense there could be a massive p.r. reception for this across the complete mainstream media.

And now the outline:

I. The Set-Up

I considered using a virtual videogame like Wii but a version called Wii Marriage. When a guy and a girl play it, it creates a marriage scenario on the giant screen TV and we would close in on it until it becomes our new *Sliding Doors* reality. I also considered going back to Pureheart's device, THE BOOK OF HALLUCINATIONS, as a way to jump-start this "Imaginary Tale/What If" premise. But I think that if I simply use the most current device in today's Archie digests, walking down "Memory Lane." This might be the simplest way to go. In this case, Archie would walk the opposite way than he previously walked down Memory Lane. He would walk UP Memory Lane. He would reach a yellow wood where two roads diverge (thank you, Robert Frost!). Archie would choose one path for 2.5–3 issues and then try the other path for the remaining 2.5–3 issues. Let me know if you concur.

II. The Time

It is just a few years in the future. Archie, Betty, and Veronica are about to graduate from college. They still look pretty much the same, but we can get some input from artist Stan Goldberg as to how he'd like to draw them. I think the closer they are to the current look, the better. The changes should be subtle.

III. The Precipitating Event

It's College Graduation Day. It's a bittersweet time as we learn that the Riverdale gang have all gone on to attend the State University and Archie, Jughead, Reggie, Betty, and Veronica are all graduating together. We also learn that their next step in life will split them up for the first time in ages as they are each going to follow his or her own path and scatter across the country or world. Facing this reality on the last day they will be together, Archie proposes.

IV. The Proposal

Each of these two alternative stories will then address in two very different ways how, when, and where Archie proposes.

V. The Ring

Obviously, there will be two vastly different scenarios here between the Betty story and the Veronica story. We see who actually picks out the ring, where they get it, and if it's true that size counts.

VI. The Reactions

Needless to say, everyone's reactions to one choice or the other will be very different. We will explore the reactions to their engagement by the girl who is NOT the bride, the parents, the friends, and the Riverdale High staff, as well as Pop Tate who has known these kids since they were toddlers. There will be real emotion, many laughs, and sentimentality.

VII. The Engagement

The Engagement period will be very short in both cases. Career choices and job commitments loom immediately ahead. And the fiancées have known each other so long that they see no point in a long engagement.

VIII. Wedding Plans

A time of chaos and stress ensues as two completely different approaches to a wedding move ahead at breakneck speed. There are plenty of hijinks and laughs and fish-out-of-water situations as the wedding day approaches. We will also keep track of the girl who is not the bride-to-be and what she is going through.

Topics addressed will include: the size of the reception; where the wedding will take place (i.e. The Ritz, Giant's Stadium, a Los Vegas Chapel filled with Elvis impersonators, etc.); the type of wedding; who will be Archie's Best Man and ushers and his bride's Maid of Honor and bridesmaids (and the role of the other girl in this); formal or not; how the expenses are being covered; the wedding planner (possibly Katy Keene or Sabrina); the band (the Archies must at least perform one song; Josie & the Pussycats); their song for their first dance ("Sugar, Sugar"); the roles of the parents; Archie's bachelor party; the bride's shower; the rehearsal dinner.

IX. The Wedding Day

The jitters the night before the wedding by both Archie and the bride; the feelings of the other girl; wedding day craziness and laughs; getting to the wedding; walking down the aisle; the ceremony. I want a double-page spread featuring every Archie character including:

Mr. & Mrs. Andrews. Mr. & Mrs. Lodge. Mr. & Mrs. Cooper. Smithers. Betty/Veronica. Pop Tate. Mr. Weatherbee. Miss Grundy. Miss Beazly. Mr. Flutesnoot. Svenson. Coach Cleats. Jughead. Ethel. Dilton Doily. Reggie. Moose. Midge. Cheryl Blossom. Frankie Valdez and Maria. Chuck Clayton and Nancy. Josie. Melody. Valerie. Sabrina. L'il Jinx and her parents. Ambrose (grown up). Alexandra and Alexander Cabot. Katy Keene. Sis. Wilbur. Pat the Brat. That Wilkin Boy. Hot Dog. Who'd I leave out?

Other events and situations in this part of the story will revolve around the reception itself; the cake (uh oh!), the tossing of the bouquet (a poignant moment as the "other" girl catches it), and the emotions of that other girl, close friends, and parents.

X. The Honeymoon

We learn where they are going and it should be a riot! I picture Jughead showing up wherever they are . . . just for starters.

XI. How Different Life Becomes

Their jobs/careers; coming home after a hard day's work; the huge difference in Archie's life if he marries Veronica and is put in charge of a company by his father-in-law or struggles to make ends meet day-to-day with Betty; the plusses and minuses of married life and a lesson in what it takes for a marriage to succeed (be best friends; communicate; have a sense of humor; don't try to change the other person; work at it every day like you do your job); *new* friends (married couples, people from work); losing touch with old friends; holidays; first anniversary; a look at what kind of husband Archie makes and what kind of wife his bride makes.

XII. "Mom and Dad . . . We're Pregnant!"

Reactions of each as well as the other girl. Talk about craziness . . . birthing classes, racing to get to the hospital, labor, delivery, twins (a boy and a girl), the reactions of everyone, learning what kind of father and what kind of mother they make.

XIII. Twins

Now little kids, the twins are duplicates of L'il Archie and L'il Betty or L'il Veronica. Lots of funny and cool moments in this section. Clearly these kids are the virtual clones of their parents and echo Archie's Mom's "curse" she put on him when he was up to his usual wackiness in high school, "May you have two kids just like you some day!"

XIV. The Loss of a Parent

Time out for a touching and emotional fact of life that must be addressed and will be a heartfelt, emotional, and important moment in this story of "Life with Archie."

XV. Archie's Family Christmas Stocking

Christmas with the Archie family. In a scene meant to evoke *It's a Wonderful Life*, while searching for just the right Xmas tree, Archie finds himself at the Yellow Wood on Memory Lane where the two roads diverge. On the way back, holding the tree, he misses the path he took and without realizing it, walks down the OTHER path . . .

The graphic novel should end with Robert Frost's poem, "The Road Not Taken":

Two roads diverged in a yellow wood,
And sorry I could not travel both
And be one traveler, long I stood
And looked down one as far as I could
To where it bent in the undergrowth;

Then took the other, as just as fair,
And having perhaps the better claim
Because it was grassy and wanted wear,
Though as for that the passing there
Had worn them really about the same,

And both that morning equally lay
In leaves no step had trodden black.
Oh, I marked the first for another day!
Yet knowing how way leads on to way
I doubted if I should ever come back.

I shall be telling this with a sigh
Somewhere ages and ages hence:
Two roads diverged in a wood, and I,
I took the one less traveled by,
And that has made all the difference.

Now, it would be easy for me to take all the above and make

each of the two stories five books in length. But I know you want Betty's story and Veronica's story combined into just five books. The hard part will be cutting the above about in half so that both the Betty tale and the Veronica tale together will be able to be presented in five or six books. I guess here's my second pitch for six. (Can't blame me for trying!) With your guidance, we can decide what from the above outline must be included and what parts we can omit.

I am around until the 16th, then will be on the road until the 31st but generally available during that time by e-mail or cell phone.

I could not be more excited about this and the potential here. Thanks for the opportunity to make this a reality.

Best,
Michael

From: Michael Uslan
Sent: Sat, 18 Oct 2008 2:48:52 -0400
To: Victor Gorelick
Subject: RE: RE: Archie no. 600

Hi Victor . . .

I wanted to get back to you right away with my thoughts about the six comic book covers and the two graphic novel covers. Here's what I'm thinking:

no. 600: Archie is on one knee proposing to Veronica at Tiffany's as he slips a HUGE diamond ring on her finger. Jughead and Betty are looking in the store window from the street outside. Jughead looks totally shocked. Betty looks crushed with tears flowing. Veronica's word balloon: **YES!!** The title: "ARCHIE MARRIES VERONICA!" and beneath that: Part 1 of 3: "The Proposal."

no. 601: The very formal, rich, extravagant wedding ceremony of Archie and Veronica at the equivalent of Giants Stadium. News helicopters are hovering. TV cameras are everywhere. Is that actually the Pope performing the ceremony?! The Maid of Honor is Betty, who is weeping, but not tears of joy. Jughead in tux and crown cap is the Best Man. Ushers in tuxes are Reggie, Moose, and Dilton. Bridesmaids are Midge, Sabrina, and Josie in world-class evening gowns. Veronica's word balloon: **I DO!** Archie's word balloon: **DO I EVER!** The title: "ARCHIE MARRIES VERONICA!" and beneath that: Part 2 of 3: "The Wedding."

no. 602: Xmas morning in the Andrews lodge. The biggest, most lavish Xmas tree, wrapped gifts galore, overflowing stockings on the fireplace, a new pony with a gift ribbon around it which Little Veronica sits on, and a kid's electric sports car that Little Archie sits in. Between them we see the family: Dad Archie (dressed like Santa), Mom Veronica, Mr. Lodge, a white-haired Smithers, a nanny, a cook, a chauffeur, and Archie's older Mom and Dad sitting with canes in comfy chairs. The title: "ARCHIE MARRIES VERONICA!" and beneath that: Part 3 of 3: "It's TWINS!"

no. 603: Archie and Betty sitting in a booth at Pop Tate's sharing a chocolate malt with two straws as Archie slips a tiny diamond ring onto Betty's finger. Behind them it says, "Pop's" on a door or wall (as he "pops" the question). Behind them, Veronica overhears and turns around and looks angrily down from over the top of the booth. Reggie is looking with her and looks totally shocked. Pop Tate in the background behind the counter has a tear of happiness coming down his cheek. Betty's word balloon: **YES!!** The title: "ARCHIE MARRIES BETTY!" and beneath that: Part 1 of 3: "Will You Marry Me?"

no. 604: A very small wedding ceremony in Pop Tate's. The guys are in sports jackets and ties; the girls are in nice dresses. Simple decorations. Through the plate glass window we can see Archie's jalopy across the street with a "Just Married" sign and tin cans attached to the rear. The guests are throwing rice. Juggie is Best Man and Veronica, shedding a sad tear, is the Maid of Honor. Ushers are Reggie, Moose, and Dilton. Bridesmaids are Ethel, Midge, and Miss Grundy. A Justice of the Peace performs the ceremony. Both sets of parents are present, too. Archie and Betty kiss. Betty's word balloon: "I DO!" Archie's word balloon: "No, **I** Do!" Betty's second word balloon: "No, I Do MORE!" Archie's second word balloon: "No, I Do FOREVER!" The Title: "ARCHIE MARRIES BETTY!" and beneath that: Part 2 of 3: "You May Kiss the Bride!" (ALTERNATIVE: "I Now Pronounce You Husband and Wife!")

no. 605: The hospital delivery room. Betty with big smile and tears of happiness in bed, sitting up. Archie in scrubs holding one baby in each arm . . . each in swaddling cloth but clearly we see a Little Archie and a Little Betty. Archie has a huge grin on his face. A doctor and a nurse are in the background. The title: "ARCHIE MARRIES BETTY!" and beneath that: Part 3 of 3: "Happily Ever After."

Your thoughts?

Best,
Michael

From: Victor Gorelick
Sent: Mon, 20 Oct 2008 15:14:22 -0400
To: Michael Uslan
Subject: RE: RE: RE: Archie no. 600

Hi Michael,

For the most part these cover ideas look good. However, I do suggest some changes:

no. 600—The point of view is Archie and Veronica in the foreground, inside the jewelry store, Archie is slipping the ring on Veronica's finger. In the background is the store window where we see Betty and Jughead looking in, crushed, crying and shocked, respectively. Copy all stays the same.

no. 601—I don't know if the artist can fit all this in without everything looking too small. However, let's see how much we can fit in without losing focus on the bride and groom. The ceremony should appear non-denominational. Bridesmaids should be Midge, Ethel, and Nancy (African-American). Leave Sabrina and Josie out of the storyline (with the exception of possibly using Josie and the Pussycats playing at one of the weddings).

no. 602—This scene should take place at the Lodge mansion. Show both Archie's and Veronica's parents sitting and/or standing around Christmas tree, somewhat involved with their grandchildren, while Archie and Veronica look on (Smithers, too, if he fits). I would not want to show them sitting with canes, looking ancient. Think about it, Michael. You could possibly be a grandparent in the next couple of years. Do you see yourself looking like that? I don't.

no. 603—Looks good as is.

no. 604—Looks okay, with the exception of replacing Ms. Grundy with Nancy.

no. 605—Looks good as is.

As far as the graphic novel goes, it looks like we're going to do one 160 page book. Maybe with a cover showing Betty & Veronica both in wedding gowns, Archie in the middle (as

always) with a nervous/frightened look on his face. Copy: "Decisions, Decisions." Or something else. Or no copy.

Your thoughts?

Victor

From: Michael Uslan
Sent: Thu, 20 Nov 2008 10:44:03 -0400
To: Victor Gorelick
Subject: Archie Graphic Novel

Hi Victor—

I'm being pressed by the *LA Times* reporter about his being allowed to break the story about Archie getting married, *Archie* no. 600, and his first ever graphic novel. Is it OK to give him the scoop?

Michael

From: Victor Gorelick
Sent: Thu, 20 Nov 2008 14:55:17 -0400
To: Michael Uslan
Subject: RE: Archie Graphic Novel

Hi Michael,

I guess it would be okay to break the news about Archie getting married. However, the graphic novel will be well over a year away. The first story of Archie marrying Veronica is scheduled for *Archie* no. 600 which goes on sale in September 2009. Do you think it's a little premature to say something now? Your thoughts?

Victor

From: Victor Gorelick
Sent: Wed 31 Dec 2008 15:38:51 -0400
To: Michael Uslan
Subject: Archie no. 600

Hi Michael,

I just finished reading "The Proposal- Part 1." Great job. I really liked the way you handled the characters and kept the dialogue to a minimum. My only criticism: Please try to avoid seven panels on a page. Keep them to no more than six.

HAPPY NEW YEAR TO YOU AND YOURS.

Victor

From: Victor Gorelick
Sent: Tue 27 Jan 2009 14:28:18 -0400
To: Michael Uslan
Subject: Archie no. 601

Hi Michael,

You need to make some changes with regard to the wedding reception. It should be at the Lodge Mansion and not Yankee Stadium. Also, you need to work Veronica's mother in a little more. Also, Riverdale is not near NYC. It's not a place they can get to in an hour or so. While Josie and the Pussycats can be playing at the wedding, I'm eliminating all the other characters as guests, such as Katy Keene, Wilbur, etc. Please call me if you have any questions.

Victor

ANNOTATIONS

Chapter 1, *Archie* no. 600

Page 9, panel 5: The first of many references to *The Wizard of Oz*.

Page 10, panel 5: One of my mother's favorite sayings.

Page 10, panel 6: An expression frequently used by my mother.

Page 11, panel 2: The corner of Memory Lane and Red Circle (Red Circle was the Archie Comics Group's super hero publishing label in the seventies and eighties).

Page 11, panel 3: Lots of Archie history here:

Vic's Blooms: Vic Bloom wrote the first Archie story in *Pep Comics* no. 22 (December 1941).

Belmont Books: A sister company of Archie Comics, they published the book *High Camp Super-Heroes* in 1966, reprinting many Archie/MLJ super hero stories.

Coyne's Stamps: Maurice Coyne was one of the three founders of MLJ Comics—he was the M in MLJ.

Shorten Sweet Shoppe: Harry Shorten was a key editor and writer of the MLJ line of comics.

Mighty Comics Shop (formerly Radio Comics): Radio Comics was an Archie Comics subsidiary that published super hero comics in the fifties and early sixties. When the company named its super hero line of comics Mighty Comics Group, its flagship title became *Mighty Comics*.

Silberkleit & Son Travel: Louis Silberkleit was one of the three founders of MLJ Comics—the L in MLJ.

Daily Jet Service to Montana: Bob Montana drew the first Archie story and created the likenesses of Archie and his friends.

Goldwater for Prez: No, not Barry Goldwater, circa 1964, but John Goldwater, one of the three founders of MLJ Comics—the J in MLJ.

"MLJ for USA": Not Lyndon Johnson, circa 1964, but MLJ Comics, which became the Archie Comics Group.

Page 11, panels 5–6: A reference to the 1915 poem by Robert Frost, "The Road Not Taken."

Page 15, panel 1: One of my father's favorite quotes. It's from Ralph Waldo Emerson.

Page 16, panels 3–4: Yep, Josie and the Pussycats are playing at their graduation. Who else?

Page 17, panel 1: "Uncle Joe" would be my dad, Joe Uslan. The Uslan family is originally from Bayonne, New Jersey.

Page 17, panels 2–3: I patterned Dilton after my brainy friend, Bobby Klein, who also went to MIT, and Reggie after my college roommate, Marc Caplan, whose fraternity nickname was "Used Car Salesman."

Page 20, panel 1: This has become a mystery on the Internet, with fans trying to decipher the secret meaning of "Osteria Al Rösen." The truth? A combination of my favorite restaurant in midtown Manhattan, Osteria Al Doge, and my Bayonne pal and Cedar Grove, New Jersey, jeweler, Al Rosen.

Page 21: I believe this is the first full-page splash panel ever in an Archie story.

Page 27, panel 5: This scene between Archie and his father is really a scene between my son David (who called my dad "Pop") and his grandfather (who called my son "Sonny Boy," and always sang him the song of that title).

Page 29, panel 1: Joann was really my daughter Sarah's wedding planner, Joann Gregoli.

Page 29, panel 3: Rob Y, who designed Veronica's wedding dress, is dress designer Rob Younkers. Sarah Uslan *is* my daughter, a top Hollywood make-up artist, trained by Bobbi Brown.

Page 29, panel 4: My dad, Joe Uslan, is the mason Mr. Lodge calls to construct Archie's office.

Page 29, panel 5: Throughout the mid-forties and fifties, Katy Keene appeared in various MLJ/Archie Comics titles. Her character was an actress, singer, and model, and was known as "America's Queen of Pin-Ups and Fashions."

Page 29, panel 6: Ben is Benjamin Melniker, my producing partner on all our Batman movies.

Chapter 2, *Archie* no. 601

Page 35: This was a riff on "Who's Who in Riverdale," from *Archie Comics* no. 1 (Winter 1942).

Page 37, panel 1: "Starchie" was the name given Archie in the parody by Harvey Kurtzman and Will Elder in *MAD* no. 12, June 1954 (when it was a comic book, before becoming a magazine).

Page 38, panel 3: Henry Aldrich was one of the radio and movie characters who inspired the creation of Archie comic books. That's why Henry reminds Ethel of Archie in panel 7.

Page 39, panels 2–6: This echoes the scene that really took place between Nancy, my fiancée, and myself the night before our wedding.

Pages 44–45: The first double-page spread in *Archie* history. Is the man officiating the wedding ceremony the legendary artist Stan Goldberg?

Page 48, panel 1: Their first dance is the number one song of 1969, "Sugar, Sugar" by the Archies.

Page 49, panel 2: A quote from my father-in-law, Dr. M. S. Osher, on my wedding day.

Page 49, panel 3: The words of my brother, Dr. Paul C. Uslan, at my wedding reception.

Page 49, panel 4: My dad recited this on my wedding day.

Page 49, panel 5: Jughead's right: In reality, it took Archie sixty-eight years to pop the question.

Page 50, panel 3: This scene was inspired by a photo from my wedding reception, when I squashed a piece of wedding cake in Nancy's face—with the urging of her dad!

Page 55, panel 4: The "David" in Human Resources would be my son, David Uslan.

Page 56, panel 3: A salute to two super heroes of the Archie Comics universe: Attorney Tommy Troy is secretly the Fly (aka Fly-Man), and Joe Higgins is the Shield.

Page 57, panel 3: Throughout this story, I kept sprinkling the titles of Archie/MLJ comic books. Here's a reference to *Pep Comics*. Fred and Ethel are a nod to Fred and Ethel Mertz from *I Love Lucy*.

Chapter 3, *Archie* no. 602

Page 62, panel 2: Nancy's and my prescription for a long, happy marriage.

Page 63, panel 6: An homage to my second-favorite movie of all time, *Citizen Kane*.

Page 64, panel 3: Yep! The grown-up kid, who was one of the best friends from *Little Archie*, owns Ambrose's

Chowhouse—Ambrose even had his own comic book briefly, way back when!

Page 67, panel 1: In the disco era, I was forced to listen to songs like "Shake Your Booty." This was my moment of vengeance.

Page 69, panel 6: A tribute to William Bendix in *The Life of Riley*.

Pages 73–74: A tribute to Dick Van Dyke in *The Dick Van Dyke Show*.

Page 79, panel 1: A reference to the comic book title *Life with Archie*.

Page 81: Here I worked in the comic book title *Archie's Christmas Stocking*.

Page 82, panel 5: A tribute to the Beatles.

Page 83: Not just my favorite poem of all time, these words by Robert Frost helped me shape my own destiny and make some key choices in life.

Chapter 4, *Archie* no. 603

Page 88, panel 1: An homage to *The Wizard of Oz*.

Page 89, panel 1: My mom's favorite quote.

Page 90, panel 1: I worked in one more old Archie comic book title, *Archie's Pals 'N' Gals*.

Page 90, panel 3: More Archie comic book titles: *Pep Comics, Christmas Stocking, Top-Notch Comics*, and *Summer Fun*.

Page 93, panel 1: Another movie I loved as a kid, *Around the World in 80 Days* (which won five Oscars, including best picture, in 1956).

Page 94, panel 4: Another 1969 hit from the Archies, "Jingle Jangle."

Page 97, panel 3: Archie is referring to perhaps the most iconic *Archie* comic book cover of all time (*Archie Annual* no. 4, December 1953), with Archie, Betty, and Veronica sharing one malt with three straws [below right].

Page 102, panel 1: A reference to the old Archie comic book title *Betty and Me*.

Page 104, panels 5–6: Reprising a real scene in my life between my daughter Sarah and me.

Page 106, panel 2: Svenson's words parallel the words told to my college roommate, Marc Caplan, by his dad, Max.

Page 106, panel 3: A riff on the theme song to the original *Archies* television cartoon show.

Page 110: Another reference to the Archies' hit "Jingle Jangle," and the old comic book title *Life with Archie*.

Chapter 5, *Archie* no. 604

Page 114, panels 3–4: References to the old MLJ comic book titles *Jackpot Comics* and *Top-Notch Comics*.

Page 119, panels 2–3: I plant the seeds for future budding relationships.

Page 120, panel 5: A salute to the bow tie Archie wore in the forties and fifties.

Page 121, panel 3: A reference to the immortal words of my idol, mentor, and friend, Stan Lee, when Spider-Man met Mary Jane Watson.

Page 129, panel 3: An homage to my favorite film of all time, *Casablanca*.

Page 131, panel 4: This character is based on my niece, Cassie Malmquist, a rising exec in the New York City fashion industry.

Page 131, panel 5: Back in the mid-sixties, *Archie* comics had this dopey, stupid narrating character called the Mighty Minstrel, who annoyed me by showing up in *Mighty Comics, Fly-Man*, and *The Mighty Crusaders* books. He actually sang, "Ki' Yippee Ya-hoo." Now I get to toss him out on his butt! That Bolling Alley sign is a salute to *Little Archie* genius writer/artist Bob Bolling.

Page 134, panel 5: Dad's quote is mine. I said it to my kids when they graduated college.

Page 136, panel 3: My tribute to the seventies television series *Welcome Back, Kotter*.

Chapter 6, *Archie* no. 605

Page 141, panel 3: My brother Paul took up yoga and became a calmer kind of guy. If it worked for Paul, I figured it would work for Moose.

Page 145, panel 1: A reference to the 2008 Spider-Man storyline "Brand New Day," where Marvel reset the comic book continuity of Peter Parker's marriage. Betty's reference is to Andy Hardy, a series of movies starring Mickey Rooney that, like Henry Aldrich, influenced the creation of Archie comic books.

Page 145, panel 4: Jessica and Samantha are the names of my nieces, Jessica Osher and Samantha Uslan. Bobby is the name of my comic book friend for life, Bobby Klein.

Page 146, panel 3: Nancy and Michael are my wife and me. Paul and Georgia are my brother and sister-in-law.

Page 147, panel 1: Archie's life here was inspired by the 1995 movie *Mr. Holland's Opus*.

Page 147, panel 3: Planting the seeds for important stories to come in the Archie universe.

Page 150, panel 1: "The Mirth of a Nation" was MLJ's original slogan for Archie in the 1940s, much like "Man of Steel" is for Superman and "Dark Knight" is for Batman.

Page 160, panel 2: Ilana is based on my cousin, Ilana Solomon.

Chapter 7, *Archie* no. 606

Pages 166–167: *Wizard of Oz* final references.

Page 168, panel 2: Reference to *A Christmas Carol*.

Page 174, panel 6: Jughead's words embody my dad's favorite quote, one we placed on his gravestone.

YESTERDAY IS HISTORY.
TOMORROW IS A MYSTERY.
TODAY IS A GIFT. THAT'S WHY WE CALL IT THE PRESENT.

—Michael Uslan

ALL NEW STORIES
4TH EDITION
BIG 116 PAGE BOOK
Archie
ANNUAL
YEAR BOOK
YOU THINK YOU CAN GET INTO TROUBLE WITH THREE ON A MATCH?...
WAIT TILL YOU SEE WHAT HAPPENS TO ARCHIE WITH THREE ON A SODA!

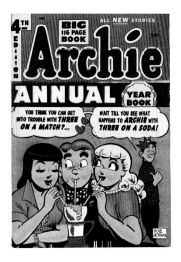

About the Contributors

Stan Goldberg is a veteran, award-winning comic book artist who has worked more than sixty years in the industry and is best known for illustrating *Archie* comics for more than four decades. He started his career at age sixteen in 1949 as a staff colorist for Timely (now known as Marvel Comics). Two years later he became the color department manager, and colored not just interiors, but every cover throughout the fifties. In 1958 Goldberg went freelance, but continued to work for Marvel until the mid-1960s, designing the color for all of their classic super heroes and villains, including Spider-Man, the Fantastic Four, the X-Men, and the Incredible Hulk. He has also illustrated for DC Comics, *National Lampoon, Redbook, Seventeen, Ms., Working Woman,* and many other magazines. Stan Goldberg lives in Beechhurst, New York.

Jon Goldwater is the son of Archie Comics founder, publisher, and editor John L. Goldwater. The Archie line of comic books is one of the most successful, longest running series of titles in the history of the comics industry (their first comic was published in 1939). Goldwater began his career twenty years ago as partner at Zak Concerts, the Japanese concert promoter. He is the former president and CEO of AFA Music Group, Ltd., and the executive producer of the film *The Return of Superfly* (1990). He has also served as president and CEO of Crash Management Inc. Using his experience in the entertainment industry, Goldwater plans on bringing the gang from Riverdale to a larger multimedia audience. He is the driving force behind the Archie Comics digital initiative as well as building new partnerships in the publishing and entertainment industries. He is also developing new projects focusing on not just Archie, Betty, Veronica, Jughead, and Reggie, but other long-standing Archie properties as well, such as Katy Keene, Li'l Jinx, the Red Circle Heroes, Sabrina the Teenage Witch, Josie and the Pussycats, Cosmo the Merry Martian, Pat the Brat, Wilbur Wilkins, Bingo Wilkins, and Suzie and Sam Hill, to name just a few. Jon Goldwater looks forward to expanding the role of his family's company, Archie Comic Publications, to prominence in the comic book medium as well as in other media.

Victor Gorelick is the co-president/ editor in chief of Archie Comics Publications, Inc., and has been working at Archie Comics for almost fifty years. He joined Archie as an art assistant in October 1958, and over the years has served as production manager, art director, and managing editor. Gorelick has unique knowledge of every facet of the editorial process required to create and publish successful comics. He has been a writer, colorist, letterer, and everything in between. He has developed a keen sense for producing good, clean, wholesome content for Archie Comics. Through the years he has helped to build a bond of trust with *Archie* readers of all ages. Gorelick has worked closely with numerous companies and organizations, designing and producing various custom comic books. For example, he has overseen collaborations between Archie Comics and Kraft General Foods, Radio Shack, Alcoholics Anonymous, the City and County of San Diego, and even the FBI. He was on the Comic Magazine Association of America's Comics Code Authority Guidelines Committee, and is a member of the Board of Advisors for the Joe Kubert School, where many of today's comics artists develop their craft. He also teaches cartooning in the College for Kids program at Kingsborough Community College in Brooklyn, New York.

Jack Morelli is an author (*Heroes of the Negro Leagues*, Abrams, 2007), artist, and designer. He has worked in production and editorial at Marvel Comics, freelance for DC Comics and Archie Comics, and has been a comic book hand letterer for more than thirty years. He lives in upstate New York with his wife, Christie Scheele, and their twins.

Bob Smith was born in Aberdeen, Washington, in 1951. Raised in Grayland, Washington, he left the family cranberry farm after graduating with a degree in fine art from Western Washington State College. He moved to New York in 1975, and found work as an inker for DC Comics. Twenty-three years and several comic book publishers later, he landed at Archie Comics. Since 1998, Bob Smith's work has appeared in numerous Archie titles and on the *Archie* newspaper strip. In 2009 he moved back to Washington, and lives in Covington.

Michael Uslan is an award-winning writer and executive producer of the Batman films, most recently *The Dark Knight* (2008), the third highest grossing film in movie history. He was the first instructor to teach comics at an accredited university (Indiana University in 1970) and wrote the first textbook on comics, *The Comic Book in America*. His autobiography, *The Boy Who Loved Batman*, is being published in Spring 2011. Uslan lives in Montclair, New Jersey.

Glenn Whitmore's comic book ambitions began at age ten, when he first attended the Joe Kubert School of Cartoon and Graphic Art. Glenn graduated in 1987. A year later he began an eleven-year run as colorist on the Superman titles for DC Comics, which included landmark storylines of the hero's engagement, death, return, and marriage to Lois Lane. For more than twenty years, Glenn has also provided color to popular comic book titles such as *The Power of Shazam, Justice Society, Nexus,* and, most recently, *Archie*. He lives in Succasunna, New Jersey.

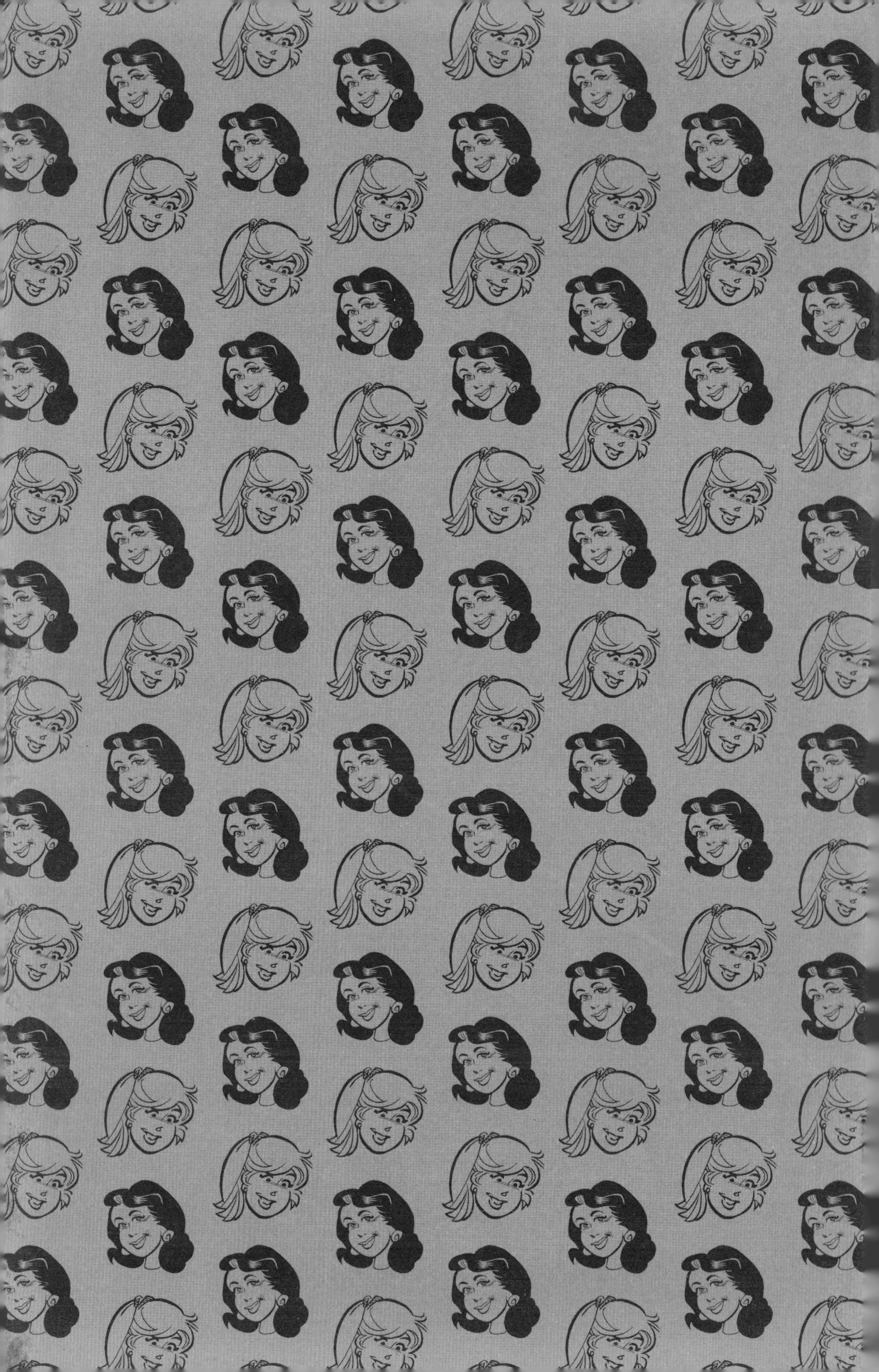